Grandfather Mountain

Grandfather

Mountain

THE HISTORY AND GUIDE TO AN APPALACHIAN ICON

Randy Johnson

THE UNIVERSITY OF NORTH CAROLINA PRESS Chapel Hill

This book was published with the assistance of Frank and Elizabeth Skidmore.

Designed by Richard Hendel
Set in Linoletter and TheSerif types
by Tseng Information Systems, Inc.

Printed in China

The paper in this book meets the guidelines for permanence and durability of the Committee on Production Guidelines for Book Longevity of the Council on Library Resources.

The University of North Carolina Press has been a member of the Green Press Initiative since 2003.

"Little Tweetsie Railroad Train" in Chapter 5 © 1975, Floyd Banner, Bannerman Music, Newland, N.C. Reprinted with permission of Louise Banner.

Photo credits: Cover photo by Tommy White Photography, www.tommywhitephotography.com; p. i, Helen Moss Davis/www.wildblueprints.com; pp. 8–9, Grandfather View, Tommy White Photography, www.tommywhitephotography.com; pp. 206–7, Rough Ridge vista, Tommy White Photography, www.tommywhitephotography.com.

Library of Congress Cataloging-in-Publication Data
Names: Johnson, Randy, 1951– author.
Title: Grandfather Mountain : the history and guide to an Appalachian icon / Randy Johnson.
Description: Chapel Hill : The University of North Carolina Press, [2016] | Includes bibliographical references and index.
Identifiers: LCCN 2015039987 | ISBN 9781469626994 (cloth : alk. paper) | ISBN 9781469627007 (ebook)
Subjects: LCSH: Grandfather Mountain (N.C.)—History. | Grandfather Mountain (N.C.)—Description and travel. | Mountains—North Carolina—History.
Classification: LCC F262.B6 J64 2016 | DDC 975.6/862—dc23 LC record available at http://lccn.loc.gov/2015039987

CONTENTS

SIDEBARS

INTRODUCTION

Grandfather Mountain

APPALACHIAN ICON

One spring day in the Blue Ridge Mountains, I was standing atop the highest crag of Grandfather Mountain's Rough Ridge, on the very flank of the mountain's loftiest summits, looking out over eighty-mile views. A group of Appalachian State University trail volunteers had asked me to point out distant peaks. A young woman standing nearby overheard as I identified the "Who's Who" of surrounding summits and queried, "Is that Grandfather Mountain over there?" Her finger leveled where a bridge could just be seen spanning a small gap between lower peaks a mile above sea level. My mind immediately turned to Hugh Morton, the legendary North Carolinian who had once owned thousands of acres of the mountain land under our feet. For an instant, I marveled at how incredibly successful Morton had been in making his bridge synonymous with Grandfather Mountain. "Yes," I said, "that's the Swinging Bridge at the Grandfather Mountain attraction."

Then somehow, that answer didn't seem adequate; I wanted to offer greater geographical precision. "That *is* the Swinging Bridge," I continued, "but you're *on* Grandfather Mountain right now." She wrinkled her nose and looked puzzled. She had parked on the Blue Ridge Parkway, far from the Mile-High Swinging Bridge, and she hadn't driven up a winding road to a visitor's center or to the enclosed animal habitats that comprise another element of the famous tourist attraction. "That's just a small part of Grandfather," I explained, pointing at the bridge, "and all of that above us," I gestured, waving my hand from the Linn Cove Viaduct up to the soaring whaleback of rock that included the highest peaks of MacRae, Attic Window, and Calloway, "all that is Grandfather Mountain, too. The Swinging Bridge is just a tiny spot on the mountain." She was starting to get it. "And if you were way down there," I said, turning to point 3,000 feet below at clouds among the foothills, "you'd still be on the mountain and everything you saw up here would be Grandfather, too." She looked left and right and all around, and started to grasp the reality of the grandiose mass that encircled her.

From Rough Ridge, it's a very big view of Grandfather Mountain's plummet to the Piedmont. Like the person questioning the view in the text, if you look closely at the ridge rising to the right, you'll see that the last little evergreen bump at the edge of the picture is really a peak—with the Swinging Bridge barely stretching to it. Photo by Tommy White Photography, www.tommywhitephotography.com.

Grandfather Mountain is a far bigger mountain, and a more multifaceted topic, than people imagine—and that's why I wrote this book.

I learned to appreciate the true size and significance of Grandfather over a forty year period, starting in the 1970s, when college friends and I set out to find the snowiest, most spectacular summit in the South. On one return trip, "No Trespassing" signs greeted me on the Shanty Spring Trail. Hugh Morton had closed the dangerous and deteriorating trails after a hiker had died from hypothermia. I couldn't imagine the possibility that the mountain's highest peaks would be off-limits to hikers, so I set out to meet Morton. Luckily, he was receptive to a hiker fee-funded, safety registration program I devised to keep the trails open. Over more than a decade, I reopened historic trails, built new ones, and implemented a backcountry management program that eventually created the hiking experience we still find today on Grandfather. Ever since, growing awareness of the once-ignored backcountry has ensured hiker access, but also helped usher-in a focus on preserving what locals for generations have called "the Grandfather Mountain."

Adding "the" to the mountain's name is a figure of mountain speech, but I hope this book will demonstrate how particularly appropriate that turn of phrase is. There is only one Grandfather Mountain. And the fact is, when it comes to the peaks and ridges of North Carolina's "High Country" near the towns of Boone, Blowing Rock, Linville, and Banner Elk, earlier generations simply would have said they were "on the Grandfather." Sadly, even as we've glorified Grandfather Mountain over the years, a greedy web of roads has girdled it, constricting and encircling this once unencumbered landmass, bringing us closer, and higher. The mountain today is whatever lies above our vantage point. Despite that diminution, Grandfather defies our impertinence. This massive, sprawling eminence is an escarpment of the Blue Ridge worthy of the term "massif." Hugh Morton turned one edge of that landmark into a commercial attraction, and along the way he helped forge an identity and a

mental boundary that still shapes how many see the mountain he used to own.

But it wasn't always that way. This book will lead you back, centuries ago, when a magnificent mountain held all but the hardiest travelers at bay. Along the way, we'll appreciate how Grandfather came to be what I argue is the quintessential Appalachian summit. We'll follow the early explorers, scientists, and adventurers who gained Grandfather's flanks on faint trails, then climbed on, to wild, virgin-forested peaks that inspired some to song. Later, settlers crept into Grandfather's shadow on rough routes only laughably called roads. It took even longer for a romantic era of railroading to bring the screeching "twee-ee-t" of trains nicknamed "Tweetsie" to valleys below. Only in the mid-1950s did a highway finally cross the high spur that radiates for miles around and below what we now call Grandfather Mountain.

This book invites you to appreciate that past, but we'll start by exploring the truly astounding size and natural character of what many call North Carolina's most distinctive peak, a mountain that has become an important symbol for the entire ancient Appalachian range. This dramatic summit, visible from all over western North Carolina, is the climax of the Blue Ridge front. Grandfather towers above surrounding foothills, and nearly twenty ecosystems plummet directly down its flanks, from crag-capped, almost alpine Canadian zone to piney western piedmont far below. Grandfather is a kingpin of the Eastern Continental Divide, dispatching mighty rivers to Atlantic and Mississippi estuaries half a continent apart. Grandfather Mountain's biological diversity is second to no other mountain east of the Rockies. How appropriate it is that Grandfather's far-flung acreage is protected by agencies as diverse as Pisgah National Forest, the East's first national forest, and the Blue Ridge Parkway, the most visited unit of the National Park System. The most significant Appalachian summit to remain in private hands into the twenty-first century, Grandfather was named in the 1990s by the United Nations as the world's only privately owned International Biosphere Reserve. Most

From Yellow Mountain, near the Appalachian Trail, Grandfather is still the "serrated" sentinel that caught the attention of early travel writer Charles Dudley Warner in an 1885 issue of the *Atlantic Monthly*. Photo by Tommy White Photography, www.tommywhite photography.com.

recently, in the early 2000s, North Carolina purchased the highest peaks to create Grandfather Mountain State Park, and Hugh Morton's Swinging Bridge travel attraction became a not-for-profit private preserve.

The story of Grandfather Mountain's significance as an attraction begins long before the Swinging Bridge. Native Americans roamed the mountain's environs for centuries before early naturalists and famous explorers like Daniel Boone traced its tempting summits on the horizon. It lured legendary adventurers and enterprising settlers, and Civil War deserters and even Union sympathizers hid out among its caves and crags. In the late 1800s, affluent families seeking cool weather in summer led to the birth of North Carolina resort towns like Highlands and Blowing Rock. That put Grandfather Mountain on the radar for Wilmington's MacRae family. They bought the mountain, founded Linville, and enticed generations of elite visitors. Meanwhile, on Grandfather's slopes, adventurous hikers came for the rugged terrain and abundant cool weather. Grandfather Mountain's road to becoming "Carolina's Top Scenic Attraction" is just part of how the mountain has shaped the history, culture, and modern tourist industry of the surrounding region. Grandfather is a big reason why the High Country corner of northwestern North Carolina can claim to be the ski capital of the South and a nationally visible symbol of the enviable Appalachian lifestyle—a place where second homes, all arrayed to gaze upon Grandfather's face, dot ridges. The mountain's rich heritage includes the founding of America's most significant Scottish cultural event, a story as stirring as the bagpipes that wail in MacRae Meadows.

Most importantly, Grandfather's transition from private ownership in the twentieth century to preservation as public land in the twenty-first makes it a fascinating study of contemporary conservation. Grandfather Mountain is in many respects a microcosm of the complicated and contentious history of western North Carolina, as economic development goals have clashed with

environmental concerns. Like other iconic places along the Appalachian range, Grandfather confronted destruction by loggers and exploitation by developers, but it has now been protected as a public treasure. While tracking places, events, and personalities across time, this tale is at the center of the book.

Ancient and craggy, Grandfather is at its most venerable and distinguished when its rocky profile "face" is blasted white with the frost of a High Country winter. The mountain stands head and shoulders above its peers, rising higher above its base than only a handful of other Appalachian peaks. Grandfather is its own "geologic window," an opening that offers a glimpse of earlier eons, just as reaching the mountain's summit gives hikers a stark view of their own capabilities—and one of eastern America's great vistas. Grandfather has endured much: the disastrous "haircut" it got in the 1930s (only to grow back a new crown of evergreens), a "swinging bridge" strung between summits in the 1950s (mercifully placed between lower peaks), and the coming of the Blue Ridge Parkway in the 1980s (soaring softly above the mountainside thanks to the timely arrival of computer design and growing respect for the most iconic of our elders). In the twenty-first century, the coming of state park status means the mountain may have outlasted the worst of past challenges.

All of that and more has made Grandfather a favorite mountain for many. Grandfather is a magical place, evidenced by scenery seekers drawn to it over centuries. It's a place that generation after generation has shared with the people they love. I count myself among them. In setting out to share Grandfather with you, I've labored to be accurate, even objective in my recounting of the mountain's past. But as someone who has devoted part of his life to Grandfather Mountain, who has known many of the figures who have shaped Grandfather's recent past and immediate future, I'll feel free to offer what I hope readers will call my own insights, especially where my participation or original research provides perspective. Even as I endeavor to present the mountain's history, what

Adorned with a roaming raven, what is perhaps the most recognized of Grandfather's multiple profile faces gazes skyward. The visage descends from Calloway Peak, at the top, down to the right, or north, to a bump at the bottom, often called the chin or beard. Actually, the complete face found on that lowest bump is the classic Grandfather Profile. Photo by Randy Johnson.

you will find here is in no small part an homage to my favorite mountain, a love letter to a place that has captured the imaginations and enriched the lives of countless nature lovers in North Carolina and far beyond. As I strive to tell the mountain's story through the eyes and lives of people who loved it, we'll meet them in these pages, along with more than a few who lost their lives in passionate pursuit of the old man's secrets.

Finally, as Grandfather Mountain faces a bright future, let's reflect on the past and take a long look at the horizon. Now is a perfect time to gaze up to, and back on, a mountain whose very name makes it a patriarch of our collective family. Join me, for a hike through the history and nationally significant scenery of a truly singular summit—the great, evergreen Grandfather Mountain.

PART ONE

A History of the Mountain

Grandfather's impressive massif drops east from snow-dusted mountain ash and full blown autumn on the peaks to still-green forests far below in the Piedmont. Photo by Randy Johnson.

1 **Grandfather Mountain**
NATURALLY OUTSTANDING

You expect inspiring shapes from the world's iconic mountains. The elegant obelisk of the Matterhorn leaps to mind. At Grandfather, it's the mountain's signature profiles that put an acclaimed public face on this summit. Grandfather's distinctive patriarch is truly set in stone. Seen from both east and west, the mountain's highest ridge forms a figurative face looking skyward. Another profile gazes upward above Foscoe on the northwest ridge of Calloway Peak, from the summit to near NC 105. The most remarkably human face looks west from the lowest outcrop, the "beard" or "chin" of that bigger visage. With the sad loss of New Hampshire's "Old Man of the Mountains" on May 3, 2003, the anthropomorphic crown of the Appalachians settled solely on Grandfather. Actually—no slight intended to the North Country—it was already there. Grandfather had its face-based name before surveyors first sighted New Hampshire's Old Man in 1805. More than that, Grandfather's faces are more dramatic, more humanlike than the Old Man of New Hampshire's memory—and license plates still. But Grandfather's significance extends beyond a pretty face or four. Its profiles adorn a massive mountain that stands alone on the skyline at the crest of the Blue Ridge.

Geology of Grandfather Mountain

The geological term "window" may be unfamiliar, but in the case of the "Grandfather Mountain window" the concept draws the curtain on real insight into how this iconic mountain came to be. A geological window is where a layer of rock has eroded or broken open to expose a lower layer. Generally, a "window is an opening through younger rocks that permits a look back at older rocks below the surface," explains Anthony Love, a geologist and geology department researcher at Appalachian

Faces abound on the Grandfather Mountain, and they've been photographed and commented on for centuries. Early hiker D. R. Beeson captured this iconic image of the authentic Grandfather Profile in 1913. Courtesy of Archives of Appalachia, East Tennessee State University, D. R. Beeson Papers.

State University in Boone. In Grandfather's case, the upper layer is actually the older rock, the Linville Falls thrust sheet. A "hole" has formed in that upper layer—the Grandfather Mountain window—through which we see younger rock that accounts for Grandfather Mountain's ruggedness today. Grandfather's window is a triangular oval almost 50 miles long and as much as 20 miles wide. It's a big chunk of terrain that misses Boone but includes Linville and Linville Gorge.

That window makes Grandfather Mountain a great vantage point from which to appreciate how the grandeur of the Appalachians started and why so much of it remains on this special summit. "There are few places on Earth where so many people can ascend to the crest of a mountain range formed by the collision of continents," writes Robert J. Lillie in a Blue Ridge Parkway geology treatise. And there is "no other where they can drive the length of the crest." That's well known to geologists at Appalachian State, where students and researchers have been studying the Grandfather window for years. "The big hurdle we face

as scientists," Love laments, "is that our research is so laced with technical terms that it isn't simple to explain." Nevertheless, both Love and his colleague Dr. Loren Raymond, former geology department chairman, are experts on Grandfather Mountain's geology. Both men are drawn to it for more than scientific reasons—Raymond and his family to the rugged trails, and Love to Rough Ridge, one of the state's best rock-climbing sites. Each insists the creation of the Appalachians and the head-scratching concept of the Grandfather window are easy to understand if you don't get too technical. The key is plate tectonics, the notion that earth's surface consists of meandering sheets of crust and upper mantle—the lithosphere—that float atop softer, warmer matter called the asthenosphere. The collisions of those shifting plates have shaped the globe we spin on today, and the mountain we look up at. About 1 billion years ago, the collision of Africa and North America (an early continent called Rodinia) pierced the sky with peaks as high as the Alps or Himalayas. That earliest mountain-building event created what Raymond calls the "roots of Grandfather Mountain," distinctly different types of rock called gneiss that, adds Love, "contain the same minerals as granite; it's just been metamorphosed, squashed out, and compressed." Wilson Creek gneiss, Blowing Rock gneiss, and Cranberry gneiss were all formed between 1.2 and 1 billion years ago from sedimentary or igneous rocks during the intense heat and pressure of metamorphism, a force unleashed by the mountain-building collision that raised summits up and down the ancient continent's east coast. Love calls them "basement rocks"—the lowest structural level of the Blue Ridge and "some of the oldest rocks in the Appalachians."

Those "early" Appalachians, the Grenville Mountains, were ultimately eroded by water, wind, snow, and ice. As the tectonic plates that caused the collision spread apart, blocks of rock dropped down, and a continental rift zone, or rift valley, formed below, eventually filling up with layer upon layer of sediment eroded from higher ground. Love describes that process as you might see it today

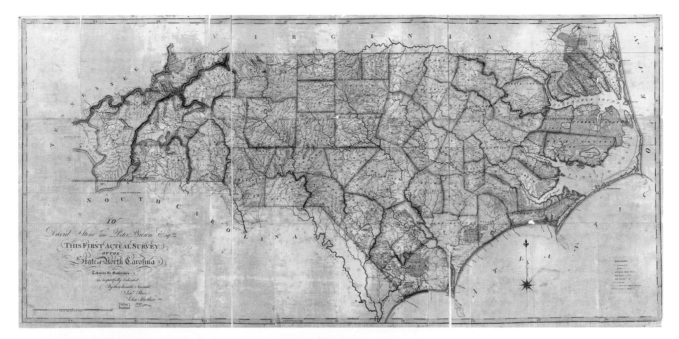

The earliest land grants bestowing ownership of property on or near the mountain in the late 1780s were already referring to the peak as Grandfather. By 1808, a possessive version of the mountain's anthropocentric name—"Grandfather's Mountain"—had made itself onto this early map in the Library of Congress, dubbed the "Price-Strother Map; First Actual Survey of North Carolina." Note that the landmarks at the time were not towns but the family-named farms of early, often noteworthy, backcountry settlers. North Carolina Collection, University of North Carolina Library at Chapel Hill.

on the scale of a small mountain stream, where an endless cycle of rains and floods generates silt and sand, layers of mud populated with pebbles and big rocks from above. Raymond calls that sediment-covered plain "the Grandfather Mountain Basin." The multilayered part of that plain that would "become the rocks of Grandfather Mountain" eventually "solidified to become rocks called conglomerate (former gravels), sandstone (former sands), and shale (former muds)," Raymond explains. Offers Love, "Grandfather Mountain's biggest contribution is that this is one of the oldest mountain-building events that we can easily recognize on the East Coast, where it's apparent that the continent was being torn apart—forming the

basin and the sediments that eventually became Grandfather." Ultimately, as Rodinia separated, an early North American continent, Laurentia, was on its own between 770 million and 600 million years ago. Cracks formed in the sedimentary surface left behind, and until about 740 million years ago, lava flows filled in the cracks with ancient eruptions. This three-quarter-billion-year-old material was the earliest form of the rock that would become Grandfather Mountain.

About 300 million years ago, "compressional tectonics" occurred again when the Iapetus Ocean between today's Africa and North America slammed shut, forming the megacontinent Pangea. That collision, the Alleghanian orogeny, pushed up

Grandfather Mountain's Backside

You're likely to overhear people talking about Grandfather's "backside." Not his posterior, but the mountain's "back side" versus the "front side." Ironically, few talk about the "front side" except by referencing the "back side." So which is which? That depends. From octogenarian Howard Byrd's side of the mountain in Foscoe, boyhood trips led "all along the back side, along US 221." Siblings Richard Chastain and Dixie Chastain Lemons grew up on the Blowing Rock side and they see it differently. "This is the front side we look at here," Richard maintains. Dixie agrees. "We have the correct view, with the outline of the man laying down. The back side is on NC 105."

In *The Carolina Mountains*, Margaret Morley concurs with the Chastains, describing a walk in Foscoe as "the back of the Grandfather," where "we see the profile from which the mountain is said to have received its name." If Morley thinks the "back side" profile is the "correct" one, is the Chastains' Blowing Rock face the wrong one? That, too, depends. Some think the "man laying down" from Blowing Rock is the best profile, and since many people first see the mountain from there, the "outline of the man laying down" must be the "front side," right? But wait. That "man laying down" from Blowing Rock looks the same from Banner Elk, so how can one face be front or back, right or wrong, especially if the true namesake "Old Man" overlooks Foscoe? Grandfather is silent on these vexing questions. It just may be that Grandfather's front side or back side is determined by which side you live on or like best. Either that or there are a lot of people who can't tell Grandfather's face from his backside.

SCENE FROM BLOWING ROCK ROADWAY

Blowing Rock's "front side" view of Grandfather is a postcard-perfect vista seen since visitors first made their way to this tempting tourism town in the late 1800s. The town's namesake viewpoint, The Blowing Rock, and the venerable Green Park Inn were early destinations, and still are. Shirley Stipp Ephemera Collection, D. H. Ramsey Library Special Collections, UNC Asheville 28804.

the Appalachians. And, Raymond points out, the massive heat and pressure of the collision changed the sedimentary rock layers of the Grandfather Mountain Basin. Metamorphism turned conglomerate into metaconglomerate, sandstone became metasandstone, and shale morphed into phyllite— all rocks still seen on the mountain. Another major geological event occurred during this collision of continents. The rock that would become Grandfather was covered up when the older rock of the Linville Falls thrust sheet was forced up and over the underlying rock. "That faulting process damaged the older rock, making it more susceptible to erosion," explains Love. All across the Grandfather Mountain window, from Linville Falls and Linville Gorge to Grandfather's rocky crest, the older, fragmented overlying layer eroded away. Gradually, the rugged, younger rock below protruded through the opening. Where Grandfather's summits rise today, a window to another time is thrown open wide. "Grandfather rock" eroded too, but those rocks also evolved, becoming intruded with other kinds of rock, some crystalizing into the erosion-resistant quartz so often seen on the mountain today. "A big part of the mountain's distinctive shape and ruggedness," Love maintains, "is the strength of the materials that are exposed." Quartz is visible all over the mountain as veins in other rock or crystal boulders, especially on the White Rock Ridge, where quartz was once mined. "The durability of quartzite accounts for the towering height of the mountain," asserts the Blue Ridge Parkway's 1997 official history of the Grandfather section of the road. It's the strength of the crags formed in that distant time that give such a striking appearance to the mountain today. The Grandfather Mountain window also provides a view into human history. Before designation of the first Southern Appalachian national parks—Shenandoah and Great Smoky Mountains—early national park proponents envisioned combining Grandfather Mountain and Linville Gorge as one park. Proximity recommended pairing the two, but a deeper kinship was revealed when the Grandfather Mountain window opened so long ago.

More Than a Pretty Face

Though decidedly his own man, Grandfather compares in size to other great Appalachian summits such as Mount Washington and Mount LeConte. Peaks connected to Mount Washington and Mount Mitchell complicate an apples-to-apples comparison with Grandfather, a monolith one 1950s newspaper wrote was distinguished by "its aloneness." Nevertheless, the bulk of all these mountains would fit into an imaginary 7-by-7-mile square drawn from adjacent gaps, notches, and lowlands. Grandfather's 50 square miles encompass more than just the crest we see above the Blue Ridge Parkway. Grandfather sprawls from the entrance to the Grandfather Mountain attraction on US 221 in the south, north to Holloway Mountain Road in the Blue Ridge Parkway's Julian Price Park. West to east, it runs from west of NC 105 across the main ridge and far down into Pisgah National Forest, its true base. Thanks to Grandfather's underlying geology, its many faces gaze out over a vast panorama. In *The Carolina Mountains*, Margaret Morley (1858–1923) says Grandfather impresses with its "splendid sweep directly up from the abysmal depths of the foothills with no intervening terraces. It has the effect of standing alone, its feet in the far-down valleys, its head in the clouds." The directness and size of that vertical rise distinguish Grandfather's jagged dominance over surrounding real estate. Elsewhere in the Southern Appalachians, adjacent plateaus and peaks soften the impact of elevation.

In *The Appalachians*, Maurice Brooks casts that consideration in stark relief, writing, "A mountain is impressive in proportion to its rise above the base." The essence of Brooks's point is that when a summit stands 4,000 or 5,000 feet above adjacent valleys, the immediate visual impact of elevation makes it obvious "this is a major peak." Take the Smokies' Mount LeConte, for example. From 6,593 feet, LeConte plummets to Gatlinburg at about 1,400 feet, just more than 5,000 feet. That's impressive by Appalachian standards, but more than that, Brooks notes, it's "comparable, so far as rise is concerned to standing in Estes Park and

Hugh Morton owned the most rugged mountain in the South; but he wanted more, and the "Fantascope" camera gave it to him.
If anything it made the Profile ridge even more facelike. Linville Peak and the Swinging Bridge looked like something out of Switzerland.
North Carolina Collection, University of North Carolina Library at Chapel Hill. Photos by Hugh Morton.

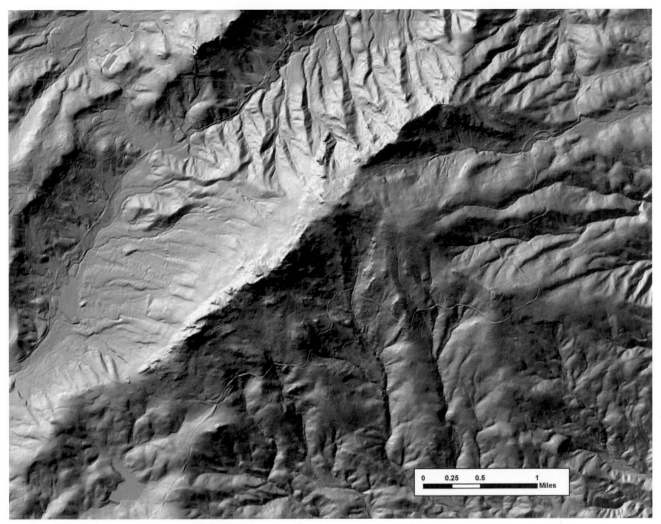

A LIDAR map, named for Light Detecting And Ranging, of the mountain nicely reflects the rugged topography even without topographic lines. This map tracks the mountain's descent far down its eastern slope. N.C. Geological Survey.

looking toward the Rockies' Front Range." That analysis yields a remarkably unappreciated accolade for Appalachia: The East's highest summits boast a Rocky Mountain–like elevation change. Grandfather is a member of that elite club, rising 4,800 feet above its base. LeConte's 5,200 feet of vertical drop and Mount Washington's maximum of nearly 5,500 feet exceed Grandfather's rise (due largely to their added height above Grandfather's 5,946 feet). Nevertheless, Grandfather's relief is among the greatest in the East, equaling Mount Washington's dramatic lift above New Hampshire valley towns like Jefferson or Berlin (pronounced BER-lin). Grandfather's perch atop the Blue Ridge gives it the airy sense of altitude found atop Mount Katahdin in Maine, another premier massif that

stands largely alone above lake-dotted lowlands. That northernmost anchor of the Appalachian Trail drops about 4,700 feet in 5 miles.

Pardon my partisanship, but I'd argue that the unobstructed plummet from Grandfather's rock-capped crest equals the impact of peaks with even greater vertical relief. Margaret Morley appreciates that when she describes the distinct edge of the Piedmont as a "shoreless sea of the lowlands." That oceanlike expanse of flatland North Carolina still impresses today. Other writers have used oceanic imagery in praise of the view. Wilbur G. Zeigler and Ben S. Grosscup's 1883 book *The Heart of the Alleghenies* compares the lowest foothills to "a stormy ocean stilled." With "cumuli building on the horizon you fancy hearing the sound

Grandfather's Shrinking Summits

The first time I saw a metal survey disk (often called a benchmark) embedded in the precariously perched boulder of MacRae Peak, I did a double take. Imagine surveying this spot in 1933, I mused. Believe it or not, says Gary Thompson, director of the North Carolina Geological Survey, even these old survey markers are not obsolete. The National Height Modernization Program is updating the disks, and that's how Calloway Peak came to shrink. Calloway was listed as 5,964 feet in 1917, back when Mount Mitchell was 6,711 feet, not its current 6,684. In 2008, GPS satellites made a switch, flopping Calloway's 64 to 46, making it 5,946 feet. Some folks seriously suggest it always was 46 until some unknown, dyslexic clerk made a typographical error. Other elevations changed too. MacRae Peak went from 5,939 feet to 5,844. The on-mountain measurements were made by Suttles Surveying of Marion. "That was the most difficult terrain we've ever been in," chuckled Ken Suttles. "We've never had to climb ladders up cliffs before." The Mile-High Swinging Bridge was also remeasured, and it lucked out. The north tower is 5,282 feet and the far end is 5,278 feet. That was a relief for Hugh Morton's grandson, who learned of the elevation changes as the mountain's president. "That means," sighed Hugh MacRae "Crae" Morton III, "there is a spot in the middle of the bridge that is precisely one mile high." Most survey disks, often called benchmarks, establish elevation or horizontal location, but MacRae's disk is a triangulation station used to plot bearings to other peaks. Benchmark replicas are available for mountains all over the world, including a version of MacRae's disk. Search "benchmark replicas" on the Internet.

1 MILE 5,280 FT

Crae Morton's incredulous but relieved realization that the middle of the Swinging Bridge is exactly a mile above sea level has become a memorable photo-op for visitors. Photo by Todd Bush/www.bushphoto.com.

of breakers." Zeigler loved grappling with big horizons. His 1895 *It Was Marlowe* first proposed that Christopher Marlowe wrote Shakespeare's plays. The impression of overviewing an ocean is most striking when inspiring, oft-seen undercast spreads below Grandfather. Morley describes the scene as "all the world blotted out, excepting the Grandfather's summit rising out of the white mists, so firm to the eye that one is tempted to step out on it." The mountain's frequent sea of cloud stretches from the great gulf to the east, across valleys to the south, where the distant Black Mountains, highest in the East at almost 6,700 feet, jut above Grandfather's encircling carpet of mist. Eddie Clark, 1980s environmental habitat manager, once crossed the Swinging Bridge with a group of Greensboro kids on their first trip to the mountains. They gasped at the cloud layer, asking, "Is that the ocean? Are we looking down on the beach?" No, they weren't, as a few lucky hikers have on Mount Washington, glimpsing the Atlantic 73 miles away. Hugh Morton's photo of the Charlotte skyline 82 miles from Grandfather reveals a similar range of vision, but you'll never see the Atlantic, 235 miles distant at Myrtle Beach, from Grandfather. At night, oceanic analogies take on galactic imagery. As a first-time camper on Grandfather's peaks, I'll never forget my awestruck surprise when pitch darkness fell on the Pisgah National Forest's foothills and distant Piedmont cities emerged as sprawling, pulsating pinwheels of light in the void beyond.

Grandfather also mesmerizes with its strikingly convoluted countenance. From Blowing Rock, Morley asserted, no other summit "can approach the Grandfather's black top in size and impressiveness, it being a landmark far and near." It impresses closer up, too, with adventurous ruggedness rare in the South. All these elements inspire the imagination. "Sometimes the Grandfather Mountain stands solidly out," Morley described, then "it is blue and seems made of mists and shadows. Sometimes the sunset glory penetrates . . . translucent in the sea of light. As night draws on, it darkens into a noble silhouette [that] draws the

curves of its summit in lines of fire." From many High Country vantage points, the view is ever changing. "Those wild shapes" that "look so near, so hard, and so terrible, at another time recede, immersed in an exquisite sea of mystical light." Ultimately, the shape of this massive mountain helps make a massive impression. No wonder those who gaze upon its heights often fall in thrall for a lifetime.

Birthplace of Rivers

With Grandfather's elevation and dramatic rise, its bowls and basins throw off streams like sparks from flint and steel. Arthur Keith (1864–1944), the first to map the geology of the Grandfather area between 1894 and 1907, wrote that "a small district around Grandfather Mountain . . . forms one of the chief watersheds of the Appalachians." Three counties, Avery, Caldwell, and Watauga (wa-TAW-ga) intersect on Calloway Peak. The verdant westward-facing ridge of the Eastern Continental Divide wrings rain and snow from clouds and splits the flow into the Linville and Watauga Rivers "rising within a few rods of each other," in the words of Swiss geographer Arnold Guyot (1807–84). The Linville flows south via the Catawba to the Atlantic; the Watauga runs west to the Mississippi and Gulf of Mexico. Not far from Grandfather, the Linville carves Linville Gorge, "a fearful and perfectly impassable chasm . . . from the plateau of the Grandfather forming magnificent waterfalls," Guyot wrote. The Watauga carves its own canyon, one of the region's favorite whitewater rides. Boone Fork drains the mountain's biggest valley and feeds the Watauga in Foscoe. Elk River runs from Banner Elk over precipitous Elk Falls. Wilson Creek seeps from Grandfather's highest springs, then plummets east steeper and farther than any National Wild and Scenic River in eastern America—nearly 5,000 feet over 17 air miles. On the way, it gouges Wilson Creek Gorge out of the oldest rocks in the Appalachians. One of Pisgah National Forest's most scenic trout streams, it's among the most challenging whitewater runs in the East. These rivers flow far and lose their early

Cars come and go on the Linn Cove Viaduct, but far beyond the inky darkness of the Pisgah National Forest, Piedmont urban areas seem to float in a void far below. Photo by Tommy White Photography, www .tommywhitephotography.com.

"Soaring in Solitude." The hang glider exhibition flights of the 1970s and 1980s may be long gone from the Grandfather attraction, but the Tater Hill Open still attracts some gliders and legions of modern paragliders to the Boone area in summer. Many soar with the Grandfather dominating the skyline. Photo by Lynne Townsend.

identities, but we can thank Grandfather for crystal water that sustains and entertains.

All of these ecological and geological distinctions make Grandfather a truly rarefied showcase of biological diversity. The Nature Conservancy calls this a repository of life second to none in eastern America, an "ecological site of global significance." New England's glaciers contributed, pushing northern plant species south, offering them an escape hatch on the heights of the Blue Ridge. Grandfather Mountain became one of the richest of those refuges, evolving over millennia as a sweet spot of biodiversity, a fitting intersection where the southernmost part of the North meets the northernmost part of the South. The ice sheet that scoured northern Appalachian summits—and shaped New Hampshire's Old Man of the Mountains—didn't reach Grandfather, whose west-facing profile and skyline face gazing at the heavens surely predated Grandfather's brother to the north. The Old Man has passed into history, but we can take heart that the Grandfather of the Eastern Mountains is still with us. As a hiker says in Shepherd Dugger's 1892 *The Balsam Groves of*

the Grandfather Mountain, "You now *see* the genuine old man of the mountains." We can't stop the natural processes that caused the Old Man to lose face recently, but with any luck, it'll be millennia before those forces change North Carolina's Grandfather. For now, he's still looking west into his sunset years, facing a bright new future of preservation in perpetuity.

Visit the Nature Museum

The Grandfather Mountain Nature Museum features the mountain's geology. Loren Raymond; Rolland Hower, former chief of natural history exhibits at the Smithsonian; and son Craig designed the museum's 4.65-billion-year geological time line. In 2003 Hower asserted that the exhibit "takes the visitor from volcanic eruptions to the . . . erosion that opened the Grandfather Mountain window." Dated rock specimens include explanations of how each type of rock was formed. The Museum of North Carolina Minerals on the Blue Ridge Parkway 26 miles south of US 221 at Grandfather is another impressive museum resource for understanding local geology.

2 The Early Explorers and Scientists

Early sun illuminates the Boone Fork Bowl and Calloway Peak from Price Lake. You can almost smell the campfire smoke from Price Park Campground. Photo by Skip Sickler/http://skipsickler.zenfolio.com.

People have gazed up at Grandfather Mountain from the earliest human habitation of the North Carolina mountains, and some imagined human profiles peering back at them. Eventually, European explorers arrived who recorded their journeys. Even as settlers scattered near Grandfather in the early 1800s, the mountain's rugged terrain deterred casual contact. You really had to want to get close to Grandfather Mountain, much less climb it. The missions of early visitors were many, but their writings reveal some of the Appalachians' most iconic incidents of exploration and discovery. Some early sojourners just reached the mountain's environs, but their experiences convey Grandfather's unique character and why it inspired renown. Part of Grandfather's allure, back then and now, is its wildness. Explorers came and went, and so did their faint trails. Grandfather was almost trackless into the twentieth century. Eventually, in the 1940s, a network of rough but formal paths was built by volunteers, but they too started reverting back to forest, a fact I discovered on my first early 1970s Grandfather hike. A few abused signs and deteriorating log ladders led me to MacRae Peak from the Swinging Bridge, but on backcountry hikes from NC 105 and US 221, one obscure, challenging path led to another. Grandfather had an air of adventure not found on crowded national park and forest trails. Only later did I realize my first encounters with the mountain were akin to those of far earlier explorers. Many a pioneering scientist climbed the general route of the sketchy Shanty Spring Trail, from Invershiel up the Eastern Continental Divide. That was the first path I cleared, signed, and blazed in 1978 to start the backcountry program. The impending Wilmor development closed that trail in the late 1980s, and today, one of eastern America's longest-lived hiking routes is completely overgrown—again. The last time I "hiked" the area, basically struggling up the former trail corridor, the mountain had largely erased the evidence of all who'd gone before. For someone who'd personally reclaimed the trail almost forty years earlier, it was a humbling experience of human transience.

One of the first white men to approach Grandfather recorded a similarly humbling experience. Moravian bishop Augustus Gottlieb Spangenberg, superintendent of Moravian affairs in Pennsylvania, was searching in 1752 to find a new Moravian base. His small party struggled into the Blue Ridge, at times "on hands and knees, dragging after us the loads we had taken from the backs of the horses, for had we not unsaddled them, they would have fallen backwards down the mountain." They saw "hundreds of mountains rising like great waves in a storm." Soon the storm they encountered was literal. As Spangenberg writes, "We pitched our tent, but such a storm burst upon us that we could scarcely protect ourselves. The ground was soon covered with snow ankle deep, and the water froze for us aside the fire." Ultimately, he and his party retreated downhill, choosing to settle in a tract of piedmont backcountry they called Wachovia, centering on a town named Salem (now Winston-Salem). Spangenberg became the first piedmont tourist to wish he'd taken warmer clothes to the mountains.

But soon another wave of explorers arrived: scientists seeking the botanic secrets of a New World clothed in primeval forests long absent in the old. To glimpse that setting, I've fantasized taking a time machine to Calloway Peak in 1794, to join French botanist André Michaux as he mistakenly proclaimed Grandfather the "highest mountain of all North America." In a way, I did take a time machine. "Bonjour, je m'appelle André Michaux," said the wizened man in the tricorner hat. It was April 2013, and I was visiting the rude backcountry residence of Colonel John Tipton, Revolutionary War soldier and Tennessee legislator. Tipton was long gone; but his 1784 home remains as Tennessee's Tipton-Haynes State Historic Site, and this was "Michaux Day." Thomas Jefferson urged Michaux to stop at Tipton's home, and he did in 1795 and '96. The historical reenactor channeling Michaux, retired Charlotte librarian

When Hugh Morton climbed into an airplane in the 1940s and took this photo over still-undeveloped Sugar Mountain, Grandfather towered inviolate above Linville Gap in a way that many early explorers and scientists might have recognized in the late 1800s. North Carolina Collection, University of North Carolina Library at Chapel Hill. Photo by Hugh Morton.

Charles Williams, was excited to know I live below his beloved Grandfather Mountain. Williams has won awards for enhancing the Frenchman's renown and, since 2000, has "appeared" dressed as Michaux, sharing the details of his life at botanical conventions, scientific meetings, and the unveiling of Michaux historical markers. I hoped my living history "visit with André" would breathe life into Michaux's experience on Grandfather.

The real André Michaux (1746–1802) was born in Satory, France, son of a farmer on the royal lands of Versailles. His agricultural talents, and a little tragedy, took him to the pinnacle of the bud-ding field of botany—and the peaks of Grandfather Mountain. When his young wife Cecile Claye died giving birth to son François André (also a future famous botanist), Michaux set out to make his mark as a scientist-explorer. He studied under botanist Bernard de Jussieu and demonstrated such pluck on a trip to the Middle East that he was named the King's botanist. Michaux was in the United States in 1785 with his fifteen-year-old son and founded a plant collection garden in Charleston, South Carolina. He took nine major journeys of exploration from Canada to the tropics and published the quintessential early book on Ameri-

Michaux reenactor Charlie Williams "goes Michaux" on Linville Peak, breaking into song as Michaux did, arms spread wide, eyes on the horizon. Photo by Randy Johnson.

can botany, the *Flora Boreali Americana* (*The Flora of North America*). Michaux strode onto the world stage with other greats, including John Bartram (1699–1777) and his son William, and John Fraser (1750–1811), the Scot whose name appends many Southern Appalachian species. Michaux found new and rare plants and shipped them to France. He also imported ornamentals from Europe that still adorn America's gardens. He encouraged mountain residents to collect and sell ginseng to the Chinese, igniting a still-thriving export plant industry. Michaux's 1794–95 Grandfather Mountain foray took him to Mount Mitchell, Roan Mountain, and the Linville Gorge and introduced him to Revolutionary War veterans like Colonel Waightstill Avery (1741–1821), namesake of the future Avery County (1911), whose grandson would later own Grandfather Mountain. Michaux engaged Avery's employee Martin Davenport as his Grandfather guide, visiting him again in 1796. In 1802, son François André saw Davenport during later travels in America.

On August 26, 1794, Michaux wrote that they started "for Grandfather Mountain, the most elevated of all those which form the chain of the Alleghanies [*sic*] and Appalachians." They paused to "herborize" and camp, then on the 30th, they "climbed to the highest mountain of all North

Sunday, August 24, I worked at putting my collection in order.
August 25, rain.
August 26, we left for Grandfather's Mountain, the highest of those that make up the Alleghany and the Appalachian.
August 27, we arrived at the base of the highest mountain.
August 28, we climbed as far as the boulders.
August 29, I continued my botanizing, among the various mosses, there were Pinus Abies balsamifera, Abies nigra, Acer pensylvanicum, etc. etc. etc.
August 30, we climbed to the summit of the highest mountain of all North America, and with my companion and guide sang the hymn, "La Marseillaise" and yelled "Long life to America and the French Republic, Long life to Liberty", etc, etc.
Sunday, August 31, we stayed in camp as it rained all day.

Michaux's original diary page from his Grandfather visit, long held by America's oldest scientific organization, Ben Franklin's American Philosophical Society. This log offers the best image we have of Michaux. No portrait exists from his lifetime. American Philosophical Society, Philadelphia. Journal of André Michaux 1794 (excerpt) translated from the French by Eliane N. Norman.

Native Americans and "The Cave of the Dawn Man"

It's known that Native Americans "passed through" the High Country on seasonal hunting trips, but Grandfather's biggest mystery may be why the rock shelter atop Attic Window Peak is called Indian House Cave.

Asheville Citizen-Times columnist and author John Parris (1914–99) romanticized aspects of mountain culture but none more so than this cave and the trail that reaches it. The Grandfather Trail was the "Trail of Thirteen Ladders" to Parris, an inspiring attraction, and the most amazing spot on that trail was Indian House Cave. "The Cave of the Dawn Man," he called it. This cave "nestles in a wilderness of trees and rugged cliffs and

A 1951 newspaper article credited Joe Hartley with building the side trail to the cave. The giant opening was "hidden by dense growth of balsam and birch," Hartley related, all of which was "cleared in order that light might enter and photographs could be made." Hartley's muddy pants attest to the effort. North Carolina Collection, University of North Carolina Library at Chapel Hill. Photo by Hugh Morton.

brooding silence," Parris wrote. Once "shrouded in the mists of antiquity," the cave was discovered in 1892 when Alex MacRae was searching for his father's sheep and "became the first white man to enter the tremendous stone room." Alex was the son of Scottish immigrant "Alick" MacRae, who lived at MacRae Meadows. In Parris's tale, "scattered about the floor of the cave were spearpoints, arrowheads, tomahawk heads and shards of pottery. Summer after summer," claimed Parris, Alex "fought his way up to the scraggly wilderness heights to fill his pockets with the ancient relics" and sell them to tourists. MacRae divulged his story in 1951, and the mountain's legendary warden Joe Hartley opened a side trail to the cave only to find "the floor was bare. There was nothing to show that man had ever lived within that great cave."

Actually, research on Indian "rock shelters" in the High Country shows that only small numbers of Indians ever lived near the mountain much less anywhere on it, maintains Dr. Thomas Whyte, an Appalachian State University anthropology professor who specializes in Southern Appalachian prehistory. All residential activity at these craggy overhangs and at the Boone area's best-known Indian location, a one-acre palisaded village called the Ward site in Cove Creek, dates to one 500-year "warming" period between A.D. 900 and about A.D. 1450. Before and after those dates, Indians were infrequent visitors, especially above 2,500 feet, which precludes "what we think of as settlements akin to the prehistoric Cherokee" anywhere near Grandfather Mountain. In fact, the High Country's few Indians weren't Cherokees at all but "members of Late Woodland societies which made them more Siouxan or ancestors of the Catawbas." Most Southern Appalachian Indians lived in deeper valleys with warmer temperatures. They "couldn't grow maize in the uplands, it was too cold," Whyte asserts. That was definitely the case during the Little Ice Age from about A.D. 1300 or so to the mid-1800s. After the heyday of the Ward site in the eleventh century, Whyte reveals, the cooling climate "restricted human settlement to individual households between A.D. 1200 and 1450 and discouraged permanent settlement thereafter."

No wonder Moravian Bishop Augustus Gottlieb Spangenberg found snow and cold near Grandfather in 1752, but no residents, red or white.

Searching for Indians

Until very recently, Indian House Cave had seen only one informal archeological survey. In the mid-1970s, Dr. Harvard Ayers, emeritus professor of anthropology at Appalachian State, dug a test pit at the cave but found nothing. Even that tentative study was sufficient to confirm that sheepherders looking for arrowheads were unlikely to have so denuded the site of related debris, called debitage, that an expert would find no evidence of Indian stone work. The picture has gotten clearer under state park ownership. In 2012, a state park employee found a bona fide "flake tool" on the upper Daniel Boone Scout Trail. Also in 2012, a Woodland period arrowhead was found in a rock shelter on Grandfather Mountain Stewardship Foundation property. In 2013, Appalachian State student Josh Goodwin studied six rock shelters in the "lower summit" region around 4,000 feet and found evidence of sporadic prehistoric use at four overhangs.

In the summer of 2015, Dr. Whyte and his students dug two test excavations in Indian House Cave and found nothing, the best evidence so far that "earlier findings of articfacts in the cave are considered untrue." There isn't yet evidence that Native Americans did more than pass the mountain and pause at lower elevation rock shelters to maintain weapons, but romantic stories abound. In 1980 when a plane crash claimed a victim on the mountain, local writer Bertie Cantrell (now Burleson) called on her Native American heritage. "The legend goes back to the Cherokees who worshipped in the cave under the Attic Window Peak of the Grandfather Mountain," she wrote. "They believed Grandfather Mountain was a 'Power Mountain,' that they could be imbued with that power by scaling its heights, and dwelling there for a space. They also believed the Grandfather claimed what he wanted for his own. With last week's plane crash," she suggested, "the legend comes alive once more, despite the talk about altimeters and tail winds." Whether Indians ever found power on Grandfather, modern hikers routinely come back from the heights refreshed by a mountain that regularly renews the human spirit.

America, and with my companion and guide sang the Marseillaise hymn, and cried, 'Long live America and the French Republic! long live Liberty!' etc." Michaux's erroneous exclamation was noteworthy early evidence that this mountain, though not 6,000 feet, has bigger scenic appeal than many a higher peak. "When Michaux got to the top of Grandfather," Williams explains, "he'd already been up on Roan and to the top of Mitchell," yet he called Grandfather "the most elevated of all," suggesting it appeared higher than other summits of his acquaintance. The mountain's near-vertical-mile relief and distinctive setting still bolster my belief that Grandfather may be the South's most striking summit. In my mind, Michaux's iconic Grandfather adventure makes him an eighteenth-century Indiana Jones, albeit one interested in plants, not pyramids. Charles Kuralt went further. The folksy, North Carolina–

born arbiter of Americana called Michaux "one of the most remarkable human beings of the 18th Century, or of any century." Speaking at Grandfather's Swinging Bridge in 1994, on the 200th anniversary of Michaux's climb, Kuralt marveled that Michaux spent "ninety nights of every hundred writing his notes by campfire or under the light of the moon somewhere in the wilderness." Kuralt argued that Michaux should occupy the "place in our imagination" afforded Daniel Boone, an explorer and self-promoter ultimately tainted by the quintessentially American shortcoming of speculating in land. "Unlike Boone and other trail-blazers of the period," Kuralt reminded, "the only wealth [Michaux] sought was scientific knowledge."

There's plenty of land speculation going on in the shadow of Grandfather today, but Daniel Boone's very real ties to the mountain don't include such things. With parents Squire and Sarah, Daniel Boone (1734–1820) and his siblings moved in 1750 from Pennsylvania to the Yadkin Valley near Mocksville. There in the Carolina backcountry, young Daniel and friend Henry Miller took their "first long hunt, inspired by Indian patterns and habits," writes Robert Morgan in *Boone: A Biography*. This "extended foray into the wilderness in quest of fur and game and adventure" led them into "the high hunting ranges that seemed to float in blue mystery on the horizon." Boone saw Grandfather Mountain on that horizon, and the sight inspired lust for the lands beyond. After he married in 1756, Boone and wife Rebecca moved to the Brushy Mountains, closer to the High Country. He met a slave named Burrell in 1760 who herded cows "near the head of the Watauga River," Morgan writes. Looking back in 1845, Burrell recalled guiding Boone on the explorer's first trip over the Blue Ridge. "On a high, sweeping meadow," he and Boone reached a cabin built by Benjamin Howard, namesake of 4,396-foot Howard Knob, the summit above today's town of Boone. Here, Boone and companions found themselves in "the backwater," asserts Morgan, beyond the Eastern Continental Divide where the Watauga and New River flow to the Mississippi. Like those waters, Boone was heading west. As late as 1892, Shepherd Dugger's *Balsam Groves* maintained that "the pile of stones that still marks the place of [Howard's] chimney is being rapidly carried away by relic-seekers." William Lewis Bryan, Boone's first mayor and a relative of Daniel Boone's wife, Rebecca Bryan Boone, claimed he used the remainder of those stones to build a memorial called "The Chimney" that still stands in Boone on Rivers Street. Not far away, another sculpture depicts Boone by a campfire with his hunting dogs.

Boone was no stranger to the High Country, and he started carving his autograph into the bark of trees. The Grandfather Mountain Nature Museum has a replica of one "tag." On his first trip to Kentucky in 1769, Boone crossed the Blue Ridge in Cook's Gap just north of Grandfather at today's "Boone's Trace" overlook on the Blue

MONUMENT TO DANIEL BOONE, MARKING SITE WHERE

29202

HE ONCE LIVED, BOONE, N. C.

Daniel Boone's presence can still be felt. The town of Boone's original very rustic monument to Daniel eventually became this postcard structure that still stands. It's lately been joined by a statue of the man. A reproduction of Dan'l's tree-carving signature at Grandfather Mountain's Nature Museum also attracts a lot of attention. *Shirley Stipp Ephemera Collection, D. H. Ramsey Library Special Collections, UNC Asheville 28804.*

Ridge Parkway (milepost 285.1). Another oft-heard connection between Daniel and the area holds that a village north of Boone was named Meat Camp for the location of a Boone hunting cabin. An intriguingly different spelling emerges from nineteenth-century Wisconsin librarian Lyman Draper's frontier research. A hand-drawn map that includes Grandfather depicts Boone's hunting forays near the mountain and spells Meat Camp as Meet Camp. "Tradition," the local informant wrote long ago, "says it was so called from the fact that it was the camp for Boone and his associates to meet for hunting across the mountain." The Boone name

The Boone name reaches all the way to Grandfather's Calloway Peak in the form of Boone Fork, the stream that feeds the Parkway's Price Lake. From a kayak on the lake or the waterside Price Lake Trail, there's a great view of the creek's headwaters, seen here high on the mountain. Photo by Tommy White Photography, www.tommywhitephotography.com.

and legend are visible all over the High Country, and Grandfather Mountain is no exception. The Boone Fork still flows there today, born in the bowl-shaped valley below Grandfather's highest summit, a chasm that dominates Blue Ridge Parkway views. But Daniel's nephew Jesse Boone is this stream's namesake, and he did more than just pass through the High Country. Born in 1748, Jesse was raised by Daniel and Rebecca Boone after the death of his father, Daniel's brother Israel. Daniel and Rebecca left for Kentucky in 1773, and in 1810, Jesse and wife Sarah McMahan settled "near Coffey's Gap" on "100 acres on the head waters of Watauga river," records an Ashe County deed (Watauga was formed in 1849). John Preston Arthur's 1915 *History of Watauga County* claimed Jesse's cabin stood "in a five-acre field four miles above Shull's Mills. The foundation stones of the old chimney and the spring are still pointed out."

Few notice, or reveal, the cabin's remains today, but a stream named for a member of Daniel's immediate family meanders from Grandfather's summit along the Parkway to the Watauga River in Foscoe.

Other than the 1940s Daniel Boone Scout Trail, there is no evidence that Daniel himself ever climbed Grandfather Mountain. Imaginings may be all we have, but the mountain definitely had what wanderers needed most: great views. Despite an almost photographic memory for topography, Boone had to look out over the land. It's hard to believe he approached a peak long familiar to him from afar, towering over the puzzle of the Blue Ridge, and decided not to look down from its summit. I'd bet Daniel Boone climbed Grandfather Mountain. Arthur left us added evidence, explaining that Boone "preferred to cross two high mountains" rather than follow "a well-worn and well-known Indian trail . . . in the direction he

Horn in the West: A Glimpse of Boone

In 2000, *New York Times* theater critic Marilyn Stasio elevated America's "outdoor dramas," writing that the best should be celebrated as "heritage dramas." That includes *Horn in the West*, a June-to-August treasure staged in Boone by the Southern Appalachian Historical Association (SAHA). The play showcases backcountry patriots who turned the tide of the Revolution by defeating British-led Tories at the battle of King's Mountain. Daniel Boone is a prominent character, but *Horn*'s iconic figure was actor Glenn Causey. He played Boone on the drama's opening night in 1952 and hung up his coonskin cap after portraying Daniel from 1956 to 1996 and never missing a performance in forty-one years, surely one of the longest-running dramatic roles in any genre of theater. "Imagine being his understudy," marvels Stasio. Causey became the area's image of Boone, appearing as Dan'l in photos and as the model for a painting of Boone at the Grandfather Mountain Nature Museum. He received North Carolina's highest civilian honor, the Order of the Long Leaf Pine, in 1999 and passed away in 2000. Adjacent to *Horn in the West*, don't miss SAHA's Hickory Ridge Living History Museum where costumed reenactors demonstrate pioneer culture. The museum's collection of historic structures includes the late 1700s Tatum Cabin, one of the area's oldest buildings. Summer Saturday mornings are a tasty time to visit when the Watauga County Farmer's Market

Hugh Morton's camera documented Mildred the Bear's countless encounters with celebrities. *Horn in the West*'s quintessential Daniel Boone, Glenn Causey, was one of them. North Carolina Collection, University of North Carolina Library at Chapel Hill. Photo by Hugh Morton.

bustles beside the museum. The route of the pioneer militia, the Overmountain National Historic Trail, passes near Grandfather, and in nearby Elizabethton, Tennessee, Sycamore Shoals State Historic Park inspiringly interprets the spot where the Overmountain men mobilized before King's Mountain (http://tnstateparks.com/parks/about /sycamore-shoals).

---

wished to go." Boone was always trying to avoid Indians and their valley paths, but, Morgan told me, Boone "sometimes followed a trail over the top of Grandfather Mountain on his way into the vast hunting territories of the Cherokees." Even if Boone never went directly over the peaks, his penchant for bear meat and pelts likely led him on an Indian trail said to cross the eastern flank of Grandfather, where US 221 and the Blue Ridge Parkway are now. The Cherokee name for that path was Yonahlossee—"passing bear" or "bear trail." Almost anywhere Boone might have walked in

that area, cliffs and crags would have revealed the endless views we see today from the Blue Ridge Parkway's Tanawha Trail.

Boone stuck to the summits to avoid Indians, but Elisha Mitchell (1793–1857) was the ultimate "peak bagger." His single-minded focus on measuring North Carolina's highest peak ultimately gained him the honor of having eastern America's loftiest summit named Mount Mitchell in his honor. Sadly, the famously multitalented University of North Carolina professor had to plunge off a waterfall and die in the effort. That "height makes right" mission could have eliminated a visit to 5,946-foot Grandfather, but even Mitchell climbed North Carolina's most spectacular peak. During the summer of 1827 he was a researcher for the state Geological and Agricultural Survey, a tour recounted in long-lost letters to his wife published in a 1905 University of North Carolina monograph. Although theologian Mitchell was born in Connecticut, the introduction credits him with "cogent arguments against the Abolitionists on the Slavery question."

Mitchell's arrival in the mountains near Jefferson was met with an irreverent jab we can appreciate today. A "fellow raised a report on the muster ground yesterday," he wrote, "that I had received from the state 9,000 dollars for passing through and looking at the rocks." He got his first glimpse of Grandfather from Mount Jefferson, then "called the Negro Mountain," proclaiming, "Oh what an ocean of mountains." Today's Mount Jefferson State Natural Area summit road still offers that vista. He also climbed "White top, an exceedingly high mountain covered with white clover and cattle." Meadows still cap Virginia's second-highest peak. "The Grandfather Mountain, as I supposed it to be, with a craggy and irregular summit was seen at the south." Mitchell was so impressed, he indicted friends who'd been in the area but hadn't climbed the ridges. "The best thing they can do in order to prevent themselves from becoming infamous in all after ages," he wrote his wife, "is to mount their horses and make the same trip again; taking in the mountains."

Mitchell passed through Boone before it was Boone, encountering the area's founding families. "Council's store was open," he wrote; "some were hunting, a waggon hauling plank; Mitchell and Calloway electioneered by the way." His climbing party included later state senator Noah Mast, "to whose father's on Watauga [River] we are going." Starting for Grandfather on a "foggy, cloudy and rainy" July morning, Mitchell "purchased small bear skin from Mr. Mast." The thoroughly soaked group paused at a Mast son's "bachelor's hall" and rode past "knobs with very indecent names."

Mitchell had no way of knowing Grandfather would become its own geological window, but he nevertheless recorded that the rocks changed as he neared the mountain. The party parked horses and ate lunch in Linville Gap, noticing, as many later would, that they could "get water from either [the Linville or Watauga River] within two or three hundred yards." Climbing the Continental Divide, "the ascent of the mountain is rough, thickety and disagreeable," he wrote, with "steep, perpendicular cliffs in places." Like hikers 150 years later on the Shanty Spring Trail, Mitchell refreshed at a gushing spring below one of those cliffs.

Mitchell was impressed with Grandfather's climate and "peculiar" summit vegetation. High-altitude sedges "constitute the principal grasses," and they still do, adding an alpine feel. Mitchell saw Fraser fir (*Abies fraseri*), a species confined to the Southern Appalachians and first described by Scottish botanist John Fraser, but he seems to have mistaken it for the balsam fir (*Abies balsamea*) that grows from West Virginia to New England. The tree "grows quite to the top but it is stunted and smaller there, and along with one other tree occupies exclusively the highest points." Mitchell saw Fraser fir growing beside red spruce. He implies that the bare crags of today may have been obscured by virgin timber, requiring an ascent of centuries-old evergreens to see the view. "The prospect was all but infinite. Table rock which appeared as a considerable eminence at Morganton was dwindled down to a Mole Hill." The hike might have encouraged Mitchell's later fixation. "I suspect the Black and Roan to be higher peaks," he wrote, and he was correct in both cases even then. It's amusing to hear the mountain neophyte admit that "the climate of the summit must be considerably colder than that of Chapel Hill." One cohort "complained bitterly of the coldness of the wind and I felt it myself."

The descending party rushed "to reach the cabin of Mr. Leatherstocking Aldridge" for a feast, but they had to camp under a shelving rock. The bear skin served "Mr. Noah Mast and myself," Mitchell recalled. "Thus furnished I lying in the middle and

"Leatherstocking" Aldridge led Elisha Mitchell up the mountain in 1827. At the time, the guide had a six-year-old son named Harrison who would become a noted 1800s bear hunter in the Grandfather Community. Harrison Aldridge still lies in his ancestors' lands, looking up as he often did at the Grandfather Mountain. Photo by Randy Johnson.

with a blazing fire at our feet we passed a pleasanter night than I had expected. I looked at my watch a good many times to see if it was not nearly morning." Days later, Mitchell's feet were "still sore with the peeling they had got in the ascent of the Grandfather." The trip yielded one cogent conclusion: "There can be no doubt that the country around the base of the Grandfather is higher than any other tract along these elevations." Mitchell had noticed why the surrounding area would later be dubbed the "High South" and then the "High Country." The good minister grasped why so many feel a little closer to heaven with Grandfather Mountain visible above.

Elisha Mitchell went on to later notoriety, but in 1841, Grandfather attracted a truly famous botani-cal visitor, arguably the archetypal scientist of nineteenth-century America. Asa Gray (1810–88) was "the go-to guy in American botany," says Michaux reenactor Charlie Williams. Gray would write the definitive *Manual of the Botany of the Northern United States*, known as *Gray's Manual*. Williams is fascinated by Gray, the scientist who single-handedly ensured Michaux's future fame by dogged pursuit of a plant discovered by the Frenchman: *Shortia galacifolia*, or Oconee Bells. As a young man, Gray had seen the unidentified plant among Michaux's specimens in a Paris herbarium labeled from the *Hautes montagnes de Carolinie*, the "High mountains of Carolina." Unlike Michaux, who "used a Linnaean methodology for organizing his plants," explains Williams, "Gray was able to give it a name without having a flower and knowing how many pistils and stamens it had." Since Gray "found" the specimen, he boldly named it *Shortia* after botanist colleague Dr. Charles Wilkins Short (1794–1863). "Once Gray named it, he wanted to find it," Williams asserts. That brought Gray and colleagues John Carey and James Constable to the High Country in 1841. Also urging Gray south was the Reverend Moses Ashley Curtis, D.D. (1808–72). Curtis was an Episcopal clergyman born in Massachusetts and a passionate botanist who lived most of his life in North Carolina. Gray claimed "no living botanist was so well acquainted with the vegetation of the Southern Alleghany [*sic*] Mountains" as Curtis. He'd warned Gray that "you will be obliged to put up with accommodations on the way, *such as you have never dreamed of*." Gray came anyway.

The botanists set off into the wilds toward Grandfather from Marion, Virginia. No doubt Gray soon recalled Curtis's warning. "With considerable difficulty," he wrote, they found a wagon piloted by "a simple shoemaker" who "proved entirely wanting in the skill and tact necessary for conducting so frail a vehicle over such difficult mountain tracks, for roads they can scarcely be called." Gray was ready. He knew Michaux as an "indefatigable botanist" who'd suffered "difficulties and privations of which few can now form an adequate conception." Gray urged, "It must not be imagined that we found hotels or taverns for our accommodation, as, except at Ashe Court House, we saw no house of public entertainment until we quitted the mountain region." But they "suffered little inconvenience," staying with local residents who were astonished that they would "toil over the mountains in quest of their common and disregarded herbs." Reaching "the termination of the road at the foot of the Grandfather," present-day Foscoe, Gray met guide Levi Moody and climbed Hanging Rock, just across the valley, with its "fine and close view of the rugged Grandfather." Then, on July 9, 1841, they bagged their main target, what Gray described as "the highest as well as the most rugged and savage mountain we had yet

attempted." He marveled that Grandfather's primeval forest bore "the most perfect resemblance to the dark and sombre forests of the northern parts of New York and Vermont. . . . Indeed the vegetation is essentially Canadian."

Above Linville Gap, Gray climbed the Continental Divide, as it "promised a comparatively easy ascent." In addition, the "rich soil of this ridge" delivered "one of the plants which of all others we were desirous of obtaining; namely, Carex Fraseriana," a sedge still found on the fertile north flank of the mountain. Gray rattled off a list of "northern species which we had not previously observed in the region." Like so many others, Gray's party climbed to the cliff later known as Shanty Spring. He was stunned that "the vegetation here is so backward" that one saxifrage at the base of this precipice "was scarcely out of flower while at the foot of the mountain it had long since shed its seeds." He was fortunate to find *Rhododendron catawbiense* still blooming in mid-July, three weeks later than the norm today. Gray was so slow to the summit, he had to delay "herborizing" until the next day. No low-impact camper, he found "the branches of the Balsam afforded excellent materials for the construction of our lodge and the large fire we were obliged to keep up during the night." The next day they reached the peaks, but bad weather forced them back "to the humble dwelling of our guide." Pondering his trip for an 1842 article, Gray attributed Michaux's now famous outburst of song atop Grandfather to loyalty for the French king rather than a reaction to the scenery. "If this enthusiasm were called forth by mere elevation, he should have chanted his paeans on the Black Mountain and the Roan," Gray quipped. Maybe, but Gray's own report says bad weather interfered with his view. As Michaux reenactor Williams theorizes, foresters looking for the low-growing *Shortia* missed it for years because foresters look up. Botanist Gray, Williams jokes, likely missed the view by looking down.

Gray failed to find *Shortia* in 1841, and he struck out again in 1843 with William Sullivant. Harvard's 2010 bicentennial celebration of Gray called

Levi Moody, Master Cabin Builder

Seven years after Levi Moody led Asa Gray to the summit of Grandfather Mountain, he built one of the most stunning structures still standing in the mountain's shadow. The Prout-Atkins House, with virgin timber logs up to 3 feet wide, still stands beside NC 105 in Foscoe. According to a history of the Valle Crucis Episcopal missionary community, Moody lived in the "wild scattered hamlet" below Grandfather Mountain and was "a good guileless man." He built his masterpiece for the Reverend Henry Hudson Prout as Bishop Levi Silliman Ives was starting the Episcopal mission in the early 1840s. The "saddlebag style cabin joins two large log pens" around a huge, double-hearth central fireplace, documents *The Architectural History of Watauga County*.

When the Reverend J. Norton Atkins bought it in 1908, downstairs rooms had dirt floors and a spring ran through the kitchen. Atkins laid a slate floor over the spring that's still "always cool, even through shoe or boot," wrote descendant Libby Legget Atkins in 1980. Like Prout, Atkins held services in the log house and taught school, too—when he was there. He "set forth as a trail priest," Libby Atkins wrote, "and for awhile, the newly named Log House was known as 'The Seldom Inn,' for he seldom was." Norton Atkins and wife Katherine died in the early 1960s, and the house continues in the family. Tradition holds that sometime after the 1938 renovation, the cabin was featured in an edition of *House Beautiful* magazine (started in 1896).

After guiding Asa Gray up Grandfather, Levi Moody built one of the High Country's most historic structures. From this massive cabin, early 1900s traveling cleric Rev. J. Norton Atkins roamed the region in his horse and buggy. Photo by Randy Johnson.

finding the plant a "botanical goose chase." Much to Gray's embarrassment, he couldn't locate the plant, and Short died in 1863 never having seen it. Years later, in 1877, the "Where's *Shortia*?" paradox finally unraveled, and Gray was on hand to see it. Plant gatherers found it on the Catawba River near Marion, far below the "high mountain" location noted on Michaux's original specimen. Mordecai Hyams and his sons were active in the state's growing medicinal herb and ornamental plant business, which even then had "reached an extent and importance of which few are aware," observed botanist John Redfield. The Hyamses didn't recognize this plant, but Rhode Island expert Joseph W. Congden did. "Something clicked" for Congden, Charlie Williams relates. "He sent it to Gray and said, 'I think we found your *Shortia*.'" That brought Gray to North Carolina one final time in 1879, with noted botanist Charles Sprague Sargent, the first head of the Arnold Arboretum at Harvard, along with William Canby and John Redfield. The group found the now endangered *Shortia* growing at low elevation where Hyams found it, but Michaux's mother lode still eluded discovery. Not needing to go back to Grandfather, Gray targeted Roan, calling it "the most beautiful mountain east of the Rockies." It was also easy to reach, while Grandfather was nearly as inaccessible as it had been in 1841. Gray's family was with him, so Roan's "well-kept hostel," a spruce-log summit lodge, was comfy and, he thought, "will become a popular resort." Gray had taken the long view on his prodigal *Shortia*, but ultimately, he wanted to know where Michaux had found it. By 1886, Charlie Williams explains, Gray was guessing that Michaux must have found *Shortia* before Grandfather, "on his first trip from Charleston to the Highlands area of North Carolina in 1787." Knowing that Sargent was heading there, Gray wrote asking him to keep his eyes open. The day Gray's letter arrived, Sargent found the plant near Highlands where Michaux had first seen it a century before. With *Shortia*'s rediscovery, late-century interest in Michaux exploded. In 1889, Sargent and James Redfield published the first-ever French transcription of

Michaux's handwritten journals, still held by the American Philosophical Society in Philadelphia.

Not long after, a man named Shepherd Dugger somehow learned that Michaux's transcribed journals mentioned Grandfather Mountain, the peak in his own backyard. Dugger was on a mission to promote his isolated home, and just a few years later, he published the first translated tale of Michaux's inspiring climb of Grandfather. With Dugger's *Balsam Groves of the Grandfather Mountain*, André Michaux's famously wrong rapture on the summit entered the heritage of the High Country. Grandfather Mountain—and Asa Gray's obstinate dedication to finding *Shortia*—had given rise to one of the most iconic stories of early exploration. A century after Dugger's book, a 1994 Grandfather Mountain speech by Charles Kuralt on the 200th anniversary of Michaux's climb consolidated ongoing greatness for the once obscure French botanist. Michaux "knew something then that most of us do not appreciate even today," maintained Kuralt, "that this place where he climbed, where we are gathered, is botanically extraordinary almost beyond expressing it." Kuralt had nailed why attaining this summit would inspire such a man to song.

Michaux's intriguing tale truly reconnected with Grandfather when Charlie Williams played his own surprising role in solving the mystery of Michaux's "high mountain" specimen. In 2002, Williams helped create the André Michaux International Society (AMIS, "friends" in French) and an André Michaux International Symposium that same year. The society's first project sent a symbolic collection of American trees and seeds to Rambouillet, France, where trees grown from Michaux's own seeds were demolished in a 1999 hurricane. Williams and society members went to France in 2004 to receive the Medal of Rambouillet, "a sort of key to the city," Williams discovered. In Paris on the way to Rambouillet, the group met French journalist Régis Pluchet, a sixth-generation descendant of André Michaux who arranged once-in-a-lifetime access for Williams and AMIS members to the Michaux Herbarium, where Gray

Michaux descendant Régis Pluchet and translator/researcher Eliane Norman (second and fourth from left) smile at the welcome they received beside the Swinging Bridge. Southern Appalachian Historical Association reenactors from left to right are Al Ernest, Travis Souther, Brian Fannon, and Dave Davis (a founder of the not-to-be-missed Hickory Ridge Living History Museum in Boone). Flag-bearers are author Randy Johnson on left and Michaux reenactor/scholar Charlie Williams at right. Photo by Rob Moore/*Watauga Democrat*.

had first found and named *Shortia* in 1839. Williams went through the "unknown specimens" folder where Gray had seen Michaux's specimen, but even that was gone. Then Williams's cold case got scorching hot. Fortuitously, French botanical historian Gerard Aymonin led Williams into the Jussieu Herbarium, a collection "that Americans didn't seem to know about," he concluded. Hundreds of Michaux's specimens were also sent to that separate archive. A little later, Aymonin and an American colleague of Williams from Philadelphia, Eliane Norman (now working with Williams on a book about Michaux), "went through the collection and," Williams revealed, "each found a previously unknown specimen of *Shortia* collected by Michaux." Gray had *not* seen this specimen; it hadn't reached the museum until 1857. Amazingly, blurted Williams, that plant "too had been collected in the *Hautes montagnes de Carolinie*—in

1787." There it was. Gray had been right. Michaux had found *Shortia* on the 1787 foray to Highlands, *below* the "High mountains." The man who today "channels" André Michaux in costume had helped definitively solve a more-than-100-year-old mystery. "If Michaux's relative, Monsieur Pluchet, hadn't invited me into the herbarium," Williams maintains, "that would never have happened."

In 2014, it was Pluchet's turn to be invited—to Grandfather Mountain on a tour of his famous ancestor's travels. Pluchet came over to help raise funds to restore Michaux's original garden in Charleston; then he went on to Michaux Day events at Tipton-Haynes historic site in Johnson City, and Grandfather Mountain. Across the Swinging Bridge atop Linville Peak, Appalachian State University's French club, Cercle Francais, sang the Marseillaise (as Michaux had), 1700s-garbed frontiersmen from the Southern Appalachian Historical Association fired muskets in celebration, and the Grandfather Mountain Stewardship Foundation's Catherine Morton presented Pluchet with a bilingual plaque. Through a translator, Jesse Pope of the foundation told Pluchet it "was really an experience to walk to the peak with a descendant of André Michaux." Responded Pluchet, "Well, André Michaux had his Davenport." Pluchet compared Grandfather to the Alps and Pyrenees, "my favorite places to be, where the trees are stunted and shaped by the wind." Pluchet returned to France in time to see his own new book about Michaux published—an interest in his ancestor first forged a decade earlier when he attended the Michaux symposium organized by Charlie Williams.

Getting the Lay of the Land

Asa Gray's titanic search for *Shortia* spanned the early and late nineteenth century, bestowing lasting fame on Michaux's exultation atop Grandfather. If the country's most eminent botanist had such a hard time sorting out just one new species found in the mountain South, imagine what a geographer faced trying to make sense of this vast rippled realm. That's exactly what Swiss-born geographer Arnold Guyot set out to do. One of his most memorable research sites was Grandfather Mountain. Maybe Gray had just been unlucky, but early Appalachian Trail proponent Myron Avery writes that the puzzling complexity of the Southern Appalachians "was not only investigated, but in fact was solved prior to the Civil War, by one Arnold Guyot." Like Elisha Mitchell, as the Civil War loomed, Guyot had elevation on his mind. He had his own system of "determining elevations by barometer," wrote Avery and Kenneth S. Boardman in a 1938 Appalachian Trail Conference publication, but he wasn't just measuring peaks. He was measuring valleys, too, assessing the relief of the mountains and the difficulty of routes through them, the task that brought him to Grandfather. Born and educated near Neuchâtel, Switzerland, Guyot met and later became a colleague of the eminent Swiss biologist and geologist Louis Agassiz, a noted glacier researcher who first hypothesized an ice age. Guyot's own glacier research revealed firsts, among them that glaciers flow faster at their center. Like Agassiz, Guyot emigrated to the United States in the mid-nineteenth century and became one of the country's most renowned scientists. He planned the first nationwide program of meteorological measurement and laid the groundwork for the precursor of the National Weather Service. Guyot's Appalachian research started in 1849 in the Adirondack, White, and Green Mountains, moved to the central Appalachians, and reached western North Carolina in 1856, 1858, 1859, and 1860. His *Notes on the Geography of the Mountain System of Western North Carolina*, Guyot's major contribution to the geography of the Southern Appalachians, was curiously enough, never published," Avery discovered. Indeed, it was lost for seventy-five years! After being sent to the director of the Coast Survey in Washington, D.C., in 1863, Guyot's study came to light in 1929. "That this survey should have been lost," Avery writes, "for over three-quarters of a century is perhaps best explained when the nature of Guyot's work and the period involved is appreciated." Avery is referring to the Civil War—and the odd and interesting later role that Guyot's research *may have* played in that conflict.

Guyot made his share of naturalistic observations—"elevation alone is not a sufficient explanation for the absence of trees" on Roan Mountain's "beautiful prairies"—but he focused on the impenetrable jumble of peaks. He saw Grandfather Mountain as a pivot point in the Blue Ridge and confessed fascination that the tremendous width of the Appalachians pinches down so lofty, high, and narrow near the mountain. Guyot was impressed by just how isolated from each other two valleys could be when separated by a high ridge. Linville Gap, where Elisha Mitchell noted that Grandfather sprawls out to form the lofty High Country, was one such intriguing height of land. It was uninhabited at the time, and though Guyot always adopted local nomenclature, he offered no name for it. "The only passage between the Watauga Valley and Burnsville" Guyot wrote, "is a rough mule path, scarcely fit for a very light wagon, which passes over the swell from which the Grandfather Mountain rises at an elevation of 4,100 feet." That description for the barrier between Foscoe and the later town of Linville wasn't far off in 1950. The gap supposedly had an 1840s "turnpike" through it, but he dismissed road maps of the day. "I was frequently deceived by them," Guyot admitted. "Some [roads] do not exist. Simple occasional paths are often marked as carriage roads. Bridges over streams belong to the rarities of the country." It's not surprising that Guyot found the roads little traveled. "The Watauga Valley, as well as the whole County to which it gives its name has a very sparse population," he observed. "There is not so much as a village for Boone, the county-seat, contains but a few dwellings clustered around the Court-house." There was a dark side to Guyot's trip to the High Country, and it wasn't the storm clouds that daily deluged him. There was a Civil War on the way that would suspend science on the Grandfather Mountain.

Hike a Historic Turnpike

Want to experience an early "turnpike" like the "mule path" Arnold Guyot took through Linville Gap? A historic route he described over Great Smoky Mountains National Park still makes an insightful stroll. Pull off the Clingman's Dome Road in Indian Gap (1.2 miles from Newfound Gap on the right) and walk a few hundred feet down Road Prong Trail. This ancient road, in use for centuries by the Cherokees before 1800s settlers upgraded it, was the only passage over these peaks till the 1920s. It was Guyot himself who disproved the long-held belief that this was the lowest gap in the Smokies, determining that today's road route of Newfound Gap was the better place to cross this "master chain of the Appalachian System." Hike the entire 3.3 miles downhill by spotting a car below at Chimney Tops Parking Area (7.1 miles south of Sugarlands Visitor Center near Gatlinburg).

It's only a short stroll past the roadside interpretive sign from the Smokies' Clingman's Dome road to appreciate the laughably rugged character of the Indian Gap Road, an early "turnpike" like the one through Linville Gap. Photo by Randy Johnson.

Civil War under the Grandfather

Though not an academic historian, early Appalachian ethnologist Horace Kephart vividly captured the conflict's unique divisiveness in the North Carolina mountains. The South, he wrote, realized "what a long, lean, powerful arm of the Union it was that the Southern mountaineer stretched through its very vitals." Union sympathizers aplenty lived below the crags and caves of Grandfather Mountain. Granted, mountain residents supported the Confederacy. A Confederate marker on Grandfather's flank adorns the grave of William W. Jestes (1845–1922). Though not uniformly pro-Union, as Inscoe and McKinney attest in *The Heart of Confederate Appalachia*, there were nevertheless mountain hotbeds of Union sentiment. A Confederate Home Guard militia was needed to suppress internal Unionist activity and incursions from pro-Union East Tennessee. It's estimated about 25 percent of mountain Confederate soldiers abandoned their units and came home or went into hiding. The mountains became the temporary home of deserters, bushwhackers, outlaws, and outliers, the latter "local men forced into hiding to evade conscription," note Inscoe and McKinney. Grandfather had its secret hideouts in rock-encircled overhangs and caves. For many, exile on the mountain was preferable to a notorious deserters' prison like Castle Thunder in Richmond. One ballad went,

> I'd ruther be on the Grandfather Mountain
> A-taking the snow and rain,
> Than to be in Castle Thunder
> A-wearin' the ball and chain.

War Stories

The Banners of Banner's Elk were Union sympathizers. Lewis B. Banner, a slave holder, had three sons who fought for the Union. Banner and other guides

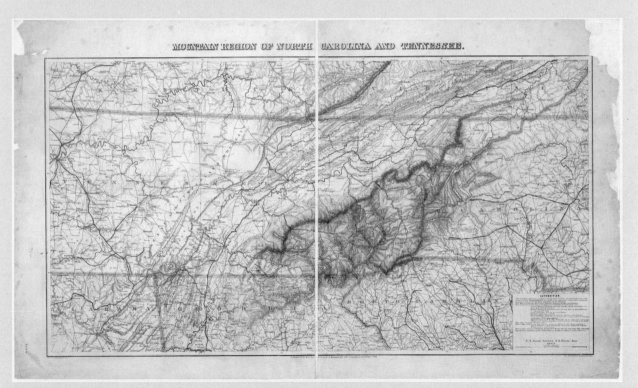

MOUNTAIN REGION OF NORTH CAROLINA AND TENNESSEE.

Arnold Guyot's research is credited as the primary source for the mountain terrain in this Civil War-era map of the Southern Appalachians. It surely came along for the ride with General John Stoneman's troops on that famous 1865 raid through Western North Carolina. North Carolina Collection, University of North Carolina Library at Chapel Hill.

funneled Unionist refugees through Blowing Rock and the wilds of Grandfather to Banner's Elk and on to Tennessee. The protagonist in Charles Frazier's novel *Cold Mountain* follows much the same escape route past Grandfather. Interpretation at the Banner House Museum in Banner Elk informs that time (http://www .bannerhousemuseum.org/). Built in 1864 by Banner's son Samuel H. Banner, "a member of the 5th Ohio Infantry," the house was "a hiding place for escapees and draft evaders." Nearby, North Carolina's Mission Crossing Scenic Byway follows the Old Turnpike Road in Banner Elk, an underground railroad route and "one of the last remaining original highways of the nineteenth century," according to the byway guide.

One of the High Country's legendary Civil War stories features L. McKesson (Keith) Blalock and Malinda Pritchard. They grew up together "under Grandfather Mountain," recounts John Preston Arthur's 1915 *History of Watauga County*. The couple married in 1861, and like other storied spouses, they entered service together with Malinda disguising herself as Blalock's brother Sam. They enlisted in the Confederate army hoping to escape North, but Keith was discharged when doctors feared his self-inflicted poison oak was smallpox. To leave with Keith, Malinda had to prove she was a woman, writes William Trotter in *Bushwhackers*, the mountain volume of his North Carolina Civil War histories. Later hounded to reenlist, Keith "retreated still further up under the Grandfather and lived in a rail pen." In one scrape, the kind of attack that sparked bad blood, he was wounded and lost an eye. The Blalocks became notorious guerrillas, what Trotter called "The Bonnie and Clyde of Watauga County." Blalock recruited for the 10th Michigan Volunteer Infantry Regiment stationed in Tennessee and came into the orbit of guerrilla leader Colonel George W. Kirk of the 2nd and 3rd North Carolina Mounted Infantry, an active Union force. The Blalocks killed, wounded, and terrorized southern sympathizers. In June 1864, a Union force under Kirk crossed Hump Mountain and captured Camp Vance at Morganton. That "emboldened the Unionists in Watauga and Blalock went about in Federal uniform, fully armed," Arthur writes.

The Banners were among the most emboldened. In an 1865 skirmish, more than 100 pro-Unionists marched from Banner Elk and captured a lightly fortified site in Cove Creek called Camp Mast, home of Company B, 11th Battalion North Carolina Home Guard. The dozen rebels who voted not to surrender were marched to Tennessee.

Stoneman Makes His Raid

Judging by the number of Stoneman's Raid historical markers, you'd think the spring 1865 Union foray was the most important event that ever happened in the High Country. Stoneman's 6,000-man cavalry offensive destroyed civilian infrastructure in six southern states—a "Sherman's March" in miniature. The raid restored Stoneman's reputation after he became the highest-ranking Union prisoner of the war in 1864 (taken with aide-de-camp Major Myles Keogh, who later died with Custer). Keith and Malinda Blalock led Stoneman's troops into Boone as scouts on March 28 and found the home guard drilling at the muster grounds. The guard, "still smarting" from Camp Mast's fall, opened fire and then scattered with nine dead and more than sixty captured, writes Chris J. Hartley in *Stoneman's Raid, 1865*. "The Battle of Boone" got as much coverage in the *Chicago Tribune* as the April 1 "Waterloo of the Confederacy" at Five Forks near Richmond.

As the war ended, the mountain towering above it was ready to again welcome scientists and explorers. Arnold Guyot, the last scientist on Grandfather before the war, wouldn't be back, but his research helped write history. In January 1863, Guyot sent his Southern Appalachian study to "Professor A. D. Bache, Superintendent Coast Survey," great-grandson of Benjamin Franklin. Remarkably, notes Myron Avery's 1938 Appalachian Trail Conference article, Guyot "strongly urges that the mountainous region and the available passes be seized by Union Forces. That the later Federal strategy achieved these objectives, may be more than a coincidence." There may not be direct evidence that Guyot's advice dictated military strategy, but his ideas likely didn't fall on deaf ears. The Swiss researcher, from a country now identified with neutrality in warfare, urged an invasion of the North Carolina mountains, and it happened right under the nose of Grandfather's profile. Most important, the U.S. Coast Survey published an 1863 map called *Mountain Region of North Carolina and Tennessee*, made "principally from a map furnished by" Guyot, according to the map's legend. You can bet Guyot's map went along for the ride with Stoneman's cavalry. For a half-century after the Civil War, it's said Raleigh ignored the "lost provinces" of the mountain counties, a well-earned honor for this border region between right and wrong. And those famous Civil War brigands Malinda and Keith Blalock are buried in Montezuma Cemetery, near Montezuma Gap, which offers one of the best views of Grandfather Mountain.

The only exploring being done would be to evade adversaries or the flow of secretive strangers passing through. As the war ended, a vast, blue-coated column of Union soldiers would ride through the High Country and turn attention back to Arnold Guyot. The geographer did more than marvel at the poor maps he had. He was making his own.

After the Civil War, the only army seeking out the Southern Appalachians was comprised of adventurous recreationists who'd eventually create a market for that rustic lodge Asa Gray enjoyed atop Roan Mountain. Grandfather's summits wouldn't even see a trail shelter until the 1940s, but scientists resumed their pilgrimages. Amos Arthur Heller (1867–1944) burst onto the botany scene in the early 1890s. With a few visits to the High Country, he added his name to Southern Appalachian species, among them Heller's blazing star. Heller found botany when his girlfriend and, later, wife, Emily, encouraged him to read "Gray's Lessons," the 1887 edition of Asa Gray's textbook titled *Elements of Botany for Beginners and Schools*. The great teacher advised readers not to struggle with technical terms; they could be "looked up." In a few years, Heller was botanizing in the eminent scientist's old shrub-stomping ground, the mountains of North Carolina. In the summer of 1890, Heller visited his older brother near Salisbury and took in Blowing Rock. A year later, the young botanist's first published paper, "Notes on the Flora of North Carolina," appeared in the June 1891 *Bulletin of the Torrey Botanical Club*. His "first visit to the mountains" impressed him with "splendid views," he wrote. "Grandfather towers above all the rest like a huge sentinel." Heller eagerly followed his famous predecessors. "Early on the morning of the 22nd, I started to tramp to Grandfather Mountain, fifteen miles distant," notes Heller's Torrey report. At Linville Gap, he turned up the trade route trod by botanists for 100 years. "It was slow and toilsome work," but "about half way up," Heller described entering "the moss belt, for the ground, trunks of trees, logs and rocks, are covered with a thick cushion." He found wood sorrel flowering in "pretty pink-veined petals." A "half-mile from the summit," Heller drank from a "spring of almost ice-cold water, which flows from the base of a large cliff." Just two years after Heller's visit, Dugger's *Balsam Groves of the Grandfather Mountain* would immortalize this same hike with an enduring, remarkably similar image of Shanty Spring. Dugger would write, "From the base of this cliff gushes and sparkles the coldest perennial spring, isolated from perpetual snow, in the United States. Its highest temperature is 42 degrees." Just above, Heller saw "large patches of Chelone Lyoni," turtleheads, their "pink-purple flowers making a very pretty appearance." To hear Heller, his rainy visit to Roan Mountain was "a failure botanically." Everybody should be so unlucky. He collected three new species on his trip, including one on Roan, *Solidago roanensis*, Roan Mountain goldenrod. Another plant, this one showy and spectacular, was collected at the Blowing Rock (where it still grows) and would be named *Liatris helleri*—Heller's blazing star. Today this rare, threatened plant grows in only eight known locations, the largest colony of which is on Grandfather Mountain.

The following year, Heller and botanizing partner John K. Small visited Grandfather Mountain three times where Michaux's "long-neglected (Carolina Lily; *Lilium michauxii*) was found in quantity." The success of Heller's two summer forays "brought Mr. Heller to the notice of American botanists," says John W. Harshberger's 1899 book, *The Biologists of Philadelphia and Their Work*. In "March, 1892, came an offer from Reverend George Vasey, Botanist of the Department of Agriculture, to join a botanical expedition." Vasey's son, G. R. Vasey, was the noted botanist who discovered the pinkshell azalea, *Rhododendron vaseyi*, in 1878, a Blue Ridge endemic that grows extensively on Grandfather. Heller's career took off and never circled back to the Southern Appalachians. He spent much of his life out west, but it's difficult to appreciate Grandfather Mountain's plants without hearing his name.

Even the blazing start of Heller's botany career pales beside the meteoric rise and sad demise of an oddly rhyming researcher named Weller. When brilliant, teenaged Worth Hamilton Weller (1913–31) fell to his death on Grandfather discovering a new species of salamander, the mountain's scientific focus shifted to herpetology and tragedy. The romantic story of this young man is one of the most compelling tales that Grandfather Mountain has yet to fully tell.

"Buzz" Weller got his start at a precursor of today's Cincinnati Museum of Natural History and Science. The venerable institution goes back to the early 1800s, and Weller's tale is one of its secrets. His fatal Grandfather hike happened on a field trip with the museum's "junior naturalists' club," founded in 1928 by Ralph Edward Dury (1899–1984), museum director from 1918 to 1975. Dury discovered a true prodigy in Weller. While still in high school, Weller was no less than the museum's curator of herpetology. Much of what's known of him comes from the memories of best friend Karl Maslowski (1913–2006), who led his own stellar career as "a trailblazing filmmaker and

Worth Weller was a handsome, brilliant young man who let the prospect of discovering a new species of salamander lure him to tragedy in Grandfather Mountain's virgin forest. Courtesy of Worth H. Weller.

photographer who was one of the first to photograph wildlife with color film," according to a *Bird Watching* magazine biography. On one of his first club field trips in April 1930, Weller found his first undescribed species of salamander and named it in honor of Dury: *Gyrinophilos porphyriticus duryi* (Weller). During the summer of 1930, Weller joined a junior naturalist's club field trip to Grandfather Mountain in August and found a brown-and-black-mottled salamander. Thinking it might be another new species, Weller asked legendary herpetologist Dr. Emmett Reid Dunn (1894–1956) to authenticate it. Weller's "long, erudite" correspondence with Dunn was so "intelligent and well-written," Maslowski wrote in 1988, that only later did "Dunn to his surprise learn that he'd been corresponding with a high school student." After that specimen somehow went astray, a second trip to Grandfather was planned for the next summer. By then, Dunn anticipated a cataclysmic career for Weller and had secured him a full scholarship to Haverford College for the fall of 1931. No one better-understood Weller's promise than sweetly soft-spoken Margaret "Maggie" Talbert, Buzz Weller's girlfriend. In 2012, at age ninety-seven, Talbert recalled, "We never even kissed. But I thought he was the most wonderful person I'd ever met. He had the most marvelous mind, and was absolutely aflame with love for science, for the natural world." Whatever might have been for Maggie and Buzz, or just Buzz, was cut short by Grandfather.

In 1930, Margaret Talbert was a shy sixteen-year-old smitten with eighteen-year-old "Buzz" Weller. At first she wasn't sure, but by 1931, the year Weller plunged off of Grandfather, "Maggie" was his girlfriend. Decades later, Weller's boyhood friend Karl Maslowski recalled, "Buzz was *crazy* for Maggie." When I first interviewed Talbert in 2012, memories of her youthful love were so distant she was "grateful just to be able to talk about him. After all this time, you can't imagine how much this means to me," she confessed. "I can't believe I'm still having wonderful things happen concerning Buzz." Randy Johnson Collection.

"Buzz truly loved Grandfather Mountain," Maggie Talbert maintained. "He spoke so eagerly about that next trip." Soon after his graduation with high honors, Weller was back on the mountain, still a vision of virgin grandeur. Maslowski missed that visit but was told that Weller, "impetuous as ever took off as soon as they arrived at camp," likely at MacRae Meadows. He took a "cloth sack he used for collecting salamanders and headed off into the woods. A short time later, a tremendous storm blew in from the west and cast the wilderness into darkness." Talbert recalls that Weller was asked "not to go out alone, but he did anyway." Night fell, and Weller never returned. Four days later a local man found him in a creek. Maslowski wrote, "They found the body at the bottom of a gorge, in a place called Stonestack Creek. In the darkness, he'd apparently walked right off a ledge. The little cloth sack was clutched in his hand." In that sack was the salamander that established Weller's second new species: *Plethodon welleri*, Weller's salamander.

Confusion has crept into what little is known about Weller. Even Maslowski's "Stonestack Creek" isn't an actual place name. In fact, it is Stack Rock Creek where Weller died. Just south of the Linn Cove Viaduct, the creek cascades below the Blue Ridge Parkway and Yonahlossee Road past towering Stack Rock (or Leaning Rock). When the storm struck, Weller was fleeing downhill in the dark, soaking wet, panicked, probably hypothermic. Not far above Yonahlossee Road, the creek exits the woods and leaps off a precipice. My guess: They found Worth Weller in the rock-pocked pool at the base of that thirty-foot cataract. Today, the Parkway spans the creek at that exact spot. If you look off the west side of the bridge, what I call "Weller's Pool" is directly below. He died there on June 22, 1931, almost exactly as Elisha Mitchell had perished seventy-four years earlier on a peak later named Mount Mitchell.

Imagine how stricken Weller mentors Ralph Dury and Emmett Dunn must have been by the tragedy. Consider the impact on Dury when a student of inestimable promise perished on a museum-sponsored field trip. Writer Anita Buck, a former employee of the Cincinnati Museum Center, concludes Dury "drove boys on natural history trips all over the eastern United States. You could never do that today." Emmett Dunn surely felt responsible for Weller's discovery of Grandfather. His 1917 article in the *Bulletin of the American Museum of Natural History* called the area "a paradise for the field naturalist," because the "country owned by the Linville Company shows the primitive conditions of flora and fauna (i.e.: a virgin forest)" and was "accessible by the splendid

Yonahlossee Road." Dunn made collecting salamanders in the area sound like sport. The "big new Linville plethodons we called 'Yonahlossees' (sp. nov. *Plethodon yonahlossee*) . . . always gave us an exciting chase." No wonder Weller went to Grandfather Mountain.

Early articles help any researcher, but I finally learned more about Weller's little-documented life when Anita Buck directed me to Margaret Talbert and she pointed me to members of Weller's own family. "Buzz is the family's legend," Talbert told me. "He's the family member they just love." But how to find them? One day I was searching for sources and a startling name—Worth Weller—was affiliated with a new hiking club near Mount Mitchell. Amazingly, this too was a Worth Hamilton Weller, the namesake nephew of Buzz. I contacted him and discovered that a precious few Weller artifacts, including high school journals, were with Worth's brother Doug in England, where his English wife, Helen Walland, was transcribing them. Realizing time was of the essence, I urged the family to donate the journal and other items to the Cincinnati Museum Center, where Weller's original salamanders still sit in specimen bottles. In August 2013, the artifacts arrived safely at the museum. "Our uncle Worth has always been a legend in our family," Doug and Worth told me in one note. "We are immensely pleased and proud that his journal is returning to a place which meant so much to him." Looking back, Margaret Talbert confessed she found beauty in Worth Weller's tragedy—the beauty of his innocent enthusiasm for knowledge, and the beauty of Grandfather Mountain and the way it captivates people drawn to its slopes. "When I was young," she told me, "I could barely accept Buzz's loss, the death of such a remarkable eighteen-year-old. Imagine—having right in his hand what established both a new species and himself as the scientist he was burning to be." Talbert paused, then concluded, "I've lived a long time, and it's beautiful, the whole story, isn't it? If there's such a thing as a beautiful death, he had one."

Soon after Weller's fall, Grandfather's virgin timber fell, too. Weller was the last scientist to savor the mountain's undisturbed natural fabric before loggers cleared the millennia-old forest. Today, we look back on that world and celebrate those researchers and reenactors like Charlie Williams, who've kept that past alive. Grandfather's now legendary natural significance is based on their stirring stories. Luckily, the future is destined to hold more such tales. Budding naturalists and emeritus professors alike still study the mountain, documenting the noteworthy and new for managing agencies and academia, or simply to satisfy their own curiosity—which is what I got out of discovering more about Worth Weller. In all my years hiking the paths and woods of Grandfather, often alone, the vaguely troubling specter of Worth Weller's solitary passing was a mystery that often crossed my mind. As I learned more about him—and managed Grandfather's backcountry to help hikers avoid a similar fate—it became apparent that Weller's story did more than just cap the mountain's first era of scientific inquiry. He was also a harbinger for what came next, an era of adventure fueled by explorers in search of excitement.

3 Here Come the Hikers

The promise of big discoveries was yielding to the quest for big views as adventurers found their way to Grandfather's flanks in the mid- to late 1800s. Factor in the clearer air of the 1800s, and we can be certain they weren't disappointed. Photo by Tommy White Photography, www.tommywhitephotography.com.

Scientists weren't the only people drawn to Grandfather's peaks. "Recreational explorers" started arriving by the second half of the nineteenth century. Among them were artists, amateur naturalists, and outdoor enthusiasts. The nation was fascinated by the devastated South after the Civil War, and the era's horseback-riding travel writers—more rightly, "travel riders"—scoured the mountains to pen postbellum magazine pieces trumpeting wild scenery and isolated mountaineers. Some visitors were adventurous New Englanders, members of the Appalachian Mountain Club (AMC), busy building trails and mountain huts in New Hampshire's White Mountains and eager to see so many southern summits that overtopped their own Mount Washington. I found those stories fascinating, having reversed that route.

By the early twentieth century, distinctively dressed tourists of the outdoorsy stripe were finding their way through Alexander MacRae's farm and onto the top of Linville Peak. When D. R. Beeson and Hodge Mathes traversed the mountain in 1913, they encountered a coed group of adventurers following a local guide. Courtesy of Special Collections, Appalachian State University, Linville River Collection.

Starting from the South, I explored New England, then tapped my own New Hampshire research with the AMC to launch Grandfather Mountain's 1970s trail program. Later, I'd learn that one of those early Yankees built some of Grandfather's first formal trails. Like northern writers who were fascinated by Grandfather, I too reveled in the mountain's New England–like climate and crags. Even when these wanderers just passed close to Grandfather, their reports painted a priceless picture of life and the lay of the land in the North

Carolina High Country. Southern locals were part of the story, as interesting sociologically as the summits were scenic.

In 1869, renowned traveler and artist Charles Lanman's (1819–95) article "Novelties of Southern Scenery" in *Appleton's Journal of Literature, Science and Art* didn't mince words pitting the Southern Appalachians against the North. Dixie's mountain scenery was "not one whit behind the Northern States," he wrote. Grandfather "is altogether the wildest and most fantastic of the whole Allegheny range." Lanman painted and wrote about the entire Appalachians, and stellar credentials back up his opinions. He studied art under no less than Asher B. Durand of the Hudson River school, America's first great art movement that elevated native scenery to an ideal of national pride. Graciously dignifying the region's rusticity, Lanman reported that the "saddle horse" had not yet been "superseded by the cumbersome coaches and the railway trains," nor were there inns with "dandified waiters and fancy napkins." The "tourist is quite contented" to find "some tidy farm-house or cabin" and a climate "beyond all praise." He described Grandfather's primary residents for many years as "a man named Jim Riddle, and his loving spouse, whose cabin was located near the summit." Lanman wrote that one of Riddle's pastimes was "to shoot at snowballs, in which *elevated* luxury his wife Betsy was wont to participate with enthusiasm." Riddle eventually "abandoned his eyry and became a preacher in the low country of Carolina." Like Asa Gray, Lanman also loved Roan Mountain. Perhaps for the first time, he popularized a Catawba Indian legend that Roan's mountaintop meadows were created when the tribe won a summit battle against rivals. After their victory, the great spirit honored the tribe by covering the mountain's crest with grass and giving rhododendrons red blooms "nourished by the blood of the slain."

Tackling the Total Mountain

Writer Jehu Lewis was another northerner, but one who climbed Grandfather on foot "at a time when recreational hiking was not yet popular in America," writes Kevin O'Donnell in *Seekers of Scenery*. Lewis recounted his summit trek in a September 1873 issue of the *Lakeside Monthly*. From a farmhouse near Lenoir he saw "a bold summit, overtopping the surrounding mountains," a "gigantic silhouette, as of an old man, with wrinkled brow, drooping nose and sunken mouth, lying as though stretched on his bier, his dead stony face cutting sharply against the tender blue of the sky." Admiring a face we still fancy, he confesses that "from the moment you first trace the lines of the wonderful profile, the GRANDFATHER becomes a reality catching the eye, and even the heart." On cloudy days, Lewis finds the mountain "tempting the eye again and again to see when the old man regains his view." For "days and weeks together" clouds could be "dark and heavy—sending forth flashes of warning that the storm-court is in session." At times, he catches a "glimpse of disrobed greatness, as the first rays of sun light up the rocky slopes and summit." Lewis found himself drawn to the mountain as so many still are. "Dwelling for months with the scene ever before you you feel a growing love for the grand lineaments of that still face. You begin to long for a closer acquaintance, to stand on that far height and look down to the utmost horizon."

From the John's River drainage, Jehu Lewis gazed for weeks at the stony visage of Grandfather's eastern profile. When he finally climbed to the peaks in 1873, he too passed through the area still known as Gragg or Carey's Flat. Longtime local musician and roadside "honeyman" Floyd Landis Gragg often said, "If you're ever in that country and encounter a man walking just say, 'Hello, Mr. Gragg.' If he looks at you mean, just say, 'Oh, I mean Mr. Coffey,' and you'll be right." North Carolina Collection, University of North Carolina Library at Chapel Hill. Photo by Hugh Morton.

Unlike explorers who ascended in steps from the west, Lewis tackled the entire elevation change from the east, a challenge impossible on an existing trail today. With "haversack of food," he set out on the last day of August seven years after the Civil War to climb the Johns River drainage over rude bridges, "caricatures of those slab benches which graced the log school-houses of the olden time." In today's tiny crossroads of Gragg, where Grandfather's "lordly summit could be seen . . . the nearest point seemed almost at hand." Like many an urbanite settling at a local cabin, he found the mountaineer "a kind-hearted, but simple-minded and uncultivated 'son of the soil.'" In one dense glade, a stone chimney stood "like a mute uninscribed monument to the memory of the household which once gathered round its blazing hearth . . . painfully common in the Sunny South since the storm of war swept terribly over it." He crossed "Wilson's Creek," now a National Wild and Scenic River, but back then, "one of the clearest, wildest, and most frolicsome streams." When he got close to the mountain, he feared proximity would diminish the "resemblance to human features." No worries. Though "every rock and tree stood out full and clear the grand outlines were still the same," complete with "a sense of its overwhelming vastness, and my exceeding littleness."

Welcomed at a house in Grandmother Gap, Lewis was "startled at the icy coldness" of a spring and plentiful "evidence that this region belongs to a climatic belt far different from that of the Atlantic slope." The next day, he emerged into an early version of MacRae Meadows on a "faint cow-path" among "Sugar maples, with sap-troughs at their roots." New Englander Lewis fell into revelry at the sight of maple sugaring—and lost his way. Depending on "instinct and observation," he plowed ahead, shouting, "Hurrah! That must be the summit! . . . lo! It was only a jutting prominence, while beyond was a fearfully rugged, tangled wilderness of rocks" where "a huge pyramidal mass rose half a thousand feet above me." It was Linville Peak, subject of countless future Hugh Morton photos. He savored the view, then scrambled up sheer

Casual tourists weren't meeting the mountains, but affluent, educated adventurers were. Hikers and horseback riders were encountering rustic local residents and marveling at the hardscrabble existence found in the isolated wilds around Grandfather Mountain. Courtesy of Special Collections, Appalachian State University, Linville River Collection.

rock "with scarcely enough roughness of surface to afford a footing." Scaling a crag, he "stood upon the brink of a precipice. The only living thing in sight was a solitary hawk hanging motionless over the abyss, and then sailing swiftly and noiselessly away. Not a sound came up from those far depths; not a cloud marred the spotlessness of the crystalline sky." Finally, he gained "the last remaining rock, the coping of the pyramid. But behold! it was not a pyramid at all. It was the projecting chin bone of the Grandfather!" Lewis gazed across the defile a swinging bridge would span eighty years later. Looking northeast, he "could trace the whole of the profile." He took in the view west and mistakenly thought he saw "several farms upon the mountain tops"—likely just the balds that still sprawl across Hump Mountain. "One long, lingering gaze upon the landscape of grandeur and beauty; one reluctant, sad and final adieu, and bending my eyes upon the pathway, I began the descent." He recalled that view countless times in later life. He didn't take photographs, but we have the wonderful word picture he painted.

Culture Shock "under the Grandfather"

About twelve years after Lewis's hike, Charles Dudley Warner and Yale University English professor Thomas Raynesford Lounsbury rode on horseback through Boone to Roan and Mount Mitchell. These aristocrats would rely on the "remunerated hospitality of the widely scattered habitants"—nineteenth-century cabin accommodations—but they would "have some larn'in to do." They barely missed Grandfather, but amusing parts of their education took place in its shadow. If he'd known better, world traveler Warner wrote, "they would not have started without a supply train." Warner's series of 1885 articles about the trip for the *Atlantic Monthly* is a masterpiece of scornful satire. As editor and eventual publisher of the *Hartford Courant*, he lived beside Mark Twain and coauthored *The Gilded Age* with him. Warner and Lounsbury started for "White-Top Mountain," a peak they'd been urged "to ascend without fail," but Warner's curmudgeon companion nixed that. Warner had to agree that "no mountain under six thousand feet is worth ascending." That eliminated "White-Top"—and Grandfather—but the tale of their close call is priceless. Warner "further agreed that any mountain that is over six thousand feet high is too high to ascend on foot," thus narrowing the choice to mountains higher than 6,000 feet climbable by horse. That would have given New England a single mountain "worth climbing," Mount Washington, with its bridle trail. After the men left their hotel comfort zone, each evening's stopping point was "magnified in our imagination—the nobility of its situation, its cuisine, its inviting restfulness," and invariably these "places

of royal entertainment" dashed all hope. One destination, Ramsey's, offered their first encounter with folks "undisturbed by debt or ambition." After eating, the men "went gayly along the Laurel, in the slanting rays of the afternoon sun," amid oaks "gigantic in size." The rhododendron "now began to strew the water and the ground with their brilliant petals," but these guys were focused on the travail of travel. "It was difficult to say whether the road was laid out in the river, or the river in the road." They were heading to Egger's, "the destination of our great expectations," but the riders "saw nothing but mean shanties and people looked miserably poor." Their next host was the "thriving man of the region, [who] lived in style in a big brick house." They worried they'd lack "apparel fit for the society we were about to enter." When they rode up to a "gaunt two-story structure of raw brick, unfinished," they encountered a man who "carried on face, hands, and clothes so much more of the soil than a prudent proprietor would divert from raising corn, that we set him aside as a poor relation." But this *was* Egger, "no gentleman of the old school," but one who "dated from the time when there were no schools." The food was dismal, but Egger's pricing was fair—"either high or low, as the traveler chose to estimate it." The men rode on, meeting a local "school-mistress," an "Esmeralda who as she talked on, she turned from time to time to the fireplace behind her, and discharged a dark fluid from her pretty lips, with accuracy of aim, and with a nonchalance that belongs to our free-born American girls." The shocked Yankees fled to Elk Cross Roads, today's Todd, a spot recommended by a "member of the coast survey." Sadly, this wasn't the coast. It was a "country literally barren," where chickens were "not put forward as an article of diet."

Signs and converging roads "notified us that everything in this region tends toward Boone as a centre of interest," revealed Warner. They rode down Boone's "single street and landed at the most promising of the taverns" about twenty years after Stoneman's Raid. Warner recalled that Boone's residents believed it to be "the highest village east of the Rocky Mountains." That might be so, retorted Lounsbury, but it was "a God-forsaken place." In their dismal tavern, at least "the flies enjoyed the heat," Warner lamented. "How they swarmed!" Warner concluded that "the only amusement" in town was when court was sitting, and people "take sides; for the region is litigious." The lack of alcohol dismayed the tippling travelers. The visitor "is doomed to disappointment. If he wants to make himself an exception to the sober people whose cooking will make him long for the maddening bowl, he must bring his poison with him." They "left the country as temperate as we found it." Visitors would say the same until the 1980s. "There is nothing special to be said about Boone," Warner wrote. "We were anxious to reach it, we were glad to leave it." He did allow, "This country is settled by genuine Americans, who have the aboriginal primitive traits of the universal Yankee nation." "Valle Crusis," the Watauga River vale that would become North Carolina's first rural National Historic District, was back then "a blacksmith shop and a dirty, fly-blown store," surely the new Mast General Store that Charles Kuralt would call an American classic a century later. Warner "carried his weariness of life without provisions up to a white house on the hill, and negotiated for boiled milk." This house too "was occupied by flies. They must have numbered millions, in black swarms. Alas! if we had been starving, Valle Crusis had nothing to offer us." The despondent writer rode "eight miles to Banner's Elk," passing under "Hanging Rock . . . the only outcropping of rock we had seen." The peak blocked their view of far rockier Grandfather.

Shepherd Dugger was our travelers' host in Banner Elk. Less than ten years before Dugger published *The Balsam Groves of the Grandfather Mountain* to promote travel to the area, the men reached "the residence of Dugger to which we had been directed, nearly exhausted." They lamented "the heat and the road and the discouraged appearance of humanity." Fair warning, fans of Banner Elk and Shepherd Dugger. Warner admitted Dugger "is an excellent man," but "it is impossible to say that Mr. Dugger lives in a clean and attractive house, or that he offers much that the pampered child of civilization can eat. But we shall not forget the two eggs, fresh from the hens, nor the spring-house, a refuge from the flies and the heat." The weary sojourners were fed up with the primitive High Country—and likely record heat in a place now known for cool. They struggled on in pursuit of a good meal and a comfortable bed, finding it in Cranberry "at the Iron Company's hotel, the first wedge of civilization fairly driven into the northwestern mountains of North Carolina." The mines and railroad were owned by a Philadelphia company that had "spoiled some pretty scenery" but created a "hotel ordered by a Philadelphia landlady, who knows a beefsteak." They had passed Grandfather Mountain without mentioning it, escaping a region that an American Automobile Association map still represented as a blank spot in 1920.

Finally at Roan, they found the summit road "very well-engineered, in easy grades for carriages." Hikers still travel those winding, gradual switchbacks on the Appalachian Trail above Carver's Gap. A decade before the resort town of Linville was born below Grandfather, the urbane New Englanders checked in to the same rustic log hostel atop Roan that Asa Gray's party had praised five years earlier. Warner and Lounsbury found a surprising number of sociable women at the facility. A stay at the lodge was "a lot like camping," an experience duplicated by New England's Appalachian Mountain Club when it built its first stone hut on the Presidential Range a few years later. Warner found Roan's dark evergreen forests depressing, saying New England's "naked granite rocks in sun and shower are more cheerful." Save for a companion who wouldn't get off his horse, Warner would have loved craggy Grandfather, the distant "serrated ridge" they repeatedly admired from Roan.

A Local Sets the Record Straight
The Balsam Groves of the Grandfather Mountain was a landmark assault on the silence sur-

rounding Grandfather. Shepherd Dugger was a teacher and Watauga County superintendent of schools, but he was a promoter by passion, a late-nineteenth-century Hugh Morton without a camera. Mainstream writers were beginning to direct the nation's attention to the High Country. Dugger surely read Charles Dudley Warner's disparaging 1885 *Atlantic Monthly* article about him, Boone, and Banner's Elk. Describing his own 1892 book, Dugger wrote, "The object of the author has been to introduce to the outside world a section of the country which, until recently, has been almost unknown and obscure." The book's Victorian mores and purple prose take getting used to, but Dugger's story literally takes us on a hike up Grandfather.

The tale starts with Tom Toddy and his wife, who live in a humble log cabin where the clock "consisted of a knife-mark extending north from one of the door facings. When the mark divided the sunshine that fell in at the door it was noon. All other hours were guessed at: on cloudy days the clock stopped." The Toddy's young son is heading home with a sack of freshly ground flour on his ox, Buck. When Buck duels with another ox, the flour falls off, and he pleads to the surrounding silence, "Oh what shall I do? Ef I Go home without, they'll be no bread for supper; ef I stay here till dark, the painters [panthers] will ketch me." Luckily, along come three tourists, "two men and a lady, mounted on good steeds." Tears and bloody nose addressed, the trio take the lad home and spend the night. The tale parallels local history when Dugger identifies the older gentleman, William West Skiles, as "an Episcopalian clergyman, who kept a school at Valle Crucis." The Valle Crucis Episcopal Mission School still contains one of the area's most historic structures. Skiles was with a Mr. Leathershine, who'd been "expelled from an institution of higher learning in the eastern part of the state and afterwards received at Valle Crucis, a sequestered spot," with "no land for the culture of wild oats." Years before Banner Elk's Lees-McRae College and Boone's Appalachian State, Dugger imagined education as an excuse for students to head to the High Country.

Miss Lydia Meaks, the lady tourist, was a private-school teacher from Raleigh, an "elegant figure" with "raven-black hair." According to Dugger, her "mouth was set with pearls," and "her eyes imparted a radiant glow to the azure of the sky." Oh, yes, and she was "probably the fairest of North Carolina's daughters." With this Eve roaming Dugger's elevated Eden, sparks were gonna fly. Mrs. Toddy was self-conscious cooking for "the big bugs," demurring, "We are poor folks but you are welcome to sich as we have. Come in, ef you can get in." Skiles tactfully led the group into "the breezes of the yard" for views "of the great evergreen Grandfather, to whose lofty summit they were going on the morrow." Skiles points out the pantheon of High Country summits, and likely for the first time in print, Dugger relates how Grandfather got its name. "Yonder Grandfather," muses the minister, "has two heads with human faces, either of which is as perfect as the face of the ordinary man. The one that we shall see tomorrow stands up and faces to the north," seen above Foscoe on today's Profile Trail. "The one that I shall show you now," continued Skiles, "lies down and faces the sky." The party perceived the "face" visible today from the west in Banner Elk, the view Warner missed, the one that tempted Jehu Lewis from the east. Awed at the "high-flown conversation," Mrs. Toddy confesses, "I've got nothin' fit fur quality, and I wished they'd a stayed at home."

Meanwhile, ten miles west on the "jubilant banks of the Linville River," two "high-born gentlemen" had checked into luxurious lodging with a Colonel Palmer and his two young daughters, Mabel and Lotus. At first, Mabel thought Mr. Bodenhamer "had a big hump on his nose" and his face "was long as a fiddle." But alas, Bodenhamer's sonorous "Thank you, Miss Mabel" responses to her "womanly attentions" greatly diminished his nasal swelling, shortened his face, and enhanced "his beautiful complexion and fine brown eyes." Along with the rhododendron, love was blooming in the High Country. By the time Dugger is done, three separate couples have hooked up and we've met family names you still hear in the area.

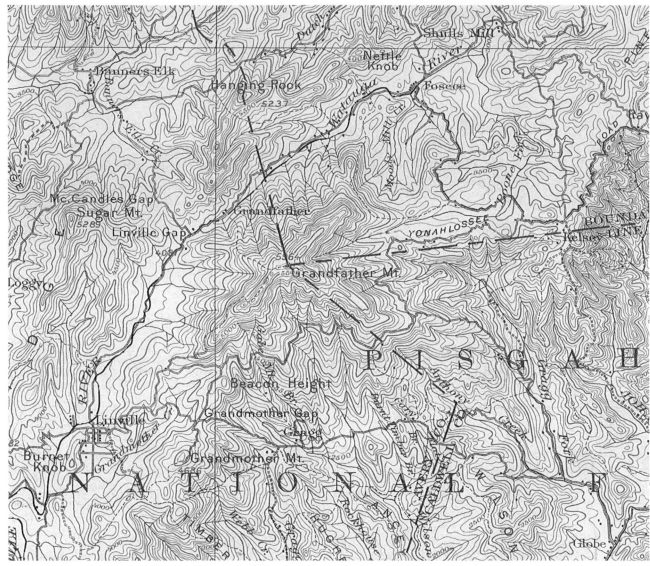

This 1902 topographic map (surveyed in the 1890s) offers a wealth of insight into turn-of-the-century Grandfather. From Alick MacRae's home in MacRae Meadows, a farm road rises toward Linville Peak that would later become Grandfather's first travel attraction. Note how the trail from there stays below the peaks, only attaining the ridge in MacRae Gap. The path seems to reach Calloway Peak, but none exists where the Boone Trail is today. A path also descends toward Linville Gap, but that veers north of the later Shanty Spring Trail to the site of Shepherd Dugger's Grandfather Hotel. And notice the road from Linville Gap to Linville. It was likely just a trail. N.C. Geological Survey.

Along the way, Dugger gives us plenty of heaving bosoms and a hike up Grandfather encountering landmarks hikers see today. The love story may not tug deftly at twenty-first-century heartstrings, but it succeeds in tying his character's best times, and readers, to the virgin backdrop of Grandfather Mountain. How pleased he would be to know that Grandfather's trailside settings still elevate the embrace of lovers.

The backstory on Dugger: Charles Dudley Warner's *Atlantic Monthly* criticism must have stung. Everything from Dugger's use of classical poetry, philosophical asides, and "high-born gentlemen" on horseback suggests indebtedness to Warner's travels with the erudite Lounsbury. Dugger seems intent on making "his" High Country a worthy destination for elite adventurers and his story a literary yarn equal to Warner's. To seal that deal, he offers us "the great evergreen Grandfather," an icon that would have changed the complaining Warner's tune if he hadn't missed it. Ironically, Warner showed up again, seven years after his first visit, as the brand-new resort town of Linville celebrated the 1892 grand opening of the Eseeola Inn. As author of the new *Balsam Groves*, Dugger was part of the program, and he surely felt vindicated at the area's evolution. Almost unbelievably, Dugger's book was the result of a Linville Improvement Company–sponsored contest "among writers to produce the best novel featuring Grandfather Mountain and the Linville area," writes Howard Covington Jr. in his centennial book *Linville: A Mountain Home for 100 Years*. Dugger's book, published with a subsidy from the Linville Improvement Company, was nothing less than a local's formal rebuttal to an uppity outsider.

Dugger set the stage for a new view of Grandfather Mountain's High Country. It wasn't long before a true icon of the outdoors turned up to second his lofty opinion. Scotland-born John Muir (1838–1914) became America's most famous proselytizer for wild nature. Often called the "Father of the National Parks," he visited Grandfather about a hundred years after Michaux and, like the Frenchman, was literally overcome with the view. Muir went to school in Wisconsin, moved to Canada to evade the U.S. Civil War, then discovered the Southern Appalachians in 1867 (recounted in his 1916 book *A Thousand-Mile Walk to the Gulf*). He returned again in 1898, having ensured preservation for Yosemite Valley in 1890 and founded the Sierra Club in 1892. Muir was a national figure; but most of his books had yet to be written, and he hadn't taken that 1903 camping trip to Yosemite with Theodore Roosevelt where Teddy awoke dusted in snow and destined to awaken the country to conservation. Muir traveled south with Harvard Arboretum director Charles Sprague Sargent and naturalist William Canby—the very men who were with Asa Gray on his visit to Roan Mountain in 1879. Gray had introduced his friends to Muir in 1878, and after an 1897 group visit to Alaska, Sargent suggested an autumn Southern Appalachian sojourn, expecting "the time of my life." The men were fast friends. One Canby letter addressed Muir as "Dear old streak o' lightning on ice." After the Sierra's arid alpine scenery, Muir wanted autumn,

Roan Mountain's once-primitive spruce lodge may have attracted Asa Gray, but after the palatial Cloudland Hotel supplanted it, even more naturalists flocked to the summit. John Muir was one of the most noteworthy visitors. Courtesy of Archives of Appalachia, East Tennessee State University, D. R. Beeson Papers.

writing, "I don't want to die without once more saluting the grand, godly, round-headed trees of the east side of America that I first learned to love." Sixty-year-old Muir had a tough train ride, but he'd bounced back by the time he got off the East Tennessee & Western North Carolina (ET&WNC) Railroad at Roan. The mountain's log summit lodge had become the massive, clapboard Cloudland Hotel, the popular resort Asa Gray foresaw. "This air has healed me," Muir crowed in a letter on hotel stationery.

Muir's climb of Grandfather in late September 1898 was a high point of his life that recalls one of scholar Charlie Williams's favorite Michaux anecdotes. Williams reminds people that Grandfather Mountain's early June event, the Singing on the Mountain, may date back to 1924, but, winks Williams, "it was André Michaux who did the first singing on the mountain." John Muir, may have been the second. A year after Muir's death, a friend shared an anecdote from that Grandfather Mountain hike. Muir was all about giving in to nature—which Michaux surely did when he sang out atop Grandfather. One of Muir's traveling companions was not of that stripe. Muir left this curmudgeon friend anonymous in his telling of the original tale, but the butt of Muir's story was likely Charles Sargent, that staid Harvard academic whom one biography called "colder than the notoriously chilly, Boston society." On their fall trip, Muir "got the better of him once," wrote Muir friend Melville B. Anderson in a 1915 book, *The Conversation of John Muir*. "The autumn frosts were just beginning, and the mountains and higher hill-tops were gorgeous," Anderson recalls Muir telling him. "My friend and the rest were making a little fun of me for my enthusiasm," recalled Muir. "We climbed slope after slope through the trees till we came out on the bare top of Grandfather Mountain. There it all lay in the sun below us, ridge beyond ridge, each with its typical tree-covering and color, all blended with the darker shades of the pines and the green of the deep valleys." Muir admitted, "I couldn't hold in, and began to jump about and sing and glory in it all. Then I happened to look round and catch sight of [the anonymous sourpuss] standing there as cool as a rock, with a half amused look on his face at me, but never saying a word." Muir asked Sargent, "Why don't you let yourself out at a sight like that?" Sargent retorted, "I don't wear my heart upon my sleeve." Cried Muir, "Who cares where you wear your little heart, man? There you stand in the face of all Heaven come down on earth, like a critic of the universe, as if to say, 'Come, Nature, bring on the best you have: I'm from BOSTON!'" Robert Underwood Johnson, who published Muir's writings in the magazine *Century*, wrote, "He sung the glory of nature like another Psalmist, and, as a true artist, was unashamed of his emotions." Like Michaux, John Muir burst into song atop Grandfather Mountain.

Muir largely left plant collecting to Canby, but the seventeen hand-picked specimens he did choose still survive, discovered years later, annexed with Muir's penciled notes within the pages of his personal copy of Shepherd Dugger's *Balsam Groves of the Grandfather Mountain*. Dugger, like Muir, exhorted people to open themselves to the world around them—especially the world of Grandfather Mountain. As Muir made his way

among the summits in Dugger's backyard and jotted notes in his book, you can bet the archetypal environmentalist of all time felt kinship with this man of the North Carolina mountains. That wasn't the case when the group took the train to Asheville to see George Vanderbilt's early forestry focus at Biltmore. They were "royally entertained," Muir wrote, but "as for Vanderbilt's magnificent Chateau, and drives, I soon tired of them." Nevertheless, pronounced Muir, "the drive from Roan Mountain to Lenoir is I think the finest in America of its kind." And that from a well-traveled man, indeed.

Inviting the Masses

Back when travelers still walked and rode horseback, Margaret Morley's 1913 book *The Carolina Mountains* urged readers across the nation to take their own mountain tour. Her classic still epitomizes how we see and appreciate Grandfather Mountain. Morley had visited the Continent, and she shares a worldly awareness that the Southern Appalachians are as distinct from the South as the Alps are from Europe. Morley gushes like the streams she admires. "What mountains ever offered themselves to the sun so enchantingly?" she asks. "This battlement of heaven was not named [the Blue Ridge] by accident. It was named Blue because . . . It is blue; tremendously thrillingly blue; tenderly, evasively blue."

The Carolina Mountains is also a sophisticated argument for conservation. Morley arrived as portable sawmills began to denude the mountains. Riding among hardscrabble farmers who'd soon cut down Grandfather Mountain's forests, she saw beyond to a future economy based on a "vast army of pleasure-seekers whose coming will bring to the inhabitants of these noble heights a material wealth vying with that in the forests themselves." Like Dugger, she wanted to entice the scenery-seekers. Morley's "favorite mountain" was Grandfather, where "trees stand apart" in virgin groves, "tall, clean columns beneath which little green things and wild flowers grow." Morley maintains that the mountain impresses "not because of its superior height—we know how many higher mountains there are—but because it is so commanding. Forty mountains may measure higher, but to those who know the Grandfather, not one is really quite so high." In an analogy apt for this patriarchal peak, she writes, "Nature fashions mountains as she does men, here and there is one so striking that it becomes a landmark for its era."

Like Mitchell and Guyot, Morley attributes the "peculiar charm" of "the country back of Blowing Rock and the Grandfather Mountain" to the lofty uniqueness of 3,000- to 4,000-foot valleys. "It is the walker's paradise, deliciously cool all summer. There are no finer views anywhere than from the high summits of the Grandfather country." Morley walked a loop of primitive roads from Blowing Rock to Boone, Valle Crucis, Banner Elk, and back. After so many bad reviews from early visitors, Morley exults in "that first visit to Boone!"—the "pretty snuggle of houses running along a single street at the foot of Howard Knob." She sets off to Valle Crucis amid pastures that look "for all the world like a summer meadow in the New England hills."

From Banner Elk, Morley took "the short walk over to 'Calloways,' close under the shadow of the Grandfather," the rustic Grandfather Hotel below Linville Gap, co-owned by J. Ervin Calloway and Shepherd Dugger. Even when she stops at Dugger's hotel, Morley never mentions him, whose *Balsam Groves* she'd surely read. Morley too climbed the Continental Divide. She took a leftward side trail to a view of the "clear-cut profile of the Grandfather," absent from the later Shanty Spring Trail but visible today on Profile Trail. "Continuing the ascent, the way grows wilder. One has a sense of rising spiritually as well as physically." Then she reaches "the famous Grandfather Spring that is only ten degrees above freezing throughout the summer," phrasing that recalls Dugger's in *The Balsam Groves*. She again doesn't mention him, but neither writer credits an even earlier reference to this spring in another memorable book, 1883's *The Heart of the Alleghenies*. Authors Wilbur G. Zeigler and Ben S. Grosscup conjured wording that both Dugger and Morley seem to emulate. "Under

a tall, dark cliff bubbles a large spring," Zeigler wrote. "Its water is of a temperature less than eight degrees above the freezing point. This, as far as is known, is the coldest spring south of New York state."

On "a staircase winding about moss-trimmed rocks through the spruces and the balsams you mount in the resplendent day," she writes, to "'Calloway's High Peak,' the highest point on the mountain." That was perhaps the first time that name appeared in print, explained by the part-owner of the hotel far below. On Calloway, the hikers stretched out on Allegheny sandmyrtle "to rest and receive the view." Morley marvels at vistas so compelling that "one shares the feelings and faith of Michaux. The view is very impressive," she writes, "because of that steep descent of the mountain into the foothills, the long spurs sweeping down in fine lines to a great depth." Morley's hike ends with a startling admission. She may have been among the first "recreational hikers" to walk along the apparently trailless main ridge of the mountain toward today's Swinging Bridge. Hunters and other bushwhackers preceded her, but "the men of the camping party blazed out a rude trail so that we could all take that wonderful knife-edge walk up in the sky, one seldom taken by anybody." Morley may have witnessed the very beginnings of what we know now as the Grandfather Trail. No wonder she called it "the great event of the season."

Another important book focused the national spotlight on the Southern Appalachians in 1913, Horace Kephart's *Our Southern Highlanders*. Overcome by "nervousness," library science innovator Kephart (1862–1931) looked for a place to escape. In a comment that could easily have applied to Grandfather, he wrote, "When I prepared, in 1904, for my first sojourn into the Great Smoky Mountains, I could find in no library a guide to that region. Had I been going to Teneriffe or Timbuctu, the libraries would have furnished information aplenty; but about this housetop of eastern America they were strangely silent; it was terra incognita." Kephart fled into the Great Smokies never to return to his family. *Our Southern Highlanders* debuted unprecedented anthropological and even linguistic insight into the Appalachians. The clannish mountaineers, he explained, saw visitors as people from beyond their own "country," so they elegantly expected "outlanders" to exhibit "outlandish" behavior. The book opened a door on the entire region, inspiring people to find the Great Smokies—and ultimately Grandfather. As a successful author and outdoor magazine writer, Kephart popularized a place where campfire light still danced overhead on virgin timber. Sadly, Kephart and friends like photographer George Masa (1881–1933) were watching that timber disappear. Both were a force in the establishment of Great Smoky Mountains National Park, and each has a Great Smokies summit named after him. Kephart was killed in an automobile accident in 1931, but he left transcendent accounts of the Southern Appalachians. Americans were listening, and they still are.

Two of Kephart's readers didn't have far to travel. Johnson City, Tennessee, architect Donald R. "Don" Beeson (1881–1983) and friend Charles H. "Hodge" Mathes (1879–1951), an original faculty member at the precursor to East Tennessee State University (ETSU), answered Kephart's invitation to explore North Carolina's peaks. "*Our Southern Highlanders* had come out in 1913 and Don and I read it with interest and delight," Mathes recalled. Kephart described dissuading a tenderfoot from tackling the Smokies' forty miles of wilderness, and Mathes said, "That sounds like a dare, don't you think?" Beeson and Mathes took Kephart's dare. Their first expedition, from August 31 to September 7, 1913, combined Roan and Grandfather. Over ensuing years they tackled the Smokies, Mount Mitchell, and Linville Gorge.

Bound first for Roan, the boys rode the Carolina, Clinchfield and Ohio Railroad to Toecane station west of Bakersville. A week later, they'd head home from Elk Park on the ET&WNC Railroad. They'd trudge between Roan and Grandfather on day-long walks of up to twenty-seven miles. The men reached the imposing Cloudland Hotel in

time for dinner and "ate about enough for a half dozen normal people." The dining room was split down the state line, with alcohol served only on the Tennessee side. They camped and were back for breakfast to hear one guest complain the "cooking was dirty." Beeson and Mathes didn't care as long as supply outlasted demand. They nevertheless left for Grandfather, indicting "the dirty proprietors." With few guests and that negative review, Beeson suggests why the hotel would close a few years later and fall into ruin.

They "struck across the country for Linville," and in Montezuma Gap they stopped at an ice house by a high lake to watch a massive storm "brewing on the head of the Grandfather. The sight of the start and growth of that storm from the grandest mountain I have ever seen so far baffles description that I won't try to paint in words what my eye beheld. I doubt if anything on the trip will equal it." The duo camped their "coldest night yet" in Linville, then walked the Yonahlossee Road and a path toward Linville Peak. From today's Cliffside Overlook, what Beeson tells us was "called McRae View," they took a long-established trail up Linville Peak. By 12:30 A.M., they consumed a "can of pork and beans, 2 hard boiled eggs, and 1 pint of coffee" in a box canyon just beyond today's Swinging Bridge. It was the most beautiful col on the mountain until Hugh Morton turned it into a parking lot in 1952.

After reading hike descriptions in Beeson's journal at ETSU and not being certain of his route, I dug deeper into his archive and discovered an empty folder simply labeled "Maps." An architect had to have made maps, so I asked the archivist to check further. Some time later, she wheeled out a folder that covered an entire table. I flipped it open to find Beeson's trail maps. But these weren't just maps; they were creations. To make them, Beeson had painstakingly cut out uniform rectangles of a topographical chart and pasted them on linen. A half-inch border of cloth separating each piece permitted the map to fold without bending the paper. On this Beeson drew the dotted lines of his hiking routes—solid evidence that the trails back

When Beeson and Mathes paused for lunch beyond Grandfather's first peak, they settled into a stunningly beautiful gap on the summit ridge. Even when Hugh Morton photographed it not long after the logging, it still appeared pristine. A Swinging Bridge would change all that. North Carolina Collection, University of North Carolina Library at Chapel Hill. Photo by Hugh Morton.

then differ greatly from today's paths. Now, the Grandfather Trail runs the very crest of the ridge over MacRae Peak and beyond. But Beeson's 1902 map shows a formal trail—already printed on the map—to the west of the peaks, below the main ridge, only gaining the crest near Attic Window Peak. Architect Beeson overlaid the dashed line of his route atop that trail—perhaps the only corroboration we have today that the path actually ran in that location. Thus, Beeson and Mathes likely missed MacRae Peak, now the location of ladders. Their lack of photos supports that conclusion.

On the evening of September 3, Beeson and Mathes were in a cave. With the weather "blowing a hurricane" and a fire blazing "in front of the cave mouth," Beeson wrote, "I doubt if I have ever enjoyed a supper more." They had come "only about four miles, but such miles." The trail was "hanging to the face of a precipice where a step of a couple of feet to the side would land you 500 feet below." In what may be the earliest photo of a trail ladder on a mountain now known for them, Beeson includes a shot of himself climbing a short, rustic affair made of on-site materials. Beeson and Mathes were having an epic day. "The outlook from the three main peaks of the mountain is magnificent and so far surpasses Roan that I think I will remember this trip as a journey to Grandfather Mountain." It was just another September day on the great, evergreen Grandfather. "We saw quite a

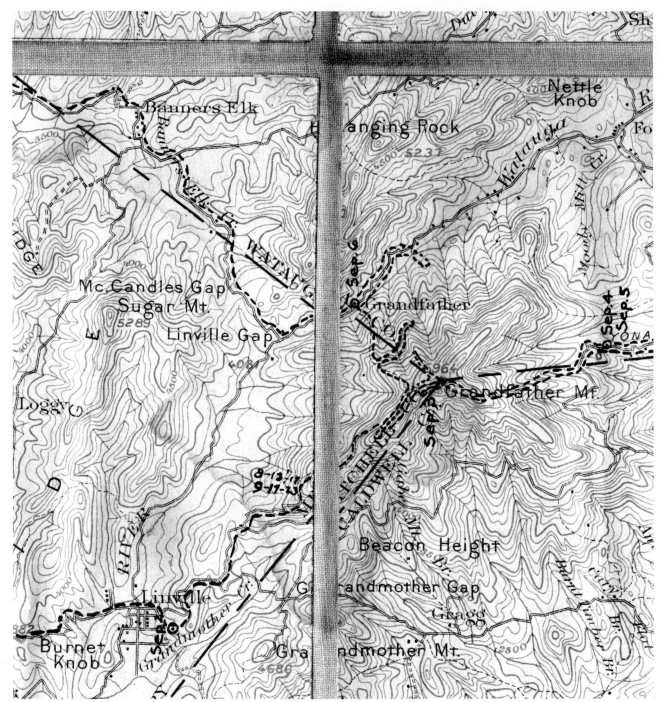

Beeson's ingeniously foldable linen map exactly plots the convoluted explorations of "the boys"—a hike that greatly informs which, if any, formal trails were in use at the time. Dates on the map suggest they returned in later years. Courtesy of Archives of Appalachia, East Tennessee State University, D. R. Beeson Papers.

few snow flakes this afternoon," Beeson observed. The men bushwhacked off the Blowing Rock side of the mountain, and by 8:00 P.M. that night were "sleeping in a bed for the first time since we started." They bunked at the Gragg family farm within feet of the Yonahlossee Road. The next day, Mathes and Beeson's longest walk led to Blowing Rock and back. They visited the Blowing Rock, "North Carolina's Oldest Travel Attraction," where they took their single picture of the day. Beeson

The duo camped in a cave and braved spitting snow squalls on their September hike that Beeson called "a vacation long to be remembered." Note that Beeson (right) is taking this photo with a string attached to his camera. Courtesy of Archives of Appalachia, East Tennessee State University, D. R. Beeson Papers.

confessed his preference for Linville over Blowing Rock, but the architect thought the Rock's fine cottages and homes were "in perfect taste and harmony with their locations." Though not blatantly bigoted, he was cool to the new guy in town— Moses H. Cone. "A rich jew has bought up a couple thousand acres to spread himself like Vanderbilt at Asheville." His "big frame house of a style that would do all right in a city . . . looks like the deuce in a mountain." Cone's 3,500 acres are today part of the Blue Ridge Parkway. On their last night at the Graggs' "our schedule went a little wrong," Beeson confessed, due to "Mrs. Gragg getting up on the N.E. corner of the bed when she was scheduled for

the S.W. side." Apparently, frequent guests beside the best turnpike in the mountains left her craving some privacy. Regardless, "the weather looked great" and "the air seemed clear as crystal."

The "air got colder and colder and soon we had frost thick on our hair and clothes," Beeson wrote. The views were "immense and wonderfully clear," but the vistas flashed in and out of clouds so fast he "failed to get a single picture." The guys climbed the general route of the 1940s Daniel Boone Scout Trail and crossed Calloway Peak to "the bluff, a jumping-off place with about 700 feet between you and the landing." They were beyond Watauga View on a bulge of Profile ridge where peregrine

The Gragg House

Six miles south of Blowing Rock on US 221, slow down to notice the Gragg House, the still-surviving, classic log structure where Beeson and Mathes stayed with the Graggs in 1913. It's uncertain when this historic, scenic cabin was built, but the 1870s sounds right based on John Preston Arthur's early 1900s conclusion that "Finley and Jesse Gragg [the latter was the likely builder of the cabin] probably moved to the top of the Ridge after the Civil War." The house "has inspired the admiration of generations of architectural historians," attests *The Architectural History of Watauga County*. This saddlebag house was called the "state's finest example of the type of log construction in which all four surfaces (of a log)

were so carefully hewn that the effect was of a sawn plank." The logs are so tightly meshed that no chinking is needed—a masterpiece of the cabin builder's art perched under snowy Grandfather Mountain. The structure appears on a 1952 Blue Ridge Parkway planning map that shows where exhibits interpret the road's "Pioneer Culture"—places like Tompkins Knob Parking Area, just north of US 421 at Deep Gap, where visitors see the Jesse Brown Cabin, Cool Spring Baptist Church, and a springhouse (milepost 272.5). That Parkway map called this the "5 Log House," likely because the side walls required only five massive, virgin logs to reach the required height. This cabin is still privately owned and never became a Blue Ridge Parkway exhibit.

What the Blue Ridge Parkway called "the 5 log house" is still a stunning 1800s reminder of what life was like below Grandfather Mountain. Beeson's overnight stay there invites us to imagine coming down off the mountain and staying with the Graggs a century ago. The detailed grain of the logs is amazing evidence of age. Photo by Randy Johnson.

falcons would be released in the 1980s. Before heading down, they tagged Attic Window Peak, "the best outlook of the three," judged Beeson. The map records this as their first visit, more evidence the "existing trail" skirted west of the main ridge. They accomplished their "best feat of mountaineering when we blazed a trail of our own that hit exactly the good view of the face." Beeson's hike also verifies that a rough path descended the Continental Divide at that time, likely the one Dugger wrote about, trod for years by botanists, hunters, and hikers. By 5:30 that evening, they had a bed at Calloway's, the "old landmark" Grandfather Hotel. Next morning, they walked to the train at Elk Park, "so tough looking" that if they'd asked at a house for help, they would have been "turned away,

empty-handed." Back in Johnson City Sunday afternoon, they'd walked 127 miles.

After generations of scientists and explorers had suffered privation in the serious pursuit of new knowledge on Grandfather, you can bet D. R. Beeson was among the first to call a climb of the mountain "a vacation long to be remembered." Though still covered in ancient evergreens, Grandfather was no longer isolated. Beeson and Mathes didn't have far to hike to catch their train to Tennessee. The two friends teetered between an earlier era of arduous exploration and a rising tide of tourism. As the twentieth century took hold, destructive winds of change were heading for Grandfather Mountain.

4 **Owners, Settlers, Sophisticated Resorts**

One of the best views of Grandfather comes from the Blue Ridge Parkway's Flatrock Nature Trail south of the mountain. Photo by Skip Sickler/http://skipsickler.zenfolio.com.

Speculators started hearing of the High Country by the late 1800s. Major mines were operating near Grandfather, and encroaching railroads meant timber harvesting would arrive in the twentieth century. With Blowing Rock a growing summer getaway, the Grandfather Mountain area was taking its first steps as a travel destination.

That spelled relief for Grandfather's owner, a one-legged Civil War veteran named Walter Waightstill Lenoir (1823–90). After decades of postwar hardship, Lenoir was ready to sell his beloved mountain and thousands of acres of surrounding land. He found willing buyers when the MacRae family of Wilmington arrived, intent on building a new summer resort below the mountain. That took decades, but the MacRaes' efforts to entice tourists and exploit natural resources would define the Grandfather's modern history.

None of it might have happened without Lenoir, a tragic figure whose family tree had roots deep in the soil of early America. Paternal grandfather General William Lenoir (1751–1839) was a captain at the Battle of King's Mountain, a militia general, and speaker of the North Carolina Senate from 1790 to 1795; he was also "one of the largest landlords in western North Carolina," writes William L. Barney in *The Making of a Confederate: Walter Lenoir's Civil War*. His plantation, Fort Defiance, is today a top-notch Caldwell County historic site (http.//fortdefiancenc.org/). Lenoir's maternal grandfather, Waightstill Avery, was also a Revolutionary soldier and North Carolina's first attorney general. Avery's sometime affiliate Martin Davenport was Michaux's guide on Grandfather.

As the Civil War approached, Walter Waightstill Lenoir opposed both slavery and secession and almost moved to Minnesota. But when Lincoln called up troops, Barney argues, Grandfather's future owner and most southerners felt forced to fight. Lenoir enlisted, became a captain, and lost a leg in the 1862 Virginia battle of Ox Hill under Stonewall Jackson. Afterward, he and many southerners struggled to blame the Yankees for an apocalyptic war the South had started to defend an inhumane institution. Lenoir and his fellows had years of suffering ahead. He moved deep into the mountains onto thousands of acres of family land and nearly became a hermit—not far from Cold Mountain, where Charles Frazier set his novel about a wounded Civil War deserter who retreats home for solace and solitude. But Lenoir was no deserter; he was a real estate speculator intent on making money from the one thing he had: land. He struggled for decades to sell property, but no one had money, especially the squatters who targeted huge tracts like his. In the spring of 1867, Lenoir gained thousands more acres from the estate of his brother William, who'd committed suicide in 1861. He moved to Watauga to sell his "Beech Creek lands close to the Tennessee border," just above

W. W. Lenoir was an avid explorer of Grandfather Mountain. On an August 1854 camping trip near Calloway Peak he'd failed "to kindle a fire" and "danced and frolicked to keep warm . . . the roughest and rarest night's lodging that ever anyone did have." After the Civil War, Lenoir continued hiking despite his low-tech wooden leg, on display today at Fort Defiance. Photo by Randy Johnson.

Banner's Elk, writes Barney. "He created seventeen small lots priced at slightly under a dollar per acre. He had no wish to return to the area anytime soon. Not only was it remote, most of its settlers were poor Unionists, some of whom were trespassing on Walter's land." Amazing as it sounds, Walter Lenoir was selling the first lots on Beech Mountain a century before it became a ski area.

Lenoir ran a gristmill and a sawmill and raised cattle above Shull's Mill, but he was desperate to sell property. He set aside a preferred parcel, "the cream of my Watauga lands," 1,200 acres along the Boone Fork. "I am rich enough to feel how poor I am," he lamented, "rich enough in land to be very poor till I get rid of it or have the means to improve it." Eighty years later, after World War II, wounded veteran Hugh Morton likely felt the same when he became owner of Grandfather Mountain. Former slaveholder Lenoir made one sale, to African American Henry Moore. With "whites in Watauga more intent on poaching his timber," maintains Barney, Lenoir hiked as many as ten miles a day patrolling on his Civil War–era wooden leg. Lenoir "was looking forward to the day when he could retire at Linville," notes Barney. "His favorite spot lay there at the foot of Grandfather Mountain. He referred to it as Under the Pinnacle and pronounced it 'one of the loveliest places in all the mountains.'"

When the East Tennessee & Western North Carolina Railroad (ET&WNC) reached the iron mines at nearby Cranberry from Johnson City, Tennessee, in 1882, Lenoir believed "the coming of the railroad would open up the scenic wonders of Watauga to outside visitors and promote the economic development he had long wished to see." Lenoir had a mild stroke in 1884, and a dream "transported him to the warmth of Florida, where he could spend his winters under the watchful eye of a good physician and nurses." Imagine, in the virgin forests under Grandfather Mountain, a dream had foreshadowed the modern seasonal lifestyle of alternating between Florida and the mountains, possibly for the first time. Lenoir's real estate prospects brightened "in 1885," Barney argues, "with the opening of the Watauga Hotel as a fashionable summer resort" in Blowing Rock. In a letter to James Gwyn, Lenoir hoped Watauga would "soon be 'spoken of as a favored land, destined ere long to become a delightful region. Behold the realization of my idyl!'" A railroad wouldn't haul timber from Shull's Mill for another thirty-one years, but just as Lenoir was about to log valuable cherry trees off his property, a man named Samuel T. Kelsey showed up wanting to build a new tourist town. Kelsey offered to buy 8,090 acres in Linville and on Grandfather for $28,000: $10,000 down, the rest in eight years. "The offer was a godsend," Barney writes. But Lenoir was partially paralyzed by a second stroke in May 1889. Nevertheless, he thought "the sale of my Lin-

ville lands will soon put me out of debt & in easy circumstances."

Kelsey had optioned Lenoir's land, but the ultimate owners of Grandfather Mountain would be a clan of Highland Scots, the MacRaes, who arrived in Wilmington from Scotland's western coast in 1770. Their influence would stretch across the state. Family patriarch Roderick MacRae died in 1807, and by 1814, grandson Alexander MacRae (1796–1868) was amassing family wealth building the Wilmington and Raleigh Railroad, North Carolina's first rail line and the longest in the world when it opened in 1840 (later renamed the Wilmington and Weldon Railroad). Alexander served in the war of 1812, was the railroad's president from 1847 to 1863, and became the oldest officer in the Confederate army. One of his nine sons, William MacRae (1834–82), would further the family's fortune. The sixteen-year-old started out like his father in the railroad business, but an obituary records that he disdained life "in the lap of affluence" and hired on building locomotives in Philadelphia. He came home at twenty-one, went "into the machine works of the Wilmington and Weldon shops," and acquired astounding expertise as a railroader. Motivated to equally stellar service in the Civil War, William became the youngest brigadier general in the Confederacy and one of the South's ablest brigade commanders. In the ultimate irony, his victory at the 1864 Virginia Battle of Ream's Station saved General Lee's essential supply line to the still-open port of Wilmington—his family's own rail line, the Petersburg and Weldon. After the war, according to his obituary, the "life-long bachelor" returned "penniless," rose to management at several major railroads, and brought the Wilmington and Manchester Railroad "back from ruin." William revived family finances, but older brother Donald MacRae (1825–92) would look west to the mountains. "Though he weighed just 125 pounds [MacRae] was a business heavyweight," read a career overview in *Wrightsville Beach Magazine*. "President of Wilmington Cotton Mills and Wilmington Compress, he also had interests in banks, railroads, Florida real estate and five blockade runners." Just weeks before the war ended, Donald and his wife, Julia Norton MacRae, had a son, Hugh MacRae (1865–1951). Twenty years later, son Hugh was in the mountains. He studied mining engineering at the Massachusetts Institute of Technology and with his father's support began investigating mountain property with mining potential, including for mica near Burnsville. Samuel T. Kelsey was scoping out the same part of western North Carolina in the mid-1880s. Wealthy lowland families were starting to vacation in the cool uplands, and Kelsey was a prophet of that Appalachia-wide travel trend. He expanded that summer-escape concept by building the town of Highlands, North Carolina, in the mid-1870s. He wanted to duplicate that success near Grandfather Mountain, not far from where the ET&WNC Railroad to Cranberry was delivering a growing number of botanically inclined tourists to Roan Mountain's Cloudland Hotel. Kelsey had begun amassing property and by 1888 had acquired options on 16,000 acres of land, including Grandfather Mountain. Kelsey contacted Donald MacRae to discuss collaboration, and MacRae dispatched son Hugh to tour the region.

If any southern soldier's grave deserves the trappings of Confederate commemoration, it's Lenoir's. The Lenoir cemetery is just one of many fascinating aspects of Fort Defiance, the family plantation in Caldwell County. Photo by Randy Johnson.

With options on Lenoir's land, Kelsey sat down with Hugh MacRae at the Cranberry Hotel to talk vision. Starting a new town had appeal, but MacRae needed to explore the property first. Kelsey and MacRae roamed Lenoir's entire tract, including the virgin valley of the Linville River. A compelling image of that riverside ride was penned a few years before their trip in the 1883 classic *The Heart of the Alleghenies*. "I entered a wilderness unbroken by human habitation for nearly five miles," wrote Wilbur G. Zeigler. "Linns, birches, and hemlocks met overhead, rendering dark the shadows. So deep and luxuriant was the foliage and so cold the waters of the stream, that the air was chilly and must be so even at noon-day. . . . In only one place did the branches of the trees separate themselves sufficiently to see the black summit of the Grandfather. That was all. A more

dismal woodland for a twilight ride could not well be imagined." Suddenly, there was an opening with "a meadow and small house. Over the house and farm loomed the rock-crowned summit of the Peak of the Blue Ridge." They were in Linville Gap. Walter Lenoir knew his land would impress Kelsey and MacRae. He had outlasted decades of exile and poverty, and "at long last," Barney asserts, the sale of Lenoir's land gave him "a 'crown of glory' to his old age which would handsomely benefit the seven family heirs in his will." A week after Lenoir met with the MacRaes, he "was stricken, never to rise again," recorded niece Selina. He died on July 26, 1890, "his favorite season in the mountains," according to Barney, when "Watauga dons her summer costume [and becomes] the fairest of the daughters of the land of the sky." Walter Waightstill Lenoir is buried at Fort Defiance.

A Dream Gets under Way

The dream of a resort town below Grandfather started to become a reality in the autumn of 1889 at a meeting in the Cranberry Hotel. The Linville Land, Manufacturing and Mining Company, immediately renamed Linville Improvement Company, had Donald MacRae as president and Kelsey as vice president before the elder MacRae ceded this position to son Hugh. Early promotion promised Linville would be a hub of business activity "for a large fertile section of the country," but Donald MacRae was more practical. He questioned the "benefits of manufacturing or mining" in favor of "making Linville a place of beauty and a popular resort for health and pleasure for the best class of cultivated people." The MacRaes wouldn't succeed if tourists couldn't get to Linville first. Stage transportation from the rails in Cranberry helped, but in 1890, the Linville Improvement Company set out to build a road to the nearest popular resort, Blowing Rock, where good roads reached Lenoir. With Linville under way, Hugh MacRae was traveling the East promoting the project. During a stay at the Cranberry Hotel on one return trip, he met his future wife, Rena Nelson of St. Louis. Another time, at the still-surviving High Country classic the Green Park Hotel in Blowing Rock, MacRae started talking to his dining room server, Joseph Larkin Hartley (1871–1966). The bright, charismatic eighteen-year-old would become a true character, a quintessential mountain man. At that moment, two families met that would prove pivotal in Grandfather Mountain's history. For more than a century, Hugh MacRae's family (and then the Mortons) would rely on Joe Hartley and his progeny in the evolution of Grandfather Mountain from wilderness to timber tract and travel attraction.

The Hartleys arrived in America in 1740, and by 1800 Ruben Hartley (Joe Hartley's great-grandfather) was "among the earlier settlers" of Ashe, later Watauga, County, maintained Joe Hartley's son Robert Hartley (1922–2010). Robert was general manager of the Grandfather Mountain attraction from 1968 to 1984 and the mountain's historian until he died in 2010. Robert's grand-

father, Elbert Joshua Hartley, was a Confederate veteran who farmed by the Watauga River in the Shull's Mill area. It was there Joe Hartley was born in 1871 and "raised where Hound Ears Golf Course is now," recounts Robert. Much of that "bottom land" was owned by the Shull family, and "when Pop was sixteen, he plowed that land with a yoke of oxen for 50 cents a day." At about eighteen years old, Robert recalled, Hartley "got him a job, waiting on tables at Green Park Hotel," where MacRae told him about the resort he was going to develop. "Dad said MacRae wanted to build a golf course! Imagine," exclaims Robert Hartley. "Who wanted a golf course in 18 and 88?" Not long after, Joe Hartley saw MacRae again and "offered himself up for a job. MacRae told him to go and see Mr. Alexander MacRae."

Lest the forest of family trees grow too thick, this Alexander MacRae is not the grandfather of Hugh MacRae, who started the Wilmington clan's railroad empire and died in 1868. Believe it or not, yet another MacRae family had settled in Linville *before* the Wilmington MacRaes arrived. These more recent emigrants from Scotland are nevertheless thought to be earlier arrivals to the flank of Grandfather Mountain. It was this Alexander MacRae whom young Joe Hartley went to see. MacRae was building a road to Blowing Rock for the Linville Improvement Company, and he needed all the help he could get. In Joe Hartley, MacRae hired a future legend. In Alexander MacRae (1842–1929), Hartley saw "a real Highlandman in appearance," wrote one Scottish visitor in the early 1900s. He was "of giant build, with a strong, rugged face, lighted by bright blue eyes. His speech had lost nothing of the soft gentle inflection peculiar to the Highlands." Born in Glenelg (pronounced Glen Elig), Inverness-shire, Scotland, just across from the Isle of Skye, Alexander MacRae immigrated to the United States with his wife Mary MacLennan MacRae, seven sons, and one daughter in 1884. He was a fisherman in Scotland with an impressive, more-than-100-foot, two-masted, steam-powered fishing boat of substantial value. Instead of "Alex," people called him "Alick."

After owning a prodigious steam-powered vessel and fishing Scotland's west coast near the Isle of Skye, Alick MacRae adapted well to working highland meadows with a hoe in his hands. His sons Johnny and Alick Jr. grew up under the peaks of Grandfather but later found themselves in Linville. This Hugh Morton portrait of Alick Jr. standing in the mist under Linville Peak speaks to the brothers' disappointment. They concealed their private conversations by speaking Gaelic. William S. Caudill Collection, North Carolina Collection, University of North Carolina Library at Chapel Hill.

MacRae almost returned to the old country—as many did in this wave of emigrants organized by North Carolinians to encourage post–Civil War immigration. He found the lowland Carolinas far too hot and made his way up in elevation, where Joe Hartley found him, naturally enough, above Linville at "MacRae Meadows." There is doubt about exactly how that move happened. Some

sources say he missed the ocean, went to Wilmington, and was hired by the "other MacRaes" to come to Linville. In a 1997 interview, Alexander MacRae's grandson Robert Carswell (1928–2013) asserted that the Wilmington MacRae's "took my grandfather up there and he persuaded them to sell him a small tract of land near Linville." But it's likely Alick MacRae was in the mountains before the Wilmington MacRaes. In 2009, Grandfather historian Hartley maintained that Grandfather's "original owner," Walter Waightstill Lenoir, "brought Alexander MacRae up here to raise cattle and sheep on his mountain land." William Caudill, a scholar of North Carolina's Scottish immigration of 1884, also buttresses that, describing Alexander's garb as befitting "a gamekeeper or estate manager in Scotland." Howard Covington Jr. agrees in his Linville centennial book. And in 2013, Hugh MacRae II, grandson of Hugh MacRae, remembered, "The MacRaes were living there before we ever bought the property." However he got there, MacRae became the meadows' namesake, living with his family in their twenty-room "MacRae House," taking in boarders, and playing his bagpipes.

Covington says Hugh MacRae "liked this Scottish [music] connection and volunteered to help Alexander find new reeds for his bagpipes," surely elusive items. "'We will be glad to get the bagpipes,' the young MacRae wrote his brother Donald, 'especially if they are loud, as we can hear them from the surrounding hills.'" Margaret Morley called on the MacRaes for her 1913 book *The Carolina Mountains*. "Sooner or later," she concluded, "you will find your way to McRae's [sic] which is to the south side of the Grandfather what Calloway's [Calloway's Grandfather Hotel] is to the north side, a farmhouse where one can stay awhile." It must have been quite an experience. "Mr. McRae has not forgotten how to play on the bagpipes those ancient airs that have so stirred the blood of his race," wrote Morley. She liked his piping, "but you will have to coax him to do it." Or maybe not. Scholar Caudill, himself an expert piper, discovered that Carswell remembered hearing that "gatherings sometimes included local musicians who would play and dance in their kitchen with MacRae playing his pipes. In essence," asserts Caudill, "true traditional Highland ceilidhs were held at the MacRae House." Seventy years before a Scottish picnic became the first Grandfather Mountain Highland Games in 1956, the sound of bagpipes was echoing across MacRae Meadows.

Until their deaths in the early 1960s, the MacRae sons lived in Linville, where their father's vintage bagpipes and sporran were on display. The brothers eventually lost the family meadowlands to the Wilmington MacRaes. They were known to converse in Gaelic when they didn't want to be understood.

Alexander MacRae would have been the perfect employee for either Walter Lenoir or Hugh MacRae. After the war, Lenoir wondered who would work in the postslavery South. Slaves would "never be self-supporting" and "Native whites had few skills," Barney writes, so "foreign-born whites were the ideal solution thought Lenoir, who preferred northern Europeans, especially the Scots, who were noted for their thriftiness." In the 1920s, a middle-aged Hugh MacRae would start importing northern European immigrants to his successful eastern North Carolina farm colonies. Had the old Confederate given Hugh MacRae the idea? Suffice it to say, by the time Hugh MacRae sent young Joe Hartley to ask Alick MacRae for a job, a thrifty, hard-working Scot was building Linville's new road.

A Link to the Outside World

The High Country was full of trails, but privately built "turnpikes" were few and quickly fell into disrepair. One of the best was the Lenoir Turnpike, leading traffic up the Blue Ridge to Blowing Rock. The Yonahlossee Road, eighteen long miles across one of the ruggedest mountains in the East, would be a critical link between Linville and that artery to the outside world. Luckily, the road traversed gradually from Linville at 3,800 feet to Blowing Rock at 3,600 feet, "scarcely changing its grade for nearly twenty miles," observed Morley. A crew of up to 100 men excavated a road up to fourteen feet wide entirely by hand, with picks and shovels, oxen and mules. The project cost $18,000 and stretched into 1891. It's uncertain who engineered this masterpiece. Morley thought it was Samuel T. Kelsey who "had yet greater genius for making roads than towns." Maintained Robert Hartley, "Mr. Alexander McRae just eyeballed it through the

Meeting Alexander MacRae

A 1907 issue of *The Scottish-American* published a surprising story about a group of Scots who found themselves on Grandfather Mountain.

Alick MacRae may have been Grandfather Mountain's first real attraction. This "real Highland man" offered hospitality and stirring music at his MacRae House. And it was not a long walk above his meadows to a viewpoint that the Wilmington MacRaes would one day turn into a tourist attraction. William S. Caudill Collection.

The Bagpipes in the Mountains Of North Carolina

In the States south of the Mason and Dixon Line when one Scot meets another it is of more mutual importance than it would be in the North. During the Christmas holidays three Scotsmen (including myself) took a horseback trip through the mountains of Western North Carolina. The region is sparsely settled, and the natives are rather poor and illiterate, living in isolated log cabins, and varying the monotony of their lives by indulging in periodical fights among themselves. This digression explains the unusual curiosity aroused in us when we learned that a Scotsman by the name of MacRae lived a few miles away on the slope of Grandfather Mountain. We heard he was a Highlandman, celebrated through the country for his performance on the bagpipes. When we arrived at his place, he was absent, having gone to his farm near the top of Grandfather Mountain (the summit of which is 6,000 feet above sea), but when Mrs. MacRae learned the nationality of her visitors she dispatched a messenger to bring him. Numerous pipes were smoked and the log fire replenished again and again, and the conversation never flagged. At last, at our joint request, our host took his bagpipes and stepped into the hall. After a moment a long strange wail arose (very strange in that part of the world), and when the piper got his wind up, the tune resolved itself into "The Campbells are Comin'," and was accompanied by the steady tramp of his feet. We could see a most solemn and almost reverential look upon his face, as he fondled the ancient instrument and brought forth upon it one after another of our Scottish airs. It was a most unique experience for we three travelers in this wildest part of North Carolina.

—J.G. Jr.

woods and the mountain people built it." Hartley's father "got 65 cents a day and gave Mrs. MacRae 30 cents a day for his room and board" at MacRae House. Covington quotes Joe Hartley saying "it was really something to build . . . hewing and grubbing from daylight 'till dark six days a week. Oh, but it was a marvel to behold." Alick MacRae reveled in his road for years as the contracted mail carrier between Linville and Blowing Rock. The route was called Yonahlossee—"Bear Trail" or "Passing Bear" in Cherokee—after an Indian hunting path said to traverse that side of the mountain and Grandfather's reputation as a bear-hunting haven. From the start, the road earned high praise. Early 1890s state highway engineers deemed it "excellent for summer travel through one of the most beautiful and interesting portions of the mountain region." The road crossed rustic rock bridges. The double gusher bridge across Wilson Creek was documented in many a photo. Besides bounding bruins, roadside attractions included the towering, tilted pillar of Stack Rock (or Leaning Rock) and Nose End Rock, projecting its proboscis over the road. Bridal Veil Falls was a roadside cascade. Linville would struggle into the mid-twentieth century, but sights on the Yonahlossee Road were an easy out-and-back drive from bullish Blowing Rock. Yonahlossee's landmark design and views of the peaks and Piedmont made it a nineteenth-century equivalent of the Blue Ridge Parkway's Linn Cove Viaduct. Ironically, the National Park Service later rejected converting Yonahlossee into the Blue Ridge Parkway, in part because it was not considered scenic enough. From 1900 to the eve of World War I, a toll was charged.

As soon as the first cars chugged up to Blowing Rock, motorists made an adventure out of the well-graded Yonahlossee. Dates differ, but according to a 1974 obituary in the *Hickory Daily Record*, James C. Shuford made the first auto trip to Linville in June 1909, "the first time a motorcar had traversed the rutty and rocky route." When "the daring automobilist" died at eighty-six, articles highlighted his early auto adventures. The trip from Hickory to Linville took four and a half hours,

and as many did, he drove to the edge of the cliff at The Blowing Rock. To gain better maintenance and public funding for Yonahlossee, the Linville Improvement Company granted the state highway commission a ninety-nine-year lease on the road in 1922. As the Good Roads movement started improving state highways, the Yonahlossee was paved a few years after Alexander MacRae died in 1929. In a sad twist, highway workers staying at the MacRae House left wet clothes near the fireplace, and the landmark burned down while they were away paving the road. Yonahlossee grew in importance. Long before interstate highways, tourism interests linked roads into "trails" to promote long-distance travel. US 221 became part of a paved route from Canada to South Florida called, believe it or not, the Black Bear Trail. Named after bears to begin with, the Yonahlossee Road found itself marked with a black bear plaque on Nose End Rock (then also called Bear Rock). Later, the Yonahlossee was routed on a more direct descent to Linville from MacRae Meadows, but the original route is still unpaved and called Old Yonahlossee Road. It passes Donald's Crag, a view ledge above Linville named after Hugh MacRae's brother Donald MacRae Jr. Much more than a tourist route, the road pierced the area's isolation and became popular with locals walking or riding to neighbors and stores. The road made Grandfather Mountain more accessible for hunting, gathering berries, or "pulling Galax." Howard and Blanch Byrd of Foscoe, in their eighties in 2013, remember the Yonahlossee Road leading to riches plucked from the mountain. Howard "walked all the way along the backside and picked our way to the top before they ever thought about the Swinging Bridge. We'd pick blueberries and carry many a gallon back off to that highway." The road was so long, people pulled off to picnic, cook over a fire, or camp. One of the most popular campsites was "Bear Rock, they called it," remembers Byrd. "I slept behind that rock many a time, yes, sir." For years, the sheltered area below another rock beside Wilson Creek was enclosed with stone and wood to create what mountain residents called a "rock house," a

With a crew of mountain locals and primitive horse-drawn equipment, Alick MacRae built the Yonahlossee Road, a turnpike that well-traveled Margaret Morley called "the best road in the North Carolina mountains." Whether you drove a new motor car or a covered wagon, the road's points of interest were an experience worth writing home about, and many postcards depicted spots like Bridal Veil Falls, shown here. North Carolina Museum of History.

Joe Hartley, Mountain Man

Born and raised in post–Civil War Southern Appalachia, Joseph Larkin Hartley was an iconic figure in Grandfather Mountain's history, a rustic man revered for his character and chiseled Scots-Irish countenance. To Hartley, walking was a spiritual act, a way of leading the mind to new insights as the feet found new settings. Hartley wrote a few pamphlet-books, and in *Walking for Health and Traveling to Eternity*, annual entries tallied up 120,572 miles walked from 1877 to 1957. Walking on Grandfather turned Hartley's mind to the Creator, and his poems praised the mountain's virgin majesty. He counted

Joe Hartley was an original, a mountain man of character and native culture sufficient to sire a family that, like the one born to Hugh MacRae, would influence Grandfather Mountain for a century. Here he appears to be standing on Attic Window Peak, wearing his fire warden's badge, seeming to shake his finger at anyone who'd abuse his beloved mountain. North Carolina Collection, University of North Carolina Library at Chapel Hill. Photo by Hugh Morton.

himself lucky to have gone to a log cabin school in 1887 "at Shulls Mills to Dr. B. B. Dougherty, who learned me most I know." It was Dougherty's "first place to teach." Incredibly, Hartley found himself tutored by the 1899 founder of Watauga Academy, which would eventually become Appalachian State University.

Hartley arrived in Linville in 1889 to build the Yonahlossee Road. After working as a bellboy at the Eseeola Inn, he met the new century with a job he'd keep for life: fire warden for the Linville Improvement Company's backcountry lands. "I crossed [Grandfather] sometimes twice a day and would sleep under rock cliffs," he recorded. Hartley was always on the mountain, building trails, surely encountering the Muirs, Morleys, and Beesons. He grew up with a hoe in his big, beefy hands, gaining gardening prowess and becoming legendary as a one-man farmer's market for hotels and cottagers in Linville. Joe Hartley, Christian gentlemen, stood by his neighbors in the Depression. "Uncle Joe was a lifesaver," Jim Hughes recalled in 2013. "I loved apples and ours were always gone." Uncle Joe would walk by Hughes's house on a trail and say, "'James if you want to I'll give you some apples.' I'd walk up there and he'd give me half a bushel. I'll always remember him for it." Robert Hartley recalled that author Shepherd Dugger would stay awhile. "Dad and Dugger were great friends," insisted Robert. "We got put off the bed to sleep on the floor!" In 2009, pointing to an upstairs window in his house, Robert mused, "Right up there is where Shepherd Dugger revised *The Balsam Groves of the Grandfather Mountain* in the early 1930s."

In later years working on the Grandfather attraction maintenance crew, Joe Hartley regaled motorists with stories and relished his role as "old time mountain man." The fissure-faced native scything the roadside was a vision of the past. Uncle Joe "was always looking for pretty rocks," notes crewman Winston Church, recalling an entire week Hartley spent tending one stretch of road after fellow workers planted fool's gold. Walking gave Hartley a long, healthy life. Church remembers a full day of trail work on the high peaks in 1962 when Hartley was ninety-one. In the mid-1960s, Hartley got "broke up pretty bad" in an auto accident and "didn't last too long after that," relates Church. A year after Hartley died in 1966, Mary K. Crawford wrote a seventy-fifth-anniversary town overview and praised Hartley as a "first citizen of Linville." He was, she wrote, "affectionately known as Uncle Joe, but respectfully addressed by the summer residents as Squire Hartley." The "orator, poet and author" was "the archetype of the great mountain men we have known here." After quoting Hartley that nature "will live on as monument to my glory when I shall be in Eternity," she'd simply written, "Amen."

Hartley took pride in his sixty-year employment by Hugh Morton's grandfather, writing, "I doubt if any man ever worked longer for any one man than I did for Mr. Hugh MacRae." As MacRae neared the end of his life (he'd die in 1951), Morton took Hartley down to Wilmington so the men could reminisce. "It was the first time this old mountain man had seen the ocean," Morton marveled. "At Wrightsville Beach he picked up a seashell, dipped up some water and tasted it, and said, 'It *is* salty.'" Many a Morton photo immortalizes Joe Hartley. One of the best enshrines the dignity of this old man of the mountains, standing with the surf to his back, gazing westward to the hills.

traditional shelter prevalent among High Country hunters, gatherers, and guides from the days of the earliest explorers.

Linville Comes to Life

When Yonahlossee opened, the massive Eseeola Inn was under way but money was tight. In late 1891, Hugh MacRae resigned as president, and the family seemed destined to leave the Linville project. Eseeola debuted in 1892 at a July 4 soiree attended by many noteworthy northerners, including Charles Dudley Warner. The inn's first summer started successfully, but the Linville Improvement Company was still losing money. By fall, Donald MacRae had died in Linville (some attributing his passing to the stress of Linville's difficulties), and Hugh MacRae was back representing family interests. In the summer of 1893, the company was in debt, and president Thomas F. Parker reported "there was not sufficient money to pay the help," writes Covington. The Linville Improvement Company was "taken over by court-appointed receiver after Thomas Lenoir filed legal papers to insure [*sic*] payment of the remaining $16,000 the Lenoir estate was owed for the property." The following year, Covington explains, MacRae was back, holding mortgages on the resort's 16,000 acres after he and a few other investors had "raised enough

money to pay off Linville's debts, get the company out of receivership and secure a majority of the company's stock." The back-and-forth between allies of MacRae and Parker continued until 1900, when the MacRaes bought out their opponents and Hugh MacRae's brother Donald MacRae Jr. took over as Linville Improvement Company president. During Donald Jr.'s tenure, architect Henry Bacon undertook a new vernacular design for Linville summer homes. Bacon, who'd later design the Lincoln Memorial, christened his now classic chestnut bark–shingled style of resort architecture on Donald MacRae's home. MacRae improved the town's golf course, and by the 1910s, Scottish golf pros were being hired.

A central figure at Linville into the early 1900s, Hugh MacRae eventually turned his attention back to Wilmington. The influential man who bought Lenoir's Grandfather lands would consolidate his fortune at the coast, but he'd also figure prominently in sparking what's been called the Wilmington Race Riot of 1898. In the only coup in U.S. history to successfully overthrow an elected government, blacks were murdered and driven from their businesses, homes, and elected offices. The direct result was the passage and spread of Jim Crow laws in North Carolina and throughout the South, successfully rolling back progress made by

In 1909, James C. Shuford made the first motorized Yonahlossee Road ramble to Linville in his Reo. Posing with friends atop the Blowing Rock as many motorists did, he was all about pride of ownership. Busy gazing at the Rock's Grandfather view, the guy in the background was oblivious to posterity. William B. Stronach III Collection.

By the 1930s, with the Yonahlossee Road a U.S. highway and part of the Black Bear Trail, Nose End Rock found itself emblazoned with a bear plaque. North Carolina Museum of History. Photo by Frank Clodfelter.

For years, traveling photographers took aim at the Yonahlossee Road's atmospheric, indeed primitive, "rock shelter" accommodation built under a boulder beside Wilson Creek. The Eseeola Inn it was not. One such observer was now-legendary Southern Appalachian photographer George Masa. His image includes the "double gusher" stone bridge that became a focal point for travelers. Another picture by an unidentified photographer gives a closer look. Photo by George Masa, North Carolina Museum of History. North Carolina Collection, Pack Memorial Public Library, Asheville, North Carolina.

This young couple didn't take the Yonahlossee Road to a room under a rock. Theirs was tastefully encased in bark at Eseeola Inn, courtesy of architect Henry Bacon. For the Lincoln Memorial, Bacon's stone of preference would be marble. Collection of Hugh MacRae II. Photo by Nelson MacRae. North Carolina Collection, University of North Carolina Library at Chapel Hill.

blacks during Reconstruction. The event ensured that it would be another fifty years before the civil rights movement further enfranchised blacks. At the 100th anniversary of the riot, grandson Hugh MacRae II was credited with participating in a Truth Commission to ease lingering hard feelings and mitigate the family's association with the conspiracy.

Hugh MacRae's businesses were booming on the coast by the early decades of the twentieth century. He expanded the family's railroad empire, including electric streetcars in the mix, eventually developing a variety of properties in Wilmington and Wrightsville Beach, among them the Oceanic Hotel and oceanside Lumina entertainment pavilion. The shift to electricity brought decades of opportunity, and Hugh MacRae merged enterprises engaged in transportation and power generation. In the early 1900s, he launched those innovative "farm colonies" where he settled European immigrants on land in eastern North Carolina, earning consideration for the position of secretary of agriculture under Presidents Woodrow Wilson and Herbert Hoover.

The High Country was coalescing as an appealing "area" by the 1920s, and Grandfather was its heart. A folder from the Asheville Postcard Company called Blowing Rock, Boone, and Linville "Cloudland," much as "Land of the Sky" denoted Asheville. Twenty-four images, a quarter of them featuring Grandfather or scenes along the Yonahlossee Road, showcased a "section rapidly becoming a foremost resort of Eastern America. Nowhere is there more beautiful or rugged scenery than is heaped into this mountainous region."

A loop drive around Grandfather wouldn't happen for almost fifty years, but good roads arced from Boone to Linville via Blowing Rock. The railroad was just a few miles from Linville in Montezuma, and in 1915, the Linville Improvement Company sold a rail right-of-way through town on the way to Foscoe and eventually Boone. A new era was emerging. Linville got its own station, and by 1919 the ET&WNC Railroad rolled into Boone. One look at Linville today would surprise anyone that this classic resort town had a tough start. Sadly, the postcard appeal of the High Country hit roadblocks. World War I hurt tourism, but the war and expanding railroads sparked a logging boom in Linville. That would help the local economy and the Linville Improvement Company for a while. But it would also eradicate a priceless treasure, the millennia-old ecosystem of Grandfather Mountain's towering virgin timber.

5 Grandfather Gets a Haircut

This late 1800s illustration by R. E. Piguet exhibits more artistic license than depictions often lavished on mountains in the New England Appalachians. Piguet's work made him a member of the New York Etching Club in 1878. This illustration aptly epitomizes the wildly romantic identity of the Appalachians in the nineteenth century. Shirley Stipp Ephemera Collection, D. H. Ramsey Library Special Collections, UNC Asheville 28804.

A Forest Waiting to Fall

Poetic prose is as close as we come to imagining what Grandfather Mountain's virgin forest looked like. Shepherd Dugger described a hiking group pausing at Shanty Spring amidst "one of the most beautiful, most bewildering, and extended evergreen forests in the whole south." Here, he wrote, "ancient trunks of fallen trees [are] only revealed by a soft, deep, bright, yellowish-green moss. Delicate ferns and young balsams wave and tremble to feeble breezes which stray off from the stronger ones that moan in the trees above. Such were the exquisite beauties along the winding step-way."

In 1902, Theodore Roosevelt gave us a remarkable look at that world in *A Report of the Secretary of Agriculture in Relation to the Forests, Rivers, and*

Artist Richard Tumbleston's popular images are synonymous with the High Country and Grandfather Mountain, often picturing the peak above settled valleys. In this painting simply titled *Grandfather*, he takes us back in time, long before settlers arrived to cut the trees. Before the logging, recalled Foscoe resident Creed Taylor, "the Grandfather wasn't infested with undergrowth. The trees were so big and beautiful you could just walk where you wanted without trails." Painting by Richard Tumbleston.

Mountains of the Southern Appalachian Region. Grandfather, Roan Mountain, and the Black Mountains "are occupied by spruce and balsam forests" that are "virtually primeval," the report read. European settlers had cleared fields for crops by girdling trees into "deadenings," but there were only isolated clearings near Grandfather Mountain. In 1903, Arthur Keith of the U.S. Geological Survey wrote that "fine bodies of timber occur," with the best "on the headwaters of Linville and Watauga rivers. . . . Clearing in the valuable forests has little more than begun." The invitations were in the mail. Some of the last—and very best—stands of Southern Appalachian timber were on the chopping block. Grandfather was protected by the same remoteness that stymied success for Linville, but that isolation wouldn't last. There were no national forests in the East, and America's new "hiker" president was urging that forest preserves be established to stem devastation of "a mountain region whose influence flows far beyond its borders." Forest preservation was essential to stem floods and erosion and to secure a sustainable timber supply, but Roosevelt saw a bigger picture, eloquently capturing the geologic scale of this living wilderness. "More than once in the remote geologic past [eastern forests] have disappeared before the sea and before the ice. But here in this Southern Appalachian region they have lived on to the present day."

The Globe—Where It Started

Decades before anyone would sharpen a saw on Grandfather's summits, timbering started so far below the mountain's famous faces the old man might not have noticed. That vast area, often just called "the Globe" by locals, is the rippling backdrop for Grandfather Mountain's most dramatic views and home to tiny settlements, Globe, Edgemont, Gragg, Mortimer, and more. Few would imagine today that cabin-dotted Mortimer was once a booming timber town of 1,000 people. Thanks to William McClellan Ritter, owner of the world's largest timber company, a locomotive-led logging boom was headed for the High Country. In 1899, Ritter's Linville River Railroad linked Tennessee to white pine forests near Saginaw, today's Pineola, south of Linville. He also owned extensive timber tracts on Grandfather's lowest slopes, far below Linville, where the Carolina & North-West Railway (c&n-w) connected Lenoir to Chester, South Carolina. Railroad magnate William Barber's c&n-w was popular with summer travelers catching stagecoaches on to Blowing Rock and Linville, but luckily for Ritter, Barber also had a smaller railroad called the Caldwell & Northern that extended toward Grandfather. Two great minds were thinking alike by 1904. William Barber and his lumber baron buddy Ritter agreed their

If any place could be called a poster child for environmental armageddon, it was the lower slopes of Grandfather Mountain. The rippling ridges far below the peaks were stripped of trees, singed by fire, and eroded by floods. After the 1911 passage of the Weeks Act, the area became the birthplace of the East's first national forest, Pisgah. National Forests in North Carolina, D. H. Ramsey Library Special Collections, UNC Asheville 28804.

railroads would meet in the woods below Grandfather—in the brand new, tiny town of Edgemont, named for its location at the "Edge of the Mountains," explains Wayne Beane, president of the historical society in nearby Collettsville.

The railroads linked up in early 1906, turning Mortimer and Edgemont into an industrial logging center with electric power, a movie theater, and "all the modern conveniences," noted one newspaper. The main mission was logging, but Barber hoped to further tap tourism by connecting the c&n-w across the mountains. That dream never materialized, but Edgemont became a resort of sorts at the base of Grandfather. Posters dubiously proclaimed it the "City in the Clouds" and the "Queen of the Mountains." One article promised "days are comfortably cool if one keeps in the shade." At 1,600 feet, Edgemont couldn't compete with the seductive climate of 4,000-foot Linville and Blowing Rock, but excursion trains toured "the Grand Scenery of the Gorge of Wilson's Creek." In 1912, the *Charlotte Chronicle* called faster service to Edgemont "too good to be true"—no doubt because any improvement in rail access made it even easier to reach the High Country beyond.

Ritter's Pineola timber eventually played out, but he kept his railroad near Linville and shifted his entire operation to Mortimer and Edgemont (the two rail lines were actually linked down the Blue Ridge for a while). Ritter's narrow-gauge trains explored a spiderweb of lumber lines across Grandfather's waterfall-laced flanks. Newspapers chronicled the high-tech, steam-powered machinery and touted one of the state's longest logging flumes, a water-fed wooden trough that flushed logs seven miles. There were accidents. Trains derailed, hands were mangled, limbs were lost, and people were killed, crushed, and even scalded to death. The communities under the Grandfather were riding a whirlwind. By 1914, even timber there was dwindling and the scenery was suffering. A 1913 excursion passenger wrote, "The grandeur of the Wilson Creek Gorge brought loud exclamations of admiration," but "the only thing marring the attractive beauty of the mountains and gorge are the denuded mountainsides devastated by fire." The writing was on the wall. The timber, and the jobs, weren't going to last.

And the Rains Came

For years, conservationists urged establishment of an Appalachian Forest Reserve. Charles S. Sargeant, Gray's and Muir's companion in the Grandfather area, first suggested a reserve in 1892. The North Carolina Press Association petitioned Congress for one in 1894. North Carolina and five other southern states voted for protected forest parks in 1901. The *Watauga Democrat* maintained in September 1907 that "the progressive West 'went after' these forest reserves and got them by the dozen . . . where thousands of people go annually for pleasure and sight seeing. This is just what most of us wish to see here." But some feared property would be condemned. An editorial duel in the *Democrat* pitted Frank Linney against Moses H. Cone. Linney asked if Cone would "let the government have any of [his] land," and Cone replied, "I would not hesitate one minute about deeding my whole estate

In 2011, Grandfather district ranger John Crockett and Parkway superintendent Phil Francis dedicated a Blue Ridge Parkway interpretive plaque saluting the 2011 centennial of the Weeks Act. Directly below, once denuded forests now flourish. Photo by Randy Johnson.

to the government without one dollar for it." After Cone's death, his lands were indeed donated to the Blue Ridge Parkway. The effort to create reserves took two decades, with "fiscal conservative" Congressman "Uncle Joe" Cannon of Illinois pledging "not a cent for scenery." Fortunately, the February 1911 passage of the Weeks Act authorized national forests in the East, and by 1916 denuded tracts had been purchased in the Globe.

Then a freak series of storms brought biblical flooding to the stump-littered landscape. Heavy rain fell in early July 1916, and a hurricane on the 15th poured twenty more inches on saturated soil. One newspaper reported there was "death and destruction on every side." At Mortimer, "the whole village was washed away. . . . The whole population of the town stood on the mountainside and watched the houses" float down Wilson Creek. The *Hickory Daily Record* described a woman and child swept from their bed. The husband barely heard her say, "Oh, Lord, I am gone." Logging company infrastructure was decimated. Also obliterated was the Globe Academy boarding school attended by B. B. and D. D. Dougherty, founders of Boone's Watauga

Academy in 1899, forerunner of Appalachian State University. The flood, a report read, dropped stinking "black loam that covered the first floor of every building to a depth of from two to five feet." As Roosevelt had warned, the soil of a millennia-old forest had washed down the mountains to clog the valleys. The new national forest's benefits soon surfaced. On tracts approved for government purchase, trails replaced washed-out roads.

A year later, Ritter's lumber mill was being dismantled. Other local companies continued to harvest hardwoods for the area's furniture industry, writes Matthew C. Bumgarner in *Carolina & N-W: The Legacy of the Carolina & North-Western Railway*. Passenger rail service continued as a cotton mill operated in Mortimer, and in 1933 the Civilian Conservation Corps (CCC) opened Camp F-5, Camp Grandfather Mountain, turning 400 men to reforestation and road building. The economy slowly shriveled. After the last excursion train to Edgemont in 1938, the CCC turned railroad grades into roads. The C&N-W, what rail fans called the old "Cain't and Never Will," never did chug beyond the blue ridges. So symbolic of destructive logging were Grandfather Mountain's eastern slopes that the Pisgah National Forest was the East's first "forest reserve," and the Grandfather Ranger District is the first on that forest. On the 100th anniversary of the Weeks Act in 2011, the Forest Service placed an interpretive easel on the Blue Ridge Parkway at Laurel Knob Overlook above the very first Weeks Act tract. One glance from that overlook at milepost 349.2—or down from Grandfather—shows just how dramatically the scene of destruction has recovered in a century. Today, a drive through the Globe area's dirt roads is one of the best day trips in the Grandfather area, complete with spectacular trails, a Forest Service campground at Mortimer, and Caldwell County's Wilson Creek Visitor Center.

Railroad to Ruin

Logging was getting closer to Grandfather. Ritter sold his Linville River Railroad to the East Tennessee & Western North Carolina Railroad (ET&WNC) in 1913, the same year William S. Whiting bought

By 1915, Tweetsie Railroad was bound for Boone, slicing through virgin timber beneath the rocky peaks of the Grandfather. Linville finally got its train station, and it too had Henry Bacon's bark-sided style. You can visit the well-preserved building today, now on display at Newland's Avery County Historical Museum. Collection of Hugh MacRae II. Photo by E. Hardy.

timber rights to the northern slopes of Grandfather. By the summer of 1915, Hugh MacRae and company stockholders agreed to permit the railroad's passage through Linville. The still-struggling town would finally get rail service. In 1916 the tracks reached Shull's Mill where Whiting's massive timber mill was being built on the bottomlands beside today's NC 105. Previous opportunities to tempt rail service to Watauga County had been so fruitless, the *Lenoir News* opined in 1908, that county residents "have become almost desperate in their desire to get a railroad." This time, Boone lobbied hard for an eight-mile extension from Shull's Mill. The town was asked to donate the right-of-way and land for a train station. Whiting, who also wanted to cut timber north of Boone near Elk Knob, had to contribute $10,000. "After a spirited campaign," relates Joe Quinn in his Appalachian State University thesis about logging in Watauga County, "the citizens of Boone passed a bond referendum in February of 1918." The railroad whistled its way into town in 1919. Nowhere has railroading had a more romantic history than it did while the ET&WNC chugged its way past the peaks of Grandfather Mountain. Affectionately dubbed "Tweetsie" for its sharp-whistled wail, the train to Boone was the longest narrow-gauge railroad in the world and the highest passenger railroad in the East. And it was the train that carried away Grandfather Mountain's virgin forest.

When Roosevelt warned against unchecked timber harvesting, the East's archetypal virgin forest still reigned on Grandfather Mountain. "A dense mixed forest covers the northern slope and extends across the valley of Boone Fork of Watauga River," the report revealed, "which is yet uncleared for more than 5 miles from its head." In a 1937 *Greensboro Daily News* story, Joe Hartley recalled this virgin stand as "the great north woods" and claimed there was "no older forest in the world." Whiting's Boone Fork Lumber Company targeted that tract. His railroad would reach Grandfather Mountain's highest, most pristine valley and snatch almost 3,000 acres—nearly five square miles—of the South's tallest trees between 1916 and the mid-1920s. At Shull's Mill, the biggest sawmill in the Grandfather area was a vision of environmental armageddon presided over by William S. Whiting. "If you saw the mill from a long way off," related Anthony T. Lord, a blacksmith at the mill in 1917, "you could tell whether it was running or not by the long, beautiful plumes of steam which came intermittently out of the exhaust pipe." Workers flooded in. The population surged from fewer than 100 in 1915 to more than 1,000 in 1917. Shull's Mill was at one point the county's largest town and "seemed likely to become the county seat over Boone," predicted Kyle Grove, producer of the 2010 documentary film *Just a Stop along the Way*. Dam-generated electricity powered a movie theater, a barber shop, Dr. R. L Hardin's hospital, and the forty-room Robbins Hotel.

A year after the mill opened, 300 men were laboring behind Whiting's Shay locomotives in high-elevation coves where rich soils, ample rain, and a perfect climate produced northern hardwood, spruce, and fir of dramatic stature. "It was the best boundary of timber in Carolina," claimed Blowing Rock lawyer and surveyor George "Bull"

Sudderth. Quoted in one of William G. Lord's story-filled Blue Ridge Parkway guides, Sudderth recalled he saw "poplars six feet through." One "was a hundred feet to the first limb." Milking the ridges for rise, the railroad switchbacked through the gaping portal that guards Boone Fork's headwaters. It trestled over the creek one final time to a jutting rock formation called Storyteller's Rock today. The awesome mechanical muscle of steam-powered America wreaked destruction on the entire valley. It was total war on trees, a campaign epitomized by the American Model D, a self-propelled steam log loader described as "a locomotive crane" by the American Hoist and Derrick Company. If need be, the Model D could turn around an entire train in the narrow confines of Boone Fork by swinging empty flatcars around itself, then loading them for departure in the downhill direction. These and similar machines could cable and drag logs a thousand feet and stack them onto railroad cars. Cables were strung across crags and cliffs all over the Boone Bowl. Alert hikers still spy cable-carved grooves in rocks and notice pieces of thick wire rope beside the Nuwati Trail, itself the former railroad grade. It was estimated the logging would take twenty years, but Whiting took less than ten. So much timber came out of Boone Fork, ET&WNC crew foreman Dewey Stout told me in the 1970s, outbound trains required two engines to climb from Foscoe to Linville Gap—and only one from there all the way to Johnson City. The timber and Whiting's mill were gone by 1928.

Logging Linville

After Boone Fork, the bulk of the mountain remained uncut until the 1930s. But while Whiting was at work, the Linville Improvement Company started logging its own lands. Early in the century, the company had asked the forest service to advise on how logging could be done with respect for the land. In 1915, the board decided to sell its timber "at any time that an advantageous offer for same may be obtained." Even though strapped for money, the directors approved on "the condition that the timber must be cut under the regulations

Newland

Site of MacRae
Lumber Co.

WEST FORK

Modern-day
Linville Ridge
Resort

West Fork
Trestle

BRIER
KNOB

Railroad Grade
Still Visible Beside
NC 105

Site of 1940
Linville Washout

Combination
Station

Modern-day
Old Hampton
Store

181

105

Modern-day
Grandfather Golf
& Country Club

WT

ET&WNC Railroad/
Linville River Railway
Tracks

L I N V I L L E   R I V E R

Linville

Eseeola
Lodge

G R A

221

221

181

G R A N D M O T H E R   C R E E K

BLUE RIDGE PARKWAY

G R A N D M O T H E R
M O U N T A I N

The ET&WNC Railroad offered easy access to Grandfather Mountain's virgin timber. As it passed Linville in 1916, Tweetsie followed the Linville River below the peaks and into the Watauga River watershed beyond. It passed many a railroading landmark on the way. The railroad reached Shull's Mill in 1916, and from then into the mid-1920s, Boone Fork Lumber Company logging trains climbed high under Calloway Peak to denude the Boone Fork valley. By the early 1930s, logging trucks were bouncing up board roads from Linville Gap to strip western slopes. Soon after, board roads from the Yonahlossee Road (today's US 221) claimed the timber on the mountain's east side.

0   ½   1   2 MILES

SCALE

ET&WNC/LRRy Tracks ⊢──────⊣   Boone Fork Lumber Co. Tracks -----------   Board Logging Roads ⅢⅢⅢⅢⅢⅢⅢ

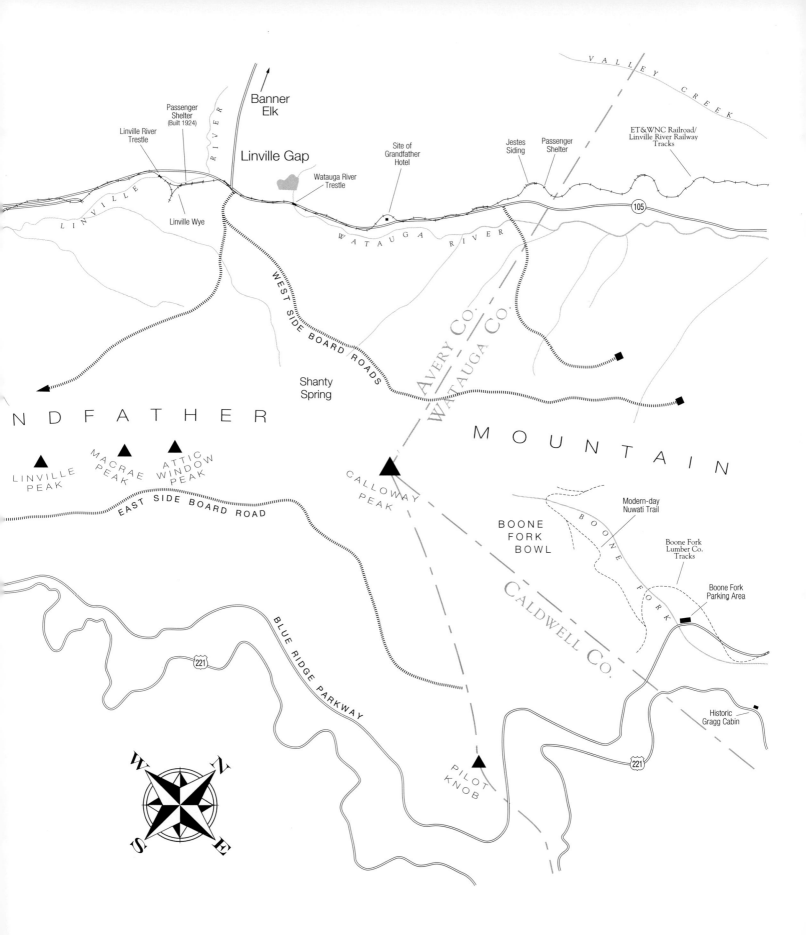

VALLEY CREEK

Banner Elk

Passenger Shelter (Built 1924)

Linville River Trestle

LINVILLE RIVER

Linville Gap

Site of Grandfather Hotel

Watauga River Trestle

Jestes Siding

Passenger Shelter

ET&WNC Railroad/ Linville River Railway Tracks

105

Linville Wye

LINVILLE

WATAUGA RIVER

WEST SIDE BOARD ROADS

Shanty Spring

AVERY CO. WATAUGA CO.

NDFATHER

MOUNTAIN

LINVILLE PEAK

MACRAE PEAK

ATTIC WINDOW PEAK

CALLOWAY PEAK

BOONE FORK BOWL

Modern-day Nuwati Trail

BOONE FORK

Boone Fork Lumber Co. Tracks

Boone Fork Parking Area

EAST SIDE BOARD ROAD

CALDWELL CO.

221

BLUE RIDGE PARKWAY

Historic Gragg Cabin

221

PILOT KNOB

W N E S

© Chris H. Ford 2016

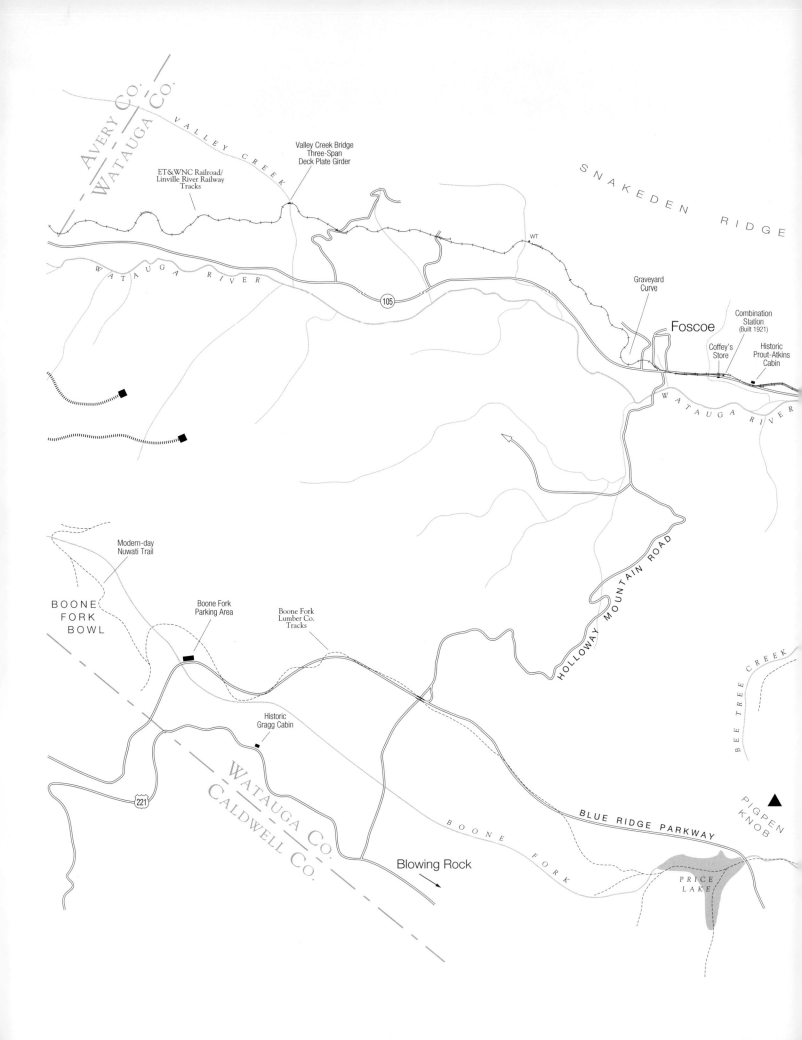

AVERY CO.
WATAUGA CO.

VALLEY CREEK

SNAKEDEN RIDGE

Valley Creek Bridge
Three-Span
Deck Plate Girder

ET&WNC Railroad/
Linville River Railway
Tracks

WATAUGA RIVER

105

WT

Graveyard
Curve

Foscoe

Combination
Station
(Built 1921)

Coffey's
Store

Historic
Prout-Atkins
Cabin

WATAUGA RIVER

Modern-day
Nuwati Trail

BOONE
FORK
BOWL

Boone Fork
Parking Area

Boone Fork
Lumber Co.
Tracks

HOLLOWAY MOUNTAIN ROAD

BEE TREE CREEK

Historic
Gragg Cabin

PIGPEN
KNOB

221

WATAUGA CO.
CALDWELL CO.

BLUE RIDGE PARKWAY

BOONE FORK

Blowing Rock

PRICE
LAKE

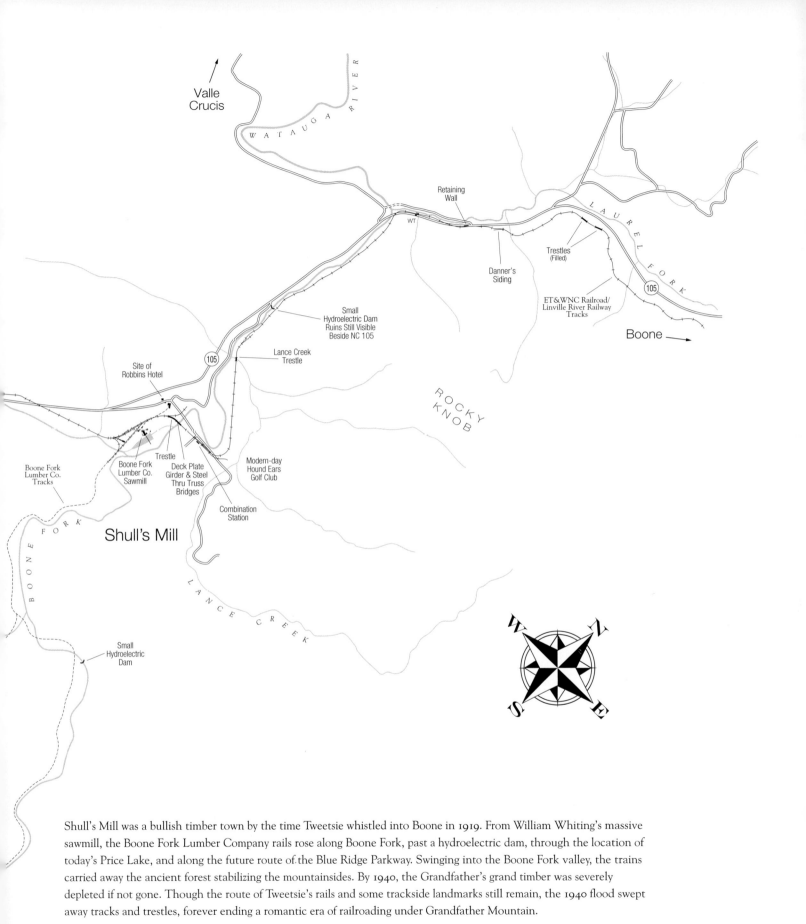

Valle Crucis

WATAUGA RIVER

LAUREL FORK

Retaining Wall

WT

Trestles (Filled)

Danner's Siding

ET&WNC Railroad/ Linville River Railway Tracks

105

Boone →

Small Hydroelectric Dam Ruins Still Visible Beside NC 105

105

Lance Creek Trestle

Site of Robbins Hotel

ROCKY KNOB

Boone Fork Lumber Co. Tracks

Trestle

Boone Fork Lumber Co. Sawmill

Deck Plate Girder & Steel Thru Truss Bridges

Modern-day Hound Ears Golf Club

Combination Station

BOONE FORK

Shull's Mill

LANCE CREEK

Small Hydroelectric Dam

W N S E

Shull's Mill was a bullish timber town by the time Tweetsie whistled into Boone in 1919. From William Whiting's massive sawmill, the Boone Fork Lumber Company rails rose along Boone Fork, past a hydroelectric dam, through the location of today's Price Lake, and along the future route of the Blue Ridge Parkway. Swinging into the Boone Fork valley, the trains carried away the ancient forest stabilizing the mountainsides. By 1940, the Grandfather's grand timber was severely depleted if not gone. Though the route of Tweetsie's rails and some trackside landmarks still remain, the 1940 flood swept away tracks and trestles, forever ending a romantic era of railroading under Grandfather Mountain.

0   ½   1   2 MILES

SCALE

ET&WNC/LRRy Tracks ├────┤   Boone Fork Lumber Co. Tracks ----------   Board Logging Roads ""''"'"'"'"'"

© Chris H. Ford 2016

The town of Shull's Mill was dominated by the massive, steaming, smoking sawmill of William Whiting's Boone Fork Lumber Company. At lower right the Robbins Hotel sits in the curve of a road still in use as a junction with Shull's Mill Road near Hound Ears Club. The barn across the street remained into recent years. The John Waite Collection.

The railroad climbed Boone Fork and brought industrial timber technology to a forest growing undisturbed for millennia. The loggers displayed bravado at their derring-do. Grandfather Community logger Vance Coffey points a logger's peavey at his handiwork as a loader prepares to transfer a log to a flatcar. Collection of Carolyn Davis Curtis.

The famously powerful Shay locomotives, like this one pausing not far from town, hauled wood to the mill's processing pond. Local logger B. G. Teams stands in front of the train. The John Waite Collection.

This very rare photo taken a few miles above Shull's Mill shows how water was funneled from a makeshift dam into a hydroelectric system that powered the town. The descending grade of the stream produced pipe-popping pressure. Remnants of railroad ties and the dam are still visible on the Boone Fork Trail in Julian Price Park. Courtesy of Special Collections, Appalachian State University, Shulls Papers.

of the US Bureau of Forestry." Ultimately, the bulk of Grandfather would be less-heavily handled than many summits. The MacRaes likely strove to be judicious with timber harvesting, but it still wouldn't be pretty. That process started in Linville, nicknamed Stump Town in the late 1800s even before the Linville Improvement Company arrived. Modest timber harvesting, sawmilling, and stumps were facts of life on the fringes of Grandfather Mountain, but by 1920 Connecticut-based Sanford and Treadway Lumber Co. had set up shop in Linville. They were aiming north of town where the West Fork of the Linville River reaches onto Sugar Mountain and Flat Top. Sanford and Treadway's big timber mill sat in meadows just beyond the Ruffin Street/Joe Hartley Road junction north of Old Hampton Store. A logging camp higher up housed and fed workers. Like Whiting's plant at Shull's Mill and Ritter's at Mortimer, this was a highly mechanized logging railroad operation unlike anything that would be used later on most of Grandfather Mountain. Until it was dismantled, the enterprise engaged the entire town and fueled welcome employment.

Loggers fanned out up the slopes in teams of five men called "wood hicks," writes Joe Quinn. A "fitter" calculated the best direction for the tree to fall, and two "sawyers" felled it with a six-foot, two-handled crosscut saw. "Swampers" would limb it, then sawyers "bucked" the tree into logs. (These logging terms are still used today.) Then "teamsters" and their teams of horses dragged the logs to trains. All this was done with the famously powerful Shay and Climax logging locomotives. A steam-powered, flatcar-mounted crane stacked logs on cars for the trip to the mill. Logs were dumped in a pond, then dragged up a ramp into the mill by a massive bull wheel. An employee rode the carriage that fed the logs to a saw powered by scrap- and sawdust-fueled boilers. After separate machines edged the planks and trimmed the ends, the boards were graded and stacked in the lumberyard for shipment on Tweetsie. Avery High School teacher Thomas Webb and Linville residents wrote a newspaper article in the early 2000s that named the people

behind the process. With horses dragging timber, a blacksmith was needed, and that was Willie Stout. We also know Ed Lewis and Johnny Riddle ran the steam log loader and that Riddle died in a log fall. The sawmill was eventually purchased by Donald and Hugh MacRae and operated as the D&H MacRae Lumber Company, then Linville Lumber Company. The names on the locomotives changed, but the workforce didn't, managed by John Frank Hampton, an able man always seen in coat and tie above with rough pants and high boots below.

Timber came from more distant MacRae tracts, a process embodied by George Tate Davis (1878–1946). The Linville Improvement Company timber warden lived in Linville Gap amid meadows cleared in the late 1800s by Walter Waightstill Lenoir. Tate, as they called him, got $100 a month and farmed rent-free to keep an eye on the area, which he did with one of Avery County's first telephones. Tate's crews of woodsmen worked Sugar Mountain and the river valley toward "Grandfather City," as Lenoir called Linville. Tate marked trees to be cut and spared and managed activity at the gap, the logical place to gather logs, prep them at small sawmills, then load them onto trains. The gap had a wye, a Y-shaped track arrangement where an engine could turn around. Davis coordinated crews for more than a decade using small notebooks to record hours worked and species and board-feet cut. He listed the locations of the logging and the men he worked with. There was trail work, too. "Building trail on Grandfather" noted one 1923 entry. He also tallied activity at the small mills. "Mill stopped six times," one entry read, usually "for logs"—meaning the saw outpaced teamsters dragging timber. Telling vignettes emerged. "Mill stopped for logs at 9:35. Mill burnt down on night of October 23, 1923. 3 inches of snow on Ground." Tate's crew got back to work in snow-covered autumn color.

The men of the High Country who claimed the "timberworker" trade were pros. Outside companies recruited them with ads in the *Watauga Democrat*. The job was dangerous. Soon after Tweetsie reached Boone, Tate injured his right arm in a log loading accident and "refused to go to a

The entire process climaxed in the mill where workers rode the carriage that delivered logs to the band saw. The John Waite Collection.

Linville Gap was an isolated outpost until the railroad appeared. Even then, automobile traffic was a rarity. North Carolina Collection, University of North Carolina Library at Chapel Hill. Photo by Hugh Morton.

doctor until the pain became unbearable," recalled his granddaughter Carolyn Davis Curtis. "By then it was too late to save the arm." He did everything left-handed afterward, including writing his logging records. Reports of accidents were rife in newspapers of the time. A man from the Grandfather Community "working at a [log] skidder last Saturday was caught with some logs and badly

injured." Arley Cornett of Mabel was riding a logging train near Boone when he fell and had both legs cut off. He died at the Shull's Mill hospital. Brakeman Thomas Harmon tried to jump between cars and fell to the tracks. "No one saw the accident and the train didn't stop. The unfortunate man was dragged and luckily was dropped where some men were cutting wood near the tracks," quite possibly Tate's crew. A train at the Linville Gap wye rushed Harmon to Shull's Mill. He lived but lost a leg. Tate relied on neighbors, the men of the Grandfather Community, where there's still a lane named Sawmiller's Way. His notebooks are full of surnames that fill the cemeteries under the Grandfather: Berry, Fox, Porch, Presswood, and others.

Logging the Peaks

Hugh MacRae's son Nelson had been running the Linville Improvement Company since 1920, opening a golf course in 1928 designed by Donald Ross, but even the wealthy weren't traveling during the Great Depression. Logging was helping, as was a new attraction called Observation Point. Starting in the mid-1930s, the mountain's first "tourist attraction" permitted motorists to drive to a rocky crag above MacRae Meadows. Still, times were tough. Robert Hartley recalled "people standing at my dad's back door begging, asking, 'Uncle Joe, could you let me have a few potatoes. We don't got nothin' to eat.'" In the 1930s edition of *The Balsam Groves*, Dugger complained, "The destroying agents are fast at work. The citizens who ought to save a part of their forest in its natural beauty are right into it with fire and smoke for tan-bark and lumber." Others saw opportunity. "Fortunately," Ted Shook (1920–2012) concluded in his Grandfather Community genealogy, "Will Smith from Canton, NC purchased the timber rights of Grandfather Mountain." The Linville Improvement Company board voted on August 16, 1930, to sell "all of the spruce and balsam timber eight inches in diameter and up at the stump, on the upper slopes of Grandfather Mountain" for $30,000, a fourth in cash, the rest in six semiannual installments. Canton's massive Champion Fibre paper mill sucked

Photos of the board roads are hard to come by. Those that do exist are as evocatively out of focus and vague as the memories of the dwindling number of people who recall them. They undulated into virgin forest and ended where trucks could turn around. Theodore and Agnes Shook Collection.

up much of western North Carolina's virgin timber. Smith had ravaged Roan Mountain, but he'd agreed to leave smaller trees on Grandfather. Ironically, to generate cash and sustain operations during the Great Depression, Champion sold 90,000 acres in 1931 to help create Great Smoky Mountains National Park. In essence, saving the Smokies would support stripping the trees from Grandfather. The mad dash to log the mountain was on.

No railroad climbed the mountain this time. Instead, "board roads" would be built, permitting trucks to roam the mountainsides on decklike roads constructed by sawing trees into thick planks and assembling them into stable surfaces. The roads were at times high above the ground,

supported by posts, wooden trestles, and even trees that had been sawn at a certain height. Horses dragged timber down to the trucks. At places along the roads and where they ended, wider staging areas permitted trucks to load or turn around. Wade Hall Fox lived in the upper Grandfather Community. "It was real engineering to build a plank road for a big truck with loads on it," he pronounces. A friend told him, "'You could hear those old truck engines a screamin' and a roarin' coming down outta there.'" Barrels of water were stationed to cool the brakes. Jim Hughes of Linville, whose father worked in the timber industry, went up the roads as a kid "just to go for the ride," he remembers. "Those were dangerous roads. It was dangerous just to look off of it! It's amazing no one was ever killed." The routes and length of the roads can only be guessed at today. A major board road rose from Linville Gap up the Continental Divide. Another turned across Little Grassy Creek and "went right off under the old Singing Ground," or MacRae Meadows, recalled Fox. The main board road passed above Grandfather's Profile face and leveled off high on White Rock Ridge. Another road forked higher near Shanty Spring. The lowest road originated below Linville Gap at a Tweetsie Railroad siding. Logging camp cabins and barns were built, though their locations are not now common knowledge. Graffiti is still visible scratched into rocks at the spring, long a gathering spot. A few carvers claim the late 1850s—including a J H and J A Mast. "G II Bunch" carved the rock in 1934. Proof that 1930s loggers left their marks is a "July 4 32" date carved by "Dolph"—Tate Davis's son, a logger at the time.

Timbering on the west side got a slow start, but by the summer of 1931 Smith was eyeing Grandfather's southeastern flank, the final parcel of virgin timber. In 1932 he "needed ten men to start to work," recalled Shook, and "the next morning, more than 100 men showed up." By the fall of 1933, the west side had been cut, and "most all men moved to the south side," recorded Shook, who at fourteen joined his uncle Harrison Church laboring on the mountain. The main board road on that side stretched from "right below the entrance gate [at today's Grandfather attraction] to above Rough Ridge," remembers Robert Hartley. It ended in the gap west of Pilot Knob, "the split between Whiting and the MacRae land being logged by Smith." Early twentieth-century photos attest to amazing timber in that location. A 1930s topo map actually shows the logging road (but not trails visible on maps thirty years earlier, understandably obliterated by logging). Evidence of timbering still remains. One spring day I set off with my son Christopher, longtime Grandfather trail volunteer Robert Branch, and an old map to find remnants of the road. We hiked to where the old logging route likely crossed our trail, then we angled off into the woods, hoping to intersect it. "This doesn't look like a logging road

to me," Bob commented. That was good news for Grandfather—the elevated board roads eliminated grades gouged into the soil. Soon Christopher asked, "What's that over there?" Barely protruding from the leaves was the headlight bezel of a 1930s-era truck. We took a picture, replaced the artifact, and retraced our steps to the trail. Robert Hartley told me the flat where we found the headlight was the site of an old logging camp that longtime Grandfather attraction maintenance man Johnny Cooper had frequented as a logger. In a 1991 interview, the eighty-one-year old recalled camp cuisine was "mostly beans and stuff like that." By "fall of 1936," Ted Shook reveals, "all timber was taken from the south side," and the plank roads were removed as lumbermen left. Neither roads nor loggers vanished overnight. Jim Hughes recalled his father, Lum, logging off a leftover board road above the Yonahlossee Road. "One truck had a log so big," he laughed, "when it crossed a railroad track in Linville the front wheels bounced off the ground and stayed up."

"Armageddon" Arrives

After logging came fire. Luckily, Grandfather had a dedicated local fire warden in Joe Hartley. In 1929 he wrote, "My heart was in the work." Hartley's writings recall fires from more than two decades of logging before 1940. "The Grandfather had a bad forest fire" in 1916, he noted. This blaze was likely in the Globe during logging, and early Pisgah National Forest ranger Monroe Coffey's crew extinguished it. In 1923, as Whiting's Boone Fork logging ended, Hartley witnessed "one of the first forest fires on Boones Fork," a severe fire that "burned in the turf for 30 days." This historic fire likely seared the entire valley from today's Daniel Boone Scout Trail across the Cragway Trail to the crest of the White Rock Ridge. The North Carolina Division of Forestry was organized in 1915, but accurate early data on fires is hard to come by. By late 1925 the agency's fire wardens, Hartley among them, were visiting logging sites, checking sawmills, and lobbying workers against practices that sparked wildfire. Best of all, the Linville

George Masa: A Hike at the Height of the Logging

Japanese photographer George Masa (1881–1933) was one of few people to decry the logging of Grandfather. Born Masahara Izuka, Masa came to the United States to study engineering and worked as a valet at the Grove Park Inn in the 1920s. He fell in love with photography and the mountains before the Appalachian Trail existed. Masa and author friend Horace Kephart helped create Great Smoky Mountains National Park. Imagine the unfathomable fantasy of an American doing that in 1920s Japan. His surprising life came to light in a 1950s magazine profile titled "The Little Jap," and Ken Burns featured him in the series America's Best Idea. In 1960, friends were petitioning to have Masa Knob named in the Great Smokies, and Leonard Rapport, a founding member of the Carolina Mountain Club (CMC), recalled Masa measuring trails with a "handlebars-and-

George Masa hiked Grandfather while logging was under way, and he hoped the U.S. Forest Service would intervene before the east side was cut. The forest, he wrote, had "beauty as like as Great Smoky." Years earlier, he'd visited Linville and taken this picture from what today is called Point Sublime—later one of Hugh Morton's favorite viewpoints of the mountain and especially of the Highland Games. This is Masa's portrait of the virgin Grandfather. The MacRae House stands to the right in Alick's meadows. North Carolina Collection, Pack Memorial Public Library, Asheville, N.C. Photo by George Masa.

bicycle-wheel device." Many CMC hikes used Masa's maps and mileages. Masa earned only enough in his Grove Arcade photo shop to "spend the rest of his time in his beloved mountains," reported Rapport. Friends learned what that meant when they had to pay for his 1933 burial in Asheville's Riverside Cemetery.

Rapport joined Masa on a weekend CMC hike to Grandfather in May 1932. Masa's party asked a man "in house back to left if ok to camp here," and Tate Davis said yes. From just below Grandfather, they had a "fine view of his rugged peaks." Next morning, the CMC hikers and locals dressed in their Sunday best had the loggers' board roads to themselves on a mountainside presumably laid waste, but no judgment was recorded. Past "the authentic profile of Grandfather," Masa

"climbed up rocky washout" to the ridge and peered over Linville Peak, which he'd photographed from Point Sublime on an earlier trip to Linville, later a favorite picture spot of Hugh Morton's. This report may not have commented on the condition of the mountain, but in one note Masa exclaimed, "Hells bells! All spruce cut down skinned this old Grandfather and the lumber ship to Champion Fibre Co. Indeed west side of Grandfather just terrible." In that heartbreaking note, he offered to "send you some photographs for your file." Tragically, most of the photos from Masa's lifetime "file" are gone—stolen, it's thought, by a competing Asheville photographer who claimed ownership, even authorship, and then destroyed irreplaceable images of the Southern Appalachians as the virgin forests fell.

Remnants of the logging days aren't that hard to find if you know where to look. This 1930s headlight bezel was found near an old logging camp. Photo by Randy Johnson.

Improvement Company was trying to reduce the impact of logging. The board not only voted to follow forest service practices. Unlike the situation in other parts of the mountains, this private company had owned Grandfather before timbering, and it intended to retain ownership afterward. The board had also tasked one of their own, Squire Hartley, with overseeing the cuts. He was a respected local icon and preservationist, dedicated to restraining a process he detested. Robert Hartley strongly maintained that his father made "sure the timber cutters were cutting timber of a certain diameter. He'd go through the woods with a measuring stick and as a little boy I'd go with him." Loggers could only cut trees bigger than eight inches in diameter, and apparently Joe Hartley was a stickler with his measuring stick. "Daddy always fussed at 'em," said Hartley. "He wasn't happy when they took the virgin forest off of Grandfather Mountain. He was a naturalist, he'd say 'this is God's country and man is tearing it up.' You hear that more now than you used to." Other locals agreed with Joe

Bayard Wootten's photo on a cloud-castle day shows virgin evergreens spilling down from the summits across Grandfather's eastern slope, a site soon to be desecrated by a major board road. North Carolina Collection, University of North Carolina Library at Chapel Hill. Photo by Bayard Morgan Wootten.

Hartley. When Smith started logging the mountainside, Tate Davis was in the thick and thinning of it, carrying his 1920s *Conservation Laws of North Carolina*, a cherished volume passed down through family. However it happened, a "lighter on the land" approach prevailed. We can only speculate whether scenery or sensitivity influenced the way logging was managed, but perhaps only by luck, the rockiest, ruggedest mountain in the South had defied the loggers, a little.

Return of the King

By the time timbering was done, a forest once "thick as hair on a dog's back," Jim Hughes recalls, had been substantially thinned but not completely cleared. "It was impossible or impractical to cut the timber in many spots," he asserts, "so there were trees left in a lot of places." Hugh MacRae II watched the logging from the plank roads. "I remember it as a fairly neat job," he stated. "There were still a lot of small trees that covered the mountain." Roosevelt's 1902 logging report had concluded that "areas in the southern Appalachians are only saved from entire destruction by the generally scattered distribution of the merchantable timber." Grandfather was a poster child for that point. So much of the mountain's timber was hard to reach or compromised by climate that ample tree cover remained to reseed the slopes and crags. Modern research supports that. The mid-1980s "Assessment of Spruce-Fir Forests in the Southern Appalachian Mountains" evaluated forests on Grandfather Mountain, Mount Mitchell, Roan Mountain, and elsewhere. Of three separate plots on Grandfather above 5,000 feet, only one contained sampled trees that averaged 55 years,

The east side's main board road slices through a vanishing virgin woodland. Carolina Mountain Clubbers from Asheville hiked the roads one weekend, but "walking the board roads on Sunday was our only fun," recalls Agnes Shook, wife of logger Ted Shook. "The log roads went far up on the mountain but we weren't hiking. Girls and boys got together and that's all us poor kids had to do." Courtesy, National Park Service, Blue Ridge Parkway.

the age they would have been if logged in 1930. Trees in another plot averaged 81 years (predating all logging), and trees in the other plot, located in the heart of the 1930s logging area, averaged 155 years. Beyond "average age," trees sampled in two plots were as old as 217 and 254 years, the oldest growing since 1681. Comparing that data to Roan Mountain, which suffered mightily in 1930s timbering, the average age of trees in most plots on Roan was less than 50 years—strong evidence that Roan lost all its trees to the saw and Grandfather got special treatment. No wonder another regional spruce-fir study concluded that Grandfather's boreal forest has returned more fully to its original acreage than the evergreen zone of any other Southern Appalachian summit. Nevertheless, coming at the very end of the logging era, the timbering of Grandfather was a sad act of utter folly.

By 1940, the mountain stood frazzled and forlorn. Fortunately, reliance on teams of horses and an absence of railroad grades outside Boone Fork had preserved the mountain's contours and soil structure. Today Grandfather's niche ecosystems reassert their dominion. In 1913, Margaret Morley urged loggers to leave trees to "preserve those picturesque skylines," for who, she asked, "can wait a hundred years for the trees to grow again?" Morley is gone, but those 100 years have almost elapsed. Best of all, timber will never again be harvested from the Grandfather Mountain.

A Romantic Railroad Tale

Tweetsie Railroad did more than carry away Grandfather's trees. To appreciate the railroad's impact on life in the High Country, step back in time before the trains. If you were going from

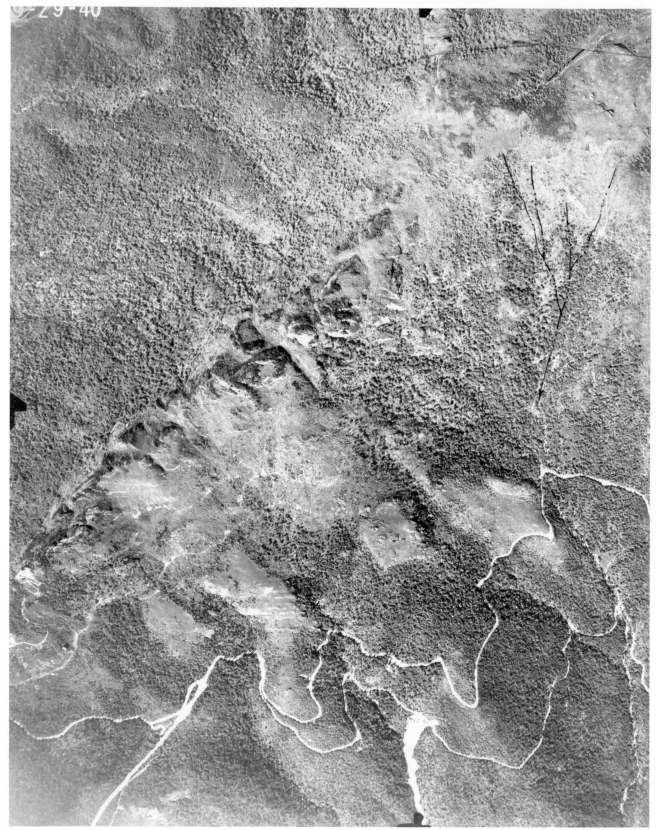

To see how thoroughly the eastern side was logged, just study this U.S. Army aerial photo taken September 29, 1940, soon after the flood that washed away Tweetsie Railroad. There's extensive timber in many places, but the routes of board roads and even evidence of likely logging camps are plainly visible. N.C. Geological Survey.

Eustace Conway:
Logging the Old-Fashioned Way

Frank Aldridge has plenty of stories from his family's eight generations under the Grandfather. He remembers "my dad saying his father would leave in the morning by the light of a lantern to go logging on the Grandfather. And he'd come back by lantern light, too." Eustace Conway knows what that was like. His 1,000-acre Turtle Island Preserve below the Blue Ridge Parkway teaches traditional skills such as logging with horses. Elizabeth Gilbert's 2002 book *The Last American Man* sparked a compost heap of media coverage about Conway's offbeat

life, which includes a role on the reality TV show *Mountain Men*. "Young men didn't have a weight problem back when they were logging the Grandfather with horses," he asserts. Conway holds up two chain-connected "grabber" hooks that are driven into logs, then attached to a horse's harness by a connecting bar. He still uses antique equipment like the 1930s gear hanging in Frank Aldridge's tool barn. "This may look like a garage sale," Conway cautions, "but it goes with a horse like a tail and nose." To log with horses "among so many competing hazards," maintains Conway, "you can't grow up answering multiple choice questions. There is no way to do that work and not exist totally in the moment." It truly focuses the mind, Conway pledges, to drag logs on a slope so steep you have one foot on the ground and the other foot on a horse's back. When the dragging's done, "you hit that grabber at the right spot and it pops out like a jumping flea." Conway admits that pulling logs through the forest creates visible damage, "but logging with horses is way more environmentally sensitive than any form of industrial logging. It's the roads and rail routes gouged out of the slopes that do the damage. Cutting trees, especially if you're not taking them all, can have relatively insignificant impact."

It's not certain whether this Linville area logger was part of the larger timbering of Grandfather in the 1930s, but his "board (or log) road" and team of horses is emblematic of what happened there. That includes the log at lower right, its edges beveled to avoid snagging while dragging. Collection of Hugh MacRae II. Photo by Nelson MacRae.

Linville to Boone, you took the Yonahlossee Road through Blowing Rock. A former "turnpike" in Linville Gap was barely a trail through the virgin evergreens spilling down from the peaks. The gap had yet to be severed from the summits by our "shrink-wrapped" concept of Grandfather. This source of great rivers was a true beauty spot, now compromised by the water-diverting dikes

of modern roads. Today, a once-pristine northern cranberry bog sits trapped behind a gas station. But back then, it was the kind of barrier Arnold Guyot meant when he wrote that ridges "are by no means inconsiderable obstacles to the inter-course between the various valleys." Linville Gap was a place relatively few people passed through on their way anywhere else. Tweetsie Railroad

Engineer peering with pride from the cab, smoke belching from the stack, Tweetsie engine #11 charges an uphill grade on the run to Boone. It's a stirring image from a romantic era of railroading. Courtesy of Special Collections, Appalachian State University, Thomas Reese Railroad and Printing Collection.

breached that divide, connecting communities long separated by dark forests.

That legendary era in railroad history got started in Johnson City, Tennessee, founded as a railroad station in 1856. Mining lured the narrow gauge ET&WNC Railroad into the mountains in 1866. The ET&WNC reached Elizabethton in 1872 and Cranberry's iron mines in 1882. When Tweetsie hit Boone in 1919, it brought game-changing mobility to the High Country. Robert Hartley remembered unprecedented new freedom. "People would go to Johnson City to the doctor or just to go shopping," he marveled. They'd get married and go off on unimaginable honeymoons. Long before Boone called itself "The Hub of the High Country," intercity buses met trains in startling scenes of modern travel. Tweetsie left Boone in the morning and was back by afternoon for the night. Boone's train station (torn down in 1977) anchored Depot Street. A wye turned trains for the trip to Tennessee. A plaque on a restaurant today notes the building's role in railroad maintenance—Tweetsie's only remaining remnant.

Tweetsie reinvented tourism. Even before the route from Johnson City through the Doe River Gorge to Cranberry reached Boone, the 1890 *Lindsey's Guide Book to Western North Carolina, Illustrated* called the canyon "the wildest gorge of the Alleghanies with precipitous sides of solid rock, twelve to fifteen hundred feet high." It was a renowned feat of engineering, an eye-popping passage above churning waters. An early 1920s brochure had photos of "indescribably beautiful" Linville taken by talented Nelson MacRae. "You will search the world in vain for a more delightful and invigorating summer climate," the pamphlet boasted. Along the way, "beauty gives place to grandeur" where the line "half encircles the Grandfather Mountain," affording "one of the most magnificent panoramic views to be had in the entire Appalachians." The extension of the rails made reaching Valle Crucis and Blowing Rock a snap via "auto service from Shulls Mills." Sadly, Shepherd Dugger missed success as an hotelier. His Grandfather Hotel had been struggling to tempt visitors over rocky trails since 1885. By the time the building burned around 1913, Dugger had sold his part-ownership, but he surely regretted missing trains gorged with potential guests. Hartley recalled day trippers "got off at Linville Gap with a picnic basket to have a day in the mountains." Traditions got started. A 1937 home movie shows a train taking football fans to Boone for a game at the future Appalachian State University. Soaring across Linville Gap, people hung out of the doors to gaze up at Grandfather. Everyone dressed up. Young soda jerks walked through the cars selling cold drinks from ice buckets. Another film, *Tennessee Tweetsie*, was made by Universal Studios in 1938. Special excursions were organized, but Tweetsie became critical to daily life. Robert Hartley was bussed from Linville to grade school in Newland. When he was late, "you'd hear the train a'coming, cut through and get a ride on Tweetsie."

Once Tweetsie gained Linville Gap, a welcome pause often permitted people to mill around amid views of surrounding summits. Some even got off to picnic or camp, returning on later trains. Today, they'd no doubt be buying burgers at the Linville Gap McDonald's, highest in eastern America. The John Waite Collection.

Students at Newland High got Tweetsie tickets at county expense. In winter, 1970s Newland postal clerk Florence Hampton remembered engineer Sherman Pippin would drop off students closer than the normal stop. Her memories included "walking across a brilliant white field of snow from the train, crunching to the school house." Food baskets sent to her sister at Appalachian State Teachers' College arrived with the contents still hot.

Tweetsie's simpler times were gentler, too, thanks to railroad men like engineer Pippin and Charles Grover Crumley. "Cy" Crumley was the conductor on the first train into Boone in 1919 and on the last train out in 1940. He devised a heart-shaped ticket punch to fit the railroad's culture. In a *Johnson City Press-Chronicle* article in 1976, Crumley told how the train got its name. An old couple were riding for the first time, related Crumley, and "the engineer gave them a good show, tugging hard on the whistle cord for a shrill twee-ee-t." Some say children of summer residents coined the name Tweetsie. Crumley made special stops to deliver people's kids to friends' houses and knew them all by name. He'd drop off physicians at Linville Gap, and they'd walk off into the mountains to see patients. He spent weeknights in Boone living in a black, wheelless caboose named Black Mariah. If mischief erupted, Crumley found it first. "My dad and them used to run and jump on the back of the train and ride to Boone," says Frank Aldridge, a descendant of Foscoe's earliest settlers, the railroad grade still winding through his property. "Sometimes the engine would get to spinning going up into Boone and it'd actually stop. One time, Cy Crumley came back through the train and said, 'Ain't no wonder! Half of Foscoe's a'hanging on back here!'" In the logging days, Crumley once stopped in a forest fire to rescue a mother and her five children. The train escaped as flames flanked the engine. That incident got Crumley

Not long before the 1940 flood, this train packed with Cannon Mills employees and flying its own trainside banner became the last excursion to cross Linville Gap. On the long haul up from Foscoe, Grandfather Mountain rose on the horizon (sadly omitted from the photo) and it was stand-in-the-doors and all eyes left. Courtesy of Archives of Appalachia, East Tennessee State University, Kenneth Riddle Collection of Cy Crumley Photographs.

invited to New York in 1938 to tell Tweetsie tales on Gabriel Heatter's *We the People* radio program. A few years later, Heatter devised his hopeful World War II sign-on, "Good evening, everyone—there is good news tonight." Tweetsie was a "good news" railroad. The little trains didn't match the scale of the mountains, but they fit the size of the lives of the people who lived there. Tweetsie meshed with their modesty, their sense of themselves as survivors, people putting their heads down for the long climb, never assuming the downhills would be much easier. During the Great Depression, Tweetsie's ET&WNC acronym became "Eat Taters and Wear No Clothes" or "Every Time With No Complaint." The people of the mountains loved Tweetsie and its crew, lifted their heads to smile at the whistle, and relied on its regularity and the crew's legendary kindness. Free rides were

common. The crew, it was rumored, often said, "We're heading there anyway." And for a generation, they were.

The Flood

Then came "the forty flood," states Wayne Beane, "and I don't mean the 1940 Flood. There's no '19' needed in front of it." Tate Davis opened a new notebook with "Notice: Worst storm and flood that has ever hit this country come on August 13 1940. Washed houses away." The deluge destroyed trestles and track. The 1916 flood had crested on the Watauga at 22.10 feet. The '40 flood rose to 29.60 feet. Sixteen people died in Watauga County. In the Grandfather Community, Wade Fox remembers his great-grandfather Julius Barlow and wife Tempie McClurd Barlow "barely stepped off their back porch when the house went floating off."

Two corn-grinding steam engines washed away from Ruffin Berry's gristmill below Linville Gap, and decades later Fox's nephew unearthed "one of them boilers two miles down the valley. My sister still plants flowers around it." Aerial photos revealed a swath of destruction that's now covered with homes and businesses. Whatever was left at Shull's Mill washed away. The ruins of one hydroelectric dam are still visible. In a tribute to the beauty of the valley, old logger Whiting stayed on to watch the forests grow back from his hilltop mansion, high above the floodplain overlooking the mill site. Remnants remain, integrated into the Hebron Colony alcohol outreach facility. Winter reveals the river rock entrance columns of the old Robbins Hotel. The 1863 Shull's Mill General Store still stands opposite Shull's Mill Baptist Church near Old Turnpike Road. The cottage at that junction is an original mid-1800s home.

Thinking of the pre-railroad isolation of his own academic institution, B. B. Dougherty stepped up to save the railroad after the flood. He and Bob Rivers, editor of the *Watauga Democrat*, had helped bring the tracks to Boone, and Dougherty begged ET&WNC officials to rebuild. They agreed, then reneged. The railroad was gone, a second world war was on the way, and like Tweetsie struggling up a steep grade, time seemed to shudder and slip backward a little. "After the flood," Frank Aldridge remembers, "my dad got 75 cents apiece to load the 33-foot long rails on the side of the truck and take 'em to Johnson City. They left the windows rolled down and had to crawl in and out." Tweetsie's last run into North Carolina left Elk Park on October 16, 1950. A 1951 article in *Trains* magazine called it "the funeral train." On this run, "nostalgia had gripped the railroad men" and put a "far-away look in their eyes." Mountain residents waved goodbye from porches.

Tweetsie wouldn't be gone for good. For a brief time in the 1950s a children's "ride-on" train attraction, "Tweetsie Junior," looped Mayview Lake in Blowing Rock. Then the real deal came home. By the mid-1950s, Grover C. Robbins Jr. set out to acquire the last remaining ET&WNC engine, #12, built in 1917, that had for years run the route to Boone. In 1954, the engine was flooded out of a tourist railroad in the Virginia Blue Ridge and was headed to Gene Autry in California. Robbins stepped in, and on July 4, 1957, the Tweetsie Railroad attraction debuted on a three-mile track in Blowing Rock. The old steam engine had been rebuilt by Frank Coffey, for decades the foreman at the Hickory maintenance facility of the C&N-W, the rail line that helped log Grandfather's lower slopes. When the C&N-W engine shop closed in 1958, Coffey moved to Tweetsie to pass on a lifetime of steam-train experience. In the ultimate irony, Foscoe's Frank Aldridge—with the old rail bed in his backyard and Grandfather overhead—found a future in railroading's past. With major rebuilding planned for engines and cars at Tweetsie, Frank Coffey invited Aldridge to be "the lowest man on the totem pole," he smiles. Aldridge's grandfather and uncles worked on Tweetsie, but when "people ask me how I got interested in steam trains," he admits, "I say, 'I didn't! I don't even like trains, I'm a drag racer.'" Eventually, Coffey's torch was passed to Aldridge. Coffey was not only shop foreman at C&N-W, but his father was foreman before him. Aldridge found himself the repository of steam engine experience reaching back to the 1800s. Tweetsie's story has a surprising future. Theme park steam trains nationwide need maintenance, and with Aldridge's help, the 5,000-square-foot Tweetsie Railroad Steam Locomotive Shop has cornered the business. Frank Coffey died in 1999, but his and Tweetsie's legacy live on through employees like Aldridge, his coworkers, and owners Chris and Cathy Robbins.

When the ET&WNC disappeared, it took the hearts of mountain people with it. There was music in Tweetsie's whistle, and Newland musician Floyd Banner heard it. A great-great-great-grandson of the original Banner family of "Banner's Elk," Floyd lamented Tweetsie's loss in his 1975 song "Little Tweetsie Railroad Train."

The Grandfather Community:
An Eddy in Time

The Grandfather Community was a dead end for generations. The first known settlers arrived around 1820, among them James Aldridge, likely the guide that Elisha Mitchell called Leatherstocking Aldridge during his 1827 visit to Grandfather. Aldridge's son Harrison (1821–1905) reportedly built his earliest home in 1836, the "only pioneer home standing in the Grandfather Community," wrote Ted Shook. An 1897 article in the *Lenoir Topic* said Harrison Aldridge killed his 100th bear at age seventy-five. Harrison's grave graces a meadow where Frank Aldridge lives today. Wade Fox, born in 1933, was a young man after Tweetsie washed away. For years, he'd hunt coons on Flat Top, today's Linville Ridge, with his dad, Roby Adam Fox (1907–81). "We'd walk through them meddas in Linville Gap and he'd tell me, 'one day son, there's going to be a little town here.'" Percy and Lucy Davis Shook lived in the fields above the gap, and "some of his kids was buried out in that field and they built houses right on top of 'em," maintains Fox. The couple had a daughter and son who died in infancy, and many a Grandfather Community elder claims their graves indeed were "lost to development." A mid-nineteenth-century "old turnpike road" up the valley was joined circa 1885–90 by the River Road. The two rough tracks played tag up the Watauga until NC 105 obliterated them, but remnants remain. Shepherd Dugger's Grandfather Hotel opened in the 1880s, and by 1906 its post office had moved down to Monroe Gragg's 1880s country store that still stands on NC 105.

Transport Tales

After Tweetsie's demise in 1940, transportation was dismal again until the mid-1950s, when NC 105 arrived. "The road to the gap was still one lane and dirt," remembers Frank Aldridge. "If you met anybody, you had to get out of the road. As a kid, I don't never remember going uphill past the old country store. The only people who went up there lived there." Recalls Wade Fox, "In the '40s, we'd start out to go to the movie in Newland,

Hard-nosed historians fret when life in the Appalachians is "romanticized," but surely, in the early days of the Grandfather Community, a girl doing her chores basked in a warm sun and Grandfather's gaze. Blowing Rock artist Jason Drake imagines the scene in his 2013 painting *Grandfather Mountain Reverie*. Painting by Jason Drake/www.jasondrake.com/.

but the road was so rutted out we couldn't get through. By the time we got pushed out, we were so nasty and covered in mud, we'd just go home. Or we'd have a flat tire. Sometimes two at a time." Howard Byrd (born in 1929) married wife Blanch (1926–2014) in 1946. "Sixty-seven years now she's been baking my biscuits," he crowed in 2013. That old country store "was just about the end of the dang road that traffic really traveled," he says. "Above that, it was walking." At the very top, the "old road forded that creek, barely wide enough for one vehicle to sort of go." One day in 1951, Howard Byrd and

Blanch's brothers set out to buy tires in Tennessee. "Where we had to cross was froze in ice. He got hung and tore every tire off that thing," Byrd admits. "Many a time I'd carry an ax and have to chop a ice channel to keep from sliding down the river."

Foscoe and the Grandfather Community were an eddy of activity under the Grandfather. "When I was a kid," Frank Aldridge says, "the older boys would go and drink beer at the old Robbins Hotel [remnants still exist near Hound Ears] and listen to NASCAR races on their car radios. Old George Baker, the state patrolman, would pull up and say, 'Boys, drink all the beer you want to, but don't go towards Boone.'" Wade Fox recalls, "I used to deliver the old *Grit* newspaper, from Foscoe to Linville Gap in the late '40s." *Grit* was Norman Rockwell America, the Paul Harvey radio program on paper. "Mr. Linville Aldridge was my last customer down in Foscoe and Tate Davis was my last one up yonder." Fox was fast friends with the McLean boys, Baxter, Bobby, Bruce, Buster, and Carlos. "Carlos wanted my *Grit* route, and I didn't. He didn't want his bicycle, and I did. We traded. He'd walk delivering papers, and I'd ride the bicycle beside him."

A Gathering Spot

Post-Tweetsie, Monroe Gragg's store was "the gathering place every night," recalls Wade Fox. "They'd buy your chickens and toss 'em out in the pen. Bought eggs, too. And natural products like cherry bark, roots, catnip. Took it all to Wilcox Drug in Boone." Howard Byrd remembers, "When I was courting, the school house burned down," and the country store stood in. "They wasn't a Saturday night passed that gals wuddn't fix a box supper or make a pie and bid 'em off. All the old boys around this country

at that time, they'd lay to buy their girlfriend's pie, but other boys would double team 'em, and run it up on him! I know'd many an old boy who'd spend his whole week's wages to buy that pie!" According to Howard Byrd, there was music too. "Old man Gragg played the fiddle, he had a boy who picked the banjer, and Rand Shook, he picked a banjer till he died out. He had a boy picked a guitar and they ganged up and made music about every Saturday night." Said Blanch Byrd, "In this day and time, there ain't nothing old timey like that used to be. Life was rough but by god you enjoyed it. When you was waiting for a Saturday night like that to happen, it took forever for a week to pass. Seems like a month ain't a week, now."

The elderly cherish their landmark mountain. "Under the Grandfather, it's my home place," Blanch stated, "where I was born and growed up. Where I'll die at, I guess." Allows Howard, "Let's say it this way, the good Lord put him up there and he's gonna stay there. Adder Hugh Morton died, he turned it over to his grandson, and he turned it over to the state—and there won't be a tree or nothing ever cut on his face, ever again, yeah buddy." In 2012, ninety-year-old Creed Taylor still pondered something an old man told him when he was a kid. "Maybe that old man was pulling a young kid's leg, and I guess he did that! But he asked, 'Who is that up there?' and I told him, 'That's the Grandfather.' And he said, 'No, that's not a Grandfather. That mountain is really a mother, to everyone in this valley.' It took a while, but I see what he meant. That mountain raised us all." Today is a different time for the Grandfather Community. For the shrinking number of residents who remember the way things used to be, there's a quickly changing place to go along with it.

From 1945 to the 1970s an ET&WNC railroad car stranded in Newland operated as the Tweetsie Diner, still "carrying" locals to memories of Tweetsie's past. Louise Bare Young (1918–93), shown here just after the diner closed in the late-1970s, was the longtime proprietor. It was "one of the best places to eat anywhere in this area," says local historian and writer Jimmie Daniels. Recalls Young's daughter Lois Bare Johnson, "Mother's whole life was operating the Diner. She had regular customers who ate with her every day. Her lunch special was one meat, three vegetables from her garden, and a homemade dessert. In 1945, it cost 47 cents." Photo by Randy Johnson.

When I was just a little boy, living on a hillside farm,
I used to see a little train meandering along.
It's track was narrow, its whistle shrill, I remember way back then,
Oh, how I would like to see and hear that train again.

The number of people who remember Tweetsie echoing under the Grandfather Mountain is shrinking from few to fewer. So is the group of folks who recall the logging days. But the rarely noticed corridor carved by the rails still winds around the ridges. When I found the words "Graveyard Curve" on an old ET&WNC map, I had to investigate. Turning off NC 105, something clicked as the Foscoe Cemetery appeared on the roadside. I stepped into the windy winter dusk and walked the edge of the graveyard. Directly below was a dark, arcing railroad grade. Graveyard curve. It was easy to imagine a smoke-belching train swooping into Foscoe, whistle shrieking loud enough to wake the dead (well, almost). Suddenly, everything was bathed in bright peach alpenglow as sunset caught a cloud bank on Grandfather's summits. I knew graves were placed on this hilltop to connect me with that place and its people, but I shivered at the realization that "the past" was so easy to find. On Grandfather Mountain and in the valleys that radiate from it, if you know where to look, history steps out to meet you. That evening, embraced by Graveyard Curve, surrounded by people who'd logged the Grandfather and listened to Tweetsie's whistle, I could almost hear the train myself.

Touch Base with Tweetsie

You can still ride the train that plied the line between Johnson City and Boone. "Tweetsie Country" is an enticing destination for railroad fans of all ages. Consider making a donation to the museums below.

Blowing Rock, N.C. / Tweetsie Railroad / 800-526-5740 / http://tweetsie.com/
Listed on the National Register of Historic Sites, engine #12 still shrieks on 3-mile trips looping "Roundhouse Mountain." There are bad guys and Indians on the way, but the ride through the rhododendron movingly reimagines the past—and morphs into Thomas the Tank Engine and the autumn "Ghost Train" too (late September to early November). Tweetsie's museum is made from railroad depots that served the Carolina & North-West Railway, the line that logged Grandfather's lower slopes. Choose September's Railroad Heritage Weekend for historic rolling stock, two-engine hookups, expanded museum exhibits, and tours of the Tweetsie Railroad Steam Locomotive Shop, the nation's number one rebuild facility. The weekend started as "Old Timer's Day" under Spencer Robbins, with railroad historian Ken Riddle. Today, the old-timers are gone, but Tweetsie honors them still.

Newland, N.C. / Avery County Historical Museum / 828-733-7111 / http://www.averymuseum.com/
Linville's wonderfully restored Tweetsie station and the last ET&WNC caboose, #505, sit behind Avery's historical museum in Newland. Take the Old Toe River Road west of town to Minneapolis and look across the river to see where the rails used to run on the hillside.

Johnson City, Tenn. / George L. Carter Railroad Museum / 423-439-3382 / http://www.etsu.edu/railroad/
The George L. Carter Railroad Museum in Johnson City features exhibits, artwork by railroad artist Ted Laws, and model rail layouts that track the history of the area's three major railroads, including the ET&WNC. Grab a southern bite in downtown's historic rail depot at the popular restaurant Tupelo Honey, with its own miniature railroad and passing trains.

Tweetsie caboose #505, shown here as active rolling stock in the mid-1900s, is alive and well at Avery County's Historical Museum in Newland. You can sit in Linville's historic Tweetsie station and look outside at the same caboose actual passengers would have seen—an experience that takes you back in time. Courtesy of Special Collections, Appalachian State University, Thomas Reese Railroad and Printing Collection.

Spencer, N.C. / North Carolina Transportation Museum / 704-636-2889 / http://www.nctrans.org/
This mega-train museum is worth an entire day. The collection includes a rare ET&WNC "combination car three," with passenger seats in front, a center cargo section, and mail in the rear. Frank Aldridge says, "It's one of the most fascinating ET&WNC cars that still exists," donated to the museum by the Tweetsie attraction.

Newton, N.C. / Southeastern Narrow Gauge and Shortline Museum / 828-464-3930 / http://www .newtondepot.com
Housed in the restored Newton Depot, the collection features a sheltered outdoor display area, a rare 1910 ET&WNC boxcar that hauled lumber from Grandfather Mountain, and a 1920s section car that carried work crews near Boone—"one of the most important narrow gauge artifacts of the southeast." The car includes the famous "Hobbs Box" transmission designed and built at ET&WNC's Johnson City engine house.

Wilmington, NC / Wilmington Railroad Museum / 910-763-2634 / http://www.wilmingtonrailroad museum.org/content/displays.php
The Atlantic Coast Line Railroad is the focus, but Wilmington is the home of the MacRae family's Wilmington & Weldon Railroad.

6 An Attraction Emerges

OBSERVATION POINT, GRANDFATHER, MTN. LINVILLE, N.C.

Seen from below, on Linville Bluffs, Grandfather's earliest attraction was an exciting contraption clinging to the craggy face of a towering peak. The builders of its parking deck learned from the loggers, basically creating a board road to harvest tourists instead of timber. Collection of Hugh MacRae II. Photo by Nelson MacRae.

Most people associate "Grandfather Mountain commercial travel attraction" with Hugh Morton, the man who gave us the Mile-High Swinging Bridge in 1952. But in 1935, with logging ending on the mountain, Morton was only a teenager when uncle

Nelson MacRae first started charging motorists to "drive up" Grandfather. Visitors didn't get far. The vista spot just above MacRae Meadows was long popular, but adding a primitive road and calling it "Observation Point" made it Grandfather's first tourist attraction. Surging visitation set the stage for Hugh Morton's later development, but it also sparked interest in the backcountry. A short, strenuous hike above Observation Point led to spectacular views from loftier peaks. Adventurers were heading higher despite primitive paths and logging debris. Fortunately, as the mountain's forests started to recover, a hiker appeared who'd jumpstart the mountain's post–logging trail network. Surprisingly, even then Grandfather Mountain's essential attractions—views and trails—looked much as they do today, and Hugh Morton had yet to build his bridge to the future. Also fascinating, way back in the 1880s, early owner Walter Waightstill Lenoir had his own persuasive vision of how to make the mountain a profitable "pleasure ground."

Lenoir's Vision

Lenoir spent a lifetime trying to commercialize what he called "the cream of my Watauga lands," but he also wanted to preserve them. He so strenuously encouraged preservation during negotiations to sell the mountain that Lenoir admitted it was naive to hope he could control land he'd no longer own. Nevertheless, he sketched a prescient and perhaps ultimately influential development plan for Grandfather. In an 1887 letter to Samuel T. Kelsey he envisioned a "pleasure ground" in the Linville River valley that except for "necessary streets should be kept in a grove of forest trees." The "summits and sides of the Grandfather & its spurs should be preserved in native forest," he wrote. Today, Grandfather Golf and Country Club and Linville Ridge come close to implementing Lenoir's prescription, albeit with guards and gatehouses. Lenoir urged "such structures on the summits as may serve for temporary shelter (& refreshment) to visitors. But no hotel or boarding house." This longtime Grandfather hiker and camper would likely be happy with the tent platforms and trail shelter found today in the state park. He also suggested that "the net proceeds realized from the toll fares collected on the roads, ways, and paths should be used for maintenance & improvement." Remarkably, he not only suggests access by trail and road; he says fees should

be charged to fund the facilities. Later attractions operated by both Nelson MacRae and Hugh Morton would follow Lenoir's playbook. So would the user fee trail program I launched in 1978. The nonprofit stewardship foundation also likely jibes with Lenoir's logic.

Ultimately, Lenoir doubted anyone would invest in a new resort town, and he and Kelsey would end up collaborating. Lenoir saw the mountain as sacred, but sadly, he lost the right to dictate his dream. So did Kelsey, a preservationist who launched the High Country shrubbery industry with a native plant business near Linville that still carries on as North Carolina's oldest nursery. Kelsey's town, Highlands, was "carved out of old-growth forest" so sensitively, maintains ancient forest expert Josh Kelly, that "most home owners would be amazed how old the forests in their yards really are." Had Kelsey and Lenoir been driving the bus, Grandfather never would have been logged. Almost unbelievably, the old Confederate's vision of Grandfather Mountain's future is startlingly similar to what we see realized on the mountain today.

Observation Point

Anyone looking up at Linville Peak in Linville's early days surely exclaimed, "Imagine the view from up there!" Achieving that view took a serious hike, but an outcrop below the peak was a lot easier to reach and had a great view, too. That vista is still a pull-off called Cliffside Overlook on the road to the Swinging Bridge, but in the 1930s it was just a rock outcrop reached by a bridle trail. Joe Hartley built that path "so the ladies could ride horses up there," Robert Hartley recalled. So many rode to the viewpoint that "Pop always called it 'the hitching ground.'" All that changed in 1935. As logging wound down, Nelson MacRae, Linville Improvement Company president from 1920 to 1942, turned the outcrop into Grandfather Mountain's first commercial attraction. "When I was 11 years old," Nelson's son Hugh MacRae II remembered in 2013, "my father built the original toll road to get extra income for the company."

In this photo of Robert Hartley and friends, Hugh Morton captured the Scots-Irish countenance and spirit of a family who greatly influenced the history and success of Grandfather Mountain. North Carolina Collection, University of North Carolina Library at Chapel Hill. Photo by Hugh Morton.

Ka-ching. It worked. Joe's trail was upgraded into a dirt road, and the craggy spot was capped with Observation Point, a rough-hewn wood parking deck and gift shop. Engineer and life-long Linville summer resident Theodore "Ted" Fitz Randolph III (1921–2015) remembered Joe Hartley orchestrating the improvements. "They used 'slip trucks' instead of bulldozers in those days," Randolph asserted, "blade-like devices pulled by either a mule or a horse."

Observation Point's parking deck was constructed a lot like the board roads used to log the mountain. The viewpoint's platform accommodated about a dozen cars and resembled board road staging areas where logging trucks were loaded. It was flanked by a small, angular gift shop called the Observation Center that was covered in Linville's signature chestnut bark. The shop didn't have electricity and sold cold snacks, souvenirs, and colorized postcards of the attraction. The toll road started west of today's attraction entrance, still visible as an old grade with a wooden gate leading left off the Grandfather Mountain office driveway on US 221. "Alexander MacRae's son Johnny had a little store there by his Dad's house, so they put the entrance beside it and he took the tolls," Robert Hartley recalled. Hartley helped Johnny "of

a Sunday, the first time I got on the payroll." With Robert's 1939 hiring, another Hartley was set to influence Grandfather Mountain. The toll was 50 cents for car and driver and 25 cents for each additional passenger.

Observation Point emulated other "roadside attractions" in its marketing to early motorists. Rock City Gardens of Chattanooga, Tennessee, painted farmers' barns as far away as Michigan and Texas for free if "See Rock City" was emblazoned on the side. And when bumper strips urged "See Rock City," motorists responded. Hugh MacRae II remembers, "My father ordered waxed paper bumperstickers that said 'See Grandfather Mountain.'" Wire in the ends of the wax-stiffened cardboard was twisted behind the era's big chrome bumpers. Robert Hartley, who saw the start of that tradition, said longtime Linville Improvement Company employee Tate Davis "asked people if he could put those signs on the bumpers. Most people were glad enough to have them." Twisting the wires was tricky for Tate, who'd lost his right arm as a logger.

The road opened in the summer of 1935, and by late August Nelson MacRae told an associate in Wilmington, "The toll road business has picked up considerably; and I think it will bring us a fairly nice income on up through October." MacRae marked a milestone on Sunday, August 25, 1935. "No doubt there were more people on Grandfather that one day than has ever been in its history," he pronounced. The day before, "the first North Carolina contract for the [Blue Ridge] Parkway was let." Nelson MacRae's spirits were up. The company was logging the mountain, and Observation Point had opened to raves, solidly popping into the profit picture. He sampled weekend opinion and found motorists "immensely pleased." He felt sure that "after it becomes generally known that it is possible to drive close to the top there will be a steady stream of people making the trip in good weather." Some were taking early trails to Linville Peak and beyond.

Robert Hartley got his license in 1938 and drove father Joe around the mountain. Ted Randolph also

Observation Point marked the birth of commercial tourism on Grandfather Mountain, and the staff waved enthusiastically when Linville Improvement Company president Nelson MacRae snapped this photo. One-armed early logger Tate Davis stands at left. Another time, Tate posed when his spiffy son Ford visited the attraction. Both men and Tate's other son Dolph "all worked on laying the plank road up the Grandfather," attests Tate's granddaughter Carolyn Davis Curtis. Collection of Hugh MacRae II, photo by Nelson MacRae; Collection of Carolyn Davis Curtis.

a rollicking young man fond of the mountain and his wealthy family's summers in Linville, "had a car with 15 horns, a siren, an exhaust whistle, a Bermuda Carriage Bell, and a cut out," he bragged. He was a local and a real character. "The people who ran the shack at Cliffside sure knew who was coming."

Mountain visitors penciled names and home towns in the road's registration book but rarely volunteered comments seen in guest registers today. Motorists came from Maryland, Texas, Chicago, Boston, and New York City, and from Cairo, Egypt, and Havana, Cuba, too. Emigrant residents of Hugh MacRae's eastern North Carolina experimental farm Castle Hayne brought friends from Holland. And there were locals, like Dr. R. H. Hardin and family of the Shull's Mill hospital. Nelson MacRae, his wife, and father Hugh MacRae registered (someone commented *"Too Too"* beside the power trio's signatures). Nelson MacRae personally recorded weekly pick-ups of 1936 gate receipts, and traffic was impressive. The ledger read, "Total visitors June 18 '36 to Aug 17 '36, 2,991." But when the weekend ended, traffic died. Scenic views require good visibility, and from October 5 to 9, 1936, the book noted, "Rain and Fog, No Cars." But Nelson MacRae was crowing. "The toll road to Grandfather Mountain is another source of income which I think will show excellent returns on investment; and is already proving one of the major points of interest in the Linville region," he told stockholders on March 30, 1937. At the time, with proposals being made to buy the mountain into public ownership, MacRae admitted "the principal reason" the company built the toll road, aside from "income to be derived," was to "fix in the minds of the public a fair value for the

started driving in 1938, and he remembers motoring up and down Grandfather on a road located almost exactly where it is today. Back then, Randolph maintained, "it was more or less one lane with passing places and every curve had a sign that said 'sound horn' or 'blow horn.'" Randolph,

A Coed College Outing to Observation Point

As Tate Davis tallied the toll road's take in October 1936, outdoorsy college men and women were finding their way to Grandfather's trails. Duke University freshman Elizabeth "Lib" Hatcher and her coed Explorer's Club friends drove to Observation Point and hiked high onto the mountain. It was a spectacular day; the distant Black Mountains pierced the sky. Duke Women's College chaperones were along—a good thing, with Grandfather's history of matchmaking hikes, thanks

A radiant Lib Hatcher atop MacRae Peak, long before Sugar Mountain and Flat Top Mountain (now Linville Ridge) became covered with houses, ski slopes, and the Sugartop condo complex. Collection of Elizabeth Hatcher Connor.

When Elizabeth "Lib" Hatcher and fellow Duke students found their way to Observation Point in 1936, a batch of walking staffs were already waiting for hikers, leaning against the rail beside the bark-covered gift shop. In 2015, Lib Conner recalled that this photo shows her and future husband Bob Conner "flirting." Collection of Elizabeth Hatcher Connor.

to Shepherd Dugger. More than a few shots show Lib with handsome young hiker Bob Conner, her future husband. The hike happened as logging was ending, and shots show debris and stumps but also untouched groves and smaller standing evergreens. Like Hugh Morton a few years later, Hatcher "quickly showed her talent as a photographer," says a Duke University bio. Her hike photos appeared in the yearbook, *Chanticleer*, along with photos of Duke Chapel, where she'd later marry and become Elizabeth Hatcher Conner. Another campus photo shows renowned twentieth-century artist Louis Orr (1879–1961). Between 1939 and 1951, Orr created etchings of the state's landmarks for Robert Lee Humber, a founder of the North Carolina Museum of Art. Duke

Chapel was one of those works, and Hatcher photographed him "sketching for an etching." Grandfather, too, became an Orr etching. Understandably, the couple's Grandfather hike launched a lifetime of trail enthusiasm. The Conners and their four kids hiked Grandfather throughout their lives, climbing the ladders Clyde Smith installed just a half-decade after that first hike. In the early 2000s, both Lib and Bob received awards for twenty-five years of volunteer work on the Appalachian Trail and thirty years of service to the Friends of North Carolina State Parks.

Nelson MacRae also captured the dismay and disarray in 1936 when passersby realized Linville's primary profit center was going up in smoke. The fire would turn the nearby annex, Chestnut Lodge, into today's Eseeola Lodge. Collection of Hugh MacRae II. Photo by Nelson MacRae.

Bob Conner in period "hiking boots" perched on a crag just above today's longest ladders on MacRae Peak. Collection of Elizabeth Hatcher Connor.

Grandfather Mountain in the event the government decided to purchase it. Grandfather Mountain as a developed property, showing earnings, would have a higher value." Not everything was fine. The town's main draw for visitors, the Eseeola Inn, burned in an impressive fire on June 28, 1936, during the Singing on the Mountain at MacRae Meadows. To replace it, the Chestnut Lodge, a 1929 Eseeola Inn annex, was renamed Eseeola Lodge. It still graces Linville. Nevertheless, a company meeting on March 30, 1937, concluded the "Linville Improvement Company has come through the depression in good condition." Observation Point was a big plus. The same meeting adopted the name "the Linville Company."

The Depression was ebbing. Then came the 1940 flood, forever ending the East Tennessee & Western North Carolina Railroad's route to Linville. With the start of World War II the following year, gas and tire rationing made Linville more isolated than ever. Sitting in the highland fog at the entrance gate, waiting for cars that never came, Johnny MacRae raised a bottle. "Johnny would get tipsy," Robert admitted. "Someone would pull up,

Singing on the Mountain

Since 1924, Joe Hartley's Sunday-school-picnic-turned-gospel-sing has been an authentic Appalachian original and Grandfather's longest-running annual event. "Whosoever Will, May Come" was Squire Hartley's eloquent invitation to inspiration where the Lord's message was most compelling—outdoors, under the Grandfather. Attendance started at 150 people, rose to 500 in year two, and climbed to 20,000 by year ten. It didn't rain until the twenty-third year. Billy Graham took the stage on a threatening day before 200,000 people in 1962 only to have the sun shine through. Graham "drew the largest crowd ever assembled in the mountains," Hugh Morton maintained. Nationally significant mountain musicians took the stage, among them Bascom Lamar Lunsford, who influenced the 1960s folk

A Hugh Morton classic: Joe Hartley beside his "Great Singing" poster at MacRae Meadows. North Carolina Collection, University of North Carolina Library at Chapel Hill. Photo by Hugh Morton.

revival. In 1948, Metropolitan Opera basso Norman Cordon sang "Rock of Ages," and Joe Hartley introduced "Mister Gordon" as someone who had "sung *all over the universe*, from the Atlantic Ocean to the Tennessee line!" For more than thirty years, Hugh Morton's "dear friend" and million-selling gospel musician Arthur Smith was singing master. Johnny Cash sang in 1974 with wife June Carter Cash on hand. The Singing hosted Oral Roberts's 1976 television special with musician Roy Clark. In 2000, Joe Hartley's son Robert moved the stage to the bottom of the field, vastly improving the event.

A Local Tradition

Joe Hartley didn't plan it—or did he?—but his Bridle Trail to Linville Gap connected to MacRae Meadows, and countless local families walked from Banner Elk, the Grandfather Community, and Foscoe. "I've never been to the Swinging Bridge over twice in my life," says Frank Aldridge of Foscoe, "but I always went to the Singing. It was wilder than the devil on Saturday night, a big drinkin' party," he confessed. "But Sunday it went to preachin' and gospel singing." Wade Fox anticipated the event in the early 1940s, energetically hoeing corn for neighbors "for 10 cent a hour, to spend at the Singing," he recalls. Hugh Morton once attributed the popularity of the event to Arthur Smith, who "plugged the daylights" out of it. Morton's own promotional genius helped, and by 1946 Joe Hartley annually thanked the Morton media juggernaut on behalf of his "conventions." A town history called *The Linville Ledger* included a telling typographical error reflecting Morton's role. The headline read, "Billy Graham Speaks to Hugh Crowd."

Details: The Singing on the Mountain is held every fourth Sunday in June, from 8:30 A.M. to midafternoon, with a midday featured sermon.

and ask him, 'What's up thar?' 'Well,' Johnny'd say, looking quizzical, 'there's a mountain up there. What *do you think* is up thar?'" Alick MacRae's son was among the area's first travel industry employees to be annoyed by the obvious questions to which tourists can be prone. Johnny "wasn't

working out," Hartley chuckled. An entrance station made of "Grandfather Stone" quarried on the mountain was built in 1942. It was the first facility to have electricity and is the only structure still in use from the mountain's earliest days. Nelson MacRae died in February 1942. Covington says

172—Entrance on U. S. 221 to the Grandfather Mountain Road, Linville, N. C.

© CURT TEICH & CO., INC.

7B-H1742

The 1942 stone entrance station in 1947, a postcard part of Grandfather's growing appeal. The building still stands, but it was enlarged and modernized in the early twenty-first century. North Carolina Collection, Pack Memorial Public Library, Asheville, N.C. Curt Teich Postcard.

"strain" killed him. Anne Mitchell Whisnant's *Super-Scenic Motorway* asserts he committed suicide. Julian Walker Morton took over the Linville Company, adding a new family name to the dynasty linked with Linville and the Grandfather Mountain. Morton had been a company vice president overseeing construction of the Donald Ross golf course. He was also a childhood friend of the MacRaes from Wilmington who had married Nelson MacRae's sister, Agnes MacRae, becoming Nelson's brother-in-law. Julian and Agnes had four children. Son Hugh MacRae Morton, born February 19, 1921, would be synonymous with Grandfather Mountain into the twenty-first century. During that time "everybody was in financial trouble," Robert remembers. "Imagine paying tax on 16,000 acres of land." In 2013 Hugh MacRae II confessed that "the company was losing quite a bit of money trying to keep Linville open during the war. My grandfather borrowed to do that." To save money, Eseeola Lodge was shuttered in the summer of

1943. In late 1944, the "cottagers," as second-home owners called themselves, or "the rich," as Robert Hartley dubbed them, formed Linville Resorts, Inc., and bought the resort, including Eseeola Lodge, the golf course, rental cottages, stables, clubhouse, and tennis courts. Hugh Morton's father, Julian Morton, became Linville Resorts' first president and, like Nelson MacRae before him, met an untimely end. He died of a heart attack in 1945, also attributed to the pressure of the job. Linville struggled on.

Backcountry Beginnings

Despite the Depression, Linville and Blowing Rock were becoming bona fide tourist towns during the 1920s, 1930s, and 1940s. With access from Observation Point, hikers were climbing rustic trails, and summer camps were part of that trend. Starting in 1924, a Blowing Rock camp named Yonahlossee gave girls a magical experience of the mountain, and Camp Yonahnoka in Linville, cofounded by

Not far above Observation Point (at least for the fit), a truly distinctive taste of Grandfather's grandeur emerged in the gap between Linville Peak and the rising rest of the ridge. That almost-alpine col may well have been the most scenic spot on the mountain. A parking lot and Swinging Bridge supplanted the spruce in 1952. North Carolina Collection, University of North Carolina Library at Chapel Hill. Photo by Hugh Morton.

Hugh Morton's father, Julian, did the same for boys in 1925. Yonahlossee girls made it to Calloway Peak in the 1920s. Group tourism started at Observation Point. Camp Yonahlossee began a long tradition of visiting the Grandfather attraction when eighteen campers drove up on July 14, 1936, led by founders Dr. Adam Perry Kephart and Mrs. Margaret Kephart (called Kep and Keppie by campers). Camp Yonahnoka director C. V. Tompkins signed in too. For summer residents with a largesse of leisure time to meet the mountain, outdoor excursions became a ritual part of "summer colony" culture that spanned the years and even generations. Ted Randolph and his family epitomize that tradition. Randolph's grandparents, J. D. and Katharine Kirkpatrick, arrived in Linville's earliest days. "They didn't like Blowing Rock," remembered Ted, "so they took the stage coach to Linville." His grandfather won a golf tournament on that first visit, "which probably explained why they liked Linville

best," he chuckled. The Kirkpatricks built one of Linville's earliest bark-sided homes, Fenbrook, and J. D. became the first president of the Linville Golf Club. As the age of horseback ebbed, he embraced his wife's "dream" of riding home to Birmingham from Linville, a 1914 trip surely inspired by Margaret Morley's 1913 book *The Carolina Mountains*. Somewhere along the line, the family turned to hiking and never stopped. By 1926, Ted had summited Linville Peak as a child of less than five years—and he'd be leading the way for another eighty-five years. Two years before his death in 2015, Randolph made his final hike to MacRae Peak at ninety-one.

As Observation Point revved up in the late 1930s, logging ebbed and Randolph fought slash-choked trails. Each summer the family took Tweetsie to Linville Gap to camp out. Ted recalls his Aunt Mary "hired a guide who lived at the Gap"—one-armed Tate Davis. On one hike "the trails were obliterated," recalled Randolph. "Even our guide got lost. I remember breaking through bush up close behind him when he went swinging out into mid-air over a cliff. He'd caught the stump of his arm around a tree." Tate had almost fallen off the face on MacRae Peak climbed by today's ladders. Adventures continued. A Swiss governess once led Ted and sister Serena Chesnut "Chessie" Randolph for a picnic and a nap in the spectacular gap where the Swinging Bridge Parking Area is now. Family tradition holds that a photo of Ted and Chessie on a peak of Grandfather appeared in a 1941 issue of *National Geographic*. Chessie later became Serena Randolph MacRae by marrying Donald MacRae's son, George. When Ted and his cohort went off to war, the mountain was a mess. Luckily, while he and other hikers were away, someone stepped up to formalize trails on Grandfather Mountain.

The Coming of Clyde

Clyde F. Smith (1906–76) was a quintessential New England mountain man, one of many drawn to the Southern Appalachians. His name crops up just below the radar of fame when the topic is trails. Smith launched the post-logging history of Grandfather's backcountry, giving us one of the mountain's classic trails and a fascinating life story. By 1943, Smith, his wife Hilda (1909–2009), and teenage son Clyde H. "Mickey" Smith (1931–2008) had started spending November to April in the Southern Appalachians, where Clyde F. pursued a business of making routed wooden signs. They settled in Spruce Pine, but their orbit included Blowing Rock, Boone, and Asheville. With Grandfather's forests dramatically thinned, Smith couldn't help noticing the mountain's rocky kinship to New Hampshire's White Mountains where he was born, in Gorham, below Mount Washington. Smith's involvement with Grandfather started in mid–World War II when he landed a dream job as a wintertime seasonal ranger on the Blue Ridge Parkway. Smith became a leader in Blowing Rock Boy Scout Troop 21 where he and his thirteen-year-old, later Eagle Scout, son would build a trail to the top of the High Country's most dramatic

summit. With Boy Scouts building the trail and Daniel Boone's footprints all over the area, his path to Calloway Peak would be named after that old "scout" himself, Dan'l. His double-entendre title was the Daniel Boone Scout Trail.

Smith targeted the logged and singed northeast side of Grandfather. In 2012, the earliest map of the path was found in a closet of forgotten clutter at Blowing Rock's Rumple Presbyterian Church, Troop 21's sponsor. The map dates the opening of the trail to the summer of 1943, and the builders included Mickey Smith, leader of the Hawk Patrol, James Ward "Buddy" Council, David "Junior" Banner, Robert "Bobby" Walters, Thomas Wright, Jim Benfield, "Benny" Britain, and Frank J. Brown (1932–2009), who would become a physician. Brown penned a brief history of the trail in the early 1980s after my backcountry program reopened his trail. "Each weekday morning," he revealed, "Troop 21 would load into Smith's pickup" for a ride to the work site on US 221. In 1999, Mickey Smith related how his father "made friends with an old lady who lived on the Yonahlossee Road—Miss Boyd—and got permission to start the trail on her property." The elder Smith was a master at making trail signs, and one of his creations marked that trailhead. Brown remembered that the troop "blazed a trail from a knoll just back of Ms. Boyd's store to a small grassy plateau, Troop 21's prime staging area (i.e., lunch break) in opening the trail to the top of Calloway Peak and beyond." That midpoint of the trail is still a campsite near a water source Clyde Smith named Bear Wallow Spring. In the flat just below Calloway Peak, the Scouts and their leader constructed a distinctive lean-to trail shelter Smith called Hi-Balsam. A half-century later, wrote Smith's son, "We built Hi-Balsam so the scouts would have a place to camp while working on the trails. A grand spot during thunderstorms and even some winter expeditions." Ted Randolph actually met Smith and his Scouts as they built and maintained the trail. "Ranger Smith had a lot of initiative," Randolph insisted, "and he did all he could to get things back and going after the war."

Ted Randolph:
Climbing the Stepping Steeps

On one of his earliest Grandfather Mountain hikes, Ted Randolph felt the weight of the world on his shoulders. His father told the four-year-old to lead a hiking group of adults on the trail around Linville Peak while he "took a short cut" directly up the airy faces above the trail. The frightened lad led onward, and "when I finally heard his voice up there, I almost broke down," he remembered.

Ever after, Randolph was inspired by his father's veritable rock climb up "the Stepping Steeps." The trail Randolph hiked still exists, a time machine climb into the gap below the Swinging Bridge. But to the right of the trail, projecting flakes of rock, sheer cliffs, and crack-fractured crags soar up out of virgin evergreens and into the alpenglow of golden sunlight on one of Grandfather's most alpine summits. By World War II, climbing the Stepping Steeps was quite an adventure for outdoorsy,

Betty MacRae, wife of Colin MacRae, was one climber who braved these "Steeps." Back in the day, this tree helped her up one truly scary cliff. She thought the transition was such a tricky move that her note on the back of the picture urged posterity to "remember me by this!" And so it does. Collection of George and Chessie MacRae.

The Swinging Bridge takes visitors to the top of Linville Peak, but a climb up the cliffs from below was a challenge for adventurous Linville hikers during the decades surrounding World War II. Photo by Helen Moss Davis/www.wildblueprints.com.

jitterbug-era young adults like Randolph. The Stepping Steeps dispensed with ladders. One crux move required climbing a lone spruce clinging to a cliff, then stretching across to handholds on the face.

Today, we'd call this a rock climb, which is what I called it as I joined James Randolph, Ted's son, on a re-creation of a "hike" he'd often shared with his dad. We roped up, and as we belayed each other up the route, I had the experience climber's crave of stepping upward out of shade into a sunlit vertical world. We zipped

up parkas as October warmth became early winter windchill. We made it, but not without knuckles bloodied by a climb that used to be called a hike. I've bounced across the Swinging Bridge a million times, but I'd never climbed Linville Peak like we did that day. I suddenly saw it as Jehu Lewis, Ted Randolph, and climbers had in an earlier era. Here was a secret rock climber's paradise, where climbing isn't permitted today, but for a time, members of the "Greatest Generation" took those steeps in steps.

The Chastain family of nearby Blowing Rock were among the summer residents who heard about the Boone Trail. Reginald Bryan Chastain and Dixie Herlong Chastain (the first female graduate of the University of Miami Law School) honeymooned at Mount Pisgah in 1935, then

bought sixteen acres and built a house south of Blowing Rock in the mid-1940s. Their son and daughter, Richard and Dixie, encountered the Daniel Boone Scout Trail, and "we all wanted to go to the top," Richard remembers. "Mom didn't know what she was getting into." The hikers encountered

Before discovering the North Carolina mountains, Clyde F. Smith was a fire lookout on New Hampshire's Mount Cardigan for a decade starting in the early 1930s. Here he and Hilda Smith pose with their son, later Eagle Scout Clyde H. "Mickey" Smith. Appalachian Mountain Club Archives.

fire warden Joe Hartley. He had cleared the rough path as a route for firefighters, Robert Hartley told me. "They'd cut all that timber and left all that slash and my father told them if it gets on fire, 'I can't get no men back in yonder.'" That man-way may have been one of the earliest cleared ridgetop routes. When Smith and his Scouts found Hartley's "pre-existing trail" a few years later, it wasn't much. Mickey Smith documented that his father didn't think "there was even a trail beyond the Attic Window except for some game paths. That remoteness to Calloway Peak is what intrigued him and inspired the Daniel Boone Scout Trail." In 1944, the year after the Scout Trail opened, "Troop 21 formalized the Shanty Spring Trail from Calloway Peak down to Linville Gap and the headwaters of the Watauga River," Frank Brown wrote. Ted Randolph helped locate that route. "Ranger Smith sent me word" during the war "that he'd like me to show him the trail up the other side of the mountain." Thus, Smith and his Scouts get the credit for establishing the basic paths we now associate with Grandfather. The post-1943 trail map also reflects his influence in naming trails and landmarks, including the main Grandfather Trail across the peaks. Intriguingly, he labeled today's Calloway Gap as Dry Bones Gap. An x denotes Indian House, now Indian House Cave (perhaps added later than the 1940s—newspapers claim it wasn't public knowledge until 1951). Smith's map calls the eventual Shanty Spring Trail the Calloway Trail—likely the earlier name for a path that descended not to Linville Gap but to "Calloway's" old hotel.

The Question of Ladders

The mysterious origin of the mountain's trail ladders crops up in a few spots in this book. Former Scout Frank Brown contends that in 1943 his troop constructed "some 18 ladders over cliffs, made of Balsam poles, fastened with chains and/ or steel cables to old Tweetsie Railroad spikes driven into rock crevices." The spikes were plentiful. Tweetsie had washed out three years before. The ladders I encountered thirty-five years later fit Brown's description. Robert Hartley also main-

the distinctive tin can lids Smith used to mark the trail. "I imagine the scouts' mothers over the winter saving the lid whenever they opened a can of coffee," Richard speculates. Forty years later, as I reclaimed the Daniel Boone Scout Trail, I still found rusting remnants of these white disks, a red Indian-style arrowhead painted in the center. Smith's trail signs often employed the motif of Indian arrows, fusing his fascination with Native Americans and the symbolism of Scouting.

After cutting the Boone Trail, Brown recorded, "Troop 21 then re-opened a pre-existing trail across Attic Window Peak, thence to the present day parking lot area." The mountain's rugged summit ridge had defied easy access for millennia, and the Scouts changed that. There was already a vague route across Grandfather cut in 1942 by

Florence Boyd at the Boone Trail

The early trailhead landmark on the Daniel Boone Scout Trail was Miss Florence Boyd's Store. Her life is a sad tale. Born in Lenoir, Boyd went to the Globe Academy and then became a successful "private nurse in some of the big metropolitan centers of the country," the *Charlotte Observer* recorded in 1953. After badly breaking her leg, she returned to Lenoir. As Caldwell County superintendent of public welfare, she "scoured Caldwell for crippled children," saw that they received orthopedic care, and later opened her home to kids. By the 1930s, Boyd owned 300 acres and logging cabins at the base of Grandfather where she gave children "summer-out-of-doors therapy" and "plenty of fresh milk and butter," she told the paper. Her little store on Yonahlossee Road served motorists and hikers after Clyde Smith and his Scouts built the Boone Trail. The Chastain family were early hikers. When Boyd handed kids Richard and Dixie lukewarm Cokes from an unrefrigerated case, Richard remembers asking for a colder one. "She'd hold it against your neck and say 'See, doesn't that feel cold?'" To Scout Frank Brown, "Miss Boyd was a dear sweet old lady who would throw in an extra piece of licorice for good measure." Boyd's fortunes turned for the worse. She lost her Lenoir house and was arrested for running an illegal children's home. She was cleared, but the camp burned, leaving her in a "humble dwelling on the camp property," reported the *Observer*. At the end of World War II, she was robbed and tied up while her pitiful home was set afire. She escaped, but then an acquaintance tried to defraud her out of proceeds from selling a right-of-way to the Blue Ridge Parkway. It's no surprise Scout Brown remembers that "a sign on her front door read, 'Don't Bother Me or I'll Shoot You.'" With help from Jim Hughes of Linville, Boyd set out to rebuild. As a new building neared completion in the late 1960s, she was found dead in her home. Hughes carried on for "Miss Florence," hosting indigent mountain kids. "The Robbins boys gave me passes for the Land of Oz," Hughes recalls, "and Hugh Morton gave me passes for the Grandfather." The camp failed, but from 1979 to about 2010 it became an isolated alcohol rehabilitation center called Serenity Farm that sold Grandfather Mountain hiking permits. Boyd's old store, the last of the logging buildings, burned down, but for years it was a roadside honey stand and trail pass outlet. Today, the "Florence E. Boyd Home and Vocational School for Crippled Children" still owns the property.

"Miss Boyd" owned the property at the start of the Boone Trail. The former nurse who was so concerned about the welfare of children was proud to pose when National Park Service ranger Clyde Smith and his Boy Scouts built a path from her front door. Smith's first trailhead sign was uncharacteristically simple, just painted letters on wood. Clyde and Hilda Smith Photo Collection.

(*Above and opposite page*) Smith's Scouts were "mountain boys" and they worked hard to clear Grandfather's trails. In a series of his signature hand-colorized black-and-white prints, Smith immortalized his troop's trail building, albeit with no names. Most of the photos seem to have been taken on a May ridge-walk amidst blooming Allegheny sandmyrtle. The image of a group clustered on MacRae Peak shows one boy hiking with an unsheathed hatchet, a risky style of maintenance Smith himself practiced. Other photos include a shot of the Grandfather Profile, no doubt as the boys cleared the Calloway Trail to Linville Gap. Others show a person perched on Attic Window Peak and a group atop MacRae. At the bottom of that photo, Smith's basket-type backpack and a towel sit ready to receive his camera. Clyde and Hilda Smith Photo Collection.

tained his father was involved with the ladders, but decades-long Grandfather employee Winston Church is certain "Clyde Smith was actively behind the ladders when I encountered them in 1962." Maybe Joe Hartley helped. He surely knew Smith and was keeping his eye on the northerner. As it is with credit for Grandfather's basic trails, it seems Smith and his Scouts were responsible for installing the mountain's now classic cliff-climbing ladders. But certainty eludes us. Don Beeson took the

earliest photograph of a ladder on Grandfather's summit ridge in 1913, a few years after Margaret Morley took her "knife-edge walk up in the sky." Had her guides built a few ladders? No one alive today can say. At the very least, Smith can claim to have greatly expanded the use of ladders. His New England trail ladder experience argues he would have built a ladder if one were needed—or the remains of one were found. By the time the 1940s ended, Grandfather had ladders anchored to cliffs

In 1913, a generation before Clyde Smith blazed his Grandfather Trail, D. R. Beeson likely snapped Grandfather's earliest image of a trail ladder. Beeson was feeling pretty local by this part of the hike. He tagged his image "'A Native Mountaineer' On the Trail Over Top of Grandfather." Courtesy of Archives of Appalachia, East Tennessee State University, D. R. Beeson Papers.

and Smith had connected Observation Point to the most remote summits and nearby valleys. But that was just the start. The North Carolina mountains would become Smith's second and final home.

A Lifetime Outdoors

Smith's late-1940s and 1950s work on Grandfather got its start during the desperate days of the Depression. For a decade after Clyde and Hilda's marriage in 1930, the Smith family alternated between seasonal jobs in New England and Florida. They spent summers tending a fire tower atop New Hampshire's 3,156-foot Mount Cardigan. The April-to-October job required the family to carry everything they needed to a summit fire warden's cabin. Besides spotting fires, Smith earned the backcountry skills he'd bring to Grandfather by building and maintaining trails and shelters and making the beautiful routed trail signs that he'd become known for. In winter, the Smiths called South Florida home, working in art deco hotels and

restaurants. Smith's interest in Native American culture got him into trouble at The Breakers hotel in Palm Beach. A traveling Indian show was in the area, and the hotelman gave Blackfoot elders "rides on the elevator," says Sally Smith, Clyde's granddaughter. The hotel fired him on the spot. The aghast Blackfeet gifted the young man with an eagle feather war bonnet. For Mickey, this itinerant life meant leaving school in New England halfway through the fall semester to become "the new kid" in hot, urban South Florida. The following spring, it was the same midterm flight back north. The couple's 1930s diaries describe the appeal of a "gypsy" lifestyle some upscale Floridians enjoy today—going from popcorn clouds and sultry winter temperatures in Miami to cool summers in New England or the high mountains of the South. For years they yo-yoed back and forth, with Clyde selling signs in both locations and wherever he could in between. Their Southern Appalachian saga started in 1933. Passing through Canton on their way north, Hilda recorded they saw the smoking stacks of "the largest paper mill in US"—at that very moment processing wood from the slopes of Grandfather Mountain. They "went over a red mud road out in no man's land and almost got stuck," she wrote. Actually, they did get stuck. They spent their first winter in western North Carolina in the early 1940s and would do so for decades. By then Clyde Smith had become a Boone Trail–building Parkway ranger, but in May 1952 he found an occupational anchor that elevated their seasonal standard of living, a "full-time" summer job with New Hampshire state parks. Until he retired in 1975, Smith was a master sign maker at The Flume near Franconia. During winters in the High Country, he cleared trails on Grandfather while making signs for local clients as well as the Appalachian Mountain Club (AMC). "He'd make 150 of the AMC's beautiful little basswood signs, white, with green lettering, and bring them up north when he came back," recalls Robert Proudman, onetime AMC trail crew leader, now the Appalachian Trail Conservancy's director of conservation operations. Proudman "always wondered how he created the

With an ax handle protruding from his pack basket, Clyde Smith nails an arrow sign on a tree high on the Daniel Boone Scout Trail. Seventy years later, Smith's arrow is nearly gone and the post-logging sapling is a tree. Like a few of Smith's signs on the now-closed Arch Rock Trail, this sign is no longer seen. In 2015, the state park rerouted this steep, rocky section of trail that Dixie Chastain Lemons said "always made me feel like I was going to fall." Clyde and Hilda Smith Photo Collection; later photo by Randy Johnson.

distinctive scalloped edge on his signs." One day Smith demonstrated the way he deftly shaped the wood with a sharp little ax. His finesse "was amazing to behold," Proudman admits. The Smiths were poor, but their lifestyle gave them count-less days outdoors. They were among the first to cross-country ski the Blue Ridge Parkway. Hilda learned to downhill ski at North Carolina resorts in the 1960s, and Clyde made the stylized skier logo sign still visible at Appalachian Ski Mountain in Blowing Rock. "Dad," as Hilda called him, returned to Grandfather's trails long after his Scouts were grown and gone. He met Hugh Morton, who told associates about the "close cooperation being carried on between Ranger Smith of the Blue

Ridge Parkway and the Linville Company in the protection of Grandfather Mountain." His spec-tacular trail signs became landmarks on Grand-father's trails and would find their way into Mor-ton's new Swinging Bridge attraction after 1952.

America's premier path, the Appalachian Trail (AT), truly inspired Smith. He met Stan Murray, chairman of the Appalachian Trail Conference (now Conservancy), in 1966. Murray, who later founded the Southern Appalachian Highlands Conservancy, had suggested running the AT over the Roan Highlands in 1952, and Smith's offer to make signs for the Roan area was "an 'answer to a prayer,'" Murray wrote. Smith's signs eventually marked the AT from north to south. They included elaborate club logos for the AMC in New Hamp-shire and the Tennessee Eastman Hiking Club and Carolina Mountain Club in the South. His signs capped Mount Katahdin for decades, and many are still displayed as art. Throughout lives of com-pulsive hiking, Clyde and Hilda Smith were never

Clyde Smith's Appalachian Trail signs eventually reached the length of the trail. This one is near Mount Lafayette, above timberline on the Franconia Ridge, in his native White Mountains of New Hampshire. Smith made this later-in-life hiking trip with his son, photographer and builder of the Boone Trail Clyde H. Smith (by then no longer calling himself Mickey). Clyde and Hilda Smith Photo Collection. Photo by Clyde H. Smith.

without a tool to trim or mark a trail. They often organized volunteer "work trips" for trail clubs. At Grandfather, Clyde's "diplomatic contacts" always secured "toll free passage up the mountain," noted one Tennessee Eastman Hiking Club newsletter. Clyde set a good example. Onetime club chairman Powell Foster remembers him in the lead "clearing trail with this ax in his ham-like hands, then turning around to wait for us to catch up." Many recalled the time Clyde Smith fell. He took "a major fall from a ladder in the middle of a rocky cliff," recounts Foster. "Scared us all to death! He just retrieved his basket-type backpack, took the climb again, with absolutely no comment." Smith personified the New England trail man, back when trails were steep and hiking wasn't supposed to be easy. "Parts of his Falling Waters Trail in Franconia Notch are so steep we used to call it the Falling Peoples Trail," laughs Proudman. Smith was also a talented photographer; his finest images were hand-tinted black-and-white photos. Imagine the Smiths' pride when son Mickey became a successful outdoor photographer for magazines and books.

Clyde Smith kept Grandfather's trails marked into the 1960s, but maintains Winston Church, "He just kind'a slowed down and wasn't able to keep up with it." In truth, Grandfather was a commercial attraction that did little to maintain the mountain's trails and nothing to promote them, so Smith gave the AT more attention as he aged. Asheville newspaper columnist John Parris raved about Grandfather's "Trail of Thirteen Ladders" in the late 1950s, marveling that promoter Hugh Morton ignored the trails, "quite puzzling since the owner never misses a beat on tom-toms, golden harp or delicate lyre to keep the name of his mountain before the public." Parris realized "there's a heap of folks, able and willing" to hike "if they only knew." It would be years before Morton would be persuaded that the backcountry could attract a "heap of folks." He knew who was buttering his bread, and it wasn't the Clyde Smith demographic. At least not then. Hiking Baby Boomers would arrive, but first Grandfather's trails were destined to decline.

By the spring of 1976, Clyde Smith had health problems. Hilda recorded, "Dad to Dr. Cort. All good but heart beat." On April 1, 1976, Clyde, Hilda, and dentist friend Dr. Creston Barker were maintaining the AT near Big Bald, the highest peak between the Great Smoky Mountains and Roan High Knob, near today's Wolf Laurel resort. Hilda's diary emits a silent scream from the page. "*Dad died* on the AT!" Nancy Smith Whiton, the Smiths' daughter, was told "the dentist heard Dad stop chopping." Barker found him "lying on the ground with no heartbeat." Whiton recalls, "For an instant" Hilda hoped "it was just a very bad April Fool's joke." Creston went for help. Before aid arrived, snow was falling hard on Hilda and her dead husband. Clyde had refused a pacemaker for an irregular heartbeat, fearing "he would never be able to work in the woods again," recalls his daughter. "I'd say he died the way he wanted." Nearly 150 people attended the funeral near beautiful Shelburne Birches just outside Gorham. Bob Proudman was a pallbearer. It would take five years, but Tennessee Eastman Hiking Club chair

A 1950s version of Clyde's big Grandfather trailhead sign at the Swinging Bridge parking lot. To this day, a grandiose sign marks the spot. North Carolina Collection, University of North Carolina Library at Chapel Hill. Photo by Hugh Morton.

Ray Hunt prevailed in having a Roan-area AT shelter named after Clyde Smith. Hilda never saw it. After Stan Murray died, he too was honored with a namesake shelter on the Roan Highlands he helped save. Hilda moved to Franconia and died in 2009 after reaching the century mark and outliving son Mickey, who died in 2008. The seasonal mountain lifestyle had been hard on Clyde and Hilda, but the volumes she left behind reflect no regrets. At the end of so many days on the trail, year after year, she penned "a lovely day" in her diary. Clyde

and Hilda had a lifetime of "lovely days" to savor each other and the mountains, including Grandfather. Their days gave us trails that hikers still take today.

Clyde Smith had an impact. By 1954, Hugh Morton's mother, Agnes MacRae Morton, had helped found a just-for-fun fabrication called the Grandfather Mountain Walking Club, whimsical evidence that "Ms. M" had a deft feel for Linville's summer society. She saw outdoor adventure becoming a key part of life in the High Country. "The Purpose of this club," she wrote, "is to enjoy the healthful exercise of walking and mountain climbing." Membership was open to those who "enjoy walking the trails"; the initiation fee was simply "enthusiasm," and annual dues were "continued participation." Even as Smith's involvement waned, hikers were following his paths to the peaks and falling in love with Grandfather. Today, Agnes Morton's "club of mountain climbers" is big beyond her wildest imaginings, but before Grandfather's backcountry would come into its own, hiking and the Smiths' trails would fade from view. Easy automobile access and hordes of more sedentary visitors would come to define the mountain. Observation Point started that process, but Hugh Morton's Mile-High Swinging Bridge invited even more cars and crowds—and destructive development—higher on the mountain than ever before.

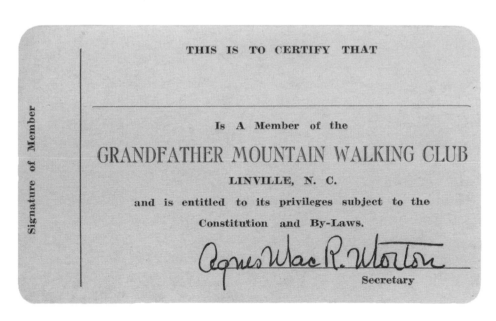

THIS IS TO CERTIFY THAT

Signature of Member

Is A Member of the

GRANDFATHER MOUNTAIN WALKING CLUB

LINVILLE, N. C.

and is entitled to its privileges subject to the Constitution and By-Laws.

Agnes Mac R. Morton

Secretary

Here's your membership card in the Grandfather Mountain Walking Club. It's already signed by Hugh Morton's mother, her name artfully abbreviated. All it needs is your name. Collection of George and Chessie MacRae.

AN ATTRACTION EMERGES

7 Carolina's Top Scenic Attraction

A new Top Shop presides over Carolina's Top Scenic Attraction. From the highest peaks of the mountain, the cities glowing on the left edge of the horizon lie nearly a vertical mile below. Photo by Skip Sickler/http://skipsickler.zenfolio.com.

Observation Point was a true tourist attraction, but 1952 saw it surpassed by a new idea from the mountain's new owner, Hugh Morton. "Carolina's Top Scenic Attraction" would emerge as a nationally known travel magnet. Between the spectacle of a Swinging Bridge, the comedy of cavorting bears, daredevil hang-gliding flights, the pageantry of a highland games, and more, it's almost as if only a photographer could have dreamed up the attraction Morton created. In fact, that's exactly how a tiny part of Grandfather Mountain became one of the most photographed places on the planet. Photography became the defining passion of Hugh Morton's life, but the story of how he came to own a mountain and devote his life to photographing it will forever link him to Grandfather.

From a Camp Yonahnoka encounter with a camera, Morton's pictures jumped into early 1940s University of North Carolina campus publications like the newspaper *Daily Tar Heel* and the year-book *Yackety-Yack*. "Enthusiasm for orchestras was probably one of the main reasons I aspired to be

Hugh Morton's World War II duty solidified his identity as a photographer. In the army's 161st Signal Photo Company, he was wounded with a camera in his hands and became a decorated veteran. North Carolina Collection, University of North Carolina Library at Chapel Hill. Photo by Hugh Morton.

a better photographer," he divulged in 1996. He shot all the major bands, including Cab Calloway's, Benny Goodman's, and Tommy Dorsey's. His best photos have the sharp immediacy of pop-culture figure Arthur Fellig, known as Weegee. Sports were a lifelong focus, from photos of Charlie "Choo Choo" Justice in the 1940s to shots from the football and basketball sidelines into the early 2000s. He never finished college, but he gave the university a lifetime of service and the institution's movers and shakers called him friend.

Morton volunteered for World War II in 1942, shooting mostly newsreel footage with the army's 161st Signal Photo Company on islands contested in the war's worst fighting. On New Caledonia, Morton traveled with USO stars Bob Hope, Jerry Colonna, and Frances Langford and received Christmas cards and visits from Hope later in life.

Combat photographers didn't film from the rear. One Philippine photo shows Douglas MacArthur with a general who was killed an hour later. "On the front line in Luzon, everyone else wore steel helmets," Morton recalled. MacArthur "stood there in his suntans and scrambled eggs hat. He set a wonderful example." As Morton filmed Philippine fighting, he walked into an improvised explosive device, his life likely saved by the camera he was holding. In a field hospital, he learned his father, Julian Morton, was dead. He went home with a purple heart and a bronze star. One weekend in Wilmington, sister Agnes brought a fellow student home from the Woman's College in Greensboro. The "bright, pretty, impressionable girl proved to be a sucker for a war hero in bandages," Charles Kuralt later remarked. Hugh married Julia Taylor on December 8, 1945.

Morton was president of the Linville Company by 1947, but the late 1940s were a busy time for his photography. Back from the war, Morton was fascinated with the elemental appeal of the mountains. Photos ranged from mountain characters to cockfights and idyllic scenes with Grandfather Mountain towering in the background. He freelanced for newspapers and magazines. Morton's photography reflects an almost Forrest Gump–like habit of turning up with major players of the twentieth century, often at events. General George C. Marshall attended Wilmington's 1949 Azalea Fest, which Morton helped start in 1948. Photographic access to famous people lasted throughout his life. Morton cultivated athletes, politicians, and celebrities, then coaxed them to Grandfather Mountain with his camera in hand.

Hugh Morton Steps It Up

Observation Point was pulling in tourists and Morton made improvements, but "the toll road just didn't make much money," Robert Hartley divulged. Morton needed a bigger idea, and Joe Hartley had it. "My daddy kept tellin' 'em, even Mr. Nelson MacRae, that if you'll put a road to the top of the mountain everyone will want to go up—it's the prettiest place in God's creation.'" Many pooh-

Joe Hartley "eyeballs" Convention Table Rock and the gap that the Swinging Bridge would soon span. He called the setting "the prettiest place in God's creation" and urged Hugh Morton to make it accessible by auto. North Carolina Collection, University of North Carolina Library at Chapel Hill. Photo by Hugh Morton.

poohed the idea. "They told my daddy, 'You can't build a road to the top of Grandfather Mountain! That can't be done,'" Hartley recalled. "I knowed you could build a road up there. Pop and I had eye-balled it." Nelson MacRae had been listening. As early as March 30, 1937, when Hugh Morton was a sixteen-year old boy, MacRae told Linville Company stockholders, "Further development [of Observation Point] should consist mainly in the extension of the road to the flat area just back of the first peak. A survey showing the feasibility has

been made." Hartley's story suggests it was Joe who urged the president higher and maybe made the survey. MacRae thought it would only cost $5,000 to reach "the most outstanding point of scenic interest in western North Carolina," but he didn't urge expansion then. Fifteen years later, Morton would extend the road and build a swinging bridge to boot.

The polio scare of the late 1940s had hit Linville hard, and according to Howard Covington Jr., Linville Resorts president Stuart Cramer was saying, "Linville is dying on the vine." Luckily, near-legendary general managers were set to start a new future. John Pottle arrived, perfecting the resort's accommodations operation as the postwar economy accelerated. John Blackburn followed in the 1980s and still refines Linville's national renown. Grandfather Mountain, too, was set to come into its own. After a long life and remarkable business success, Hugh MacRae died in 1951, and his estate was divided among family members. Part of the estate was "3,627 acres, including all three peaks of Grandfather Mountain," gained in a 1943 deal to "secure sundry cash loans" MacRae had made to the Linville Company. Hugh Morton is often said to "have inherited the mountain"; "you might say that," Hugh MacRae II specifies, "but it was a little more complicated." In the division of his estate, "the Morton group retained most of the Linville property and our family retained a lot of property down" in Wilmington. "There's no clear record," but "Hugh worked it out with other family members to either receive or buy the mountain." By the time Hugh MacRae died, some company stockholders had taken buyouts, and Hugh MacRae II relates, "the bankers in Wilmington were all advising not to be too concerned about the mountain property." On April 28, 1952, the Linville Company board met. President Hugh Morton reported he'd approached banks about a loan to "carry out maintenance and improvements" on the toll road, but none "appear interested in making the needed funds available." The board encouraged Morton to personally lend the company the money for "extension to the Grandfather Mountain Road" in return for a "deed of trust on the Grandfather Mountain property to secure same." A month later, Morton urged the company to dissolve itself, and by June the Linville Company was no more. Hugh Morton had a mountain and a toll road.

"So," Robert Hartley reminds, "Hugh says, 'What am I going to do with a rock pile? How am I going to pay taxes on it?'" Hugh Morton and his heirs would sweat paying property taxes on that "rock pile" for another sixty years. There was one bright spot, proclaims Hartley. "When Hugh Morton inherited Grandfather Mountain—he inherited my daddy. And my daddy started telling Hugh the same thing he'd been saying for 20 years, 'build a road up there.'" When Morton set out to extend the road to Linville Peak, wrote Harris Prevost, later Grandfather Mountain vice president, he "borrowed every cent he could." Robert Hartley remembered, "Wachovia was the only bank who would talk to him. People said building a road to Linville Peak couldn't be done, but Hugh Morton did it."

As Morton was building the Swinging Bridge, Robert Hartley moved "off the mountain," to Kingsport, Tennessee. "You see it a lot in these mountains," he says. "Sometimes you have to move away to come back." Robert's time would arrive. In the interim, brother Joe Lee Hartley had also moved, to Charlotte, but he was back. "One day," explained Robert, "Joe Lee and Hugh got to talking about extending the road. They walked up from Observation Point and were discussing what folks would do if they got up there. Joe Lee was a telling him that as boys we'd throw rocks across the gorge where the Swinging Bridge is now and we'd always say, 'Well if they'd build a bridge across here we wouldn't have to walk all the way around.' And Hugh said, 'Maybe we *could* build a bridge across there.'" Shaking his head and smiling, Hartley insists, "If you think something can't be done, well, tell Hugh Morton that. 'You can't do that,' some people said. You know the rest of the story." Years later, Joe Lee and Robert Hartley attended a press conference at Grandfather Golf and Country Club where "Hugh introduced us," Robert said to me

with pride. "If I am a success," Morton proclaimed, "I owe a lot of it to their daddy. He advised me what to do [build a road up the mountain]. I gambled and took the chance on his advice."

To get to "the top," the new road clung to the mountainside above Observation Point, climbing three final switchbacks to the crest, all of them dynamited into solid rock. Time has softened the destruction, but aerial photos at the time offer ample evidence why National Park Service officials long ridiculed Morton's road and doubted his proclaimed environmental sensitivity during the Blue Ridge Parkway debate. It appeared poorly planned, if not unplanned and executed on the fly, with grades gouged out and then abandoned. Robert Hartley thought the destruction might have been avoided had his dad's idea been better understood. Joe thought the road should have continued gradually past the first switchback, into the forest beyond, then turned back on a single, less visible turn to the crest. Flag-waving greeted defeat of the mountain's defenses. Once on top—perhaps chastened by the destruction or restrained by the pristine setting—Morton cleared a small parking lot in the flattest space beside Convention Table Rock. A small wooden structure became the first Top Shop. Picnic tables and grills flanked parking spots. To reach the Swinging Bridge, Jeff Hartley and Sons of Linville climbed the crag with a flight of stone steps. In 2003, Jeff Hartley's grandson, Clay Hartley, rebuilt them. Down below, a retaining wall of Grandfather stone turned the old Observation Point into Cliffside Overlook.

The Swinging Bridge anchors into rock, but it has tight ties to Greensboro. Designed by Charles C. Hartmann Jr., the $15,000 bridge was built by Truitt Manufacturing Company and assembled across the chasm by Craven Steel Erecting Company. The 228-foot span was dedicated by future North Carolina governor William B. Umstead on September 9, 1953. The most touching incident was when Hugh Morton squired his ninety-year-old grandmother across the bridge. Rena MacRae first climbed Linville Peak with her new husband, Hugh MacRae, in 1891. She fol-

This startling aerial view pairs the new summit parking lot and Swinging Bridge with Observation Point still operating far below. No visitor center or even shelter yet exists on the summit, but Clyde Smith's Grandfather Trail can be seen winding through the evergreens. North Carolina Collection, University of North Carolina Library at Chapel Hill. Photo by Hugh Morton.

lowed her grandson across, some say in tears, and said, "I thought I would never get up here again." The bridge inadvertently got its name from state tourism director Charles J. Parker. The previous evening, during dinner at Eseeola Lodge, he wondered, "Why not call it the Mile-High Swinging Bridge?" Morton and Charles Hartmann Jr. had agreed a swinging-style bridge would be more exciting and "give people something to talk about." Years later Morton concluded, "We made the right decision."

The Hartleys' Road

Robert Hartley's older brother Joe Lee Hartley managed the transition from Observation Point to the Swinging Bridge. Wind soon destroyed the new bridge, and tethers were added so the swinging

became swaying. New roads attracted more tourists. The Blue Ridge Parkway was completed north and south of the mountain. Highway 105 opened in 1956 linking Linville to Boone and Banner Elk. Just a few years before Hugh Morton passed away, he turned down a proposal to have the highway named after him, revealed Harris Prevost. Morton did not want to be linked with "shady politicians getting roads named after them," so there is no Hugh Morton Highway.

By 1960, Grandfather Mountain needed bigger summit facilities, and a massive Top Shop was built that dominated the skyline until 2008. The blocky, bulking, cinderblock-and-wood structure was also designed by Hartmann. Sheathed in Grandfather stone and rough-cut siding, it was dedicated in the spring of 1962. The bottom floor housed a gift

The new summit parking area eventually had a tiny "gift shop," grills, and picnic tables. North Carolina Collection, University of North Carolina Library at Chapel Hill. Photo by Hugh Morton.

shop and snack bar; the upper floor was a huge space called the Skyscraper Room. A three-story, window-flanked stairwell on the windward side exited atop Convention Table Rock, where a path led to the Swinging Bridge. Future employee Winston Church recalled he "first saw that big stone Top Shop looking down at it from MacRae Peak." Not long after, he stopped in to see if the mountain would sell his taxidermy, and Joe Lee offered him a job. Except for a stint in the army, he worked a forty-year span from 1962 to 2002. During those years, Prevost maintains, "Winston was one of Mr. Morton's most trusted advisors."

Church started on the maintenance crew, called the "road crew" because the mountain's unpaved road required virtually all the maintenance. In truth, it was a lot like working on a chain gang, minus chains and summer heat. "Every Friday," Church says, "a motor grader smoothed the washboards in the curves, added gravel, then we'd start at the top with garden rakes and walk it down—

two miles." Years of problems plagued the primitive road, challenged at one point by racing sports cars during a mid-1950s hill-climb event. Calcium chloride was spread to keep down dust, and it rusted out employees' cars. When the road got wet, the resulting Silly Putty surface stuck on cars like blobs of cement. When the droplets dried, they could pop paint off a vehicle. "People'd get that stuff on their cars and some of 'em would come back down wanting to fight you," Robert Hartley exclaimed. "You just couldn't maintain a crushed rock road [up the mountain] to save yore life." To Church's relief, he was drafted into gift shop sales in the fall of 1962.

By the mid-1960s, Robert was working at the post office in Kingsport and coming back to help with the Singing on the Mountain. "My brother Joe Lee was like Tom Sawyer," Robert asserts, always asking for weekend help. Robert "never thought of getting paid for it," he admits. "It was the family work." After Joe Hartley died at age ninety-five

Highland Games: A Bit of the Highlands in the High Country

The Grandfather Mountain Highland Games is more than a typical tourist event; it's an authentic expression of local culture. People the world over are moved by the stirring drone of the bagpipes, but something deeper happens when they wail in MacRae Meadows under Grandfather's peaks. It was that scene that brought Highland Scot Alexander MacRae and the sound of his pipes to the meadows in the 1880s. No wonder as the games end at dusk on Sunday some claim to see old Alick and hear his airs ebbing off over the valleys. The bite of Scotch and flickering torchlight may have something to do with that, but over four days of pageantry and parades the meadows serve up North America's most authentic Highland experience.

There's piping, individually and in moving massed bands. Friday evening's Celtic Jam complements daily Celtic Grove concerts in the woods. Dance competition offers stunning performance. Athletic contests include the Grandfather Mountain Marathon, one of the country's most demanding. Scotland's professional athletes have participated in a sheaf toss (kind of a hay-bale heft), the turning of the telephone-pole-like caber, and more. And there are sheepherding demonstrations, vendor tents, Scottish fare from meat pies to haggis, and fine Scotch whiskeys. A new feature called the Scottish Cultural Village offers expert lectures and demonstrations on aspects of traditional Highland life.

A Founder's Tale

It's all fueled by Americans' passion for Scotland and its culture. That's particularly true in North Carolina, where Scottish and Scotch-Irish ancestry is among the highest in the country. That, pronounces Games cofounder Donald MacDonald, has helped make "the Grandfather Games the largest, most successful highland games in Eastern America." The story of the Games starts in 1953. As a reporter for the *Charlotte News*, MacDonald covered a visit by Dame Flora MacLeod of Dunvegan Castle,

Scottish culture and moving massed bands emerge from the mists of time every year on MacRae Meadows, as stellar a spot as exists to stage a highland games. Photo by Helen Moss Davis/www.wildblueprints.com.

then Scotland's only female clan chief. She implored her audience to "come back and visit Scotland, your ancestral home," and the following August, MacDonald attended Scotland's premier highland games, the Braemar Gathering. That's where he heard the call. Visiting the Isle of Skye home of his clan chief, he was "commissioned to help raise Clan Donald in the US." Back home, the reporter staged events to help the cause and made sure they made the newspaper. With his "one major ambition, a highland games, still unfulfilled," MacDonald was contacted "by a down easter from Wilmington." Hugh Morton's mother, Agnes MacRae Morton, had read about his Clan Donald events. They met and agreed to collaborate on realizing Morton's "long-standing dream of rallying her clans-folk, the MacRaes" on MacRae Meadows, and MacDonald's goal of creating "America's Braemar."

The first Games attracted about 800 people in mid-August 1956. "Mostly it was like a picnic," recalled Hugh Morton. "Nobody knew what a highland games was." But Morton documented the rebirth of Highland culture below his mountain. "It was a great and a thrilling surprise to find how many Scots there are eager to attend a gathering," admitted Agnes Morton. The Games quickly became a major event. Partners emerged, including a cadre of locals such as longtime manager Frank Vance. Agnes MacRae Morton passed away in 1982, and in 1986, at the thirty-first Games, a memorial was dedicated to her. The Reverend Richard Gammon remembered her as the Games' "guiding light." The Agnes MacRae Morton award still honors special contributions to the event.

By the time the Games got going, MacDonald was immersed in reborn Scottish fervor. He'd seen a film called *Rob Roy, the Highland Rogue* and dismissed it as "a horse opera in kilts," but he was struck dumb by a duo of singing Scottish sisters. Marietta and Kitty MacLeod had set the Scottish music scene on fire singing in Gaelic. He found Scottish music recordings at the Charlotte Public Library and "Surprise, surprise!" raves MacDonald, "the Gaelic side contained songs by Marietta and Kitty MacLeod." MacDonald had launched his Games, and it was time to head back to Scotland. Staying with one of the Scots that the early Games were attracting, he went to a party, and there in the crowd MacDonald turned to meet the Gaelic songstresses. Long story short, MacDonald spent his visit with Marietta. She not only sang in Gaelic, but she was beautiful, with such perfect "gams that I started calling her 'Legs' MacLeod." Back in the States, MacDonald knew, "I would just have to see her again, and again and that perhaps she would marry me." In the summer of 1960, his Games' cofounder Agnes Morton arranged a very public, very Scottish wedding at the Wee Kirk Presbyterian Church in Linville. And that, MacDonald maintains, is how a founder of Grandfather's Games "met, wooed, and won the actress Marietta MacLeod." In 1962, that was enough to reverse his own family's immigration when he moved to Scotland with Marietta. He's lived there ever since. The print journalist for Edinburgh's *The Scotsman* and professor of journalism at Napier University has returned often for his Grandfather Games.

A Ritch Tradition
Harvey Ritch has an intriguing Highland Games story. In 1971, Ritch opened one of the country's first Scottish-themed specialty shops, Everything Scottish, Ltd., in Charlotte. A High Country tradition was born in 1973 when he moved to the mountains, enticed by an offer from Agnes MacRae Morton and her son Julian of a Scottish-style building for his shop at their Invershiel development. Much more than a purveyor of kilts, Ritch was a major force in the now widespread celebration of Scottish culture in the South and beyond. He taught and inspired more than a generation of bagpipers and personally helped start bagpipe bands. One of them, the local Grandfather Mountain Highlanders, is among the best in the world in its grade and the host band of the Grandfather Games. At age thirty-five, Ritch learned to play the pipes from Jack Smith and pipe major Sandy Jones, the latter president of the Games, whose North American Academy of Piping and Drumming in Valle Crucis has attracted students since 1971. "I don't know what sparked my interest in piping," Ritch explained. "I just loved pipe music and wanted to learn."

Ritch launched the Charlotte Scottish Pipe Band in 1971, which some "still say was the best band to come out of the South," says Sally Warburton, president, business manager, bass drum player, and original member of the Grandfather Mountain Highlanders. In 1974, Ritch added another "cofounder" credential to Agnes MacRae Morton's resume by founding the Grandfather Mountain Highlanders with her.

One day in 1985, a year after reintroducing peregrine falcons on Grandfather Mountain, Wildlife Resources Commission biologist Gordon Warburton walked into Everything Scottish. "I hadn't played the pipes in years, so I dropped in to pick up some reeds," he remembers. Thanks to Ritch, bagpipe reeds were a lot easier to find in Linville in 1985 than they were 100 years earlier when Hugh MacRae wanted them for Alick MacRae's pipes. Ritch immediately invited Warburton into the band, where he found his future wife, Sally, and spent ten years as the Highlanders' pipe major. "It's no exaggeration to call Harvey the forefather of piping in the South," Gordon says. "The bands you see today and the quality you hear can be traced back to him. He and the Grandfather Mountain Highland Games are the roots of that tree." The Highlanders boast a longtime lineup of topnotch pipers, among them Bert Mitchell, Scott McLeod, John Shell, and Ed Krintz. "Harvey was a curmudgeon," Sally Warburton claims, "a real piece of work! But he was the most generous, kind person I've ever met." Ritch's financial and moral support, even scholarship money, benefited students, pipe bands, and fledgling highland games as well. He led the entire region to greater appreciation of Scottish music and culture, and like Sally Warburton, received the Agnes MacRae Morton award for service to the Games.

There's no better example of the Games' local musical impact than Maura Shawn Scanlin. The Watauga native and member of the Celtic band called the Forget-Me-Nots picked up a violin instead of the pipes. She started competing at the Grandfather Games in Scottish fiddle, and after a 2008 qualifying event she became Junior U.S. National Scottish Fiddling Champion, then overall Open Champion in 2010 and 2012. Invited to Scotland in 2013 for the Glenfiddich Fiddle Competition, the most prestigious Scottish fiddle competition, Scanlin was crowned champion in Blair Castle. Her tartan kilt and sashes came from Ritch's shop.

As Ritch aged, he often had lunch with friend Hugh Morton at Mildred's Grill in the Grandfather Nature Museum. Everything Scottish closed for good in February 2014, and Ritch passed away in June. "The High Country's pipe major" and the Grandfather Games he embraced still inspire much of the music that echoes around Grandfather today. At the Games that July, as the Parade of Tartans began with a surge of pipes, the Grandfather Mountain Highlanders strode off over the ashes of the man who'd founded the band.

The Sound of Celtic Music

North America's premier Scottish festival has also had an undeniably global influence on Celtic music. Back in 1980, "Celtic music" wasn't even a term. The scene was set for the creation of *The Thistle and Shamrock*, Fiona Ritchie's radio program credited with inventing the modern Celtic craze. Amazingly, the idea for her show bloomed like the thistle in MacRae Meadows. Ritchie was an international student at the University of North Carolina-Charlotte in 1980 when someone asked, "Are you going to the highland games?" she recounts. "And I was like, 'Well! highland games . . . here?' And they said, 'Yes, huge! The biggest in the world.' And I thought, 'Well, I suppose I should go then.'" She put on cutoff denim shorts and a white T-shirt, and she admits, "I was walking around looking like an American, while all of the Americans were looking quite authentically like Scots. I was flabbergasted!"

Then, Ritchie confesses, "I had a powerful experience that changed my future." Sitting in the shade, "I saw a man and wife and maybe four children. And they looked poor, actually. They had a little, beaten-up tape recorder, and quite reverentially, their father was reaching up with this little microphone, attempting to record the sound of all these pipe bands. I can't describe how moved I was," Ritchie remembers. "They thought this was connecting them to their roots. That really got me thinking. I never

in 1966, Grandfather Golf and Country Club got under way, and Joe Lee Hartley was asked to join the country club team. "At first I said I didn't know who could take Joe Lee's place," Robert remembers, but a nice letter from Morton persuaded him to try. Morton told Hartley he had a "love of the mountain comparable to our own." Hartley took the job. When Joe Lee Hartley died at age ninety, Morton called him "one of the most honorable and talented people I have ever known."

The road wasn't the only continuing problem. Getting water to the Top Shop was a nightmare. Despite nearly 60 inches of annual rainfall, the Top Shop sat on solid rock. A 300-foot well was sunk with little luck. "Somebody said 'drop dynamite in there,'" Robert remembers. They did, and "water came squirting out" like Old Faithful, for a while. Then it stopped, again. "I don't know where the idea come from, but Hugh got the elevations of the building and Shanty Spring and said 'we should run a waterline through there.' Of course, they said, 'You can't do that!'" The spring was indeed higher than the Top Shop. After a helicopter dropped 8,000 feet of black, PVC plastic pipe, the water flowed, for a while. Then a decade of hassle started. Parts of the pipe were stolen; then bears got into the act. Endlessly fascinated by the sound of water running through the pipe, the bears were always biting it in two. "You got in on the tail end of that," Robert reminded me. When the trail program started in 1978, hikers filled their canteens where water gushed from an "open black pipe" at Shanty Spring. Nearby, the "closed black pipe" led off into the woods bound for the Swinging Bridge. If I didn't make sure water was gushing from the "open black pipe," hikers often further hobbled the flow. Some then disturbed the "closed black pipe" in direct opposition to a sign that read, "Do not disturb closed black pipe." I came to dread the mere existence of the ugly contraption. The maintenance crew hated it more. Under foreman John Church—not related to Winston—the crew spent days bushwhacking out to fix the pipe, and "the bears would eat into it before we could get back to the Top Shop," laments Church. Finally, a well was drilled at Black Rock parking lot that largely eliminated Hartley's headache of "coming in every morning and not knowing whether the restrooms at the top of the mountain would work."

Robert blacktopped the road in 1971 and widened the curves for busses—moves applauded by anyone who'd ever raked gravel. Twenty years after grading the first small summit lot, Morton expanded it, blasting encroaching rock and chopping down the virgin, tree-line-like forest on the west side of the gap. Brown Brothers of Boone handled the excavation. One day, Winston Church was outside the Top Shop checking traffic near the blast zone when a charge went off. "Just as I got in the back door," he remembers, "a rock as big as a basketball came crashing through the roof and landed ten feet from me." The Top Shop was always in the line of fire—from the elements. It was cold and uncomfortable, even in summer. When winter operations started, propane and kerosene spot heaters reduced the chill, but foul fumes radiated

Thousands of feet of PVC pipe, the notorious "closed black pipe" at Shanty Spring, were airlifted to funnel water from the spring to the Swinging Bridge facilities. The pilot prepares to take off from a gravel parking lot at the top of a then gravel road. North Carolina Collection, University of North Carolina Library at Chapel Hill. Photo by Hugh Morton.

The Top Shop wasn't even a year old when its roof started blowing off. The building would continually be challenged and eventually defeated by the wind. North Carolina Collection, University of North Carolina Library at Chapel Hill. Photo by Hugh Morton.

better than the heat. Worse yet, the big, uppermost floor defied the wind instead of shedding it. Howling overhead, wind literally "raised the wooden roof and you could see outside," Church attests. When it dropped, "it sounded like a shotgun going off." Roof repairs went on for years, even after concrete replaced wood. The dismal, drafty, and damp Skyscraper Room was often closed and became obsolete when a new Nature Museum opened in 1990.

Here Come the Animals

Robert Hartley's most memorable years at Grandfather were "when we got into the bear business." Unbeknownst to mountain managers, a lasting new element of the Grandfather attraction was about to be born—by accident. Wildlife interests wanted to restore the wild bear population, and "Mr. Morton wanted to help," Church remembered. Winston went to the Grant Park Zoo in Atlanta (later Zoo Atlanta) and brought back two bears for release. Church noticed something was amiss, or more accurately, a mister. "I thought we had two males, and sure enough, that's what they gave me." Church went back for a female, but unknown to him, the new bear had almost been a pet, likely raised in the zoo's office. At the mountain, the bears got a ceremonial send-off filmed for the Arthur Smith Show in Charlotte. With Arthur's brother Ralph singing "The Preacher and the Bear," the bears were freed, but only the male fled. The female started checking out the cameras. Ralph grabbed a broom, recalls Church, "shooing her away with, 'Get outta here, Mildred.'" Church still wonders "where that came from, but the name stuck." The saga of Mildred the Bear, Catherine Morton once quipped, is "a story about a bear that refused to go over the mountain." Mildred had to be watched, and one day when Church was following her, she ambled out of the bushes at the Let-It-Rain Picnic Shelter. "Boy, you talk about screaming and getting back in cars. Mildred had her a big old lunch." Mildred had become the mountain's mascot, but soon Morton got a call from wildlife officials: Mildred needed a home or they'd put her down. She got a 15-by-30-foot cage. Eyeing the caged bear, Church speculated, "Looks like we'll have a zoo." Little did he and Hartley know. By the time the animal trend ran its course, Grandfather would house and display bears and their cubs, deer, cougars, eagles, and otters and become an official wildlife viewing site designated by the North Carolina Wildlife Resources Commission.

"My Dad was a showman," admits Catherine Morton, "so it did not take long before he began bringing Mildred out to let the tourists take photographs. After the first summer he built an amphitheater." At 10:00 A.M., 1:00, 3:00, and 4:30 P.M., with help from honey and grape crush sodas, Mildred was led out to entertain guests. Morton arranged for Mildred to mate with a cub from the TV show Gentle Ben, and Catherine judged a contest to name the cubs. She was terrified when her Dad made her pose with the cuddly babies, but Morton insisted she was safe. "Sit still and smile," he demanded. "This picture is going to pay for your college education." Mildred and Catherine became fast friends, the cubs became Mini and Maxi, and "I got that college education," she remembered. In the early 1970s, planning was under way for the North Carolina Zoo, and Morton helped raise money, as he'd do for causes throughout his life (including acquiring the USS North Carolina for Wilmington in 1962). Morton toured the state with a cub in support of the zoo's $2-million bond issue. Another contest gave the cub "the appropriate name of Hobo," according to Harris Prevost, and the bond passed. When Morton met the people planning the first "natural habitat"–style zoological park in the country "he invited them up to talk about building something," explained Hartley. The experts thought Grandfather was perfect for an exhibit and designed what in 1973 became Mildred the Bear Environmental Habitat. Prevost maintains Morton was motivated by "how much better that kind of life would be for his beloved Mildred." Mildred, Maxi, and Mini would become celebrities, starting with Morton's telling their story in a cute 1970s children's book Mildred the Bear. Writing in Mildred's voice, Morton asserted she was happy

wildlife officials had turned her over to "friendly folks who seemed to know how a bear likes to be treated." It was quickly discovered that the new habitat had plenty of places for bears to hide from people, and that led to years of unhealthy, controversial food bribes from attendants. Daughter Catherine admits she was among the first to "sit next to the habitat with a bucket full of Tootsie Rolls and coax the bears into public view." The public got involved, too. The earliest addition to the habitats was a Bear Hut, where for twenty-seven years Martha Oberhelman, "the bear lady," sold mini-marshmallows and peanuts so customers could feed the animals. Guests ultimately wrinkled their noses at obese bears catching treats tossed by tourists. It was undignified and unhealthy. In June 2010, the mountain closed the hut. People started tossing healthy "'omnivore bear feed,'" says Harris Prevost. Today's animals "live 'au naturel,' with no public feeding," though habitat staff conduct "several enrichments a day to coax the bears up for guests." Cougars even get "boxed" meals that emulate interaction with prey.

Morton often drafted employees for photography duties, especially when the animals were involved. According to Church, "You could get asked to do almost anything when Mr. Morton would get some of his famous visitors and want to take their picture with Mildred." The list of famed folks memorialized with habitat habitués is too long to enumerate. Politicians, media stars, athletes, and friends all had pictures taken with Mildred or other animals, and the staff had to regulate barely controllable behavior. Church came out on the losing end trying to manage Hobo. "He was a good bear but he wouldn't cooperate," states Church. Robert Hartley and Morton had a rope around Hobo's neck, and Church, thinking he was choking, lifted the rope over a branch. "I got too close," Church admits. "He grabbed my leg and sunk his teeth together." Church felt "blood running into my shoe. He missed the bone, but I still have scars." He didn't blame Hobo. "After that, whenever I'd go in the habitat with him he'd stand up, open his mouth, and I'd grab his teeth to

Mildred the Bear posed to popularize her twice-daily shows. Cameras were always clicking at the amphitheater where she and the cubs performed, separated from the crowd by nothing more than thin air. North Carolina Collection, University of North Carolina Library at Chapel Hill. Photo by Hugh Morton.

Catherine Morton tries to keep a stiff upper lip as her dad takes a picture to publicize a contest that eventually named Mildred's cubs Mini and Maxi. North Carolina Collection, University of North Carolina Library at Chapel Hill. Photo by Hugh Morton.

play with him." Church knew a bear who repeatedly apologized for biting him. Pam Scarborough became both the attraction's first naturalist and female habitat employee in 1986. She had her own painful run-in shooting Morton's famous photo of a fawn in misty woods. "We came down the road in Mr. Morton's car with the fawn struggling on my lap," she reflects. "It jerked suddenly and almost broke my nose." Morton chose the resulting image as one of the seventy-five favorite photos of his life in 1996. "We all did frankly ill-advised things for years," concludes Scarborough. A deer habitat debuted in 1979, and maintenance crewman John Church later "got cut from belly button to sternum by a deer's antler." One of Morton's most iconic animal images shows a bear perched on a rock high above the valley. That crag, named Hartley View Rock after Joe Hartley, was once accessible to the public by ladders, a long tradition of catwalk views at attractions. The view had closed, but Morton drizzled a ladder with the universal currency of bruin bribery, honey, and Hobo climbed up. After the photo shoot, the bear wouldn't climb down. A three-day frog march ensued. Employees eventually rigged a harness, lured Hobo to the edge with golden goo, and pushed him off. Gently lowered to the ground, "Hobo walked off like nothing happened," maintains Church.

"Bears started it," admits Robert Hartley, "but I'll never forget the day Winston Church called and said 'there's a man up here with a panther!'" Like Grandfather's bears, cougars also happened by accident. Lenoir resident Silvio Martinat contacted Morton when neighbors forced him to give up his two declawed pet cougars, Rajah, a male western cougar, and Terra, a female eastern cougar, one of the most endangered of mammals. Around 1981, Mildred and her cubs got separate enclosures, and space opened for cougars. The big cats are the only animals to ever attack a guest at Grandfather. A twenty-six-year-old woman from Charlotte sustained punctures and a 6-inch scalp wound on April 10, 1983, when a cougar climbed a 14-foot rock wall into a viewing area. Employee Allen Tennant was bitten as he fought off the animal and "threw it back into the enclosure," a newspaper reported. That cat, too, came from Martinat after it mauled a 9-year-old girl two months before. Fault fell on the habitat wall, and it was reconfigured. But the mountain briefly lost its insurance and "ended up having to get insurance in the Bahamas or somewhere," reflected Prevost.

Grandfather needed a final resting place for its habitat family, and Morton chose a quiet setting near the picnic area. In June 1989 at age seventeen, Hobo became the first occupant. The end of an era came when Mildred the Bear died on New Year's Day 1993. "Her passing was a front-page story in many North Carolina newspapers," noted Harris Prevost. Mildred's daughters are there, her oldest cub, Maxi, "humanely put to sleep" at thirty-four in 2004, Prevost wrote to employees. Rajah is there, too. In 2013 the staff found a dead wild bear beside the summit road, shot by a hunter, apparently fleeing to the presence of the mountain's other bears. It too resides in Grandfather's quietest habitat. The soil on the grave of "Unknown Bear, 2013" has been repeatedly disturbed. The staff believes the bear's mate is responsible.

Morton's grandson, Hugh MacRae "Crae" Morton III, who would guide the mountain to permanent protection in 2008, urges that people view "Grandfather's habitats in terms of the values of that time period. Back then, if someone saw a bear in the mountains—very likely it was in a cage beside a gas station with kids poking sticks at it," he explains. He grants his grandfather "took it too far at times. It's hard to imagine he let people have their pictures taken with bears! But that was a different era. I'm proud of what he did." The habitats became a popular mainstay of the mountain. Splashing otters leaped onto "You Otter Be Here" ads in 1997 that won a regional advertising award. The eagle habitat got its start with golden and bald eagles that couldn't fly, but in 2012, a mesh aviary was added to display flight-capable birds that can't fend for themselves in the wild. Over the years, the urging and insistence of habitat staff lessened the number of unsafe or unsavory animal practices. Early habitat manager/biologist Steve Miller helped reduce the bears' intake of peanuts. Eddie Clark took over in 1986 "and really made the habitats shine," asserts Scarborough. In 2013, Grandfather's habitats celebrated forty years confident they equal the best animal exhibits anywhere in the private sector. The best way to appreciate that is to participate in the Grandfather Mountain Stewardship Foundation's habitat interpretive efforts, including "Behind the Scenes" tours and "Keeper for a Day" programs that visit sites like the "Bear Motel," where Grandfather's bruins slumber four months of the year.

Grandfather Mountain: Hotbed of Hang Gliding

Hugh Morton called John Harris "our Lindbergh at Grandfather." When Harris and friend John Sears became the first to hang glide off Cliffside Overlook, they launched a romantic era of kite-borne aviation. For years, daring young men and eventually women would be snatched off Grandfather's cliffs by violent, vertical elevator shafts of air and disappear with a gasp from spectators. Some circled thousands of feet overhead; others ran ridges far from launch. They flirted with fame and courted catastrophe. "Soon, pilots from all over the country were experiencing a magical place," recalls Jeff Burnett, an early flyer from New Hampshire. "Hugh Morton realized this new sport could add a popular new element to Grandfather's attractions." The hang-gliding program may be the quintessential example of Morton's promotional genius. In the spring of 1975 he hired an elite crew of pilots to entertain tourists, and Burnett would be one of them. The mere existence of a demonstration team set them apart in the sport.

Two launch sites faced opposing winds. One was across the Swinging Bridge, looking east; the other, a 500-foot cliff called Spectacular View, aimed west. "We'd make an announcement in the gift shop," remembers Winston Church. "May I have your attention," he'd say into the microphone, "a man is going to jump off a cliff in a few minutes. If you'd like to watch . . . ." People dropped would-be purchases and scurried to the launch sites. Morton would be one of them. He leaped into hang gliding without ever flying, so in 1979, at age fifty-seven, he flew tandem off Spectacular View with Burke Ewing.

The First Flyers
"People moved to Boone from all over just to fly Grandfather and get paid for it," maintains Bubba Goodman, former reserve pilot and organizer of the summer gliding competition near Boone called the Tater Hill Open. The first team included "Lucky Pierre" De Lespinois, Steve Coan, Doug Heath, John Sears, Chris Langton, Chris Huffines, and John Harris. "Later Stew

With a bird's-eye view of Grandfather behind him, John McNeely and his hawk flew into an award-winning Hugh Morton film that inspired anyone who's ever wondered what it feels like to fly with the birds. North Carolina Collection, University of North Carolina Library at Chapel Hill. Photo by Hugh Morton.

Smith, Joe Foster and Scott Buchanan joined the flock," details Burnett. "Those guys were the best of the best," pronounces Goodman. The expert gliders earned the lofty salary of $25 a day even when they weren't flying, which was pretty often on "Grandfogger Mountain." When grounded, they retreated to a secret room in the Top Shop called "the Cave." Even the elite made mistakes. "There was always something happening," Church recalls. One day, an employee "came running into the gift shop with her eyes real big, yelling that Pierre tumbled down the cliff." Church grabbed a radio and ran. There was Pierre hung in a tree, 3 feet from the ground. "The tree caught him on his last tumble," Church marveled. Hiking ahead to tell people Pierre was OK, Church came out of the woods carrying his harness and helmet "and all these pale people had horrified looks on their faces. They thought he was dead!" Paul Harvey carried the radio story, creating priceless publicity. Harvey "told about how they hang glide at Grandfather," Church explains, "how they check their harness, they check their buckles, they check everything before they take off—but this one time, Pierre forgot to tie his shoe." Later, Pierre's glider was tugged back up the cliff by rope, but bad weather left it hanging on the face. "I guess they weren't thinking," assumes Church. The phone rang off the hook. Everybody driving by on NC 105 thought a pilot was trapped on the cliff. As Paul Harvey might say, that was "the rest of the story" of why De Lespinois was "Lucky Pierre." Morton aimed his media savvy at the daring dudes. Images went out with news releases or on the wire. Morton photographed and filmed team pilot and falconer John McNeely actually flying beside his red-tailed hawk. Morton, whose movie camera helped him win a Bronze Star in World War II, won eight CINE Golden Eagle Awards, two for hang-gliding films, including *The Hawk and John McNeely*. Other CINE honorees include Ken Burns, Steven Spielberg, Ron Howard, and Spike Lee.

Just Like a Raven

The first season, pilots who remained aloft for at least an hour flying with the "locals"—the mountain's ravens—earned the Order of the Raven. In 1976, team member Scott "Buckeye" Buchanan flew three and a half hours one day and then doubled that the next. Buchanan was "known as Dangerman," Burnett remembers, "famous for his quote 'danger is my business and I'm late for work.'" Grandfather team flyer Robert Crowell set the duration record at the mountain of eight hours and five minutes. The Order of the Eagle was instituted in 1985 to honor flyers who flew cross country for a distance of more than 20 miles. Joe Foster and Stew Smith were the first two Eagles. Competition started in June 1975 with the Grandfather Mountain Hang Gliding Championships. The 1975 U.S. Nationals were also held at Grandfather,

"the first time an East Coast mountain was chosen for a National meet," reports Burnett. In attendance was Francis Rogallo, NASA engineer and "father of hang gliding" who'd invented the flexible wing. Then the Masters of Hang Gliding Championship was patterned by Morton after the golf tournament. Prize money was attractive. "Five grand was big bucks in those days," Burnett assures.

Last Flight

Stew Smith became the leader of the Grandfather Mountain Flyers. He was "a natural pilot with a strong competitive spirit," Burnett remembers. Smith was a

The hang gliders often saved their most daring flying for buzzing hikers challenging the mountain's highest peaks. Many a startled trail explorer looked up from having lunch on a rock outcropping to see a glider appear yards away with a sudden whoosh and the flutter of fabric. Photo by Randy Johnson.

former gymnast, a frequent finalist in the Masters, and a top performer at world meets. He won the Rogallo award as top individual at the American Cup meet in England in 1982 and was crowned the U.S. National Champion in 1984. Smith had married Robert Hartley's niece Kathy, and during the winter, he was a professional ski instructor at Sugar Mountain ski resort. In May 1985, Smith nearly doubled Foster's distance record by ending up 113 miles from Grandfather at Virginia Polytechnic Institute in Blacksburg. That record still stands today.

Stew Smith died in the first round of the 1986 Masters trying to land at MacRae Meadows. It was a major tragedy for the mountain, the High Country, and hang gliding. "Stew always said the Meadows landing field would get him one day," Burnett confesses. That was the last Masters, and the exhibition flights ended the following year. "Changes in kite design over the years made it more difficult for spectators to enjoy the sport," Hugh Morton's daughter Catherine explained. Gliders flew far above the mountain or long distances from it, "decreasing the appeal for onlookers." Harris Prevost urged Morton to end the program, citing surveys showing the flights only drew a small percentage of visitors. There were other drawbacks. Customers were angry when bad weather prohibited safe flying, and they clogged the summit parking area when the flying was good. But the best reason was Stew Smith. "Stew's death crushed Mr. Morton," Prevost reveals. "That was it."

Today, says Bubba Goodman, relatively few of the early hang gliders remain in the Boone area, which is why he started the Tater Hill Open. "I just don't want the 'good old days' to go away." Still, it's hard to forget the glory days at Grandfather. "For the few pilots who had the opportunity to fly daily at such a magnificent site—and get paid for it—the memories remain powerful," Jeff Burnett reminisces. In 2001, a group from "back in the day" got together at Grandfather, and "some of the 'old timers' flew off the mountain one last time," recalled Prevost. Hang gliding has ebbed as the newer, parachute-like sport of paragliding has soared—also attributed to Rogallo. "Paragliding is easier to learn than hang gliding," maintains Goodman. "You run down a meadow to launch instead of jumping off a cliff." The opposite of all that is why for a time, Grandfather Mountain was one of the most terrifying and transcendent places to take your chances with the wind.

Details: The Tater Hill Open Paragliding and Hang Gliding Competition is held in August. For information on the Tater Hill Open, visit: www.flytaterhill.com/Home .html.

Mr. Morton's Museum

Grandfather Mountain's Nature Museum really started the mountain's educational activities and filled a glaring gap in facilities. Until 1990 when the museum was built under then-president Hugh Morton Jr., the habitats didn't even have restrooms. A museum beside the habitats meshed indoor exhibits and multimedia programs with seeing animals outdoors, turning a "stop along the way" into a destination, a single facility that included shopping, education, and food with the 140-seat Mildred's Grill. Thanks to onetime manager Reeca Vance, the restaurant is still known for tasty dishes like the homemade vegetable soup Hugh Morton heartily recommended and relished almost daily. Nevertheless, the Grandburger is still the number one food visitors gobble down. On rainy days, or when the upper summit road was closed by high winds or snow, the museum not only permitted the attraction to open; it made a visit worth the price of admission. The museum is also where busses park, and smaller shuttles ferry guests higher. The Nature Museum quite literally reinvented the mountain by aspiring to unprecedented professionalism. "You didn't get to make flowers for that museum unless you'd made them for the American Museum of Natural History in New York," maintained Mike Leonard, attorney and preservationist, later board member of the Grandfather Mountain Stewardship Foundation. "That's just the way Hugh Morton was." The museum's overall designer was Dr. Rolland Hower, the Smithsonian's director of Natural History Exhibits and Research. Each exhibit has its expert, states Prevost. Paul Marchand, "the world's leading creator of artificial wildflowers," made flowers, berries, and mushrooms. Bill Chrisman of Rocky Mount, North Carolina, produced lifelike bird carvings. Professor Jack Hanahan curated geological exhibits, including a 165-pound, Morton-owned amethyst, "the finest amethyst ever discovered in North America," Prevost asserts. John White, "the top minerals man from The Smithsonian," Prevost continues, saw that Grandfather has "the finest collection of all-North Carolina gems and minerals in existence," including "the largest gold nugget on public display in North Carolina." The sculptor who crafted an Indian statue also created "the bust of Will Rogers in the Capitol Rotunda." Wildlife artist Richard Evans Younger depicted Daniel Boone making his

famous tree carving. In 1997, Morton partner John Williams surprised Morton with a massive bowl hollowed out of a 3,200-pound black birch burl found on Grandfather. For Johnpaul Harris's statue of Mildred, the sculptor actually measured the bear and her cubs. So many people touch the statue, its paws are brightly polished brass. In 2002, this popular place to pose for pictures received a new backdrop, an artificial boulder by Dwight Holland, the "Renaissance man," one newspaper called him, who created the artificial rock walls at the North Carolina Zoo (and Grandfather's habitats). The boulder "makes a much better background than bathroom doors," Morton remarked. This mountain attraction designed by a photographer also has spotlights in the ceiling to better illuminate Mildred for picture-takers. Ask someone in the gift shop to turn them on. Perfect shot, every time.

By the late 1970s, Grandfather and this billboard offered a bullish juxtaposition of attractions designed to entice people through the gate. In 1998, the mountain's reusable billboards started to be printed front and back, making the old-time marketing medium more environmentally friendly than when paper would shred off in windy weather and litter the High Country landscape. Photo by Randy Johnson.

Basking in His Presence

High Country dwellings have evolved from the almost hidden houses of early settlers to homes that satisfy their owners' fascination with "a Grandfather view." There's an instant up-charge if you want to bask in the sight of a profile that symbolizes the entire area. An ancient audience of only trees has been replaced with the homes of Grandfather's human devotees that spread like spectating sports fans across ridgetop bleachers. There were early idolaters, among them late-nineteenth-century artist Elliot Daingerfield (1859–1906), whose 1900s Greek Revival mansion still overlooks Grandfather sunsets that are "always glowing, never glaring," he wrote. Westglow Spa and Resort still bathes in that westering glow. Hound Ears Club started basking in 1964, then came ski and country club communities: Seven Devils in 1966, Beech Mountain in 1967, and Sugar Mountain in 1969. Morton family developments came along, too. All upped the value of a Grandfather view.

Linville Ridge launched in 1982, where Hugh Morton's camera captured Grandfather from the East's highest golf course.

By early 1983, Morton was focusing on something he didn't like: construction of an infamous monstrosity of a condominium atop neighboring Little Sugar Mountain. Ironically once part of MacRae family lands, the tract had become Sugar Mountain Resort when George and "Chessie" Randolph MacRae sold it. In late 1982, US Capital Corporation, based in Columbia, South Carolina, started flattening the entire summit to build a five-story condo that morphed into a ten-story urban edifice as demand increased. The eyesore made national news; outrage ensued and persists. Hugh Morton, understandably sensitive about the building's negative impact on scenic views from Grandfather, called it a blight on the landscape. Along with allies in Western North Carolina Tomorrow, an organization that the *Carolina Public Press* called a semi-public leadership

Foscoe's Echota development is one of many High Country second-home condo complexes with a great view of the Grandfather. Photo by Todd Bush/www.bushphoto.com.

council, Morton set out to draw the line on similar developments. The political movement that he helped orchestrate, the most noteworthy legislative effort of his environmental career, took only six months to achieve passage of the Mountain Ridge Protection Act of 1983. By January 1, 1984, similar mountaintop developments were illegal.

The effort was sparked, says Morton's wife, Julia, when longtime Sugar Mountain resident Al Traver told Morton "the magic words, 'What you people need is a ridge law.'" Among key supporters, Morton was joined by Liston Ramsey, speaker of the North Carolina House, who Julia Morton says orchestrated "the crafty crafting of the successful bill" that "passed with a huge majority because it allowed any county which was included to 'opt out' through a public referendum." Despite mountain residents' antipathy to being told what they can do with their own land, antidevelopment sentiment prevailed, yielding one of North Carolina's most significant conservation statutes. Julia Morton said the episode illustrated that "there is no end to what you can get done if you don't care who gets the credit."

In the late 1980s, when the U.S. Forest Service actually shaved clear-cuts below the brand new Linn Cove Viaduct, Hugh Morton was again shocked, as was Blue Ridge Parkway superintendent Gary Everhardt. Clear-cutting became a national controversy, and eventually many governmental and tourism organizations in the High Country went on record decrying the logging. Morton encouraged my own series of articles about the debate that earned the *Mountain Times* first-place North Carolina Press Association awards in community service and investigative reporting. The sanctity of the view from Grandfather Mountain had helped fuel a national protest that reined in clear-cutting across the country.

Thirty-plus years after the ridge law, more and more developments cluster around Grandfather, some likely a loophole's foot or two shorter than the law would allow. In 2014, there was widespread dismay when one of the most colorful knobs above Foscoe was stripped of trees. When a house was plopped atop it, a peak just below Grandfather's face looked more like a pimple. Elsewhere, a two-story window in an affluent former Appalachian State University geology student's mansion earned the nickname "The Grandfather Mountain Window."

To all those people basking in the view or about to build a house or development that does, keep in mind that our venerable old man deserves some respect. He and thousands of his visitors are looking back at you.

Bumperstickers had been part of the Grandfather experience since Tate Davis's single-armed efforts at Observation Point. Times had changed by 1990. "I got along very good with Mr. Morton," maintains Winston Church, "but one of the problems we did have was bumper strips." Church "told him all the time, 'bumper strips are a thing of the past.' But in the '70s and '80s, he'd come up the mountain and say, 'Winston, I saw 15 cars leaving the entrance that didn't have bumper strips. You better get somebody out there.'" What Morton meant was, get a modern-day Tate Davis out in the parking lot. "I'd say, 'Mr. Morton, those 15 people didn't want them.' We had people coming in and hollering at us." Church eventually won. "We started getting cars with painted bumpers, and when people came in red in the face, showing their car's paint stuck on the stickers—and demanding payment—Mr. Morton thought 'maybe it is time we stopped.'" A lot of input goes into Grandfather Mountain, and policy changes have come from the public and employees. One visitor suggested that people arriving just before closing get in free the next day. Great idea. Another asked that the mountain drop selling "switchblade" combs and prohibit smoking at the habitats. Both changes made. To get ahead of the customer service curve, Grandfather's employee hospitality training has come from authorities like the Disney Institute, but the mountain has its own traditions. Bill Alexander (1927–2004) worked at Grandfather from 1951 to 2003, and "he loved working on the mountain and

The bumpersticker battle in the early 1970s. Lawyer and politician Rufus Edmisten watches as Hart Hodges, grandson of Governor Luther Hodges, places bumperstickers in the parking lot. Hodges was one of many summer hires whom Winston Church would urge into the parking lot when Hugh Morton was unhappy with the stickerless cars leaving the gate. Boone native Edmisten's career ranged from working with Senator Sam Ervin during the Watergate scandal to running for governor and serving in several state offices. North Carolina Collection, University of North Carolina Library at Chapel Hill. Photo by Hugh Morton.

it showed," wrote Harris Prevost. The mountain's annual customer service award honors Alexander.

People Passing Away

In 1996, tragedy came to the Morton family with the suicide death of forty-eight-year-old Hugh Morton Jr. from an overdose of prescription medications in a Wilmington motel. "He was a good man," Hugh Morton emphasized, "and I'm just sorry he was so mixed up in his frame of mind that he did what he did. But he did a lot of really good things in his lifetime." Hugh Morton Jr. was North Carolina's director of travel and tourism from 1987 to 1989. On July 4, 1997, Hugh Morton's close friend Charles Kuralt died of complications from lupus. When Kuralt retired after twenty-five years "On the Road" and anchoring CBS Sunday Morning, the three-time Peabody Award–winner revisited his favorite people and places for his book *Charles Kuralt's America*. Grandfather Mountain was one of Kuralt's favorite places, and Hugh Morton was

one of his favorite people. Morton's old friend stayed at rustic Anvil Rock cottage, hidden just off the attraction road near MacRae Meadows.

Millions of people traversed the Swinging Bridge between 1952 and 1997, but there's no telling why two visitors suddenly fell to their deaths within fourteen months. Both tragedies happened within 50 feet of each other on Linville Peak just beyond the Swinging Bridge. Somehow, two women "lost their balance" and died. The first fatality *ever* at the attraction happened on Saturday afternoon, June 14, 1997. Thirty-four-year old Anita Harmon of Lenoir stood up from a ledge and fell 200 feet down the face. She died a few minutes after her husband and Grandfather rescue workers reached her. The circumstances were particularly sad as Harmon and her husband, Allen, had been married on the mountain and "were there celebrating their anniversary," according to a newspaper story. Harmon's minister husband got permission in 1999 to build an outdoor chapel near Linville Bluffs as a memorial. In 2013, he refurbished the rustic pulpit surrounded by log seats. The second fatality occurred Monday, August 2, 1998, when the Associated Press reported that Patsy Garmon Ashby, forty-seven, of Martinsville, Virginia, "fell about 100 feet from a ledge of Grandfather Mountain." Avery County sheriff Ed Gwyn reported that Ashby and her husband came to hike the mountain's trails. Gwyn said witnesses told him "she just started to turn around and just slipped and fell." A statement released by Harris Prevost indicated that Ashby was walking with her husband, Lloyd, when he "warned her to get back. It was too late. She lost her balance, tried to grab a rock and fell." Prevost noted "she apparently died instantly of massive injuries."

The deaths prompted reflection. Signs urge visitors to use normal care and restrain children, and a remarkable safety record is the result. But newspapers pointed out "there are no railings or fences at the area where Ms. Harmon fell." Prevost told employees the media had asked whether railings would be installed. "We doubt if this will happen," he responded, saying that "fences or guardrails can provide a false sense of security." Reporter Bill Leslie of WRAL in Raleigh quoted mountain visitor Emily Rowe, who summed up the feelings of many. "If you put up a fence, where are you going to stop?" Rowe asked. "After a while you might as well stay home and watch it on TV." Hugh Morton maintained the number of guardrails needed on Grandfather "wouldn't be in the hundreds, it would be in the thousands." The local rescue squad praised the way Grandfather staff handled the second accident, a reflection of the well-organized safety and rescue preparedness program overseen by director Steve Miller.

With cliffs abounding, the Grandfather summit was closed on the windiest days for public safety, but employees often went up anyway. On April 18, 1997, Top Shop manager Thomas Huskins remembered thinking, "We might set a wind record today." The son of longtime gate manager "Tommy" Huskins Jr. heard a "strange noise that sounded like a vacuum. It was scary." He investigated and was shocked to see "the wind blowing the outside wall of the building away from the stairwell," lifting the stairs "up and down like an accordion and I was on it!" The employees "made a run for it." The entire three-story outside wall had to be reattached, a $125,000 repair that dented that year's profits. The Swinging Bridge was next. In 1999, a routine engineering inspection revealed deterioration in the main cables. The project started November 4, 1999, with a Thanksgiving finish expected. Massive new cables were strung, and galvanized steel was used to eliminate the dangerous annual job of de-rusting and repainting the bridge. Wooden deck planks were replaced with nonslip, aluminum punched panels. Vertical metal bars made the side rails harder to climb. On December 14, local basketball star and Avery County building inspector Tommy Burleson strolled across in gale force winds and gave his OK. "Several days later," Harris Prevost wrote in a newsletter, "a strong wind tore the all-metal bridge apart. Thankfully, part of the flooring got stuck on the near tower or the thing would have ended up in Lenoir." Prevost took the rap. "I was in charge of that," he confessed.

The annual task of repainting the Swinging Bridge was nerve-racking and dangerous. North Carolina Collection, University of North Carolina Library at Chapel Hill. Photo by Hugh Morton.

"I wanted the bridge to swing more. Add a little more excitement." After a redesign that included spring-equipped stabilizing cables, the bridge reopened in April 2000 at a total cost of $300,000. Prevost now accepts that the nominally "swinging" bridge "just wiggles," but Hugh Morton noted it also "sings like a pipe organ" when wind blows through the vertical bars of the railing. A bionic Morton was among the first to cross the new span. He'd had a knee replacement and gotten a pacemaker in 1998.

Hugh Morton Has Left the Mountain
In 2003, at age thirty-three, Hugh Morton's grandson, Crae Morton, became the fifth generation of

the MacRae/Morton family to guide the mountain. With an undergraduate degree in communications from the University of Pennsylvania and graduate studies in business, Morton's grandson became president in June 2005. Crae Morton said he tackled his new role confident he could rely on the mountain's employees, especially his grandfather's longtime vice president, Harris Prevost. "Harris has been working for Grandfather Mountain for as long as I have been alive and I rely on that experience," he assured. A year later, on June 1, 2006, Hugh Morton died in Linville after a six-month battle with esophageal cancer. His ashes were scattered on the mountain. Nationwide notice was paid to Morton's passing. There were many memorial services, the biggest in Greensboro. Employees past and present paused to appreciate the daily privilege of knowing "Mr. Morton" as a personal friend. After working with him for thirty years, Prevost captured the man employees saw. "We knew a kind and gentle person who loved Grandfather Mountain and protected its beauty for us and future generations," he wrote. "We see someone who cared a lot about us, our place in life and our families. We lost a great boss, a friend and mentor." It was "the privilege" of Grandfather employees to be "passing on Mr. Morton's legacy to future guests of Grandfather Mountain." A cascade of change flowed from Morton's death. In September 2008, the Mortons sold the mountain's backcountry, creating Grandfather Mountain State Park. In November 2009, the Grandfather Mountain Stewardship Foundation came into being, dedicated to seeing "Carolina's Top Scenic Attraction" into the new millennium as a nonprofit.

A New Shop On Top

By 2007 Mother Nature had worn out the old Top Shop. More than 9 million people had browsed its shelves and heard Arthur Smith's soundtrack song touting the mountain as "a mighty good place to be."

Boone architect Bill Dixon would create a new Top Shop, but the job was bigger than he thought. "No one had ever done any master planning,"

Dixon realized. "It went as Mr. Morton wanted it to. Organically." So Dixon and his assistant Leigh Blevins started at the bottom and spent three years assessing the attraction's thirty-odd buildings. He hoped "if we did that right, we'd get the carrot at the top of the hill." While keeping its character, he doubled the size of the 1942 stone gatehouse in 2005. He added accessible restrooms there and at the museum and addressed "haphazard" evolution at the habitats. Easier access to the cougar exhibit improved other habitats, too. A new fudge shop became the mountain's first green structure. During the process, "things that don't usually happen to architects were just wonderful," Dixon reflects. He remembers a conference between habitats where he was told not to make eye contact with the bears. "I was thinking," he mused, "Can we go meet over there somewhere?"

Despite a desire to rehab the old Top Shop, it had to go. Years of planning were required to assess all types of issues. The building sits on solid rock and earned one of only two "truck and haul" sewage permits in the state that permit sewage to be transported to a secondary septic system. The search for summit water had always been fruitless, including "one well in the old building, which is illegal," Dixon whispered. "After two years and lots of money—we got water." When the old Top Shop was razed in April 2008, a basement was discovered, the perfect location for two 15,000-gallon water storage tanks. "The new building will never again be without water," he pledged. Discovering the basement was a good example of why builder G. Perry "Skip" Greene, vice president of Greene Construction in Boone, called the project "a design-build situation. We were constantly reacting to changing circumstances." All new power was needed too. No one wanted power poles, but underground power was too expensive despite Mountain Electric's offer to share costs. Aboveground power lines were encased in concrete.

No goal for the new Top Shop was more important than creating first-time wheelchair access to the Mile-High Swinging Bridge. That meant the building had to be built "around a three-story elevator. It was that big a wish for the Morton family." The entire three stories of the old building had directly confronted its nemesis—the wind—so the new building would flop that design, being lower on the windy western side and higher in the east. Curved lower roofs would lift the blast over arching higher floors that contained the elevator. Besides deflecting wind, the new building has foot-thick walls of concrete, plank-formed to display wood grain texture. For weatherproofing able to defy wind-driven rain, snow, and ice, Dixon worked with SKA Consulting Engineers, Inc., designers of the current Swinging Bridge. Heating was high-tech, too. "The old Top Shop had air heaters, so when somebody opened the door, the hot air went out," explains Dixon. "The staff froze, the public froze, and they spent a fortune." Dixon's solution: "Concrete is the best radiant disperser and holder of heat," he asserts, so a closed system now pumps nonpotable hot water through the floor on all three levels. There's an electrical generator for the "days on end when the staff can't get up there." Sadly, the summit winds were just too powerful for wind- and solar-power options. One plus: The new rounded roofline is almost invisible from NC 105. "We literally tried to make this new build-ing disappear, the opposite of what an architect usually does," Dixon admits. Though still visible from the Blue Ridge Parkway, the building has a "more natural profile." Demolition of the old shop started in the spring of 2008 while a temporary Top Shop was built to stand in during construc-tion. Construction took two years, and the critical variable, as expected, was weather. "I have lived in this area most of my life and have never experi-enced extremes like I did on top of that mountain," pledged Bill Dixon. Winter 2009–10 didn't help. Access was impossible for weeks at a time. The new building's radiant floors exceeded expec-tations. Catherine Morton said workers actually complained that their feet were too warm.

There was no way to restore the alpine beauty that was lost when the first parking lot was built in "Top Shop gap," but razing the old building yielded a rare peek into the past. When the dust cleared, Convention Table Rock was freed from the grasp of the old building. Dixon was lucky enough to see what I've dreamed of seeing: the face of the gap, standing there again in the sun and wind just as Hugh and Julia Morton saw it around 1950 when Hugh photographed his bride posing in that pris-tine setting. Interviewing Dixon in his Boone office helped me imagine that experience. "I didn't even know the rock had a name," he confessed, "but I love that cliff. Seeing it without the old building was a dramatic sight." The new structure is com-pletely detached from the rock, unlike the old Top Shop that clung to the cliff, pounded by the wind like a boxer being battered on the ropes. "I'm an intuitive architect," Dixon explains. "I listen to my belly. It was telling me to keep the building completely clear of the rock. I can only imagine what that gap looked like before development," he offers wistfully. "The fact is, if the road to the top of Grandfather Mountain and the Swinging Bridge weren't already there, it could *never* be built today."

With the building standing clear of the cliff, a new bridge was needed to lead visitors across the void to the Mile-High Swinging Bridge. "We lit-erally had to build a bridge from the upper door so we called it 'the bridge to the bridge,'" explains Dixon. Only six piers gently touch the cliff in selected spots. "It was literally designed around colonies of Heller's Blazing Star and Blue Ridge Goldenrod." Once again, the sun beams and the breezes blow on Convention Table Rock. The new building is smaller than the old one, with larger restrooms. Visitors reach Swinging Bridge level by elevator and stairs, the latter with windows and eastern views never before seen from inside. Dixon was told "they weren't making money" in the old building, so enhancing retail sales was a main goal. The new building's first floor is an attractive souvenir space, and an exhibit about the moun-tain's history is planned for the second.

The new summit facility opened June 10, 2010. In a ceremony that inspired visitors, media, and Grandfather's staff, thirteen-year-old Luke Wilcox of Vilas crossed the Swinging Bridge in his computer-equipped, speech-activated wheel-

Luke Wilcox crossed the Swinging Bridge for the first time in years on June 10, 2010. Wearing a Grandfather Mountain T-shirt emblazoned with "I Crossed the Mile High Swinging Bridge," Luke was helped across by friend Cole Hawkins of Boone. Photo by Randy Johnson.

chair. Luke has muscular dystrophy, and until he was six his parents carried him across the bridge. They stopped when he got too big. "Luke had such fond memories of crossing the bridge that he wrote a paper about it for school," his mother, Anita Wilcox, told reporters. "I never thought he'd ever cross the bridge again. This gives us faith that the world really is opening up to handicapped people." Years after his new Top Shop debuted, Bill Dixon still displays a picture in his office of a woman sitting in a wheelchair at the edge of the parking lot "staring up at her family walking across the Swinging Bridge. That poignant image," he explains, "will always stick with me as a reminder of the real importance of this project. Being able to say we achieved that still gives me goose bumps." Skip Greene literally put the final touch on the new Top Shop, recycling "every piece of stone on the outside from the old building." Fittingly, Grandfather stone continues to soften the intrusion made by humans on this mighty peak. No wonder the building seems as stout as the mountain itself. Hugh Morton's widow, Julia, donated her share of

the proceeds from the mountain's sale as a state park to build the new Top Shop. "We borrowed no money to build that building," asserted Penn Dameron, the first executive director of the Grandfather Mountain Stewardship Foundation, who departed in 2014.

Celebrating Past and Future

One of the most memorable Swinging Bridge birthday celebrations happened on the fortieth anniversary in 1992 when Charles Kuralt famously belittled the span. Kuralt claimed the "fuss in the newspapers" had given him "the impression that the Mile-High Swinging Bridge spanned a chasm one-mile deep. You can imagine," he told the audience, "how I felt when I came up here and saw that the Mile-High Swinging Bridge actually hangs about 80 feet above the ground." Kuralt wondered how many people "would have made the trip if it were advertised as the Eighty-Foot High Swinging bridge." He concluded that "the Mile-High Swinging Bridge, which is NOT a mile high, is not swinging, either. So what we have here is an 80-Foot High, tethered bridge. Big deal." While celebrating Morton's genius, the famous journalist visibly enjoyed skewering his mortified old friend. Kuralt reprised his remarks in 1996 when Morton received the North Caroliniana Society Award in Chapel Hill. He recalled Morton wore a "tight and nervous smile, for Hugh is very proud of his Mile-High Swinging Bridge, and does not want to hear any kidding around about it. And I could not help myself."

Six years after Morton passed away, on September 11, 2012, Harris Prevost remembered Kuralt's remarks at a sixtieth anniversary gathering at the bridge. Standing by the new Top Shop, Prevost fondly remembered his old boss, reminding listeners that "the sixtieth anniversary of the Mile-High Swinging Bridge is also the sixtieth anniversary of the Hugh Morton era of Grandfather Mountain." He imagined that the mountain "in a sense is crossing its own bridge, transitioning from one era to another, but still keeping true to Hugh Morton's vision." That mission was Morton's

Longtime Grandfather Mountain vice president Harris Prevost (center) celebrates the sixtieth anniversary of the Swinging Bridge in 2012 with Phil Francis (far left), the Parkway's seventh superintendent. Gary Johnson, once the Parkway's chief of resource planning and professional services and a key participant in the story of the Linn Cove Viaduct detailed in the next chapter, is between Francis and Prevost. Dan Brown (to the right of Prevost), was the Parkway's sixth superintendent. Photo by Randy Johnson.

oft-stated "very strong feeling that he didn't own Grandfather Mountain; he was its caretaker and his mission was to protect it for the enjoyment of future generations." Prevost concluded, "Just as Hugh Morton's grandmother crossed the Mile-High Swinging Bridge and was deeply touched by the beauty she saw, Grandfather Mountain has crossed its bridge. And we, too, are happy with what we see."

Hyperbole aside, the Mile-High Swinging Bridge *is* a mile high, and if you don't look straight down into the eighty-foot chasm directly below, the terrain plummets nearly a vertical mile to the rippling western Piedmont. The gasps that view elicits are the stuff of memories, not marketing. Just ask André Michaux. Or the millions who have crossed the Mile-High Swinging Bridge. Prevost turned to Blue Ridge Parkway officials in

the audience, including then-current and former superintendents Phil Francis and Dan Brown, and pointed out the irony that both the Linn Cove Viaduct and the Swinging Bridge share September birthdays. The viaduct, the "cousin" of the Swinging Bridge, was twenty-five years old the same month Hugh Morton's bridge was sixty. Prevost reminded everyone that the years have yielded growing mutual respect between officials of the Blue Ridge Parkway and Grandfather Mountain, goodwill hard-earned after deep enmity aroused when Hugh Morton and the National Park Service dueled titanically for decades over which route the road would take across the mountain. As much as the Swinging Bridge itself, that Battle of the Blue Ridge Parkway still shapes the future of Mr. Morton's mountain.

8 The Battle of the Blue Ridge Parkway

By the time the debate was settled over where to route the Blue Ridge Parkway across Grandfather Mountain, the emergence of computer technology permitted the Linn Cove Viaduct to set new standards for environmental sensitivity and spectacular scenery. To this day, when winter ice and snow close the road, walkers and cross country skiers enjoy pedestrian access to a span otherwise reserved for vehicles. Photo by Tommy White Photography, www.tommywhitephotography.com.

"America's most scenic drive"—the Blue Ridge Parkway—annually attracts almost 20 million motorists. That makes it the most visited unit of the national park system and an apt symbol of America's love affair with the open road. The crown jewel of that nearly 500-mile linear park is Grandfather Mountain, in part for its globally recognized span, the Linn Cove Viaduct. A national park tourist highway of that caliber was a pivotal event for the travel-challenged North Carolina mountains. As a witness to Linville's ongoing isolation, Hugh Morton saw the Parkway as a make-or-break opportunity to build a successful tourism business for himself and his part of the state. Regrettably, debate about where the road would cross Grandfather turned into one of the biggest battles in National Park Service (NPS) history, a saga that delayed debut of the "missing link" for thirty years, until 1987, two years after the road's fiftieth anniversary.

The idea for a Blue Ridge Parkway–style road likely originated in 1909 with Joseph Hyde Pratt, director of North Carolina's Geological and Economic Survey. A section of his ill-fated Crest of the Blue Ridge toll road was actually built south of Grandfather by 1912. Early parkways aimed to merge scenery with speed, the perfect description of the Blue Ridge Parkway's immediate predecessor, the 100-mile Skyline Drive in Shenandoah National Park. With the Public Works Administration building roads to counter Depression-era unemployment, the idea surfaced to link Shenandoah and the Great Smokies by road. That forced Tennessee and North Carolina to compete for the Smoky Mountain connection. Competition was fierce, but Interior Secretary Harold Ickes bestowed the road on North Carolina on November 10, 1934, despite Congress having never approved the project. The Parkway was "finessed" into reality in 1936 when North Carolina congressman Robert Doughton barely passed a bill that formally named the road and transferred control to the National Park Service upon completion. Luckily, the park-to-park highway would be completed—construction was already under way not far north of Grandfather at Cumberland Knob.

A Dream National Park

From the start, Grandfather took center stage in the story of how the high road came to be. Early National Park Service landscape architect Edward Abbuehl considered Grandfather "the most outstanding mountain" between Shenandoah and the Smokies, according to Brian Cleven's official history of the Grandfather section of the Parkway (written for the National Park Service's Historic American Engineering Record, or HAER). Besides the Smokies and Shenandoah, Grandfather and Linville Gorge were considered a "third" Southern Appalachian national park possibility. The

first two got the nod, but according to the HAER history "the NPS considered (Grandfather) to be a vitally needed addition." Grandfather was already on the government's wish list. Steven T. Mather (1867–1930), first director of the National Park Service, was appointed in 1917, and the Department of the Interior was soon authorized by Congress "to accept for park purposes any lands and rights-of-ways, including Grandfather Mountain." According to Anne Mitchell Whisnant's thorough Parkway history, *Super-Scenic Motorway*, the Linville Improvement Company had offered to donate 1,400 acres covering Grandfather's summits, but Mather rejected that, citing plans to commercialize adjacent property. Whisnant contextualizes that decision with Michael Frome's claim in *Strangers in High Places* that the mountain was "barren of trees" at that time. Actually, logging had barely started. Accepting that 1,400 acres—60 percent of the acreage of today's Grandfather Mountain State Park and nearly identical to Mount Mitchell State Park—would have saved Grandfather's storied virgin timber. A milestone opportunity had come to naught.

A variety of dream scenarios emerged to make the mountain a public park early in the century. Hugh Morton later lured politicians to the Swinging Bridge, but the first and only governor to climb the mountain on foot arrived in 1924 among a party of prominent people evaluating the area as a national park. "Most of the party climbed to the top of the Grandfather Mountain," according to the November 13, 1924, *Watauga Democrat*, with then-governor-elect Angus Wilton McLean (1870–1935; governor 1925–1929) "leading the way. Standing on the highest peak he remarked: 'I have visited the Alps and traveled through the world-famed Rockies but never in life have I beheld such wonderful scenery as this.'" In 1938, fabled Parkway landscape architect Stanley Abbott noted a U.S. Forest Service idea for a picnic area and trails on Grandfather's awesome eastern spur, Pilot Ridge. The desire to attain "reasonable foot access" to those "fine panoramic views" would repeatedly motivate Parkway plans.

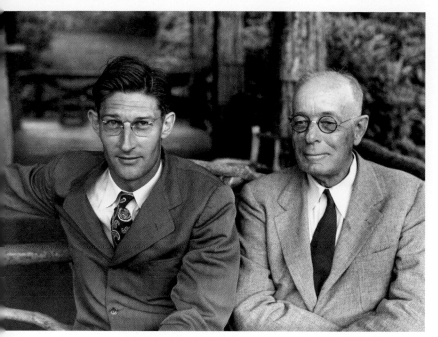

Seminal Parkway landscape architect Stanley Abbott (left) aspired for the Parkway to do nothing less than "lie easily on the ground." For that to happen at Grandfather, many thought the mountain would need to be public land first, and that's what crusader Harlan Kelsey set out to accomplish in the 1940s. That then unrealized quest brought the two men to Linville to meet Hugh Morton in 1947. North Carolina Collection, University of North Carolina Library at Chapel Hill. Photo by Hugh Morton.

By the mid-1930s, loggers were stripping Grandfather's slopes, and the National Park Service jumped at saving a route for the road. The Linville Improvement Company was certain Yonahlossee Road would be that route. In a March 30, 1937, report to stockholders, Nelson MacRae asserted that "the Yonahlossee Road, which will become part of the Parkway," was expected to net "some fair compensation when this right of way is deeded to the State and Federal Government." The HAER history says the Park Service asked "the BPR [Bureau of Public Roads, now the Federal Highway Administration] to submit preliminary right-of-way maps to the state based on the survey line of US 221"—the Yonahlossee Road. Expecting the "Linville section to feel distinct benefits from increased travel" on the Parkway, the directors of the just-renamed Linville Company voted unanimously on October 29, 1937, "to sell a right-of-way through a portion of the Company's lands to the North Carolina State Highway and Public Works

Commission . . . for the Blue Ridge Parkway." They specified "458.52 acres, more or less," along the still largely unlogged Yonahlossee Road. Ostensibly to save virgin timber, Yonahlossee would become the "low route" among three competing paths proposed for the Parkway.

Continuing interest in preserving the mountain coalesced around conservationist Harlan P. Kelsey throughout much of the 1940s. Past president of the Appalachian Mountain Club, Kelsey had ties to Linville as the son of Samuel T. Kelsey, an early Linville investor who had helped acquire the mountain from Walter Waightstill Lenoir. In 1940 and 1942, the MacRaes of the Linville Company made repeated attempts to sell the mountain into park status, and Kelsey was offered a commission to find investors. Governor J. Melville Broughton encouraged Kelsey in February 1944, urging that Grandfather "be set aside for public service." In the April–June 1944 issue of *National Parks Magazine*, Kelsey's article "Shall Grandfather Mountain Be Saved?" called the area "by far the most superlative feature along the Blue Ridge Parkway, an almost virgin area of forests, flowers and cascades in imminent danger of despoilment by lumbering." Kelsey left out that the logging was already over. A Linville Company planning map of the time had "No Wood" written on the east side of the mountain. In 1945, the Linville Company gave Kelsey an option on 5,550 acres that Park Service director Newton B. Drury (1940 to 1951) intended to be another Parkway "bulge" like Julian Price and Moses Cone Parks. The option was renewed a second time—by Hugh Morton, back from World War II and president of the company—but it expired in the spring of 1947. Between debate over what the logged land was worth and tight state budgets as North Carolina developed its parks, public money was unavailable. Private investment was similarly stymied. Led by Parkway superintendent Sam Weems (1944 to 1966), another offer was made for the mountain, and in August 1948 Hugh Morton rejected it. Annoyed at Kelsey's depiction of the company as a rapacious logger, Morton said the mountain was not for sale "at any price."

Despite support for public ownership and Linville Company openness to outright sale, Grandfather was still private property. Hugh Morton started planning a new future.

Devilish Details

Morton urged the Park Service to finish the Parkway. To do it, the agency set out to take as much of his mountain as they could get. "Settling on the final roadway alignment for this section," pronounces the HAER report, "proved to be the most difficult and drawn out ordeal faced by the parkway designers." Parkway officials eventually thought reconstructing US 221 "would leave unsightly reminders that this was a 'hand-me-down' location," so the state asked the Park Service to consider a loftier path. A 1940 Park Service study discovered an old logging grade from Holloway Mountain Road to very near Pilot Ridge, and the concept of a "high route" across the mountain emerged. This old Whiting Lumber Company railroad grade into Boone Fork inspired the idea for a tunnel through Pilot Ridge. With that "1,700′ tunnel," records HAER, the Parkway route would be shortened, "eliminating the long scar that going around the mountain would create." That line crested to great views atop Rough Ridge, then followed "a reasonably good route to Beacon Heights" through "Linn Cove, a very deep ravine . . . expected to be crossed by a standard type of high viaduct."

In December 1943, the Park Service asked for state data to compare a "higher line" with US 221, and the tunnel idea resurfaced. By 1946, the Park Service had embraced that higher route, asking the state in 1948 to start "right-of-way acquisition around Grandfather Mountain." Years of inaction followed, but the seeds of controversy were sewn when the proposed boundary included more land than a typical Parkway corridor, the HAER history concludes. The plan projected a "normal right-of-way of about 400′ on the roadway's upper side," but on the lower side "it expanded." That bigger Parkway boundary engulfed Pilot Knob, where a pedestrian overlook was planned, and then dipped lower, putting all the land between the Parkway and US 221 "in public ownership." The Parkway urged condemnation of the route, states the HAER report, and on May 27, 1955, North Carolina did exactly that. Harris Prevost remembered Morton saying he'd asked R. Getty Browning of the North Carolina Highway Commission why the official hadn't warned him that condemnation maps would suddenly appear at the courthouse. Browning said he knew Morton would be mad at him.

Then the Parkway's proposal came under scrutiny. The land desired on Grandfather Mountain exceeded the 125 acres per mile authorized by enabling legislation. Donation of additional acreage was permitted, making places like Moses Cone Park possible, but the Park Service had factored in that donated land when they calculated the number of acres they could buy in the vicinity of Grandfather. "In view of this savings and the fact that Grandfather Mountain was an outstanding scenic attraction," reads the HAER report, "the NPS and North Carolina Highway Department considered this wider than average right-of-way request a reasonable solution." Morton begged to differ, thinking it was unfair to make him sell more property just because a rich neighbor donated his. The state backed him up and the Park Service gave in. Then another wrinkle surfaced. The Park Service reduced the width of the Parkway right-of-way they were requesting from the usual 1,000 feet to 750, or "three fourths of the 1000 feet needed to average 125 acres per mile." To recoup the missing fourth, the Park Service again wanted Pilot Knob.

The debate suddenly shifted to routes across the mountain. The Parkway's preferred high route became "Line A." The Yonahlossee Road low route became "Line C." Reacting to Morton's outrage, the state asked the Park Service to study a middle route, "Line B." This route, like Line A, would still face the challenge of Linn Cove, but then it stayed more level, below Rough Ridge, avoiding a tunnel but requiring a "road cut" around Pilot Knob. It also eliminated lofty auto access to the top of Rough Ridge and an easy trail to Pilot Knob envisioned in Parkway plans. On December 1, 1955,

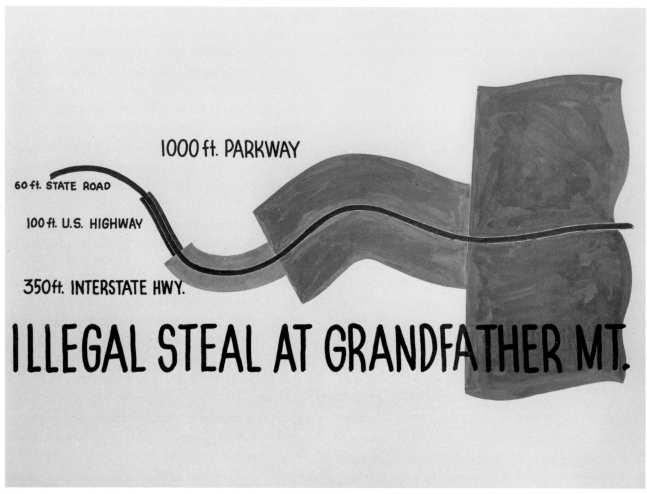

1000 ft. PARKWAY

60 ft. STATE ROAD

100 ft. U.S. HIGHWAY

350 ft. INTERSTATE HWY.

ILLEGAL STEAL AT GRANDFATHER MT.

This media image that Morton created during the Parkway debate was a pretty graphic assessment of what he thought was going on. He was outraged that the right-of-way needed for even major highways was a fraction of what the National Park Service was seeking for a scenic road across his mountain. North Carolina Collection, University of North Carolina Library at Chapel Hill. Photo by Hugh Morton.

HAER states the Park Service chose the high route again, this time over the middle route. Surprisingly, in evaluating the routes, the Park Service added that Line C, the Yonahlossee Road, was itself superior to the "middle route." Conservationist Michael Frome would later speak for many objectors to the middle route when he complained in *American Forests* that it was "chosen by Mr. Morton himself." The agency astutely recognized one major drawback of Morton's line B—which did eventually become the Parkway. They noted that US 221 and the Parkway would be very close to each other. That unfortunate visual redundancy is even easier to indict today with both roads in place. Line B would also require more "scarring," and the road would be too low for "reasonable foot access" to

Pilot Knob and Rough Ridge. At this mid-1950s point in the debate, some writers with uncharitable views of Hugh Morton claim Grandfather's owner used his superior public relations skills to score an illegitimate victory against the Park Service. Whisnant's *Super-Scenic Motorway* says Morton started winning the route battle when he sent a pivotal press release to the *Asheville Citizen-Times* on February 6, 1956. Morton cast his spell with a mesmerizingly entitled missive "A Capsule of Facts Substantiating Opposition to a Possible Change in the Established Right of Way for the Blue Ridge Parkway at Grandfather Mountain." Lucky for him, even so clumsily titled a document got a lot of publicity. Morton's detractors believe he deliberately exaggerated how high the "high route" would

No wonder the Park Service wanted Pilot Knob. The wide-angle image from the summit of my hiking-staff-holding shadow attests to how dramatically separate the peak seems from Grandfather's main ridge. At the moment I snapped this shot, Hugh Morton was photographing me from below. Some time later, I was back with a few other poseurs. I don't remember who leaped off the rock, but I was glad to be the one standing there with a radio orchestrating the photo op for Morton. Shadow photo by Randy Johnson; others North Carolina Collection, University of North Carolina Library at Chapel Hill, photos by Hugh Morton.

go, mischaracterizing the Parkway route as going "over the top" of Grandfather Mountain. Thus, with an argument designed to feign dubious concern for the environment, a self-interested capitalist would win his battle against the Parkway over the best interests of Grandfather Mountain. In this view, Morton was solely motivated by crass concern for the profitability of his destructive commercial attraction. In 2006 Whisnant wrote, "Morton has for fifty years obscured the real complexity of the conflict and created a cause no one could counter."

Unfortunately for the Park Service, says the HAER report, the "reasoned counterarguments" in R. Getty Browning's anti-Morton "Report on

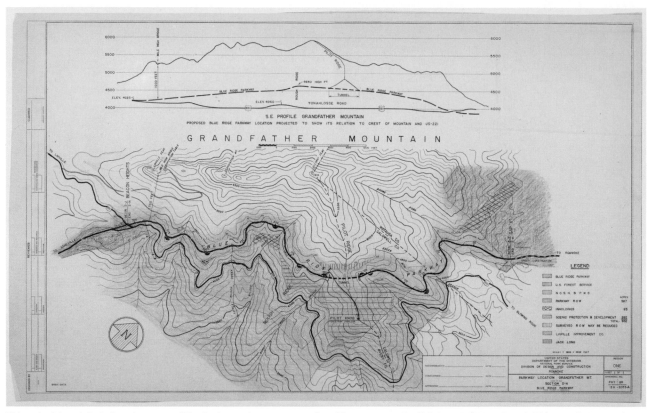

This colorful undated planning map of the Parkway shows proposed parking areas on the "high route" atop Rough Ridge and at a nearby tunnel where a paved trail would lead to Pilot Knob. The diagram at the top illustrates that the route was far below Morton's tourist bridge. Most fascinating, the planners kindly redesigned Morton's "low standard" road to the top, eliminating damaging switchbacks in favor of one long turn—a route like the one Robert Hartley said his father Joe had urged. Courtesy, National Park Service, Blue Ridge Parkway.

Section 2-H" were overlooked, perhaps due to Morton's influence in the media and state government. "While the NPS made its case," or failed to, the state gave Morton's "high route" back to him, according to the HAER history. Why is still a mystery. Whisnant implies Morton pulled strings. On April 25, 1957, the Park Service flat-hats were caught flat-footed at news from the courthouse. Morton reached back to his grandfather's 1939 agreement to sell the Yonahlossee Road, claiming he'd satisfied the Parkway land request. Back in 1955, the Park Service itself had said the lower route was preferable to Morton's line B, so why not just take Line C, the Yonahlossee Road? A year later, in 1958, the Parkway answered. After restudying Line C, the Park Service changed its assessment: This time the Yonahlossee option was inferior not only to the preferred high route but to the middle route, too. Obviously, the Park Service *really* wanted Line A. Objections to Yonahlossee included "elbows

of the old road on the inside and outside of curves" that would defeat efforts to "retrofit" it for Parkway use. Yonahlossee was too far below Pilot Knob and Rough Ridge for "reasonable foot access," and the old road wasn't scenic enough, despite tourists flocking to its waterfalls and rock formations for more than sixty years.

Dueling Banjos: The Public Debate

Both parties were jockeying for position as 1962 arrived. In early March, Conrad Wirth, then National Park Service director (from 1951 to 1964), met with the state highway commission, and chairman Merrill Evans pledged to go "ahead with efforts to complete the parkway." Morton commented the next day in the Raleigh paper that it was "high time the Park Service cut out its foolish attempts to steal the rest of Grandfather Mountain" and use the low route. Morton was trusting Governor Terry Sanford (a close political ally) to use "fairness and good judgment." The controversy came to a dramatic head when Hugh Morton squared off against Wirth at a North Carolina Highway Commission public hearing on May 31, 1962. The antagonists brought props and supporters, and Wirth depicted the routes on a three-dimensional model of the mountain (much like a relief map now displayed in Grandfather Mountain's Nature Museum). The debate covered all three routes, and admits the HAER history, "Morton was convincing in his assertion that the NPS was going to level off the top of the mountain," even though "the NPS's preferred route was not at the crest." Afterward, Morton and Wirth took their arguments to a Raleigh television show that was expected to help the Parkway, but Morton won, wielding a sharp and enduring quote—building the Parkway across Grandfather would be like "taking a switchblade to the Mona Lisa."

Later, Morton recalled friend Arthur Smith attending the television debate. As the host of the first nationally syndicated country music television show, the popular musician had strong appeal for Morton's local audience. He'd written hundreds of best-selling country and gospel songs, including the 1948 hit "Guitar Boogie," now known as "Dueling Banjos" (which one journalist suggested reflects the Morton/Parkway row). Morton remembered Smith telling the audience, "It just don't seem right for a bureaucrat to come down here from Washington and take [Grandfather Mountain] away from him." Recalled Morton, "The switchboard lit up. Wirth didn't know what hit him." A year later a highway commission committee came out in support of Morton's Line B. Terry Sanford recommended that route to Interior Secretary Stewart Udall in March 1964, but again, according to HAER, the situation stalled. Morton made new headlines in 1965 deeding 377 acres to complete the middle route. No one had asked for the land, but Morton got untold column-inches promoting his views. He contended the middle route had gained state government support, but Udall had rejected it to "pacify the Conrad Wirth faction within the Park Service." It was time to

"swing around the end of Pilot Knob," Morton concluded, and build "what is probably the most scenic section of the Blue Ridge Parkway." Still, reveals the HAER document, "NPS and the Federal Highway Administration [formerly BPR] did not abandon the high line for several years."

Commercial Conflicts

Beyond the route controversy, Hugh Morton irritated the Park Service by siding with people who thought Parkway policies were antibusiness. Businesspeople expected the Parkway to boost the mountain economy, and they objected to what they saw as antagonistic Parkway attitudes, including repeated attempts to charge a toll. Entrance fees are the norm at national parks. With just four entrances, Shenandoah's Skyline Drive was (and still is) a toll road. The Parkway's hundreds of access points made charging tolls seem impossible—at least to everyone but the Park Service. Communities also assumed Parkway signing would announce local services. Imagine the knitted brows when a national park tourist road arrived only to embargo signs directing visitors to nearby services. The same debate continues today. In 2012, the Parkway's first-ever management plan weighed whether the road should become a "commuter route" linked to local communities or stand aloof, insulated as a noncommercial experience. The "pro-isolation" argument won Park Service support, artfully defended as "historic preservation" of the Parkway's early ideal. That concept seemed antibusiness in the 1950s and 1960s, and it still seems out of touch to nearby communities today—even as the Parkway justifies its budget in press releases crowing about the park's impact on local economies. In this part of the Parkway debate, Morton seemed to be inviting the future while the Park Service was holding on to the past. Morton and tourism boosters may not have been "right," but it's not necessarily diabolical that he and his ilk believed the federal government shouldn't be competing with local businesses. No one supports billboards on the Parkway, but to this day there's only one sign on the Parkway attesting to the existence of the Grandfather attraction. The sign near US 221 was permitted in the 1990s when the mountain became the world's only privately owned, United Nations–designated International Biosphere Reserve. That's either perfectly appropriate or an absurdly lofty bar to set for one "parky" sign.

National Park concession policy also caused ill will. Locals never expected "their" national park would have its own government-sanctioned lodges, restaurants, gas stations, and even craft shops to compete with their own. Yellowstone National Park needs a grand park lodge in a wilderness, but it was a surprise when visitors could drive day after day on the Parkway and never get off. Suspicions rose further when the Park Service–affiliated organization, National Park Concessions, chose big, nonlocal businesses to run concessions. How could locals not have an antigovernment attitude? At one time, the Parkway might have needed tourist facilities, but even now, low occupancy and poor profitability still call some Parkway concessions into question. All of the above makes it easier to appreciate Morton's perception of Parkway imperiousness.

By the time of the Grandfather route debate, Morton saw himself fighting back against a National Park Service intent on ensuring that travelers wouldn't get off the Parkway at Grandfather Mountain or anywhere else. Granted, Morton had desecrated the mountain with what the Park Service called a "low standard road to the mountain's top," but his road climbed far lower on the mountain than summit developments managed by public parks on Roan Mountain, Mount Mitchell, and Mount Washington. The result was that Morton could argue with a straight face that the Park Service proposed to scar his land. Like virtually all major eastern summits, the Grandfather Mountain Morton claimed to be saving had been logged, but he didn't need to claim the mountain was pristine wilderness to justify protecting it. Even after timbering, Grandfather Mountain was legitimately less damaged than many places treasured then and now as wilderness. One of those, federally designated in 1964 as Shining Rock

Wilderness, was truly clear-cut and consumed by post-logging conflagrations. Shining Rock's most popular trails are logging railroad grades through inferno-cleared areas that environmentalists now call "scenic balds." In comparison, Grandfather was lightly logged. More than that, even skeptics of "Hugh Morton, environmentalist," might admit that the Blue Ridge Parkway is, after all, a road that has laid 469 miles of asphalt on the crest of the Blue Ridge. Legendary Forest Service preservationist Bob Marshal also regretted the Parkway's effects on wildlands. In fact, the already completed Appalachian Trail had to be moved when the Parkway came slicing along the Blue Ridge in Virginia. The rustic picnic shelter in the Parkway's Rocky Knob Recreation Area is among the earliest Appalachian Trail shelters, abandoned when bulldozers obliterated the wilderness path. In essence, the Parkway could be seen as "just another road destroying a trail."

Mona Lisa's Scars

The Parkway HAER report acknowledges that "people worried that the intended right-of-way would destroy the mountain's character." Scars made by cut-and-fill road building were an issue, but the Park Service defended the higher line, saying it had "faced these concerns about road scars from the beginning" and "for the most part they healed over or were hidden." At Grandfather, the problem was expected to be further mitigated because Grandfather stone "weathered nicely." Engineers also defended the high route thinking the road would be camouflaged by forest, odd on a peak that Morton's critics claimed was decimated by logging. The Parkway's chosen route also specified a tunnel, so there'd be no scarring there. It was therefore obvious Morton's Line B would scar the mountain more—exactly what he claimed he didn't want. Speaking of contradictions, the Parkway's high tunnel would have been the longest on the entire road, 1,700 feet, plunging a scenic road into darkness for a third of a mile.

Despite Parkway projections of benign impact, construction in the 1930s and 1940s was not gentle or sustainable, nor would it have been in the 1950s or 1960s when the Parkway might have been completed lacking Morton's opposition. Granting Park Service optimism, an amazing number of Parkway road closures today are still caused by the collapse of failing old road cuts. In 2012, Lloyd Middleton, Ph.D., an engineer long associated with the Parkway and its Grandfather Mountain segment, attended the twenty-fifth anniversary of the Linn Cove Viaduct. "When you consider the harsh environment of the high elevation areas, with so much freeze and thaw," Middleton explained, "you need to look back long ago and realize this road was built to expose the back slope," the road cut above the pavement, "and that means the area below, that supports the road, was created by fill. That was, and still is, prone to failures—all the fault of how, and when, it was constructed." That explains a major 2009 closure near Craggy Gardens, where massive repairs dictated a "solution" more visible and elaborate than the original road cut. The Parkway maintained that the impact of cuts would be minimal, but it turns out Morton's concern was either justified or somehow aimed at appearing so thirty years later. Michael Leonard, who would later guide Hugh Morton into protective covenants on the mountain, asserts simply, "In Morton's youth, he spent time on the peaks of the mountain, and I believe he wanted the Parkway to have minimal impact on the views from the summit trails. He just didn't want a road crossing the mountain at that elevation." But, Leonard admits, "some of it was just a territorial thing. He didn't want to share ownership with the NPS. He really didn't want people messing with that mountain. He owned it."

By the mid-1960s Morton had an attitude, but the end of the debate was near. Finally, with location tweaks and access agreements, 1968 saw acceptance of Morton's middle route, Line B, "the most acceptable to all parties involved," rationalized HAER. Whisnant says Governor Dan K. Moore "somehow convinced the Park Service to abandon the high route." Part of the solution may have been the departure of Morton antagonists Sam Weems, Conrad Wirth, and R. Getty Browning. On October 22, 1968, Governor Moore, Blue Ridge Parkway superintendent Granville Liles, Congressman James Broyhill, Senator Sam Ervin, former NPS director Wirth, Hugh Morton, and others attended a festive deed delivery luncheon for the Blue Ridge Parkway Association atop Grandfather. Then as now, Grandfather's summit building was tagged the Top Shop, a name that surely triggered a gag reflex among Park Service attendees. Hugh Morton had donated his Line B property, and that day a spade turned near Beacon Heights and the "missing link" was on its way to completion. But roadblocks appeared, and "passage of the National Environmental Policy Act of 1969 placed more rigid requirements on construction techniques," states the HAER report. "This particular route would require greater skill and care to protect the environment than any previous section." The final piece of the Parkway would become a landmark achievement for the National Park Service, the environment of Grandfather Mountain, and Hugh Morton.

Flagging a Route to the Future

Gary Everhardt, the longest-serving superintendent in high road history, became the fifth Parkway superintendent in 1977. The North Carolina mountain native seems destined to have completed the Parkway. He was one year old when the Parkway started in 1935, and "if there had been a 25th anniversary celebration I would have been been here for it," he asserts, referencing his earliest Parkway job. "I was also with the Parkway for the 50th and I'm still around for the 75th." He won't speculate whether he'll see the 100th. Everhardt was instrumental in the initiation, completion, or both of the Linn Cove Viaduct, Asheville's Folk Art Center, the Blue Ridge Music Center, the Parkway Visitor Center, and the park's headquarters building, linked to the visitor center by a concrete bridge—"my 'non-swinging bridge,'" Everhardt grins. He seems western, a little reminiscent of Lyndon Johnson (the white Stetson helps). Born and raised in Lenoir, he and his brothers "used to go up into Pisgah National Forest to fish and hike and I remember looking up at Grandfather Mountain." At North Carolina State, Everhardt worked for the Park Service "the summer of 1956 up in Boone surveying boundaries around Deep Gap and Grandfather." Not long afterward he jumped at an NPS engineering job, eventually rising to assistant superintendent for operations at Yellowstone in 1969, then superintendent at Grand Teton National Park in 1972. In January 1975, Everhardt went to Washington, D.C., as the ninth director of the National Park Service, overseeing a 32-million acre expansion of parkland in Alaska that doubled Park Service property. Everhardt became one of the Park Service's movers and shakers, but he was glad to be back in the North Carolina mountains in the late 1970s.

Completion of the Parkway was a major achievement in Everhardt's career. The viaduct debuted at a landmark event in 1987. Also just beginning was the legendary status of this bridge as an artful victory for aesthetics and the environment, a success story of sensitivity to nature. Naysayers claim the viaduct's reputation as a symbol of environmental preservation is another misleading claim that "retroactively" permits Hugh Morton to claim being an environmentalist. Environmental rules were just getting started, but the span's top-down construction and artfully planted piers were indeed far lighter on the land than any previous "solution" to Linn Cove would have been. Those working on the viaduct insist it was the dawning of an era when "environmental impact" really took hold. A tree had fallen in the forest, they say, whether or not skeptics want to hear it. The basics are simple. The "high route" was "the road not taken." No tunnel would burrow through Pilot Ridge. Both Morton's middle route and the high route retained the tricky passage of Linn Cove, a monumental moss-and-rhododendron-covered jumble of cliffs and boulders. "Two different geo-technical engineers confirmed the instability of the massive rock formations in this critical area," attests the HAER report. The elegant late-1970s solution was the viaduct, a radical span built from its starting point outward, over thin air, with con-

crete segments glued together and tensioned with cables into a serpentine causeway just feet from trees, rocks, and thousands of feet of air.

Nobody better understood the challenges or worked harder for success than the Blue Ridge Parkway landscape architects whose toil and travail at the hands of nature—and people like Hugh Morton—redeemed the promise of the Parkway. First superintendent and Parkway designer Stanley Abbott, a true giant in the field, thought the Parkway should "lie easily on the ground . . . and appear as if it had grown out of the soil." Nevertheless, the lake named after him at Peaks of Otter in Virginia was a fragile mountain bog when the Parkway was built. Home to the endangered Peaks of Otter salamander, it would still be a bog under today's standards. The times and meaning of "light on the land" have changed, but greater sensitivity reigns thanks to later landscape architects and planners, among them the Parkway's viaduct-era resident landscape architect Robert Allen "Bob" Hope and planner Gary Johnson.

In an oral history recorded in 2000, Bob Hope described how the plan for the viaduct came about. "We had no idea how to get through there with a road," admits Hope. "Finally after about three or four hikes around there with everybody in the National Park Service," he chuckled, "we agreed that the only way to get through here was just to bridge all these rock formations and not disturb the rocks." After decades of wrangling with Hugh Morton, Hope remembered, "we kind of designed and built [ourselves] into a problem with our back against the wall. We had to do something." The Parkway's HAER report recalled "there were so many design lines studied that workers claimed every foot of the ground contained at least one survey stake." Eventually an "ironic situation developed: 'highway engineers sobered by the formidable obstacle to road construction, favored bridging the worst sections; while bridge engineers wary about bridge construction endorsed the idea of proceeding through the area by cuts and fills.'" Gary Johnson attributes the solution to the Federal Highway Administration. The engineer who

This image of the viaduct shows the Linn Cove information station to the left of the road, a "last minute" visitor facility that Morton was surprised to learn about. The now popular visitor site required the Parkway to buy an additional ten acres from Hugh Morton. North Carolina Collection, University of North Carolina Library at Chapel Hill. Photo by Hugh Morton.

Viaduct to History

Though the Linn Cove Viaduct is lauded, it's not widely appreciated why the structure is noteworthy. The High Country landmark may be nothing less than the combined genius of the twentieth century's two top bridge designers.

The Parkway's chosen route was especially problematical below Black Rock Cliffs, a location the Parkway's Historic American Engineering Record (HAER) report called "amongst the most environmentally sensitive in the eastern United States." Fortuitously, by the late 1970s, emerging commercial computer technology had permitted designers Eugene "Gene" Figg Jr. (1936–2002) and Jean Muller (1925–2005) to reinvent bridge design. The viaduct that resulted owes its significance, asserts the HAER report, to the "respect with which it treated the site" and the "progressive method of construction it employed."

The bridge may be the best example of Figg and Muller's essential method: a "complex precast concrete segmental and cable-stayed bridge design." Each of the viaduct's 153, fifty-ton segments was cast to perfectly abut its mate. Each was epoxied to the previous segment and then tensioned with cables. The cantilevered construction method known as progressive placement had only been invented seven years before. Each piece of the bridge was lowered out from the end of the viaduct and attached, a method "originally developed to build over water." This technique created an extremely complex array of pressures on the bridge as it went from suspended and hanging to supported atop the seven piers that are its only points of contact with the ground.

Many photos documenting construction of the viaduct were taken from below or beside the bridge. But from above, on the crags of Black Rock Cliffs, the amazing construction project looked downright death-defying. Photo by Randy Johnson.

Thus the viaduct soars over an awesome boulder field with minimal impact. This was the first and longest bridge in North America to "follow the slope's contour," records the HAER report, permitting it to gracefully wind and weave. That gave the bridge "almost every kind of geometry used in highway construction," creating curvature "in two directions" and an "'S-and-a-half' or 'W' shape." Only one bridge segment wasn't curved.

Jasper Construction Company of Plymouth, Minnesota, won the contract in 1978. Work started in May 1979, and the last segment was placed in December 1982. Finalization of the railings and road surface took place in 1983. Jasper was credited with great skill and innovation in coping with unforeseen complications while still finishing on time. The company's pace of fabrication accelerated from one segment every two weeks to four a week and employed a concrete mixture that both exceeded the strength required and cured during winter's coldest temperatures. A shelter built on the end of the viaduct ensured year-round progress. The final cost was $9,863,384, more than $8,000 a foot for the 1,243-foot-long bridge.

Gene Figg Jr. cut his teeth on the Interstate Highway System, and Paris-based Jean Muller started his career after World War II as a protege of Eugene Freyssinet, the inventor of prestressed concrete. Like Figg, Muller refined his skills in Europe and the United States in the postwar bridge-building boom. They created Figg & Muller Engineering Group in 1978. Their viaduct won many honors, including the 1984 Presidential Design Award, which praised it for being "technically innovative and respectful of the environmental situation" as well as "elegant, economical, and new." The design provides "accessibility by animal life below" and "gives the motorist the sensation of driving tantalizingly on air while the earth goes by." One engineering journal concluded that when Figg & Muller "coupled the precast, prestressed concrete techniques with cable-stayed supports, they helped change the way bridges were built in North America." Figg was aiming high. "We are designing bridges for 100 years or more. It needs to be a piece of art." Parkway motorists surely agree they succeeded.

made the difference and "sold Federal Highway on precast segments placed in progressive placement," Hope remembered, was R. B. "Rex" Cocroft. The design saga started with countless planning meetings at Grandfather. "I don't know how long this process had gone on," Hope concluded, "but the outcome usually was, they would go back to Arlington and study it some more." Finally "Federal Highway decided they would stay there until they worked it out." Recalls Hope, "That night Rex had a topo map of the area and he started circling in red the points where there were suitable footings." With footing sites marked on the map, "they decided, 'Well, there, that was the design.' They just connected the red dots and there's your bridge." This road would not be gouged through a "piece of land" as it might have been decades earlier. It would float over a sensitive environment elevated above carefully chosen single spots that could support a span.

Gary Johnson was among the key National Park Service staffers overseeing the "missing link." After serving in Vietnam and earning a degree at Virginia Tech, he found himself at the National Park Service's Denver Service Center in the late 1970s. As the primary project inspector with federal highway engineers at Grandfather Mountain, Johnson was one of five people pictured in a Denver Service Center newsletter at the viaduct site, "an area undisturbed by roads or even trails." One participant was asked what he thought of the bushwhack hike. "That was two hikes for me," he confessed, "my first and my last through that part of the country, though it was beautiful." Johnson became "the enforcer" for efforts to lessen impact. Site protection was paramount, and only trees below the viaduct could be removed. Johnson handpicked and flagged each tree to cut. Once he found a mass of dirt and rocks against an ancient tree, and "I really let 'em have it," he remembers. "I told them to build tree wells and walk a lot more softly." About a week later he was called back. The contractor refused to cut an unflagged tree. "This tree was six feet tall and one inch in diameter," he laughs. Johnson suspected "these guys were messing with me but they'd gotten the message." Environmental impact statements were in their infancy. The statement Hope and Johnson had written for the viaduct was only thirty pages. "It would be a book today," he states. "We'd have botanists and biologists all over out there. Truth be told, many of the species on that mountainside weren't even inventoried. Nevertheless, the National Environmental Policy Act had set some standards. Environmental sensitivity was at the front of our minds."

The route debate had been about environmental impact from the start, and good news emerged. Scarring that the Park Service feared would result on Morton's middle route was softened or eliminated by technology. Line B forced the road lower on the mountain, with more drainages to cross and more curves and turns, one reason why the Parkway's 45 mph speed limit remains 45 mph on Grandfather. Additional bridges were needed, but even more were added as sensitive areas had to be crossed. In one key spot, Johnson specified a very low bridge to preserve the complex natural drainage of an entire boulderfield forest ecosystem. To the consternation of Federal Highway engineers, Johnson and the Parkway got the bridges they demanded, eliminating scarring that would have occurred years before. Best of all, the bridges provide wildlife with safe avenues under the Parkway, an unexpected benefit on a mountain now known as a major wildlife corridor. Another victory of design over destruction came at "The Great Wall of China," a massive retaining wall opposite Rough Ridge Parking Area that Johnson confirms "was all new technology. The wall held the road away from the mountain, reducing the cut above and con-

taining fill below." Concludes Johnson, "It's likely that the years of controversy with Hugh Morton permitted the right solution to emerge. I personally believe that the viaduct was perfect for that landscape. If the road had been built when originally planned, it wouldn't be what it is today." Johnson came back to the Blue Ridge Parkway from 1994 to retirement in 2011. During those years, he literally "wrote the book" about preservation of the Parkway's scenic views, the *Guidebook for the Blue Ridge Parkway Scenery Conservation System*. He received the Appleman-Judd-Lewis Award for excellence in cultural resource management in 2011 from National Park Service director Jonathan Jarvis. Looking back, Johnson admits, "We never realized how iconic this part of the Parkway would become, but it's hard not to be proud to have helped design and build it. I'm convinced this part of the Parkway can trace its heritage all the way back to Stanley Abbott."

By the time the Parkway opened to wide acclaim, hikers were wandering the Tanawha Trail high above the road. Early Park Service planners had been right. Views from the crags of Rough Ridge would distinguish the entire Grandfather section; that was why they wanted the high route to begin with. Despite repeated Park Service assertions that this "middle route" would eliminate "reasonable foot access" to great views, the Tanawha Trail easily delivered those vistas without the impact of a road. But Tanawha almost didn't happen. In 2000, Bob Hope remembered, "When the parkway was being funded, we knew we wanted a foot trail to connect the overlooks, but there was no project money. So the superintendent (Gary Everhardt), decided to take it on as a project. He convinced the Federal Highway that the foot trail was an integral part of the parkway. And so it was funded." Imagine—"And so it was funded." Today, the Tanawha Trail is one of the most spectacular segments in North Carolina's Mountains-to-Sea Trail from the Great Smokies to the Outer Banks. On the trail's climb to Rough Ridge from Linn Cove it crosses a boulderfield forest like those spanned by Johnson's bridges. Now listed among Grand-

By the time the Parkway was finished, even hikers were concerned about the impact the Tanawha Trail might have on Rough Ridge, much less a parking lot on the summit proposed years before. Today a boardwalk carries hikers right past this distinctive stack rock, seen here in the pristine, pre-Parkway 1970s. Photo by Randy Johnson.

father's most endangered ecosystems, this pristine place still exists on the Tanawha Trail where it might have been destroyed had the high route been built. The passage of time has called other elements of Line A into question. One proposed trail would have led to the peak of Pilot Knob from a Rough Ridge parking area near the tunnel entrance. Today, all of Pilot Knob is off limits to protect an endangered species discovered in the 1980s. More ironically, the Tanawha Trail's gradual design frequently required that it climb onto Hugh Morton's land. He readily granted the path passage, agreeing to trail easements, all but one of which were donated.

Everhardt's Legacy of Healing

"I was there when the arguments and negotiations with Hugh Morton were fresh in people's mind,"

Gary Johnson recalls. "Sometimes things just happen when they're ready. This part of the Parkway almost seems predestined to have turned out for the best." Good karma flowed at the Parkway's opening ceremony in 1987. Everhardt remembered seeing Morton meet his old nemesis Sam Weems. "My guess," Everhardt says, "is that was the first time they'd ever met. It was touching to see them talking, two old warriors burying the hatchet. Each had to know it had all turned out pretty good." One newspaper piece at the time quoted Weems concluding "Morton just outlasted the Park Service" in a political battle where the governor was "not willing to side with us against his citizens." Ultimately, Weems was convinced the completed road achieved its "objective of grandeur."

Gary Everhardt often engaged Hugh Morton and helped heal the old wounds. As Grandfather's

Gary Everhardt (left) and Hugh Morton survey the Parkway route long before the road was built. As the viaduct debuted, Bob Hope told me, "The situation at Grandfather is the reverse of most national parks. The park is usually the scenic special resource and private lands and businesses encroach upon it. Here, the scenic resource is private land and the park is having the impact." Photo by Randy Johnson.

Gary Everhardt poses in 1987 at the viaduct viewpoint Hugh Morton made famous with a variety of postcards and photos. Photo by Randy Johnson.

trail manager during those years, I remember scrambling over the mountainside during Parkway construction, exploring the future route of the road and Tanawha Trail with Morton, Everhardt, and landscape architect Hope. I feel privileged to have experienced the constructive spirit they displayed as we discussed backcountry management issues while the "missing link" came to a close. "Hugh was one of the great supporters of the Parkway," Everhardt told me in 2010. "The time that went by helped generate opportunities and alternatives. What more fitting conclusion for the Parkway could there be than the Linn Cove Viaduct? Hugh Morton deserves credit for that." Morton and Everhardt later cooperated to usher in an era of public support for preservation along the Parkway. To prevent development, they orchestrated purchase of two private tracts, one below the viaduct, and transferred them to the U.S. Forest Service. To achieve larger preservation of lands adjacent to the Parkway, Morton and Everhardt formed an alliance with the Conservation Trust for North Carolina. In late 2013, the trust purchased its fiftieth Parkway-buffering parcel, having saved more than 31,000 acres. Parkway superintendent Phil Francis (from 2005 to 2013) says Everhardt "was the right person at the right time." His tenure as Park Service director gave him "connections and political acumen that many people wouldn't possess. Gary knew better than anyone how important relationship-building is. That's why we're sitting in a building (Parkway headquarters) named after Gary Everhardt." How appropriate that the man who completed the Linn Cove Viaduct is acclaimed for building bridges between people—a skill missing on both sides during the controversy. Says Everhardt, "Almost everybody does for parks what they can at the time they're there to do it." After forty-two years with the National Park Service, if anyone can claim the title, Gary Everhardt may be Mr. Blue Ridge Parkway, or at least Superintendent Emeritus.

This remarkable image by High Country photographer Todd Bush illustrates the technical and scenic significance of the viaduct as the capstone of the entire Blue Ridge Parkway. It easily proves that the Park Service history of the bridge was correct in maintaining that the viaduct has "almost every kind of geometry used in highway construction," including curvature "in two directions." Photo by Todd Bush/www.bushphoto.com.

Seeing Past the Past

One question lingers. If the Parkway had taken the high route, would it have undermined Hugh Morton's toll road receipts? The North Carolina Highway Commission concluded that "landowner (Morton) is unduly alarmed" and "without question, the high bridge would have an enormous increase in visitors," high route or not. Turns out they were right. Attendance at the attraction closely rises and falls with Parkway visitation, strong evidence that the success of Grandfather Mountain is not in competition with the Blue Ridge Parkway but dependent on it. Despite Morton's surely unfounded fear for his "high bridge," few would deny that the long debate gave us a Grandfather part of the Parkway that's far superior to anything that might have come earlier. While the viaduct's much-touted environmental sensitivity is interpreted by some as mythology that gives Morton unjustified claim to being an environmentalist, it's difficult to deny that the viaduct's builders see their own efforts as a watershed moment in protection of the environment. Even assuming, as critics do, that Morton was disingenuous when he claimed to care about the environment, darn if the environment didn't benefit anyway! Talk about being stuck between a rock and . . . Grandfather Mountain. After years watching the Parkway battle wind down into completion of the road, I personally fear Morton's most avid detractors take their own "low route." The Parkway at Grandfather is easy to understand as a complex collision of bull-headed people with positive and negative motivations muddling through to an ultimately sound solution. A dispassionate view turns the black and white of that battle into shades of gray. Let's simply celebrate that the most visited unit of the national park system came to such a successful conclusion. Environmental preservation handily wins out over private greed as the dominant narrative at Grandfather. Thankfully, as the Parkway was opening, the pendulum would only swing further in that direction. High route or not, the verdict is in: Grandfather Mountain is the peak of the Blue Ridge Parkway experience.

9 The Path To Preservation

Winter in MacRae Meadows offers a dramatic encounter with whatever weather is challenging the survival of species on the higher summits. In this view, a departing storm bathes Linville Peak in cloud-scattered alpenglow. Photo by Tommy White Photography, www.tommywhitephotography.com.

Clyde Smith's trails were in serious decline if not gone by the late 1970s. Construction of the new Blue Ridge Parkway had severed the Daniel Boone Scout Trail, and few hikers located the old trace above the road, much less reached Calloway Peak. Grandfather's admittedly primitive paths were disappearing,

even as Baby Boomers were crowding trails all across America. Grandfather was a peak people increasingly climbed by car, and Hugh Morton's Mile-High Swinging Bridge was packing 'em in. It's hard to believe today, but one of the South's most significant natural areas was an increasingly marginalized tract attached to a tourist attraction. The private landowner did not seem intent on

On my first early 1970s winter climb of Grandfather, this Clyde Smith sign rotting in the snow made quite an impression. Years later the redwood artifact was still lying there, so I strapped it to a pack board and humped it off the hill. Photo by Randy Johnson.

development, but in fact, resort communities were envisioned for pristine parts of the mountain. Fortunately, the process of preservation was about to begin.

Birth of the Modern Backcountry

Not every hiker wanting to climb Grandfather was deterred by deteriorating trails. In the summer of 1972, I drove up to the Mile-High Swinging Bridge and tracked the brushy Grandfather Trail to find Michaux's vertical-mile vistas. Friends and I climbed Mount Washington in winter and found similar challenge camping for a week in January near Calloway Peak. Then, reeking of campfire smoke, we'd gorge in not-so-family-like style at the Dan'l Boone Inn. There was something transcendent about Grandfather, and I knew I wasn't the first to feel it. When I discovered an artistic old trail sign rotting in the snow, I got goosebumps and followed it to a lifetime of fascination with the mountain. One spring day, a security guard and

"No Trespassing" signs turned me away from the Shanty Spring Trail. Doug Coffey, the charismatic owner of Invershiel Texaco, told me hikers were getting lost and one had died. National parks and forests have professional trail managers, but try as Hugh Morton might, his mountain was a dangerous free-for-all. And when trails disappear, hikers can too. The easy answer was to proclaim "No Trespassing" and "close" one of the most significant mountains in eastern America. I drove to the attraction entrance and convinced the craggy-faced manager to let me hike. With a withering gaze, he took my money and gave me a receipt to get past the guard.

I couldn't get the fate of the mountain out of my mind that snowy fall-color weekend. Grandfather was too special to lose. A solution slowly took shape. I was finishing graduate school and aiming at a career in backcountry research and management. My focus was carrying capacity: How many hikers are too many on a trail system? My mission was to devise trail management policies that hikers would support even if restrictions were required. In a nutshell, that was the challenge at Grandfather. My idealism aside, no businessperson would permit public access without a self-sustaining solution. The key seemed to be charging a backcountry fee, a policy the Appalachian Mountain Club was exploring at busy Appalachian Trail campsites I'd been studying in New England during the mid-1970s. The fees helped pay caretakers to protect the resource, and the campers I surveyed seemed happy to contribute. That gave me an idea. I would devise something new for Hugh Morton: a self-supporting hiker fee system on private property. I'd base my plan on recreation research undergirding management of federal forests and my own studies funded by the U.S. Forest Service and the Appalachian Mountain Club. That snowy weekend, I came off the mountain burning with desire to protect Grandfather's trails. I met Hugh Morton and assured him that a (hopefully) break-even hiking fee program could make the trails safe. I knew that without public access, development would be easier to initiate, threatening any future possibility of public ownership. With the Blue Ridge Parkway destined for completion in a decade, I told him he'd never keep people off his mountain. His best option was to professionally manage it like public land. "How are we going to do that?" he asked. "We don't have anyone like that at Grandfather Mountain." I said, "Hire me." We discussed the details, including that the mountain was closed in winter. Regardless, I knew that without year-round control, continuing problems would sink a backcountry management experiment and end public access. I weighed my dedication to keeping the mountain open against leaving graduate school just shy of a master's degree and accepted a seasonal salary doled out over twelve months instead of seven. Morton agreed I'd have flexibility to subsidize my income. Asked to check in with mountain manager Robert Hartley, I strode into his office in cut-off blue jean shorts and hiking boots. Once again, he gave me that steady appraising gaze. I stuck out my hand. "Can

I call you Bob?" I asked. No, it was very obvious, Mr. Hartley could not be called Bob. Which may account for his nickname for me: "Short britches." Only years later did I realize how understandably skeptical Hartley was of a "college boy" who dared step into the shoes of his own father, Squire Hartley, a legend almost as big as the mountain itself.

Clearing the Trails

New trailhead signs explained that a hiking permit was required and available across the street. People groused at the "capitalist plot." I never knew what to expect when I said, "Hi, I'm the trail manager. May I check your hiking permit, please?" At the crux of that trailside argument—I mean, encounter—was the eco-outraged idea that "nobody should own a mountain." Hundreds thought the "filthy rich guy named Morton" actually "owns Morton Salt." Rebranding Grandfather as a "publicly accessible private preserve," I argued that Morton had protected the highest peaks while publicly owned parks had summit parking lots on Mount Mitchell and elsewhere. Grandfather welcomes hikers, I assured; all we ask is that they offset our lack of tax funding and "put their money where their feet are." That philosophy fit the times. Much improved, litter-free trails yielded converts. Hikers got a trail map, and the permit often helped people locate overdue hikers. Trail inquiries increased, and so did thank-you notes. Opening the trails was critical, but finding them came first. Slowly the vegetation gave way, downed trees were removed, and colored blazes appeared. New trail signs went up, with lettering gouged out with hand-held carving tools so I could avoid asking to buy a routing machine. Trail work became a solitary labor of love, just me and my big, black, startlingly yellow-eyed, white-bearded Irish Wolfhound Luke, a hand-signal-activated assistant ranger who stared at my trailside debates from just above the discussion. I don't know when the weedeater was invented, but months of swing-blading convinced me I knew what early mountaineers suffered harvesting hay by hand. Volunteers made the difference, especially my brother Ken, newly

Falls and Fatalities

How many people have died on Grandfather Mountain? Not as many as have perished on Mount Washington, the deadliest, arctic Appalachian summit. Counting all the likely causes, Grandfather's "death toll" is easily more than a dozen, perhaps much more when the distant past is included. Factor in close calls, and you have one dangerous mountain.

Falling for Grandfather

Herpetologist Worth Weller died walking off a waterfall. One day below Rough Ridge, a solo free climber without ropes or a belay fell thirty feet onto boulders beside me. After screaming for a while, he miraculously hobbled off.

Hypothermia

Hypothermia has claimed at least one hiker. On Friday, January 2, 1976, Charlotte friends Thomas Alva Loftis Jr. and John Kiker, both twenty-three, set out for Calloway Peak on Shanty Spring Trail in light jackets. Survivor Kiker told Avery County sheriff Howard Daniels they "got lost off the main trail," sheltered under a cliff, "and tried to stay awake to keep from freezing." The temperature dropped with Friday's rain, and the wind chill factor neared zero. When Loftis fell into a creek, Kiker went ahead for help. Saturday afternoon searchers found Loftis's body slumped over a tree. He'd likely died from a combination of hypothermia and a heart attack. His death led to the trail closure that inspired my 1978

Litter-bearers carry a casualty. Photo by Randy Johnson.

backcountry trail permit program. In the years since, the mountain's rangers have intervened when exposure might have claimed more lives.

Heart Attacks

Simple exertion, especially climbing steep, rocky trails, can induce a heart attack. In one 1980s incident, a father trying to keep up with energetic young kids was stricken on one of the Grandfather Trail's ladders. He had to be pried from the rungs. Another heart attack death happened in 2010. Always let the slowest, least-fit person set the pace.

Lightning

There's no way to know for sure how many people have been struck by lightning on the sharp summits of Grandfather Mountain. In July 1926, two young men from Cary's Flat were struck under a boulder on Yonahlossee Road. One died. In the mid-1980s, a party of hikers was hit on the whaleback cliffs of the Grandfather Trail at Alpine Meadow campsite. They'd been warned not to cross the mountain's crest with thunderstorms threatening. Several hikers were stunned, but one was catapulted off the cliff into evergreens far below. A helicopter used by a crew filming a movie nearby was deployed, and as trail manager, I located the body from the air while a litter team climbed the mountain. The rescuers had no hope of finding the body without being led, so in an amazing feat of flying, the pilot of the Vietnam-era Huey deftly hovered just feet above cliffs as I jumped out. That dangerous move is just one example of the unexpected risks responders encounter when hikers take chances in the backcountry.

out of the navy, offering unpaid labor for "room and board" from my meager salary. I recruited Boone outdoor types, Scout groups, Outward Bound crews, and ski, hiking, outing, and environmental clubs. Some got "free hiking" for their help, including Caldwell County juvenile court kids led by counselor Richard "Gerry" McDade. First intern Jim Boone tamed erosion with railroad tie steps. We replaced decaying log ladders from the 1940s. The Daniel Boone Scout Trail took a year of "connecting the dots"—crawling on hands and knees searching for tin-can-lid trail markers. It was open by 1979. In 1980, my first "Backcountry Report" found hiking was way up at Grandfather. The program had more than broken even. Clyde Smith's backcountry momentum was coming back.

Grandfather was the Rodney Dangerfield of southern summits. Hugh Morton was a master of public slideshows; but the backcountry had an untold story, and I'd have to tell it. When I first met him, I showed him postcards I had published in New England and assured him my photography and writing could cultivate support for the permit program. I was naively unaware that Morton was the very epitome of postcards and public relations. I screened my backcountry slideshow for outdoor clubs, civic organizations, and anybody else who offered me a mic. I gave tent-side interpretive talks and led wildflower walks for the High Country Host organization's 1980s Wildflower Weekends. Later trail manager Steve Miller named Storyteller's Rock after continuing campsite talks that trail crewman Ed Schultz gave there. My bigger goal became counteracting media silence about the state's most spectacular trails. Refreshingly, former Carolina Mountain Club president Bernard Elias called Grandfather the "Climax of the Blue Ridge in height and grandeur" in a guide map he published. In 1982 Allen de Hart's first statewide trail guide was the perfect example of how private ownership marginalized the mountain. I finally found Grandfather in the back of his book under "Private Trails." I devoted off-work hours to "freelance writing," publicizing Grandfather's trails gratis as an editor at the fledgling *Mountain Times*. Despite my working at Grandfather, many publications wanted stories on a hidden hiking area. *The State* magazine (now *Our State*) aptly called it

(*Left, top*) The task of bringing back a trail system that was overgrown if not gone took years of backbreaking work. Here Ken Johnson starts the task of locating the Daniel Boone Scout Trail in 1979. Photo by Randy Johnson.

(*Left, bottom*) Near today's Alpine Meadow campsite, Randy Johnson painstakingly blazes the Grandfather Trail in 1978 while brother Ken looks on. Such scrupulous attention to detail was critical in gaining public support for the fee system. Maintenance superior to that found in public parks was intended to demonstrate that hikers paying to use a privately owned preserve were entitled to customer service. Photo by William A. Bake.

(*Above*) Even the best of Smith's remaining ladders were rickety and unsafe. Realizing an accident could shut down the trails for good, we set about replacing them as fast as we could. Volunteers from the local Sierra Club chapter played a key role. Photo by Randy Johnson.

This coffee can lid trail marker is likely the last one remaining from the dark days of World War II when Clyde Smith and his Scouts marked their now classic climb to Calloway Peak. Photo by Randy Johnson.

Setting out to make Grandfather widely known as a great place to hike, I invited Allen de Hart to visit the mountain. Now a noted trail guide author and longtime force in the creation of the Mountains-to-Sea Trail, de Hart included Grandfather in his first statewide guide, written for the Appalachian Mountain Club. Photo by Randy Johnson.

"The Other Side of the Mountain." I wanted nothing less than for the backcountry to become "the dog" that wagged "the tail" of the attraction. By the 1990s, major media like the *Atlanta Journal-Constitution* and *Southern Living* had featured the trails, bestowing added visibility and appeal on the attraction. More and more hikers drove to the Swinging Bridge.

I had an ulterior motive. Today we help kids avoid "nature deficit disorder," but back in the 1940s, Ira Spring encouraged "green bonding." Beyond "the benefits it brought to the hiker; far more important," wrote John Caldbick in an essay about Spring, is "the benefit it would bring to the wilderness itself. Crowded trails were a trade-off for the creation of a citizen army of wilderness protectors." The backcountry needed a constituency, and the trail renaissance was creating it. Grandfather's designation as a state Natural Heritage Area helped. With support from the Nature Conservancy (TNC), the Heritage Program started in 1977 and began inventorying important tracts. Dr. Ritchie Bell, founding director of the North Carolina Botanical Garden, urged the

first head of the heritage program, Chuck Roe, to approach Morton about registering the mountain. I encouraged that effort and afterward touted the designation on trail maps and signs. Money to purchase conservation easements became available under the Natural Heritage Trust Fund in the late 1980s, and until my departure in mid-1990, I lobbied Morton to consider easements as a way to retain ownership while protecting the mountain and reducing property taxes. Without permanent preservation, I reminded him, someone could "rewrite your biography." Other accolades elevated the backcountry. I secured the Department of the Interior's National Recreation Trail designation for the Grandfather Trail and Daniel Boone Scout Trail in 1986, a status that required Morton's formal pledge of public access. Ironically, the certificates were signed by James Watt, the notoriously pro-privatization interior secretary in the administration of Ronald Reagan.

Research and Renown

Turning to my research roots, I encouraged the kind of backcountry scientific study conducted in national parks and forests. I met an occasional academician enjoying free trail access with students and was shocked at how many displayed disrespect for "Morton's mountain." Private ownership was tainting the status of a natural area. John C. Hendee, one of the nation's most prominent wilderness researchers and author of *Wilderness Management*, then assistant director of the Forest Service's Southeastern Forest Experiment Station in Asheville, told Morton, "Because of private ownership Grandfather Mountain may not have received the same degree of scrutiny by scientists as other locations." Just the stigma of entrance fees discouraged research. Only scientists could corroborate that Grandfather Mountain was a place worth protecting, so I started attending research conferences, presenting policy papers on the fee system. Forest Service friends referred scientists. I made part of my job cooperating with researchers studying the mountain's wildest acres. "Grandfather Mountain" started showing up on symposia syllabi, and the list of study topics grew long, from the balsam woolly adelgid to acid rain, trout populations, and even earthquakes with a solar-powered seismometer on the summit. (Sadly, the device wasn't able to count trail traffic by monitoring the footfalls of hikers.) Word got out. Peregrine falcons were reintroduced in 1984. Endangered species of bats and flying squirrels were discovered and studied. By the late 1980s, researchers with the Natural Heritage Area program and Wildlife Resources Commission joined in, taking a fresh look at the mountain, actively inventorying flora and fauna. Grandfather was becoming re-renowned for species diversity.

My private-land-user-fee ethos intrigued public land managers coping with budget cuts. In 1984, the mountain was featured at a Fees for Outdoor Recreation conference sponsored by the U.S. Forest Service's Northeastern Forest Experiment Station. John Hendee visited Grandfather to see the program in action and told Hugh Morton he was "very impressed" with "to my knowledge, the only private wilderness management program in the country." Hendee said Grandfather was "proving possible what many have claimed could not be done." Morton was an entrepreneur with "the foresight and good taste to include wilderness in the spectrum of recreation you offer." The current fourth edition of Hendee's classic book *Wilderness Management*, now by principal author Chad Dawson, still references the uniqueness of Grandfather's "private wilderness." The mountain's growing reputation as a laboratory of backcountry management policy went national in 1984, gaining mainstream coverage with a user fee debate in *Backpacker* magazine and articles in *American Forests*, a magazine covering innovations in forestry since 1895 that had skewered Morton during the Parkway debate. In 1987, the *Journal of Leisure Research* published a study that compared hiker attitudes about fees at Linville Gorge and Grandfather, recording a 98 percent fee compliance rate at Grandfather. Conducted by researchers at Virginia Tech's School of Forestry, the study was strong evidence that hikers would support "dedicated fees," jargon for fees that benefit the park where they are charged. In a 1996 *International Journal of Wilderness* article, I profiled "Grandfather Mountain: A Private us Wilderness Experiment," saying Grandfather had proven that "when wilderness protection and management are balanced against the acceptability of user fees, hikers indeed can see the forest through the trees." Recreation fees were national news, and in 1996, legislation permitted the U.S. Forest Service and the National Park Service to "experiment" with charging fees and returning them to the originating park. That program continues to authorize fees on public land—and Grandfather Mountain is part of that narrative. By 1992, Grandfather had become an International Biosphere Reserve, designated by the United Nations, in part because long-standing research in the backcountry easily met the requirement that scientific study take place in reserves. As the mountain was designated, Hugh Morton told me, "Whatever we've been doing [with research] was the right thing. We haven't changed anything to get the Good Housekeeping Seal of Approval."

When Morton decided to develop the Wilmor tract in the mid-1980s, I knew the historic Shanty Spring Trail was doomed. But as I'd hoped, by then such a popular path required replacement. I chose a trail corridor and picked the name Profile Trail for a view of the Grandfather face missing since Shepherd Dugger's days. Micro design was done later as the mountain made its own demands. Kinney Baughman, one of the principal builders, admitted, "At times, you just have to listen to what the mountain wants." He proposed to his first wife on the trail. Most construction took from 1985 to 1987, but it stretched on and got complicated. Hugh Morton asked me to hire his son Jim, and eventually the job split into contending crews that focused on different tasks. By far the greatest mileage of the trail required "benching," a numbingly arduous excavation of flat treadway akin to building a mini–road grade that I called "digging a ditch in a rock-pile." The other, more creative task was building steps with stone. Trying to complete the project quickly, I lobbied against grandiose rock work, embracing a "lighter on the land" philosophy. Nevertheless, the rock-wall-encircled bonfire pit at Profile campsite was so big I mocked it as "Virgin Sacrifice Memorial Campsite." Similar features took months. I just wanted to finish before retirement. One long stairway was named Peregrine Flight after the endangered bird released on the mountain. Sadly, winching rocks for its construction destroyed a colony of endangered plants and earned the only letter of censure ever received from the Natural Heritage Program. Volunteers showed up to receive Jim's "Grandfather Mountain Trailblazers" T-shirt, as did a growing group of unregistered hikers who didn't need to buy

permits because they knew the owner's son. Ultimately, everybody slaving away out there finally got the deed done. We all dug tread and worked with stone. When the trail finally opened—the most costly, protracted project of the entire backcountry program—I was ready to go back to just wrestling with the mountain. The challenge of the Blue Ridge Parkway had arrived.

The birth of the trail program started a ten-year countdown to the opening of the Parkway. Thousands would be crawling over the flanks of the mountain, trampling fragile plants and challenging a single person's ability to enforce the permit system. It was imperative to prepare. Luckily, Superintendent Gary Everhardt was able to fund a "Parkway parallel trail." If done correctly, I reasoned, a path above the road could help limit damage to the backcountry. The Mountains-to-Sea Trail (MST) was being built from the Smokies to the Outer Banks, with the Parkway as a designated corridor. I thought Grandfather's roadside trail should be part of the MST and got involved with volunteers building it. In 1982, the first statewide MST trek took place, and figurehead hiker Lee Price sampled views from Grandfather's crags above the Parkway. In yellow brush coats, wilderness trail specialists Jack Dollan and Robert Steinholtz from the Park Service's Denver Service Center flagged the trail's route across Grandfather from Beacon Heights to Price Park Campground. They wanted to climb above Morton's property line for gradual grades and better views, and I persuaded Morton to agree, knowing hikers would bushwhack higher if trails avoided viewpoints. I had second thoughts at Rough Ridge, where hordes of hikers could destroy the alpinelike vegetation. Rock climbing was emerging by the early 1980s, and the cliffs of Rough Ridge were called Ship Rock. Classic North Carolina climbs were being pioneered by High Country climbers Dan Perry, Tommy Howard, Lee Carter, Doug "the Beast" Reid, Vernon Scarborough, and Jim Okel. Some hikers toss rocks off cliffs, so it didn't seem smart to me to put a trail above a climbing site. I suggested that Tanawha climb to where today's boardwalks are located, then skirt

Planely an Obstacle: Crashes on Grandfather

In evergreens under Calloway Peak, I heard sobbing near the remains of a private airplane that had crashed a year before. A young woman was weeping beside her backpack, and when she looked up startled, I apologized and explained, "I'm the backcountry manager—I didn't mean to invade your privacy." After a brief talk, I hiked away full of sympathy for her and the relative who'd died on that lonely mountaintop. The incident drives home how unusual it was that Grandfather Mountain suffered not one but a string of three plane crashes, one each in 1978, 1979, and 1980.

Clouds and Calloway

On Friday, May 12, 1978, according to the FAA report, a "CESSNA 182Q" aircraft flown for "pleasure" by a "noncommercial" pilot aged "47" took off from Seven Springs, Pennsylvania, bound for Florida. Sadly, his final destination was Grandfather Mountain. The pilot was rated for "visual flight rules" and was not trained to fly solely by instruments. Expecting to see clearly during the trip, he continued to fly visually "into adverse weather conditions" with "mountain tops obscured." He "collided with trees" while "in flight: normal cruise." Also "found in wreckage" was "one outdated low altitude enroute chart." He had "inadequate pre-flight planning and/or preparation" for "low ceiling" and "rain." His injuries

In a 1980 crash, the plane literally flew into the summit boulder of MacRae Peak on the side of the peak opposite the trail. Nevertheless, one of the plane's propellers landed right beside the summit ladder and easily could have hit hikers if they'd been present. Photo by Randy Johnson.

were "F." Fatal. The plane was missing for four days and was so strewn across Calloway Peak that a pilot had to tell searchers "they were in the middle of the wreckage." The day before, two searchers had been injured when their own plane crashed. On windy days, hikers still ponder the plane's creaking aluminum not far from Hi-Balsam Shelter.

Wrong Place, Right Time

On Sunday, September 16, 1979, I was patrolling the clifftops near Calloway Gap with volunteers Keith Grogan and Ken Johnson. Clear views stretched west, but a massive cloud bank clung east of the peaks. Then at full gallop a hiker almost knocked us down. "There's been a plane crash!" Lee Kirksey yelled. Just minutes earlier he'd heard an engine and thought, "Boy, I hope that plane isn't as low as it sounds." Then, BOOM, an explosion resounded in the dense clouds. Kirksey and I jogged down to report the accident while Ken, a Navy medical corpsman, and Keith searched. Between Watauga View and Calloway Peak, air rising through a rocky notch brought them the smell of smoke and fuel. When they found the plane, the pilot was afire in the wreckage and flames had to be extinguished around the site. The man had lived near Boone and was an experienced pilot, a licensed airplane mechanic, and a flying instructor. The crash had also been heard by hang gliders dodging clouds that day in the Masters of Hang Gliding Championships.

But for a Few Final Feet

On Monday, April 7, 1980, a third crash happened. A forty-six-year-old man on his way from Myrtle Beach to Ohio was "flying between two cloud layers, by visual aid," stated the report. Those layers apparently concealed MacRae Peak. The pilot "hit mtn," directly slamming the uppermost boulder that hikers reach by ladder. Thirty more feet and he would have lived. The man held the "highest rating sanctioned by the FAA, transport pilot, a rating required of airline pilots." The plane wasn't found for two days, and searchers said the man's hand was clasping a tree root beside the rock. Tragically, under "Miscellaneous Acts, Conditions," the FAA report concluded "Alcoholic impairment of efficiency and judgment." The crash was so close to the Swinging Bridge that an entourage, including Hugh Morton and Robert Hartley, made the climb. Avery County sheriff Braswell forgot to duck under "Head Bumpin' Rock." Blood dried below a gash on his scalp. Later, the crash was broken up and concealed in a nearby cave. Grandfather looked like it was going to be "the Cape Hatteras of Southern airways" one newspaper predicted. Instead, the mountain got its own warning on aviation charts, and there have been no further crashes . . . so far.

below the climbing cliffs. But the Parkway planners wanted to cross the summit—as much, I knew, to own Rough Ridge as to build a trail. I urged Morton to grant the additional acreage, hoping a "high route" for the trail would restrain bootleg paths, concentrate use on one route, and funnel hikers back to the Parkway. Another plus: with Rough Ridge in public ownership, I wouldn't need to enforce a trail permit for climbers and hikers. Climbers weren't happy at first. Thomas Kelley was writing the state's first rock climbing book, and the Parkway folks asked him not to include Rough Ridge. In a 1986 tour with Parkway officials, Kelley was shocked at the destruction wrought by the new path. "How could any responsible organization have such a blatant disregard for such a pristine area," he wrote to climbers. Eventually, our decision to cede Rough Ridge to the Parkway pleased me most when conservation easements eliminated rock climbing everywhere else on the mountain.

The Parkway had me "running scared." The Boone Trail opened in 1979, and Hi-Balsam Shelter was rebuilt in the summer of 1981. The Parkway let the Tanawha contract in the summer of 1983. I wanted new trails to excite hikers, especially a loop hike, so I turned to trailless parts of the mountain, like the Boone Fork Bowl. On Saturday August 6,

One of the few early Clyde Smith signs that remained intact illustrates the craftsmanship that Smith brought to signs up and down the Appalachian Trail and all over eastern America. Photo by Randy Johnson.

1983, I christened new, volunteer-built trails in the bowl when the first hikers circled the view-packed Cragway circuit. That fall, Grandfather and the new North Carolina Trails Association sponsored a statewide trail construction workshop on the mountain, and Dollan wowed attendees. Organization president Louise Chatfield wanted a follow-up aimed at "building the trails we'll be hiking in the year 2000." At a second trail workshop at Grandfather in 1984, participants built steps on the Cragway Trail and watched low-tech Tanawha contractors use a rototiller to bench soil. Tanawha opened in sections as the debut of the Parkway neared. Paddling guide author Bob Benner and I, cochairs of the MST's Central Blue Ridge task force, designed and helped build a trail that joined the MST and Tanawha Trail at Beacon Heights. A trail named Tanawha—the Cherokee word for "great

hawk or eagle"—would carry the MST soaring across the flank of Grandfather Mountain.

A Bridge to Preservation

By 1990, TNC was working with Hugh Morton to acquire conservation easements on Grandfather's backcountry. Critics argue that easements create "tax free private preserves," but Grandfather was nowhere near private. The trails were overrun, and deliberately so. By creating a new kind of private preserve with public access, I'd hoped to make Hugh Morton ever more obligated to permit public use. By easement time, when some say the "preservation story" at Grandfather Mountain started, the trail fee system had already created a more-than-decade-long example of private land managed for the public good. Grandfather's backcountry "experiment" helped set the stage for

Rebuilding Hi-Balsam

For months, Grandfather Mountain's ancient maintenance man Johnny Cooper had asked, "Have you found that Boy Scout cabin yet?" No, I hadn't. Despite the magical twinkle in the old man's eyes, I doubted it existed. Johnny often told stories about the "Boy Scout Trail" that I spent a year reopening without finding the first clue about the cabin. Then one day, I decided to explore cliffs near Calloway Peak beside the highest trickles of Wilson Creek. When the terrain plummeted, I angled left into a rock wall. At a sloping ledge, I weighed the danger of falling where I wouldn't be found and pulled myself up. At the lip of the cliff, a wave of goosebumps almost dislodged me. A deflated and sagging trail shelter topped the rocks. No wonder I hadn't found it. Three sides were obscured when ice-and-snow-covered spruces were flattened by the wind. One stout branch had pierced the roof. Under the apex of an eave hung a masterfully crafted sign. It looked almost new with the crisply routed, white-painted

words "Hi-Balsam." Not "High Balsam" as in lofty. But "Hi" as in hello. Like greeting an old friend. I knew then that people would again sleep in "Hi-Balsam."

Johnny Cooper beamed when I told him I found the hut. "I told you h'it was out thar," he winked. When the time came to rebuild, a cadre of volunteers included Virginia forester Jack Corman and Outward Bound instructors Jerome "Jeep" Barrett of Jonas Ridge and Steve Owen of Boone. Except for logs, everything was carried up (cedar shakes arrived by llama). A shoestring budget dictated secondhand materials. I found a trove of planks in the mountain's decaying "dry shed," an old building in Linville once used to season lumber sawn from the mountain's virgin timber. I mentioned at the office that I hadn't bought planks and was cautioned not to use "a special stack of Mr. Morton's antique rock maple lumber." Too late. The triple-weight boards from Grandfather's ancient forest were back on the mountain—as the roof and floor. On Friday, August 21, 1981, I installed signs and pruned open a path. Years later

A 1940s photo of Hi-Balsam hand-tinted by Clyde Smith shows the shelter's wonderfully serrated sign. Positioned under the eave, it survived in pristine condition for years after the roof was pierced by a tree limb. Clyde and Hilda Smith Photo Collection.

Virginia forester Jack Corman (right) and Jerome Barrett of Jonas Ridge, longtime chief climbing instructor at the North Carolina Outward Bound School, pause as the new Hi-Balsam takes shape. Photo by Randy Johnson.

I got a letter from Clyde Smith's son, Clyde H. "Mickey" Smith, who helped build the original shelter. He hiked to the peak alone one day and was shocked to find a rebuilt remnant of his youth. I can only imagine how he felt pondering his dad's picture on a poster in the shelter. "I think my father's spirit will continue through the rebuilding of Hi-Balsam," he wrote. Thousands have camped at the shelter, including Hugh Morton, who spent the night while filming the nearby release of peregrine falcons. Luckily, when Morton lay back in his sleeping bag, he didn't recognize the "special" lumber he was looking up at.

Changing maintenance policies and personnel take their toll on any high-altitude structure. In recent years, maintainers may have missed regularly sweeping away duff from the shelter, and on one corner the lowest logs have sagged into decay. A shelter in use for three-quarters of a century now needs repair. Thankfully, first state park superintendent Sue McBean says she'll rebuild, and possibly relocate, Hi-Balsam—plans that seem to fit the shelter's historic cycle of renewal.

the "era of easements," introducing Hugh Morton to the researchers studying endangered bats in his caves and releasing falcons on his peaks, all of them praising increasingly renowned trails. Grandfather Mountain's lasting protection is a story that involves many people, not least of which were hordes of hikers who opened their wallets to buy backcountry access and support trail maintenance. A shift was happening. The lure of the wild became a reason to visit Mildred's mountain and not just to "drive a golf ball off of Linville Peak" from Billy Joe Patton's kitschy 1950s golf tee. The now discontinued "National Park experience" of watching a bonfire pushed off Yosemite Falls is gone too. Travelers had a more environmental ethic, and hikers no longer dismissed Grandfather as a "tourist trap." More importantly, the successful marketing of private wilderness at Grandfather reflected the emergence of environmental tourism we have come to call eco-tourism. Before that term was coined, it was being practiced on Grandfather Mountain, and Hugh Morton found himself ahead of that curve. His eventual openness to conservation easements (much less an outlandish self-supporting backcountry management system) reflects our new reality: Private landowners are of pivotal importance to the future of conservation. The bottom line, as they say, is that Hugh Morton found profit in preservation at Grandfather Mountain. That's a "development" even an ardent environmentalist should applaud.

The Era of Easements

Grandfather's backcountry was no longer a forgotten backdrop to a tourist attraction. Preservation of the peaks started coming into focus. North Carolina's network of Natural Heritage Areas was providing preservationists with a "road map to the most important areas in need of conservation," asserts Fred Annand, longtime North Carolina Nature Conservancy activist and key figure in Grandfather's preservation. The mountain showed up on that road map, and program director Chuck Roe, later founding director of the Conservation Trust for North Carolina, recommended that

Besides founding North Carolina's influential Natural Heritage Area program, Chuck Roe actively worked to ensure public access and protect Grandfather's backcountry. Here he explores the still trailless beauty of the White Rock Ridge, one of the most scenic, environmentally sensitive parts of Grandfather. Photo by Randy Johnson.

Annand and TNC target Grandfather for permanent protection. "It made sense that TNC would get to know the Morton family, to stay in touch," Annand reasoned. After funding became available through the Natural Heritage Trust Fund, "the Mortons apparently began to discuss the possibility of permanently protecting the most significant parts of Grandfather Mountain." One day in 1990, remembers Annand, Morton "had his son Hugh Morton, Jr. call me. We chatted and, out of the blue, he said, 'Well, the family has been talking about the future of Grandfather Mountain and we've decided we want to give it to The Nature Conservancy.' You can imagine my shock," exclaims Annand. Easements would ultimately foreclose future development on 1,460 backcountry acres, with Grandfather retaining the right to maintain the trail system. In December of 1990, the first 146-acre easement was donated. New easements were added over the years, each dedicated to the memory of a Morton family member or friend, including Morton's father and mother, Julian Morton and Agnes MacRae Morton; his grandparents Hugh and Rena MacRae; Uncle Joe Hartley; Hugh Morton Jr.; Charles Kuralt and Susanna Baird Kuralt; and Dr. and Mrs. Billy Graham. Morton was

extremely savvy in the way he took "full advantage of the charitable contribution," notes Annand. "Morton and his consultants came up with that first 146-acre figure to offset a specific dollar figure of income taxes owed." That was very attractive at the time. "Gifts" of land to qualified charitable organizations like TNC weren't just a tax deduction, but "a dollar-for-dollar tax credit," he explains. Morton reduced federal and state taxes by the full value of the easement. According to Annand, "Near the end of every year, Hugh Morton's tax advisers would look at the income at Grandfather Mountain, Inc., then look at the tax liability, and decide how many acres they would donate. It was a very smart way to go about it." So smart, some indict easements as giveaways. Annand feels Morton would have donated anyway, but the tax incentives "certainly benefitted him and the family."

The Wilmor Controversy

Just as Hugh Morton started garnering publicity for granting backcountry conservation easements, controversy exploded over his plans to develop nearly 1,000 acres above NC 105 on the ecologically rich route of early explorers. The news reminded people that "conservationist Hugh Morton" had already developed some of the mountain's true beauty spots, and lacking a binding preservation plan, only time would tell whether he had more developments in mind. Morton's early enterprises are the backstory to Wilmor. In the mid-1960s, Hound Ears debuted, ski resorts were on the way, and Morton's brother and mother developed Scottish-themed Invershiel. Hugh Morton built his own first residential community at Grandmother Lake, excavated below a Blue Ridge Parkway overlook near Grandmother Mountain. His own longtime residence occupies one of the exclusive homesites. Among influential friends who moved in were Governor Luther Hodges (1898–1974) and wealthy Linville resident John Williams (1918–2013), Oklahoma oil pipeline builder and CEO of the Williams Companies in Tulsa. Both men engaged Charlotte's most famous architect, Harry Wolf, to design lakeside summer homes that

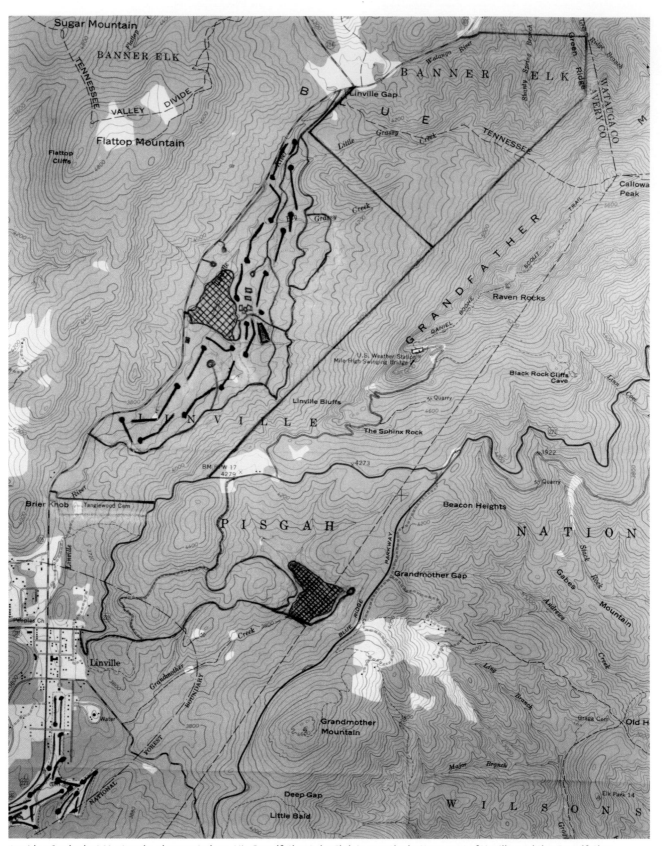

A mid-1960s look at Morton development plans. His Grandfather Lake Club is near the bottom, east of Linville, and the Grandfather Golf and Country Club sprawls west of the summit ridge. Both projects involved lake excavations. North of the club, the Wilmor tract awaits development. North Carolina Collection, University of North Carolina Library at Chapel Hill. Photo by Hugh Morton.

today are considered among the state's modernist masterpieces.

Also by 1965, Hugh Morton and his sister Agnes Morton Cocke were developing what would become Grandfather Golf and Country Club (GGCC). "Aggie," who was "one of the South's finest amateur golfers," according to the club's twentieth-anniversary history, inherited 1,968 acres along the Linville River beside NC 105. An Ellis Maples golf course was initiated; but unseen springs and other obstacles trebled the cost, and the project "was about to go belly up," Morton told TNC's Fred Annand. In 1967, Williams and Morton came to the rescue, forming G. F. Company, Inc., to complete the development. Williams asked attraction manager Joe Lee Hartley to join the developers, and brother Robert replaced him on the mountain. With one golf course complete and another planned, GGCC needed a master plan in 1968. Harry Wolf recommended Dan Kiley, of Charlotte, Vermont, renowned today as "the father of modern landscape architecture in the United States," according to Harvard, where Kiley's design papers include the GGCC master plan. Collaborating at the club with Kiley were Wolf and Jack Smith, the latter designer of Utah's Snowbird ski resort. The relationship crumbled, according to Wolf. The liberal-minded architects abruptly quit, but the country club went on to stability and success. In the early 1980s, continuing development and expanding membership threatened the resort atmosphere at GGCC, and in 1982, the 1,000-acre club bought out G. F. Company's remaining assets. Under the name Wilmor Corporation, majority owner Williams and junior partner Morton ended up owning 900 acres north of GGCC. "When the timing was right," Annand explained, they'd establish another exclusive community on Grandfather Mountain. By 1990, the time had arrived to develop the Continental Divide, and the Profile Trail was completed to permit closure of the popular Shanty Spring Trail. Morton and Williams "got a lot of push back from the homeowners at GGCC," Annand recalls. In "one of these typical 'not in my backyard' situations," the wealthy people already enjoying the mountainside lifestyle did not want to diminish their exclusive location.

Environmentalists soon formed the Friends of Grandfather Mountain to oppose development. Leaders Kim Isaacs, Martha Stephenson, and journalist Miles Tager decried an "environmentalist" who was "donating" conservation easements while developing adjacent acreage. Stephenson wrote to the *Charlotte Observer* in August 1992 railing against creation of "66 exclusive homesites" in a development named "The Divide," calling it "a sad case of misplaced values to take pride in a classy nature museum when rare species are being sacrificed for profit." Referring to the trail fee hiking program and the end of the Shanty Spring Trail, she asked, "Wouldn't you rather pay an access fee to see a thriving community of rare wildflowers than pay admission to a museum showing plastic replicas of what used to be?" Ouch! Morton was outraged that a group could even call itself the Friends of Grandfather Mountain, when Hugh Morton thought he was the only friend his mountain needed. "These people have yet to save their first acre," he groused. "I've already saved a lot more acres than they have." Years later, when Anne Mitchell Whisnant wrote an unflattering history of his victory in the Blue Ridge Parkway debate, Harris Prevost says Morton consoled himself believing that "environmentalists' biggest enemies are always other environmentalists." Despite Morton's wanting an environmental legacy, business is about profit, and he felt obligated to help John Williams cash out. But the proposed development exposed an intriguing gap in Morton's thinking. He told *Charlotte Observer* reporter Bruce Henderson that "I never considered this [the Wilmor tract] Grandfather Mountain. We feel the summit, which we do control, is the strategic part." Morton had so segmented his mountain mentally that he thought the leading ridge of the Continental Divide wasn't considered Grandfather Mountain. Another article quoted him saying, "Development is going to occur everywhere, and the best thing you can do is try to make it good." Morton *had* persuaded his partner to preserve the new Profile Trail.

Invershiel: "Another Way of Life, Not Just Another Resort"

There are a million places in the mountains to buy a cabin, but if you dream of owning a castle, Invershiel was the place to be. The mid-1960s resort was designed to be a colony of castles straight out of Scotland. Invershiel's founder and president, Julian Morton, was Hugh Morton's brother. Agnes MacRae Morton, mother of Julian and Hugh, was board chairman. Writing in *Palm Beach Life*, Betty Raveson maintained Julian was "convinced that he could transplant the sixteenth-century charm and unbelievable livability of those Scottish homes to the Linville domain." Her gushing 1967 article "Invershiel: A New Old World" reveled in the first sight of the resort still seen today (renamed Tynecastle). "There, before the eye, lies a meadow and mountainsides so reminiscent of the Scottish Highlands that it appears as in a dream."

With Highland Games cofounder Donald MacDonald as their guide, Julian and his mother had searched Scotland in 1964 for architecture to emulate. They borrowed "Invershiel" from a rural area near Eilean Donan Castle, the MacRae clan's iconic ancestral home. Their resort's signature Tolbooth was modeled after the 1600s tower MacDonald showed them in Culross. Harvey Ritch, owner of the Everything Scottish shop that

Agnes MacRae Morton and Julian Morton stand outside an Invershiel Croft House, complete with goat munching the sod roof. North Carolina Collection, University of North Carolina Library at Chapel Hill. Photo by Hugh Morton.

On their "Invershiel architecture tour" to Scotland guided by Highland Games cofounder Donald MacDonald, Julian and Agnes MacRae Morton visited Eilean Donan Castle, the stunningly scenic MacRae ancestral home. In ruins since 1719, the castle was rebuilt and reopened in 1932. Photo by Randy Johnson.

Invershiel's Highland Stable Club was as upscale as its embossed matchbooks.

"Fortunately," Annand concludes, "Hugh Morton had a relationship with The Nature Conservancy." With the anger of environmentalists ringing in his ears, Morton "invited TNC to see if that 900 acres was biologically significant enough that we might acquire it." The conservancy called on Natural Heritage Program biologist Alan Weakley to refine his earlier studies, and "as you might guess 95 percent of the property was biologically important," Annand states. Weakley's Natural Heritage Program partner, ecologist Mike Schafale agreed. "If Wilmor is lost," he told the *Charlotte Observer*, "it's going to diminish the mountain as a whole" and likely destroy the entire tract. TNC started negotiating, but Annand had no idea "where The Nature Conservancy would have found the resources to buy that land." The Friends of Grandfather Mountain had motivation, not money. "We were on our own," Annand thought. The principals dickered for a year about price—not unlike the ambiguity national park advocates faced when they negotiated with Morton's ancestors. Ultimately, "work by us and Alan [Weakley] led to serious discussion about selling 700 acres of the tract." The land eventually sold in "a bargain sale, below fair market value." The unrealized land value gave Wilmor a tax break. Ironically, in 1990, Morton had told the Associated Press he'd "like nothing more than for a conservation group to buy this land and keep it in trust."

The land purchase wouldn't have happened without what Annand calls "the champions of the day": Fred and Alice Stanback. Longtime TNC board member Fred Stanback Jr., former partner in Salisbury's Stanback headache powder company, cured a major headache for Grandfather when he and his wife and two sons, Brad and Lawrence Stanback, pledged more than $3 million toward the Wilmor purchase. Regrettably the deal did not stop a shopping center from being built on NC 105. The Stanbacks, stellar exemplars of wilderness preservation by the wealthy, earned the National Parks Conservation Association's first-ever Sequoia Award in 2013. Annand attributed "outrage about the Wilmor controversy and shopping center" to Morton's managing the backcountry "like it was public land. People assumed it was public property." Nevertheless, decided Annand, a shopping center "was a small price to pay compared to what could have happened." As the controversy closed, Friends of Grandfather Mountain president Martha Stephenson wrote to Hugh Morton calling the result a "win! win! deal." Morton wasn't ready for a handshake. He predicted the Friends would "take credit" but chose to see the sale as an extension of his own legacy. In reality, his critics had played the decisive role in saving an irreplaceable piece of the mountain. Grandfather's visibility rose to the top of the national conservancy community, and Wilmor had coattails. In the summer of 1993, with the Stanbacks' help, TNC purchased another 300 acres on the mountain's Foscoe flank that

The Shanty Spring Trail corridor, route of the early explorers and scientists, as it appeared in the path's heyday during the late 1970s. Chestnut stumps then visible from the logging days are now increasingly hard to spot on Grandfather. Photo by Randy Johnson.

On April 7, 1993, Hugh Morton (far left) and conservationists held a press conference in the rainforest at Charlotte's Discovery Place to announce the purchase and preservation of the bulk of the Wilmor acreage. Beside Morton (left to right) are quintessential conservation philanthropists Alice and Fred Stanback; Katherine Skinner, executive director of North Carolina's Nature Conservancy; Bill Hollan, a Nature Conservancy trustee; and Fred Annand, associate state director of the conservancy and a preservationist pivotal in the Grandfather Mountain story. News release photo, courtesy Grandfather Mountain.

included an old quartz mine. In 1996, Wilmor Corporation donated an "absolutely gorgeous" 45 acres near Grassy Creek once reachable on the Shanty Spring Trail.

Casting About in Boone Fork

As preservation progressed, Fred Annand thought Morton seemed reluctant to grant easements along the Boone Fork. Every time he asked about Morton's plans, Morton delayed, saying Boone Fork was one of the "'few places where the private landowner could enhance habitat for native brook trout,'" Annand explains. He asked conservation lawyer Mike Leonard for help. "Fred Annand called," Leonard reveals, and said, "'Mike we can't get this done. Could you go talk to him?'" Leonard had unusual insight into Hugh Morton. Leonard had "saved" substantial acreage in a variety of states and was a partner in the Winston-Salem law firm of Womble, Carlyle, Sandridge & Rice, where he handled litigation for international companies. Leonard had grown up in Lenoir and "can't remember not being fascinated by Grandfather Mountain." His father "hated to go anywhere near Grandfather because I'd start pitching a fit if we didn't go up to the Swinging

Bridge." He hiked to Calloway Peak in 1970 and later gave his first wife an engagement ring there. Morton met Leonard when Hugh chaired the Year of the Mountains in 1995. The duo capped that observance orchestrating a conservation easement on the 18,000-acre Asheville watershed, sealing a relationship that saw Morton attend Leonard's May 2001 wedding as best man. He "finally figured out" that Morton had a resort development planned for the Boone Fork Bowl, a project attributed, Leonard was told, to a Vermont-connected designer, possibly Dan Kiley, GGCC's onetime master planner. Annand concluded Morton knew he "wasn't going to live long enough to see even the full 1,400 acres donated," much less develop a resort, so Morton asked if there was "another way we could accelerate this." Knowing development was planned, Leonard realized Morton "sees value back there" and that offering him money was key. "Once we positioned it that he was going to be paid for the land, he was OK with it." To gain a grant from the Clean Water Management Trust Fund, Morton donated half the value of the easement and was paid the other 50 percent. The same process secured the route of the Profile Trail.

Gated communities like GGCC meant jobs and progress in the 1960s. By the early 1990s, times had changed. Development was proliferating around Grandfather. The ecological and recreational importance of the Shanty Spring Trail, much less the Continental Divide or the entire backcountry, had been firmly established. All were considered Grandfather Mountain, at least by the public. Annand suspected Morton wanted his children to develop Boone Fork, but when the Wilmor project failed, it was obvious future development in "the Grandfather backcountry" had become impossible. Morton sold easements on the last unprotected parts of his mountain. The press and even environmentalists had always been kind to Morton. At the height of the Wilmor controversy, the president of the North Carolina Sierra Club, Bill Thomas, confessed, "Our perception is that it would be counterproductive to irritate Hugh Morton." By the mid-1990s, with the end of the Wilmor controversy

Mike Leonard has been influential at key points in Grandfather's path to preservation. After returning to North Carolina in 1986 from Alabama, where he founded the Alabama Trails Association, one of the first things Leonard did was write to me and volunteer to replace the temporary plastic signs still lingering on Grandfather's new Cragway Trail. He would become one of the original board members of the Grandfather Mountain Stewardship Foundation. Photo by Dan Root, courtesy of WNC magazine.

and increasing easements, the stream of media coverage turned into gushing praise and elder statesman status for the "guardian" of the mountain. Leonard was one among many who was certain Morton "was serious when he repeatedly said, 'I'm just an interim steward of a place like this.'" When the mountain became a Biosphere Reserve, the *News Herald* of Morganton wrote that if people "in positions of power, in government, business and industry, were as careful in their stewardship of public natural resources as Morton, ours would be a far safer and more beautiful world." Morton reveled in the esteem and friendship of scientists

focusing on his mountain. He delved into topics like forest decline with Robert Bruck's acid rain studies on Mount Mitchell and worked with Walter Cronkite on a documentary called *The Search for Clean Air*. By the end of his life, Hugh Morton had a long list of conservation credentials.

Evolving Priorities

In 2003, Morton tapped grandson Hugh MacRae "Crae" Morton III to guide the mountain into the future. Son of Morton's deceased eldest son, Hugh Jr., and great-great grandson of Hugh MacRae, Crae brought an irreverent new view of his grandfather's vision. "When people think of Grandfather Mountain," he states, "they think of bears and bridges, cheeseburgers, t-shirts, and that reflects my grandfather's ability as a promoter. I'm not going to apologize for Hugh Morton creating that image, he did what he did, and he did it well." Crae spent a year working each of the mountain's employee roles. At a certain point, he relates, "we were thinking, 'what is the mountain, what is it all about?'" He answers, "We started to focus on the backcountry. The tourist attraction gets so much attention, but if you look on a map, at the geological boundaries, the Swinging Bridge and the bears border on insignificance." Crae emphasized stewardship and added programs that still shape the mountain's future.

The visitor experience evolved toward nature appreciation and interpretation, a transition that would turn the attraction into a not-for-profit foundation. Designation as a Biosphere Reserve mandates environmental education; but that was not happening, and employee Jesse Pope had an idea. The graduate of Banner Elk's Lees-McRae College had started as a seasonal trail ranger and then worked full time at the habitats. He was embarrassed when "a 5th grade class called and wanted to talk about the bears and we were gonna bring out some bear fur!" Crae Morton knew a naturalist program "had been tried before and didn't work," but Pope's 2004 proposal to become the park's naturalist made "the same economic argument for education," explains Pope, "that was

Purchasing conservation easements on the rushing waters of Boone Fork got complicated when Fred Annand and Mike Leonard realized Hugh Morton had development plans for the Boone Fork Bowl. Would another lake have been part of the plan? It wouldn't have been the first lake scintillating at the bottom of a "glacial cirque." Photo by Tommy White Photography, www.tommywhitephotography.com.

made for trail management back when the back-country program was proposed." Pope was certain he could draw school groups in slow shoulder seasons, but he calls Crae Morton's enthusiasm "an important part of this story." Pope, now credited with bringing state- and national-park-style inter-pretation to Grandfather, quadrupled the number of visiting schoolkids the first year curriculum-based programs were offered. When a 2005 focus group found Grandfather visitors were likely to return for educational offerings, Harris Prevost told employees, "Our 'Naturalist Department' is really our 'Marketing Department.'"

In June 2006, as Crae Morton was shepherd-ing the mountain beyond his grandfather's way of doing things, Hugh Morton died. Young Crae's openness to change—indeed correction—signaled a culture shift that empowered and acknowl-edged the mountain's employees. "That was the biggest time of change at Grandfather Mountain," remembers Pope. No one faulted Hugh Morton for the past; after all, he owned the mountain. But a more modern culture emerged under Crae. A less-commercial approach included "truth in advertising." More accurate wind gauges were installed on the mountain. And when new mea-surements reduced the height of Calloway Peak to 5,946 feet (from 5,964) in November 2009, Crae ended Grandfather's claim as the "Highest Peak in the Blue Ridge."

Buying the Backcountry
A State Park

Crae Morton was looking to the future. The family business had earned tax breaks and income by granting easements on the backcountry, but finances were an issue. In May 2007, Chimney Rock Park, a longtime private attraction not unlike Grandfather, became a state park and set a prece-dent. Lewis Ledford, now-retired, much-respected director of North Carolina state parks, wanted to expand the public foothold in spectacular Hickory Nut Gorge. The Morse family who owned Chimney Rock wanted to sell. With funding through Mike Leonard of the Conservation Trust, the Stanbacks,

and a state appropriation, the $24 million sale happened. Leonard told the Mortons he had "some ideas about the future," and some time later, Crae Morton called. "The Mortons knew there was state money available," Leonard remembers. Lewis Led-ford maintains the state's creativity at Chimney Rock argued for a state park at Grandfather, but so did Hugh Morton's past. His battle with the Park-way forever soured him on the mountain going to the National Park Service.

The parties settled on fee simple purchase of the backcountry with restrictive state park ease-ments on the attraction. However, the attraction needed its own easement over the state park. Leonard realized the state suspected the moun-tain's trail ladders were incompatible with official trail standards. That was "the closest I saw the deal come to falling apart," he recalls. The state park people made "it sound like they were going to have to put in escalators," eliminating one of east-ern America's renowned adventure hikes under bureaucratic "safety" standards. Negotiators feared even preexisting ladders would be closed under the Americans with Disabilities Act. That didn't happen, and Jim Morton gets the credit. "I didn't think Jim would kill the whole deal, but I thought, if we don't get this straightened out this could fall apart," Leonard reasoned. Leonard suggested that Grandfather sell the land but keep a trail ease-ment to Attic Window Peak with responsibility over the trail. That's how the Grandfather Trail's lad-ders were "grandfathered in." Concluded Leonard, "It all worked out." Sue McBean, the state park's first superintendent, thinks "that agreement was in the best interests of everyone," especially as it preserved revenue at the attraction generated by hikers heading to the ladders. Lewis Ledford later said he doubted compliance with the disabilities act would have been necessary, so hopefully, if the state ever takes over maintenance, sanity will pre-vail when the fate of the ladders is considered.

A New Park

Grandfather Mountain, Inc., a corporation owned by the Morton family, received $12 mil-

High Winds? Or Just Hot Air?

Mount Washington's 231-mph record wind speed makes it the Appalachian wind champ, but for decades, high winds have also enhanced Grandfather's image. My mid-1980s book *Southern Snow: The Winter Guide to Dixie* called Grandfather the "Mount Washington of the South" for the 161-mph highest wind recorded at its official National Weather Service (NWS) station at the Top Shop. Nevertheless, some skeptics complained that Grandfather's wind speeds were grossly exaggerated by the anemometer's placement atop the three-story building. The long-held suspicion was that Hugh Morton purposely created astounding wind records to generate a slew of newspaper articles. The mountain's wind "made news" even when it just destroyed weather gauges. In truth, Grandfather was more like a wire service than a typical weather reporting station. The mountain's publicists often sidestepped the NWS and fed data directly to the media. That's how Grant Goodge got involved. He worked for the National Oceanic and Atmospheric Administration's National Climatic Data Center in Asheville and authored an unpublished 1980s study questioning Grandfather Mountain's wind records. When the NWS stopped putting their official seal of approval on Grandfather's weather data, Hugh Morton "took it as a personal attack," Goodge maintains.

Goodge retired in 1997 but came back to oversee an improved data collection system as the climate change debate emerged. His U.S. Climate Reference Network would avoid inaccuracies like Grandfather's anemometer location. When the mountain reported "really high numbers" in the 2000s, the debate flared anew and the NWS pulled its instruments. Remembers Goodge, that prompted "a very hurtful letter" from Hugh Morton blaming him and another meteorologist. "Hugh Morton was very well connected, very well known," Goodge admits. "No one crossed him lightly." In a fit of pique, Morton had "complicated" and some say almost ended the career of a scientist genuinely dedicated to accuracy. Morton put up less-expensive instruments in the winter of 2006, and again nearly 200-mph winds caused

From the early days of the old Top Shop, measuring the weather and winds were important parts of Hugh Morton's mission to publicize the mountain and its distinctive extremes. For the employees involved, it was never easy. North Carolina Collection, University of North Carolina Library at Chapel Hill. Photo by Hugh Morton.

controversy. "I got e-mails asking about accuracy," Goodge reveals. In February 2006, the Weather Channel staged a live remote at Grandfather and included an off-site interview with Goodge demonstrating how winds that blew up, and not across, an anemometer's conical cups created dramatic over-speeds. Using data from NASA's Howard's Knob windmill in Boone, Goodge estimated Grandfather's reported wind speeds were double what they really were. Again the NWS expressed concern about the "unbelievable winds"; but this time, Crae Morton was president, and he convened a "weather summit" of concerned experts. Crae not only invited state climatologist Dr. Ryan Boyles, Appalachian State University geography professor Dr. Baker Perry, and Ray Russell of the Ray's Weather website, but he welcomed

Goodge. "Crae Morton told us, 'I don't want the data coming out of here to be a laughing stock,'" Goodge says. Then came a moment of drama. "First thing I know," Goodge confesses, "the doors open and they wheel Hugh Morton into the room. We shook hands. I learned three months later he was deceased."

Crae Morton started afresh. The group urged placing a new anemometer atop the Swinging Bridge to measure air moving unimpeded across the mountain and not the maelstrom swirling above the Top Shop. A few years later, Grandfather's old gauges again measured a 200-mph wind, and Goodge proved his hypothesis. The new gauge read 103 mph. Whether or not Morton had intended to mislead, by 2009, the new anemometer fit the Grandfather Mountain Stewardship Foundation's less promotional approach. Since then, the mountain's highest recorded wind was 120.7 mph on December 21, 2012. Goodge looks kindly on Hugh Morton. He once attended a photography lecture and "learned a lot from him. Except for that wind speed issue, we could'a been the best of friends."

Today, Grandfather's weather is monitored by the Appalachian Atmospheric Interdisciplinary Research Program at Appalachian State. Mountain visitors can participate in daily weather observations, and data screens at the attraction and on Grandfather's website report the latest weather conditions. A 2013 NASA grant promises to make the mountain a mile-high weather teaching and learning tool for visitors and students.

The deal to sell Grandfather Mountain to the state was announced in a MacRae Meadows ceremony, with Crae Morton, at right, representing Grandfather. Governor Mike Easley and wife Mary are left of him. Looking on from left are Bill Ross, secretary of the N.C. Department of Environment and Natural Resources; Mike Leonard, vice chair of the Conservation Fund board of directors who helped negotiate the agreement; and longtime director of North Carolina state parks Lewis Ledford, whose tenure was capped by a number of important new state parks. Ledford went on to become director of the National Association of State Park Directors. Photo by Helen Moss Davis/www.wildblueprints.com.

lion for the 2,600-acre backcountry that would become North Carolina's thirty-fourth state park. On September 29, 2008, the Mortons announced the deal in a MacRae Meadows ceremony with Governor Mike Easley. "If you can get a Grandfather Mountain for $12 million," Easley urged, "you'd better get as many as you can." The media noted that the state bought "more than three times as much land as the Chimney Rock deal at half the price." Proclaimed Crae Morton, "Grandfather Mountain is protected for good, over and done, period. Grandfather Mountain is too significant for anyone ever to ruin it." Morton's aunt Catherine Morton pronounced it "an emotional satisfaction to know we're working on something more important and bigger than we are." She seconded Crae's conclusion that Mike Leonard was critical to the success of the deal. The "Grandfather Mountain attraction" remained nearly 800 acres, including MacRae Meadows, but state restrictions govern management. That easement, Leonard sums up, "basically says the attraction can't be used for anything except what it's already used for." New structures, roads, and parking are prohibited,

Hugh Morton: A Profile

Charles Kuralt famously joked about the fellow who bragged he was "a good friend of Hugh Morton and his wife Mildred." Morton's grandson Crae recalls that countless times he heard someone say, "'Oh, Hugh Morton, yes, we were good friends.' And he had a lot of friends, but I think very few people, maybe a handful, actually knew him. He was always the man behind the camera. Not necessarily a participant, but an observer." Morton's "observer" attitude fit the task of promoting his mountain, which explains why so many events became a "photo by Hugh Morton" and not a photo of him.

Longtime employees had a window on "Morton, the Man," asserts Sally Gideon Warburton, who worked at the Top Shop for years as a teenager and knew Morton into late life. He was "a very common man, a regular guy," she concludes. He was also a dog lover whose current pooch was often riding shotgun with the rabid fan of North Carolina college sports. One day near the Swinging Bridge, team loyalties came up, and Morton got his curly gray poodle to intervene. "Would you rather be a dead dog or go to Duke?" Morton asked his pet. "Duchess laid down and played dead and everyone erupted in laughter," recalled Warburton.

Even those who say Morton was a "simple man" would admit he was also complex and at times contradictory. He was modest, but he could display towering ego. Some picture Hugh Morton in the black-and-white film once found in his cameras, but he's best appreciated in the Fujichrome color the old wounded World War II combat photographer started using after years of shunning "Made in Japan." Crae maintains the "best way to get to know him was to get in a car with him." Luckily, Morton was always going somewhere to take pictures or driving across the state, and I had many an opportunity to ride with him. Throughout his life, he drove big, often rear-wheel-drive American cars, the quintessential "old guy's ride" with a "GMTN" vanity plate. In winter you'd see him spinning up the icy road to the mountaintop, spurred onward by a trunk full of camera gear. Grandfather Mountain was the ultimate focus of Hugh Morton's often stunning shots, but "no one knew a lot of times he was taking the same picture again and again," reflects Warburton. "He was always looking for the perfect shot."

By the end of his life, Morton's focus shifted from "making the mountain" to appreciating how the mountain was making him. "He wasn't just somebody who inherited a mountain," Sally Warburton concludes. "He was a man possessed by a mountain." But Morton wasn't always the man who would preserve Grandfather the way it is protected today. Mike Leonard saw "a definite pivot in Morton's thinking toward environmental concerns later in life." Ultimately, Morton called himself "a steward of Grandfather" so many times that only preservation and public ownership would redeem the image he'd created for himself. He developed, through the encouragement of economic incentives, the friendship of scientists and naturalists, even the opposition of opponents. At the end of his years, Morton became more interested than ever before in protecting his mountain—and his legacy as a conservationist. To his credit and to the benefit of Grandfather Mountain, times changed, and Mr. Morton found a way to change with them.

Hugh Morton's photography defined him and helped define his times. Here he keenly observes a football game at Kenan Stadium in Chapel Hill in October 2003. Over his lifetime, many thought Morton was one of the University of North Carolina's most famous alumni, though he never graduated. AP Photo/Jeffrey A. Camarati, File.

and there are restrictions on expansion, explains former Stewardship Foundation executive director Penn Dameron. "We're very limited in our ability to handle more people."

The Stewardship Foundation

Crae Morton assured observers that the state park sale wasn't motivated by financial difficulties, but Dameron admitted a string of bad years "really got the state park conversation started." Recalls Jesse Pope, "The big question Crae and Mr. Morton were asking was 'how do we pay the property taxes?'" Without the "backcountry tax burden," attraction managers hoped Grandfather would be better off financially. A year after the state park sale, the Grandfather Mountain Stewardship Foundation was formed to put the mountain on an even less taxing footing. The foundation received 501(c)(3) not-for-profit tax exempt status on September 10, 2009.

Many assume that nonprofit status means the Mortons sold the attraction. Not true. The deed to the attraction's land is still held by the for-profit, family-owned corporation Grandfather Mountain, Inc. What did occur was that all the stock in Grandfather Mountain, Inc., was transferred to ownership by the Stewardship Foundation, "which means," explained attorney Dameron, "that the Foundation owns all the personal property, the vehicles, and things that were not land and fixtures." The reason for not actually selling the land, maintained the foundation's first executive director, was to "get control over the mountain, but not have to spend a large portion of your endowment paying the U.S. government capital gains tax." To achieve that, the Mortons granted a "triple net lease" that transfers "every aspect of the ownership of the property" to the Stewardship Foundation while Grandfather Mountain, Inc., keeps the title to the land. For that, the foundation pays the corporation $360,000 a year in rent, which is then donated back to the foundation—minus "Grandfather Mountain, Inc.'s business expenses, including tax returns, accounting fees, legal fees. It's a brilliant, elegant solution," offers Dameron.

On day one of the foundation, Crae Morton resigned after achieving a new trajectory for his grandfather's mountain. He was chairman of the foundation board of directors until 2011, and then he departed on a more entrepreneurial track. "I love not being important anymore," he admitted in 2013. "I was there for the blink of an eye in the history of Grandfather Mountain." No longer just another business, the proclaimed goal was to be preservation not profit. To Harris Prevost, that future looked a lot like the past. "All along," Prevost noted, "Mr. Morton was putting all the profits back into making the mountain better and that's what nonprofits do." The foundation wanted to be self-sustaining through gate receipts and retail income, but raising funds from outside sources was an important new opportunity. "The other thing that's changed," explains Jesse Pope, "is our focus, it's more on protecting and interpreting the resource and less on profit and the tourist attraction. We want folks to leave inspired to take care of whatever resources they're entrusted with."

For more than half a century, the Morton family seemed destined to be synonymous with Grandfather Mountain, and Stewardship Foundation bylaws ensure Morton family members a prominent place in the mountain's management. The foundation's board of directors was initially all Morton family members; but it grew in 2012, and by 2014, there were four "public" board members and four family members. It is unknown how the board will evolve, but the foundation requires a simple majority vote to remove a public board member. To remove a Morton family member, however, it takes unanimous agreement among all other family board members and all public board members. Excepting voluntary resignation or death, the foundation board seems to bestow lifetime membership on the Mortons. "Some have expressed concern about the degree of influence that one family is having over the foundation," Dameron admits, but he emphasizes that observers need to understand that the Mortons (via the MacRaes) have "been the owners of the mountain since the 1880s and they felt like they had the best interests of the mountain at heart more than anybody else." In 2014, Avery County complicated the foundation's future by challenging the exclusivity of its educational emphasis, eliminating its tax-exempt legal status and reinstating payment of property taxes.

As 2016 dawned, the mountain's longtime 1970s-style obelisk entrance sign was replaced. Like Mount Mitchell's aging geometrical eyesore of a summit tower replaced in 2009 by an accessible, rounded ramp, Grandfather's new oval logo sign features a flagged summit spruce instead of a swinging bridge strung between peaks. Harris Prevost says the sign largely came courtesy of Jim Morton, the stewardship foundation's president as the second decade of the millennium matures. At the same time, Jesse Pope became the foundation's second executive director. "I've done it all," he admits, "parked cars on busy weekends, scooped ice cream, made food, cut fudge, headed the naturalist program, worked at the entrance gates and as a trail ranger." That experience uniquely equips him to convey "what's so unique about what we offer, including what makes Grandfather Mountain so special and rare."

Ancient Mountain, New State Park

When 2,600 acres of Grandfather became a state park in April 2009, the mountain was a bustling backcountry destination with trails that had been maintained and monitored for more than thirty years. The state eliminated trail fees, but "other than that," says superintendent Susan McBean, "there haven't been any major changes in management." McBean, former superintendent of Haw River State Park near Greensboro, arrived in April 2010. For the first year, rangers from nearby state parks, especially Elk Knob, patrolled trails and installed signs. The founding staff included rangers Andy Sicard (a transfer from Elk Knob) and Luke Appling (former trail manager at the attraction). By 2015, a larger workforce was installing more signing and rerouting sections of trail. For McBean, Grandfather is a dream come true. "I always knew I wanted to work on a mountain," she confesses, and she definitely got her wish. "I

Sue McBean, the first superintendent of Grandfather Mountain State Park, was in for a surprise when she traded the Piedmont scenery of Haw River State Park near Greensboro for what she called "a real mountain." Photo by Randy Johnson.

knew how rugged this mountain is and how hard this job would be, and boy is it! It's an all day event just to get up there." She often hears "people say they're happy that the mountain's being 'preserved forever.'" McBean emphasizes that Grandfather "is different from so many parks" where the primary facility is a campground, picnic area, or beach. "Our closest claim to facilities is that trail system." McBean, whose "mantra is, if a trail is too steep or unsustainable, reroute it," realizes that a wealth of steep trails will create a long to-do list on the Grandfather Mountain. A bigger Profile Trail parking area and a new connector trail were expected by 2016. A visitor center is another possible improvement that a bond referendum might get under way in the aftermath of the state park centennial in 2016.

McBean's favorite place changes with almost every hike. "Cragway is one of my favorites," she says, "and you can't beat the Profile Trail for wildflowers." Wildflower walks are among ranger-led offerings, as are volunteer workdays. In 2014, lower Profile was designated a TRACK-Trail, one of a nationwide network of interpretive paths devised by the Blue Ridge Parkway Foundation. Change will come slowly to the mountain's moody summits. State park stewards, like the slow and steady hikers who climb the trails, have time on their side.

Seek and Ye Shall Find: Mountain Search and Rescue

When a hiker twists an ankle, much less dies of a heart attack, somebody has to do the difficult, dangerous work of search, rescue, and recovery. Passing a litter hand to hand down a rocky trail is the most arduous "hike" you'll ever take, especially if it lasts all night. "We're often working in situations where the rescuer can easily get hurt," admits Steve Miller, Grandfather's safety manager and backcountry manager from 1990 to 2006. Under the hiking permit program I launched in 1978, oversight of Grandfather's trails greatly improved with regular patrol and the first use of radios. To Miller's credit, rescue response got even more formal in the 1990s after my departure with help from the Linville Central Rescue Squad in Pineola. Since 2009, Grandfather Mountain State Park has led the way in search and rescue. For help, rangers can call on other state parks, attraction staff, and agencies like the U.S. Forest Service and Wildlife Resources Commission. In 2010, Grandfather started hosting an annual, multiday Winter Alpine Search and Rescue Training program that includes practice on local ice floes and ski slopes. The group stages rescue scenarios on MacRae Peak "no matter how bad the weather," assures Stephen Sudderth, emergency management coordinator for Watauga County.

Preventing problems is best, and that's why it's paramount that hikers follow backcountry regulations. Posted warnings at Grandfather require hikers to be off the trail by a given time, but some hikers ignore warnings or just take longer than expected. That prompts what may be the classic search situation: day hikers are overdue at the trailhead in the dark or the cold or both. An "abandoned" vehicle at a trailhead may just mean an unauthorized camping trip. But if a car at the Profile Trail doesn't have a camping permit or there's a vehicle inside the attraction after the gate is locked despite "no camping" signs, something could be very wrong. At these times, rescue crews never just race into the woods but in fact pause to consider whether a crime may have been committed. The irony of modern wilderness search and rescue is that if rangers hit the information jackpot, a solution can be as easy as "running" the car's license plate and calling the "missing person" at home or on his or her GPS-enabled cell phone.

It's not always that easy. When canine search teams are needed, they're available at Grandfather through the North Carolina Search and Rescue Dog Association, Inc. (NCSARDA), the country's oldest canine search organization. "NCSARDA and its members in the High Country work up to 80 calls a year," reports Richard Schaeffer, a "team leader" in the Boone area. One typical trailhead dilemma employed dogs from the Swinging Bridge Parking Area. A missing hiker's vehicle contained children's clothing, so law officers opened the car to find "scent articles," Schaeffer explains. "One item was cut into pieces and saved in separate plastic bags in case more scent was needed later." Happily, searchers found the rule-breaking family snuggled in a tent atop Attic Window Peak. "All's well that ends well," offers Schaeffer, but Grandfather's trails are a challenge during the day and even more so in the dark. Canine or human searchers could have gotten hurt.

There are great experiences to be had on Grandfather, but there can also be accidents and tragedies. The wild card is Grandfather itself, and High Country rescue crews know just how wild that card can be. On this mountain, even the most experienced outdoor people should err on the side of safety.

"People love these trails and this mountain, so protecting what we have is what's important," McBean believes. "As our former state park director Lewis Ledford always said, 'in state parks, we're in the forever business.'" For McBean, that means "we have time. We, and this mountain, are going to be here forever."

Layers of Protection

Unprecedented layers of protection shield Grandfather. Conservation easements acquired on the mountain specifically prohibit development. "The basic idea," maintains Mike Leonard, "is that since nothing can be developed back there, who would buy the land?" In this case, that undevelopable acreage was bought, as a state park. Though surprising, those two overlapping financial transactions impose different, at times conflicting, sets of restrictions, a situation that is "absolutely unique," asserts Fred Annand. The irony is that these competing sets of rules create potential complications for the environment and recreation. One example is the Boone Fork, that native trout stream Hugh Morton was concerned about. TNC easements prohibit fishing, but state parks allow angling and stream management. Easements forbid rock climbing, but state parks allow that, too. Under TNC guidelines, the mountain's logged forests are "preserved" status quo, but state park flexibility might permit active restoration of the spruce-fir ecosystem. Conflicts like those seem destructive at worst, dysfunctional at best. Why would the Nature Conservancy want to tell rangers how to manage a state park? Ultimately, believes Fred Annand, "We'd be open to the possibility of transferring our ownership into the park." A glimpse of that future occurred when the park built a new Profile Trail parking area and TNC simply donated the property for the connector trail. TNC retains ownership of only a fraction of its protected land; the rest, Annand notes, "has been transferred to other agencies." That may not happen during the state park's infancy; the park "has its hands full." But a future land transfer could bring simpler administration, new opportunities, or even old trails. The historic Shanty Spring Trail was closed by the proposed Wilmor resort development—that thankfully never happened. Now owned by TNC, the land, Annand speculates, could become part of the park. Among all the possibilities we see in Grandfather's future, it makes a trail guy smile to think a sustainably redesigned Shanty Spring Trail, the route of the early explorers, might reappear on Grandfather Mountain's trail map.

Conclusion

The preservation of Grandfather Mountain started with Pisgah National Forest—eastern America's first—protecting public land well below the peaks. The Blue Ridge Parkway draped a national park's protection across the mountainside. A state park now shields the summits. TNC's tracts are sheltered by conservation easements. On the mountain's most heavily developed peak, a nonprofit Stewardship Foundation is exploring environmentally responsible private ownership. Along the way, protection has involved the North Carolina Wildlife Resources Commission and Natural Heritage Program and the U.S. Fish and Wildlife Service; even the United Nations has bestowed international Biosphere status. That remarkable path to preservation has united countless people whose love and labor have made Grandfather Mountain one of the nation's, indeed the world's, epic achievements in conservation. Marvels Fred Annand, "What a wonderful, amazing, jigsaw puzzle of preservation we have put together on Grandfather Mountain."

That differs from uncertain times not so long ago, when conservation easements did not exist, Grandfather Mountain State Park was just a dream, the mountain's trails were closed and unknown to most, new resort developments were envisioned for Grandfather's backcountry.

That came back to me one day as I hiked down the Nuwati Trail carrying a wonderfully shaped piece of bark found sloughed off a tree by the trail. It bore a dim blue trail blaze I'd painted decades before. "What's that?" a hiker asked. "It's a souvenir," I said, of an earlier time when the Boone Fork Bowl was an unseen place. I painted those blazes hoping to change that. More and more hikers found their way to Boone Fork, and today the bright metal markers of a state park are nailed over fading paint.

People have fallen in love with Grandfather Mountain for centuries, and thankfully, they'll continue to do so. Like earlier visitors, they'll bring along acquaintances who become friends for life and lovers who become wives and husbands. Like the Randolphs of Linville and the Chastains of Blowing Rock, they'll raise families whose love of the mountain spans generations. Experiences like theirs truly convey the meaning of this mountain.

For years, the Randolphs' big annual outing was a trailless climb of "Haystack Rock," a soaring, but to me, misnamed crag above the Profile that I always called "the spire." Their 1981 trek attracted fifty-year-olds born in 1931. In the excitement, Ted Randolph's wife, Jane, lost track of their eleven-year-old son James. As the group lunched on Haystack, with Jane wondering where he was, "suddenly this little face pops up over the cliff," she exclaims. "He'd climbed the highest, sheerest face!" Looking back, Salisbury attorney and rock climber James Randolph recalls "how weird it was to see everybody casually eating lunch when I'd just stared down death as a pre-teenager."

Blowing Rock's Chastains track four generations of family hikes on a wall plaque. Ever since their first 1940s climbs, the mountain has helped "break-in the boy friends and girl friends," laughs Richard. "One time I took my wife-to-be across the mountain and my father told her about the water fountains and benches. She never found the water fountains—just ladders! That was her one and only hike." On Richard and wife Linda's fiftieth anniversary in 2009, married kids and grandkids hiked across and documented the adventure. "It's a family rite of passage," Richard announces. "There's something special about touching the earth on that mountain."

Too much potential change lies over the environmental horizon to be certain the backcountry will always tell tales like those. Mike Leonard actually thinks multilayered restrictions on the mountain may be valuable "so the state can't do something bizarre like sell the backcountry" to diminish a deficit or spur privatization. Nevertheless, we can be pretty confident that hikers on the Asutsi Trail will never be displaced by cars with ski racks—even though that gradual grade under the Parkway was once a right-of-way intended to permit development of Boone Bowl.

In cutting my own path in life and writing this book, I have followed Grandfather's trails, both literal and figurative. After I tracked down century-old notebooks from Tate Davis's logging days, I reverently opened one, and when spruce and hemlock bark scattered my desk, it hit me: this was as close as I'd ever get to Grandfather's virgin forest. Tears hit the page before I pushed his book away with my linen-gloved researcher's hand. I wondered if Tate regretted snatching the Grandfather's centuries-old cloak to feed eleven kids. Were Shepherd Dugger or Joe Hartley ever moved to tears by the fate of Grandfather's forests? In 1959, Squire Hartley proclaimed, "If you could have seen this land as it was 75 years ago, you'd go into tears." Perhaps he had shed tears—one of many experiences I suspect I share with a man who found his life's work on Grandfather Mountain. The drops on Tate's notebooks were likely rain in his day. A few of those drops, I confess, are tears in mine.

I missed the earliest part of that past, but I count myself fortunate to have encountered the mountain at what I call "the end of the Appalachia of old." I stepped in to reopen the mountain's trails just forty years after the great forests fell, alive with longing for their grandeur. Forging the backcountry program involved me for a time in the future preservation of Grandfather Mountain, but in retrospect, those years actually drew me closer to the past. Despite lacking the craggy features of the Scots Irish, I used the tools of those early times, stood in the woods in wet wool, and was beaten up and defeated by the power of the mountain. I felt kinship with gray misty days and went home to wood heat. I am deeply privileged to have reopened the route Shepherd Dugger trod in *The Balsam Groves* and walked in the same woods

Multiple generations of the Chastain family are enjoying Grandfather in this twenty-first-century photo at Calloway Peak. There are two Chastain sons-in-law (from left), Mark Stubblefield and Bill Jones; grandson Jack Stubblefield; granddaughters Emily Sloop and Amanda Robinson; and their husbands, Scott Sloop and Justin Robinson. A poor quality 1940s family photo shows Richard, Dixie, and their dad at the same spot beside a Clyde Smith sign on the summit that read, "Calloway Peak." Dixie insists it ought to be replaced. "Talk about a great place for a photo," she says. Chastain Family Collection.

as André Michaux, Elisha Mitchell, Asa Gray, and others. I imagined the sun-pierced shade of the tall timber they admired, found the rusty spikes of logging railroads, cleared paths to the peaks, and lured people to my favorite mountain.

Most of all, I was honored to feel the skeptical, appraising gaze of a mountain man like Robert Hartley and see not only him but through him, to his father and the men and women before them, used to hardship, hard work, and the sharp edge of life in these mountains. Far from setting me apart, I now know that seeing myself reflected in their

eyes connects me to them, their culture, their heritage, and the Grandfather Mountain. My youthful days on the summits link me to many a solitary logger or hunter of a century and more before. It's decades ago now, but that history is still alive for me each time I step (ever more gingerly) onto the trails. My hope is that the wild beauty still found on the mountain's peaks, and the rich history explored in this book, will open a door to appreciation and inspiration for whoever finds their way to our great, evergreen Grandfather.

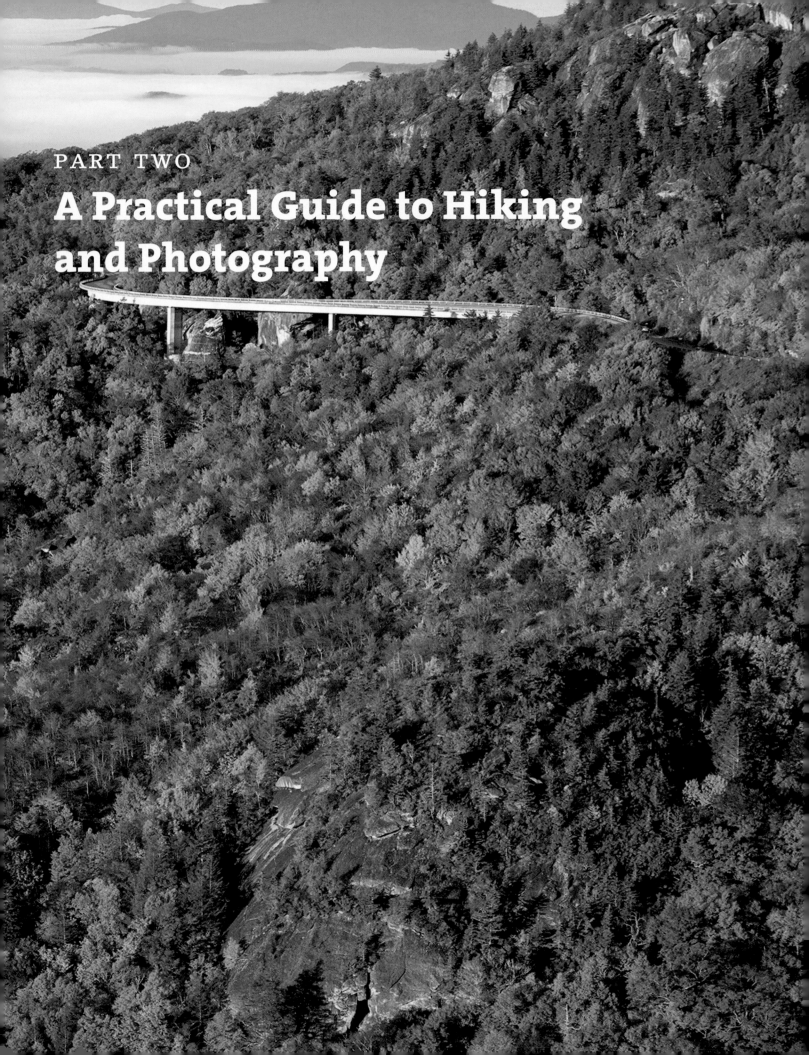

PART TWO

A Practical Guide to Hiking and Photography

Cliffs, Cracks—and Cirques?

Grandfather Mountain's majesty, northern character, climate, flora, and fauna all arise out of elevation and location. Geology explains the mountain's origin, shape, and size, but don't despair if the details elude you or make your eyes glaze over. It is easy to find places on the mountain where geological concepts inform what visitors see with their own eyes.

For Appalachian State geologist Anthony Love, MacRae Peak is a favorite spot to see signs of earlier times. Near the uppermost ladders, where the mountain's metaconglomerate underpinnings are dramatically thrust up through the Grandfather Mountain window, "we see Grandfather's essential rocks exposed," he asserts. Embedded in the cliffs are cobbles of granite, rhyolite (silica-rich volcanic rock), and basalt, all "shaped by water transport," evidence of origin as a "long-ago sedimentary rock layer" that metamorphosed when colliding tectonic plates forged rugged peaks. The same rock is seen in a "conglomerate wall" where the Underwood Trail squeezes below MacRae Peak and on the motor road in the boulder called Split Rock.

Understanding the role weathering plays in creating the mountain's crags is as easy as a hike on the Grandfather Trail. Love explains that the mountain's "layers of rock are tilted ever so slightly up from east to west," logical given the collision of continents. When "weathering and erosion take advantage of that exposure," they create west-facing cliffs. Horizontal layering of the once sedimentary rock sets the stage, then the rain, snow, and freeze-thaw cycles on the mountain's windward side cut "perpendicular to those layers," instructs Love. An insightful place to see that is between Indian House Cave and Calloway Gap. Two separate ledges, perhaps 70 feet apart, flank a cliff that plunges between the vistas. Horizontal strata delineate the cliff face, but vertical joints fracture the rock, causing slabs to cleave off in blocks. One seems poised in midface, tipped slightly outward, not so quickly creating a cliff.

It's a perfectly flat place to sit—if anyone dared! Warmer, sunnier weather on the peaks' lee side eliminates that type of weathering where big domes dive downward.

Another of Love's favorite spots to sense geologic scale is Rough Ridge. Everyone knows about regional faults like California's San Andreas Fault, where rocks slide past each other on a massive scale. But on Rough Ridge, Loren Raymond and Love found evidence that rocks had done the same in a smaller setting, creating "cliff scale faults." Discovering "how harder rock in the mountain had metamorphosed and deformed, while other weaker rocks slid past one another along fractures," may sound like a footnote in the "big picture," but that rock-shattering tectonic collision is still visible in the fissure caves and debris strewn across Grandfather's eastern spurs. Raymond and Love published those findings in a 2006 issue of *Southeastern Geology*, evidence that scientists are still unlocking the secrets of the Grandfather Mountain window.

One of the most fascinating geological debates about the mountain is whether a hanging mountain glacier shaped the Boone Fork valley. The issue arose in the August 1973 *Science* magazine with the controversial assertion that the valley was the East's southernmost cirque, a Dixie relative of the famous "ice cream scoop-shaped" bowl of Tuckerman Ravine on Mount Washington. That conclusion was drawn by Anthony Love's colleague Loren Raymond and associate James O. Berkland. The men found "polish, grooves, and striations" of "alpine glaciation" far south of the recognized southern limit of ice and called their find "the Boone Fork glacier." Promoter that he was, Hugh Morton marketed the discovery, taking photos of the smiling scientists beside grooves on Storyteller's Rock. The men crowed about their discovery in a *Winston-Salem Journal* article, calling the evidence "incontrovertible," and "absolute proof." A later opposing article revealed that the grooves were made by logging cables during the 1920s and "in no way resemble the polished, striated, and grooved outcrops we have seen in glaci-

if the bowl were a cirque, the evidence would be concealed beneath the massive deposition of vegetative matter generated in the South. Perry maintains, "There's no question there were incipient snowfields that survived summer melt season and quite possibly some small glaciers as recently as 19 or 20,000 years ago." Nevertheless, Perry does not see cirquelike steepness where the valley should display a "headwall," a cliff carved where the glacier hangs at the head of a cirque. But the next time you're standing on Storyteller's Rock with no leaves on the trees, look into the upper valley, and right where you might expect to see a headwall, notice a cliff that some observers call "the headwall." In a different political climate, Perry suggests, "the topic could use some fresh science."

Mining the Mountain

Western North Carolina was a major mining district when Arthur Keith published his 1903 geological overview of the Cranberry Quadrangle. Well before Hugh Morton envisioned "rich crops of tourists" on Grandfather, veins of the mountain's minerals were being mined, including gold. Keith said, "Considerable ore has been taken out" of one gold mine "located on the north side

When geologist Dr. Loren Raymond and James O. Berkland thought they'd found grooves made by a glacier on a rock in the Boone Fork Bowl, Hugh Morton set out to promote the discovery. Local United Press International photographer George Flowers went along and documented Morton creating a photo that widely announced the find in newspapers. Scottish heritage was so ingrained at Grandfather by this time that Morton's press release map called the bowl a "corrie," the Gaelic-derived word for cirque still applied to glacier-carved climbing routes and ski runs in Scotland. Courtesy of Special Collections, Appalachian State University, George Flowers Collection. Photo by George Flowers.

ated areas," wrote John B. McKeon, John T. Hack, and Wayne L. Newell. They cited a retired local lumberman who maintained cable marks could be seen "all through the woods," made when logs were dragged by cable to a logging railroad. Johnny Cooper, who also logged the area, went further, finding pieces of the old cables right beside the logging railroad grade the scientists and Morton had followed to reach the rock. The grade later became the Nuwati Trail, where cables are still visible.

While I was Grandfather's backcountry manager, I coined the term "Boone Fork Bowl" on trail maps to reference the debate and highlight the valley's similarity to cirques in New England. Well-traveled hikers and mountaineers were intrigued by the comparison. "It's definitely a u-shaped valley," asserts Appalachian State geography professor Baker Perry, "but I wouldn't characterize it as cirquelike necessarily." Perry thinks that even

From Storyteller's Rock, site of the "glacial striations" caused by logging cables, a winter hiker looks up into the supposed cirque at rocky cliffs some call the headwall. Photo by Randy Johnson.

High on aptly named White Rock Ridge, state park ranger (and former Grandfather backcountry manager) Luke Appling surveys the scene from a once-mined outcrop of quartz. Photo by Randy Johnson.

Carolina concluded gold deposits "are generally too small to be worked profitably." Old maps show crossed-pick mining symbols elsewhere on the mountain. Above the Foscoe gold mine near the crest of the aptly named White Rock Ridge, quartz was mined in the twentieth century. Drill holes are still visible in the milky white outcrop reached by a steep old road. The easiest way to see the mine is to look down from Watauga View in winter. Stone was also quarried from the mountain. Praised by Parkway landscape architects for the way it weathers, this "medium grained, light greenish gray" rock was "Grandfather Stone" to Bryant and Reed. With "cleavage parallel with bedding," the "metamorphosed sedimentary rock" was easily quarried "south and east of Grandfather Mountain." The entrance station and Top Shop are built or faced with the rock. Old quarries also existed near the Grandfather Mountain Nature Museum and in the Boone Bowl below the Cragway Trail.

An Island of the North in the South

When outdoor writer Horace Kephart moved to the Southern Appalachians, his early-1900s research revealed, "Here was news. We are wont to think of the South as a low country with sultry climate," yet in the mountains "one sleeps under blankets the year round." Grandfather's cool summers and snowy winters decidedly debunk that "Sunny South" stereotype and help give North Carolina the most diverse climate in eastern North America. The mountains see temperatures and snowfall akin to those in the far North, while the southeastern coastal climate emulates interior Florida's. Mount Mitchell claims the state's lowest average annual temperature, just 43.8 degrees (measured at 6,240 feet). But Grandfather, justifiably famous for keeping his cool, comes in second at 44.8 (despite recording data a thousand feet lower at 5,200 feet). Towns below the mountain are the coolest places in North Carolina—figuratively as well as literally.

Climate is key to Grandfather's natural world, and no variable is more important than elevation. Many meteorological factors play a part, but

of Grandfather Mountain" just above Foscoe on what's called Gold Mine Branch. Ted Shook's *Grandfather Community* book records that early settler Ben Davis's son Will "discovered gold in a creek" in 1870 and found "the mother lode" in 1876. Shepherd Dugger "knew of people in New York who were interested in mining," and he helped form the Grandfather Mountain Mining Company in 1899. Shook's description still holds. The shaft is 8 feet in diameter and runs about 200 feet inside Grandfather. A dike of rock and dirt at the entrance has flooded the tunnel. Ore was initially "hauled to Cranberry by oxen and wagon, loaded on the ETWNC (now Tweetsie) and shipped to New York." As the mining era ended, ore was hauled to Lenoir, but at $18 per ton "the mine could not continue" and shut down in 1905. In his 1930s boyhood, Shook "picked many a nugget out of the walls" and would later "lose them or throw them away thinking nothing of it." Another mine was worked on the east side of Grandfather below Pilot Ridge, but Bruce Bryant and John Reed's 1966 U.S. Geological Survey paper *Mineral Resources of the Grandfather Mountain Window and Vicinity, North*

Weathering the Weather

Automatic instruments usually record Grandfather's weather now, but for decades Winston Church "took the weather" with gauges locked in a louvered box behind the Top Shop. True to the publicity value of severe weather, Church asserts recording that data was job one in winter. There was no snow-removal equipment. "If we couldn't drive up, we walked," often through drifts so deep "it could take two hours." Church "often looks back at doing things that were kind'a foolish, especially when the wind was strong enough to blow the measuring cups right off the roof." One time, the all-important anemometer had been down for days, Church was by himself, and he thought, "Well, it's not too bad today. I believe I can install a new set of cups." To raise the flag or fix the gauges, employees reached the roof with a 14-foot ladder placed on a landing. By the time Church was done, "the wind got up and when I got back to my ladder, it was gone." Church was dressed pretty warmly, but "I had to get down," he maintains. It was 6 above zero, and "I didn't expect anybody anytime soon." Those were the days before cell phones or even radios on the mountain. "If things went wrong," Church was certain, "I knew I'd fall a long way." Hitting the parking lot would be fatal. He only had one option. "I figured, they taught us how to jump out of helicopters in the Army, hit and roll. I'm just gonna have do that." That's what he did. "The best I can say," he concludes, "is I didn't break any bones." Sadly, when plowing started, he rolled the plow truck on a particularly challenging day and broke his arm.

By the 1980s, bullish traffic at High Country downhill ski areas made plowing the road and giving the Swinging Bridge a winter season worthwhile. North Carolina Collection, University of North Carolina Library at Chapel Hill. Photo by Hugh Morton.

air temperature generally declines from 2 to 5 degrees per thousand feet of added elevation. The average temperature difference between the high mountains and Charlotte is 10 to 15 degrees, but mountain temps can be as much as 20 degrees cooler than Columbia or Charleston, South Carolina. July 1, 2012, illustrates how that weather works. It was the hottest day ever recorded on the mountain—83.2 degrees. On Calloway Peak, 658 feet higher than the mile-high weather station and often in cloud, the temperature might have been in the high 70s. That was also Charlotte's hottest day ever—106 degrees. Charlotte's average high for July, the hottest month in the city and on Grandfather, is 90.1, versus 69.2 on Grandfather. In Boone, which lacks an annual occurrence of 90 degrees, July 1 hit 92, significantly warmer than Boone's average hottest July day of 76.4 at 3,300 feet. The average July low, by contrast, is 70.6 in Charlotte, while on Grandfather and in High Country towns it's the mid- to upper 50s. That contrast creates a summer worth savoring. As Swiss geographer Arnold Guyot wrote, "The climate of this elevated region is truly delightful." In "summer the temperature scarcely rises above 80." Margaret Morley praised summer as "sweet beyond words, and the thermometer goes no higher here than in the North—and not so high very often—and the nights are cool." Summer temps dip further during August as the season slides toward fall. Wrote Morley, "Down in the plains and in all the cities, it is August. Up here, it is some celestial month not mentioned in any calendar." Late summer on Grandfather is a wonderful time when a golden glow bathes the peaks and infuses the very air itself.

Elevation also affects cloud cover and precipitation. Air masses rising over summits condense to create clouds, making a warm day cooler or triggering rain and snow, a process called the orographic effect. Lying in opposition to prevailing northwest winds, Grandfather often produces a vaporous summit plume. Many an old-timer has warned of rain because "the Grandfather has his hat on." That cloud-generating pattern is a plus

for visitors to the Swinging Bridge. Linville Peak is lower and often in the clear when clouds wreath MacRae and Calloway. That impact on the atmosphere nets Grandfather more than 63 inches of average yearly rainfall served up in steady doses of 4 to 6 inches per month (5.25 average), with half the days of every month receiving precipitation. Guyot pointed out a "remarkable rainy season, apparently confined to the mountains" that lasts from the end of June to the end of August. By noon, he writes, "thick clouds suddenly rise to the zenith" and "thunder-storms follow accompanied by copious rains for an hour or two. By 4 P.M. the sky is clear again and the night cloudless." These showers instantly cool down the hottest days, but sometimes it just gets wet. The mountain's rainiest year was 1979 with 89 inches. The second-rainiest was 2013 with 85 inches. That July was the wettest on record, with almost 24 inches of rain pelting down on 28 of 31 days. Imagine camping on the mountain's rainiest day ever, September 8, 2004, when 11.3 inches fell. That helped make September 2004 the record rainiest month, with almost 33 inches.

September and October step down in temperature with respective average highs of 63 and 54 (and lows of 50 and 40). Dipping temps and waning sunlight drain chlorophyll from the leaves, revealing all those hidden colors. New England's often quicker descent to cold and dimming daylight can bring brighter colors, but Grandfather and the High Country come close. By the end of September and early October, the alpinelike vegetation above the Blue Ridge Parkway flames with Grandfather's brightest, earliest autumn color. Summit leaves usually reach peak by October 10, then get swept away by wind, hoarfrost, and early snow. The second to third week of October is best for color in the High Country, but—best kept secret—err to the slightly early side and come midweek. It's a head-shaking marvel to locals how many flock to see the colors on October's event-filled third weekend to find most leaves down due to wind and rain. October through December is the least rainy time, with November and early December ushering in superb atmospheric clarity. Add the

Orographic lift is the culprit as rising air creates shredding clouds that spectacularly obscure Grandfather's rugged ridge. Photo by Tommy White Photography, www.tommywhitephotography.com.

absence of leaves on trees, and late fall is a great time to savor the mountain's scenery. November and December highs average 47 and 39, with lows about 32 and 24.

The Old Man in Winter

Grandfather's northwesterly location can create weather not shared by the rest of the region. When a sinking jet stream brings snow, Grandfather can be in the southern tail of a storm that stretches to New England, illustrating why the mountain is a southernmost outpost of northern flora and fauna. Thus, Banner Elk proclaims itself "Ski Capital of the South," and skiers at both Beech and Sugar ski areas gaze out at Grandfather. The mountain's average annual snowfall of about 56 inches pales beside Mount Mitchell's 104 inches, but that places Grandfather just slightly below Denver with 57.5 inches and above Chicago (38 inches), Boston (41), and Minneapolis (49.9). Beech Mountain, at 5,506

feet, nets 90 inches of snow, close to the 94 inches that fall on Buffalo, New York. And Roan Mountain likely gets 120-plus inches. Grandfather can blame its deficit on the orographic effect. The mountain hides in the "precipitation shadow" of state-line peaks to its west like Beech and Roan, the first to face rising air masses that wring rain *and* snow out of storms. A similar situation makes Asheville the driest place in the mountains. Nevertheless, Grandfather's earliest snow fell on September 10, 1964, meaning snow-dusted fall foliage isn't unusual. In 2012, Superstorm Sandy launched the High Country ski season in October. November has a 3-inch average, and ski areas often open by Thanksgiving. December is winter's fourth-snowiest month with just under 10 inches. Serious snow enthusiasts should focus on January, February, and March, which bring the year's greatest snowfall, just under 14 inches in February, with January almost identical. Third with more than

It's always awesome when seasons collide. Grandfather is a place where snow and ice can arrive early or stay remarkably late. As Clyde Smith might have admonished his Scouts, "Be prepared." Photo by Randy Johnson.

11 inches is March, a month when snow-poor winters often rebound. Grandfather's snowiest winter, 1960–61, totaled 128.7 inches of snow, with 64 inches falling in March. One of the heaviest snows on record brought almost 30 inches during March 12–14, 1993. Grandfather is one of the South's best targets for a snowy winter experience. Watch the weather, arrive when the snow is deep and likely to stay, and multiple feet are not hard to find.

Truth is, "We don't know how much snow falls on Grandfather," admits Appalachian State geographer Baker Perry. "We have data, for a long time, but there are quality issues." Ideally, snow measurements would be taken on a high sheltered site and not on a windy summit. And days go by without the staff being able to reach the instruments. The bottom line, Perry advises, is take Grandfather's snowfall stats with many grains of salt. But more than snow accounts for Grandfather's winter

majesty. Hoarfrost, those frost feathers that build up on the windward side of trees and rocks, can make the mountain a monument to winter anytime from September to May. As the feathers fall to the ground, a spring or fall hike can become a wintry one.

Despite Grandfather's lowest temperature of minus 32 on January 21, 1985, the average daily high temperature is above freezing each month of the winter (from about 35 in January to 45 in March). But those average highs do not mean every day is above freezing. In fact, there are stretches of dangerously cold weather, often after snowstorms and cold fronts. At the summits, subzero wind chills are the norm, and nighttime temperatures dip subzero a handful of times a winter. Average low temperatures are well below freezing all winter—19.89 in January, 21.90 in February, 23.95 in December, and 28.41 in March. Also, mean

With so much wind and exposed rock, even the best efforts at measurement have produced dubious snowfall statistics on Grandfather. Photo by Skip Sickler/http://skipsickler.zenfolio.com.

winter temperatures, the average of the maximum and minimum, are also below freezing from December through February, and that can preserve snowy conditions for long periods.

Appalachian spring may be Grandfather's most inspiring season. Aaron Copland's symphony is the perfect soundtrack when greening summits and waving wildflowers are music to the eyes. With each passing week, bud-burnished trees creep higher up the flanks, a sneak peak at autumn's future colors before chlorophyll covers them up all summer. It's an amazing sight when Grandfather breaks across the horizon like a massive, lime-green ocean wave, a top stripe of hoarfrost masquerading as foam across the rocky crest. Snow is still a possibility—just under 4 inches is average for April, a quarter inch in May. But by then spring has sprung, and as Charles Kuralt once said, in May, Grandfather Mountain is the best place to be in America.

The Flora of Grandfather Mountain

Kuralt's "best place to be" is the "single most important site for rare plant species in eastern North America," according to the Nature Conservancy. The mountain's 4,000 acres are home to seventy-three species of rare or endangered plants and animals, more than are found in the half-million acres of Great Smoky Mountains National Park. Many of Grandfather's plants, animals, and entire ecosystems are ranked as critically imperiled, imperiled, or rare and uncommon. Many are unique to the mountain or found in a few special places on the entire planet. Some of those species came south with Ice Age glaciers, forming "relict" and "disjunct" communities that are today northern enclaves trapped in a few lofty southern spots. Grandfather stands out as a rare-species refugium for its unusually complex topography and the abruptness of outcrops and cliffs on this rugged summit. Remarkable geography and an assort-

Jesse Pope is always aiming his binoculars at the peaks. In 2015, he was chosen as the Grandfather Mountain Stewardship Foundation's second executive director. Top priorities include getting the public and civic organizations engaged in preserving Grandfather and funding the foundation. A new volunteer program permits fans of the mountain to assist visitors, and a field trip scholarship fund helps school groups defray the cost of a visit. The scholarships honor Nathan Pribble, a young man from Apex, North Carolina, who loved hiking on the mountain and died in 2014. The ability to fund that and other specific projects at Grandfather permits donors to target their support. Photo by James McKay Morton.

ment of microclimates give Grandfather a mind-boggling sixteen separate ecosystems.

That means that over a few memorable miles of trail, the mountain compresses a thousand miles of climatological contrast into a climb to the peaks. Grandfather Mountain Stewardship Foundation executive director Jesse Pope has seen the mountain's incredible biodiversity firsthand, thanks to his former role as the foundation's director of education and natural resources. Pope likes to focus on the "miniature aspects" of a monumen-

tal mountain. "I look for these truly unique little microclimates that may not be representative of Grandfather as a whole, but where little populations of plants are here and nowhere else." Pope isn't referring to a major ecosystem, such as the **red spruce–Fraser fir forest**. He means the tiniest microclimates, where the deepest secrets of biodiversity are revealed. One example is a spectacular meadow far from any trail. It hides high on the south side of the mountain but on north-facing terrain where no north slope would be expected. That's what geographers call "aspect," the orientation of the slope. In these out-of-the-way places, the vegetation is very unlike that on the south slope, and it is unlike the north slope's, too. This "high elevation seep is very wet, almost like a bog but better drained," Pope explains. Profuse herbaceous plants grow here, among them one of the rarest on the mountain, **bent avens** (*Geum geniculatum*), found only in three locations in the world. Amazing microhabitats like these undergird Grandfather's deeper natural significance, but the mountain's major ecological zones stand out most to visitors.

The Mountain at Its Peaks

The whispering cool of the Canadian forest zone covers Grandfather's peaks in **red spruce** (*Picea rubens*) and **Fraser fir** (*Abies fraseri*). The spruce grows north to New England and Canada, but Fraser fir is endemic to western North Carolina, eastern Tennessee, and southwestern Virginia. Firs have achieved major economic importance as the staple of the Christmas tree industry. Prized nationwide for their shape, needle retention, and longevity, they've been chosen many times as the White House Christmas tree. Remarkably, the very earliest sales of Fraser fir Christmas trees can actually be traced to Grandfather Mountain. In a study of the state's Christmas tree industry, Dr. Jill Sidebottom credits late-1940s and early-1950s tree sales to Denver Taylor, Foscoe nurseryman and, later, grower. She writes that he would "hike up on Grandfather Mountain and carry out 4 or 5 little Frasers which he would sell as Christmas

Though not truly alpine as in "above treeline," many places on Grandfather appear to be timberline ecosystems. This open enclave among evergreens near Attic Window Peak is home to Alpine Meadow campsite. Photo by Randy Johnson.

trees along the roadside for $1 each." Around 1950, the invasive pest the **balsam woolly adelgid** (*Adelges piceae*) started killing Fraser fir, inflicting one of the Southern Appalachians' major eco-catastrophes. Insecticide kills the pest in commercial fields, but trees on the mountaintops have been hit hard. Luckily on Calloway Peak the fir reaches impressive verdure in solid stands that seem to resist the pest. Even red spruce has shown evidence of decline. Starting in the 1980s, Dr. Robert Bruck's research on Mount Mitchell faulted acid rain for spruce and fir mortality. Bruck found air pollution ozone levels acidic enough to burn evergreen needles. Recent research offers hope. Bruck's student Stephen Banks reported resurgent

growth in Mount Mitchell's spruce-fir forests, saying reduction in air pollution under "1990 amendments to the Clean Air Act may have potential implications for increased forest resilience." In New England, red spruce shows even greater growth. Hugh Morton created a slideshow and actively lobbied for the stricter provisions in the 1990 Clean Air Act. At Governor James G. Martin's urging, Morton showed the program to the North Carolina congressional delegation, and all but Jesse Helms ended up voting for changes that may now be easing the impact on summit forests. Nevertheless, the spruce-fir ecosystem is still vulnerable as long as politicians threaten to weaken clean air laws. The summit evergreen zone has

The Year of the Perfect Christmas Tree

With some of the earliest Fraser fir Christmas trees coming from Grandfather's slopes, it's fitting that the mountain lies at the heart of a classic children's Christmas book. *The Year of the Perfect Christmas Tree* tells the tale of Ruthie and her most memorable Christmas Eve. Her father is coming home from World War I, but Ruthie and her mom fear he won't arrive in time to climb the Grandfather Mountain and cut the perfect tree he marked with a ribbon from the little girl's hair. Ultimately, mom and daughter claim the perfect tree themselves—but that's just one of the gifts she gets. Avery County native and author Dr. Gloria Houston grew up under the mountain, and her classic 1988 book is rich with a sense of times past. "I put the perfect tree on Grandfather because it is my favorite place on earth," insists Houston, who as a kid often went up the mountain with her parents. "They had to hold on to my clothing because I truly believed that if I walked off of the cliffs," she admits, "the mountain had magic that would support me on thin air." During college at Appalachian State, Houston worked at Eseeola Lodge and used the inn's key to visit the Swinging Bridge at all hours. The tours she leads to the settings of her books always visit Grandfather. Two-time Caldecott Medal winner Barbara Cooney's paintings capture the way Grandfather's snowy summits dance in the Christmas memories of many a High Country resident. Houston and Cooney climbed the mountain to take photos as inspiration for the book's wonderful paintings, and Hugh Morton opened his photo archive to her. She's "hiked much of the mountain. My favorite memories are of the Tanawha Trail on Rough Ridge." Houston confesses, "For reasons I don't quite understand, the mountain has remained an emotional touchstone in my life. Whenever I fly over and look down on Grandfather, it always brings tears. I can't explain it. I've just given in to having such a special place in my life!" Houston's book captures the magical sense of place felt by so many who live with Grandfather Mountain on their mental horizon.

The loftiest, most wind-gnarled, climate-challenged Fraser firs on Grandfather Mountain are decidedly not "perfect" Christmas trees. But in the particularly verdant evergreen forest below Calloway Peak, where Fraser firs and red spruce bear up under heavy blankets of snow, the scenery is worthy of the most atmospheric Christmas card. Photo by Todd Bush/www.bushphoto.com.

Catawba rhododendron blooms all over the mountain, including below the peaks at Half Moon Overlook. Photo by Skip Sickler/http://skipsickler.zenfolio.com.

been linked to local culture for generations. Fraser fir was the "she-balsam" to mountain residents because resin could be "milked" from its bark blisters, not possible with the "he balsam," red spruce. Elisha Mitchell encountered the tradition in 1828, calling the resin a "precious fluid . . . the panacea or universal remedy of the mountains."

Spruce and fir aren't the only ebbing Southern Appalachian evergreens. The filamentous fringe-like beauty of the hemlock has long darkened Grandfather's lower slopes. Sadly, the **hemlock woolly adelgid** (*Adelges tsugae*) is wiping out the **Canadian hemlock** (*Tsuga canadensis*) and the **Carolina hemlock** (*Tsuga caroliniana*). Some of the High Country's most towering trees are ancient hemlocks, growing on Grandfather Mountain near US 221 and along the Blue Ridge Parkway. In many places, choice stands are being treated with pesticides, including a towering grove of 350- to 400-year-old hemlocks below the Grandfather face.

Deciduous trees also populate the peaks (though it's June before some bud). Among these are **mountain ash** (*Sorbus americana*), **yellow birch** (*Betula alleghaniensis*), **mountain maple** (*Acer spicatum*), and **striped maple** (*Acer pensylvanicum*). In late May, the whitish pink flowers of **hobblebush** (*Viburnum lantanoides*) are the first signs of spring up high. The red-blooming **Catawba rhododendron** (*Rhododendron catawbiense*) flowers in late June here and on Roan Mountain's meadows. **Southern lady fern** (*Athyrium asplenioides*) and **mountain wood-fern** (*Dryopteris campyloptera*) adorn the forest floor, as do cloverlike **wood sorrel** (*Oxalis montana*) and the waxy yellow flowers of **Clinton's lily** (*Clintonia borealis*). The ghostly stalks of **Indian pipe** (*Monotropa uniflora*) are easy to spot, as are the red bell flowers of **Gray's lily** (*Lilium grayi*), **Michaux's twisted stalk** (*Streptopus roseus*), and large-flowered **trillium** (*Trillium grandiflorum*).

True alpine and "pseudo-alpine" plants are everywhere on Grandfather, easily appreciated on the paved path between the Top Shop and Swinging Bridge. Preeminent nineteenth-century botanist Asa Gray maintained that sedges like those above and tufted bulrush, among other grasslike plants, gave Grandfather a "truly alpine aspect." Also visible are the purple flowers of Heller's blazing star and the tiny yellow tufts of Blue Ridge goldenrod. North Carolina Collection, University of North Carolina Library at Chapel Hill. Photo by Hugh Morton.

A rich assortment of mosses and lichens include **Grandfather Mountain leptodontium** (*Leptodontium excelsum*), growing on the bark of summit spruce and fir and first found on Grandfather. There's also **northern peatmoss** (*Sphagnum*), which Clyde Smith used to chink Hi-Balsam shelter, **pale-margined leptodontium** (*Leptodontium flexifolium*), and **matted feather moss** (*Brachythecium populeum*).

High Elevation Rocky Summit

Where rock crops out—and where doesn't it on the Grandfather?—**high elevation rocky summit** ecosystems face the elements. In New England, a true tree line occurs at about 4,800 feet. Grandfather would need to be 8,000 feet to have an alpine zone, but where the South's weather is at its worst, "pseudo-alpine" plants cling to thin,

dry soils. Grandfather Mountain has more of that plant community than any other Southern summit. Where wind-flagged spruce and fir shiver in savage gusts, a tree-line-like appearance prevails. Sedges—alpine and subalpine grasses—add to that effect, turning autumn blonde in late August. The true alpine plant **tufted bulrush**, or deerhair bulrush (*Tricophorum cespitosum*), is found on New Hampshire's Presidential Range and on Grandfather in disjunct populations widely separated from northern neighbors. **Appalachian fir clubmoss** (*Huperzia appalachiana*) also grows here and in northern New England. **Wretched sedge** (*Carex misera*) is a local endemic found where Grandfather's rarest plants bloom in alpinelike settings. The Nature Conservancy maintains Grandfather is "one of only a few strongholds" for **Roan Mountain bluet** (*Houstonia montana*). Half of the world's rare **Heller's blazing star** (*Liatrus helleri*) may be on Grandfather. Ninety percent of the globe's **Blue Ridge goldenrod** (*Solidago spithamaea*) grows in "several scattered locations along the summit ridge," the "primary stronghold" of the species, according to the Nature Conservancy. **Allegheny sandmyrtle** (*Leiophyllum buxifolium*) is a relative of the alpine azalea growing above tree line in New Hampshire. Asa Gray said the plant's matlike growths added a "truly Alpine aspect" to Grandfather. All three of the latter plants populate the paved, wheelchair-accessible path between the Top Shop and the Swinging Bridge.

Heath Bald Haven

Grandfather's uppermost ecosystems are not rigorously delineated. They ebb and flow, wrapping an infinite natural tapestry over the peaks. One of those is the heath bald, an alpine-appearing zone adjacent to rock outcrops and granitic domes in sunnier, drier conditions. Many are relatively low in elevation: near the Blue Ridge Parkway's Linn Cove Viaduct and on Rough Ridge, the Cragway Trail, and White Rock Ridge. Shrubby ground cover includes **smooth highbush blueberry** (*Vaccinium corymbosum*), **black huckleberry** (*Gaylussacia baccata*), and **teaberry** (*Gaultheria procumbens*). Bench Huckleberry Patch on White Rock Ridge was long popular with berry pickers from the Grandfather Community, but bears and birds also favor these fruits. **Galax** (*Galax urceolata*) grows in shiny clusters under the bushes. The showy oblong cluster of stem-top flowers on **Eastern turkeybeard** (*Xerophyllum asphodeloides*) is seen in June. **Pinkshell azalea** (*Rhododendron vaseyi*) grows mostly in southwestern North Carolina, but 1980s botanical investigator Alan Weakley called it "locally abundant" on Grandfather, its "northernmost outpost." That abundance is easily seen in mid-May just above the Nature Museum on both sides of the road at Forrest Gump curve, literally the filming location for one running scene in the famous Tom Hanks movie.

Grandfather is the northern limit of the pinkshell azalea (*Rhododendron vaseyi*), blooming here amid crags on the Grandfather Trail in Grandfather Gap. Photo by Randy Johnson.

The Realm of Rock

Rocky outcrops, cliffs, and crags create special sites. At the base of cliffs and in sharp gaps between the peaks, ice and snow accumulate, creating **high elevation seeps** where poor drainage collects water and rare plants like the fuzzy-leaved **Michaux's saxifrage** (*Saxifraga michauxii*). The composition of the rock separates different plants in the **montane acidic cliff** and **montane calcareous cliff** communities. Climbing is an issue on these faces because the species are sensitive and their habitat can be displaced into midair by one swipe of a rock climber's hand dislodging dirt in search of a handhold. **Rock gnome lichen** (*Gymnoderma lineare*) is one of the mountain's most endangered species. Only "200 square meters of the lichen are known to exist in the world," and Grandfather's crags sport "50 square meters," according to the Nature Conservancy. **Rock tripe** lichen (*Umbilicaria*) grows in drier spots.

Mid-Mountain Richness

Upper slopes range downhill through deciduous woods, including the northern hardwood forest, the high elevation red oak forest, and the rock-strewn **boulderfield forest**, one of the most interesting ecosystems on the mountain. This scatter of rocky blocks is draped in mosses and sparse soil, with water often heard gurgling just below. Periglacial freeze-and-thaw cycles are the presumed cause. The Profile Trail traverses exemplary boulderfield forests from Profile campsite to Profile View. In that area, Asa Gray's hike found many northern species and inspired comparison with New York, Vermont, and Canada. He mentioned sedges, hobblebush, and bent avens. The Nature Conservancy estimates "roughly eighty percent of the world's Bent Avens" is on Grandfather. Gray also saw the **purple turtleheads** (*Chelone obliqua*) that Amos Arthur Heller found growing from Shanty Spring almost to the ridge. Yellow and orange **jewelweed** (*Impatiens pallida* and *capensis*) is profuse in these moist boulderfields, as is **bee balm** (*Monarda didyma*). Yet another similar ecosystem is a **boulderfield subtype** of the red spruce–Fraser fir forest that is completely unique to Grandfather. Michael Schafale, coauthor of *Wild North Carolina* and a longtime ecologist with the North Carolina Natural Heritage program, asserts that these "well-developed boulderfields have near 100 percent ground cover of large rocks and may be the rarest of Spruce–Fir forest subtypes, known only from Grandfather Mountain." Hardwoods encircle the uppermost ecosystems. Yellow buckeye, **black cherry** (*Prunus serotina*), and **American beech** (*Fagus grandifolia*) are dominant, with **yellow birches** (*Betula alleghaniensis*) prevalent. **Trout lily** (*Erythronium americanum*) and **red trillium** (*Trillium erectum*) are often seen. On the south side of the mountain, as precipitation declines below the peaks, **high elevation red oak forest** finds **red oak** (*Quercus rubra* var.

ambigua) keeping company with yellow poplar, or **tuliptree** (*Liriodendron tulipfera*), black cherry, and American beech. **Flame azalea** (*Rhododendron calendulaceum*) and **mountain laurel** (*Kalmia latifolia*) are seen near the Blue Ridge Parkway and below. Deep soils of the **rich cove forest** offer the iconic Southern Appalachian habitat of towering trees. Tuliptrees, generally considered the tallest of eastern trees, soar to heights up to 150 feet. There's also **Fraser magnolia** (*Magnolia fraseri*) and **cucumber tree** (*Magnolia acuminata*). **Acidic cove forests** have more acidic soil and trees such as yellow buckeye and especially Canada hemlock and Carolina hemlock. These forests, famed for biological diversity, have played host to centuries of scientists marveling at the scenery and species. **Fraser's sedge** (*Cymophyllus fraserianus*) grows on Profile Trail near Shanty Branch. On the old Shanty Spring Trail, the multi-sedge-covered expanse of "The Glade" once inspired botanists and hikers. A cranberry bog sprawls in Linville Gap, where University of Tennessee botany professor A. Murray Evans reported "a rich stand of cranberries" (*Vaccinium oxycoccum*) and **crested wood fern** (*Dryopeteris cristata*). In eastern foothills far below, where hot days tempt swimmers into the waters of Wilson Creek Gorge at 1,400 feet, the **low mountain pine forest (montane pine forest subtype)** meets the western Piedmont. **Pitch pine** (*Pinus rigida*) and **Table Mountain pine** (*Pinus pungens*) are ubiquitous, and there are hardwoods too. Even these "less unique" ecosystems below the mountain are special in an unexpected way. Just a few air miles from the Canadian climate of Calloway Peak, the near-seamless transition from high to low habitat creates a welcoming environment for birds and animals, offering travel corridors that greatly amplify Grandfather's ecological importance.

The Fauna of Grandfather Mountain

Grandfather's native wildlife ranges from major mammals, like the black bear, to tiny mollusks and crayfish in streams and pools. There are unique bats, birds, and even insects. Species of fauna

Dainty orange and yellow jewelweed are often seen high on the mountain bobbing in chilly breezes near seeps and streams. Photo by Randy Johnson.

range from common to rare and endangered, some discovered on Grandfather.

The **American black bear** (*Ursus americanus*) leads any list of Grandfather's iconic animals. To Margaret Morley, "the Grandfather was once a famous place for bears"; then came decades of hunting by Daniel Boone and the likes of Foscoe's famous Harrison Aldridge. The Wildlife Resources Commission has helped bears rebound across 60 percent of the state. In 2009, mountain bear sightings made TV news in Charlotte with trail closures on Grandfather and Mount Mitchell. The attraction now has bear-proof trash receptacles, and the state park requires that food be hung at backcountry campsites. Today, Grandfather is back at the heart of a bear corridor stretching from the Pisgah National Forest across the peaks to woodland tracts in Tennessee.

You'll see **groundhogs** (*Marmota monax*), those puffy-cheeked, roly-poly rodents calmly munch-ing away beside the Blue Ridge Parkway. They experience a true winter hibernation of three or more months. **Red fox** (*Vulpes vulpes*), introduced in the 1700s from Europe, and the native **gray fox** (*Urocyn cinereoargenteus*) live on the mountain. And the **coyote** (*Canis latrans*) has moved into the area. Squirrels are plentiful, especially my favorite, the **boreal red squirrel** (*Tamiasciurus hudsonicus*), or "boomer" to local residents, often seen chattering down at hikers. The endangered **Carolina northern flying squirrel** (*Glaucomys sabrinus coloratus*) calls the mountain home. These nocturnal gliders hang on where spruce-fir meet northern hardwoods. Nest boxes have been placed in trees as part of ongoing research on this symbol of the Grandfather Mountain State Park Junior Ranger program. There wouldn't be carnivores without prey, and the latter include the endangered **Allegheny woodrat** (*Neotoma magister*). Another furry favorite of predators no doubt is the

Appalachian cottontail (*Sylvilagus obscurus*), a higher elevation, smaller bunny more accustomed to a northern climate than the typical **eastern cottontail** (*Sylvilagus floridanus*).

Grandfather Mountain's insects are many. Another of the most endangered species is the globally critically imperiled **spruce-fir moss spider** (*Microhexura montivaga*). "One of the last viable populations occurs in Fraser Fir forest on Calloway Peak," concludes the Nature Conservancy. The **green comma** (*Polygonia faunus smythii*) is a high elevation butterfly, and there's also a rare **caddisfly** (*Micrasema burksi*).

Holy Bat Cave

The Black Rock Cliffs Cave Trail opened in 1958, but by the late 1970s, speleologist and Old Fort dentist Dr. Cato Holler, now director of the Carolina Cave Survey, had discovered big-eared bats in Black Rock Cliffs and an even bigger cave on the mountain. The news spread, and Robert Currie of the U.S. Fish and Wildlife Service; Mary K. Clark, curator of mammals at the North Carolina Museum of Natural History; and her husband, David Lee, the museum's curator of birds, visited the cave and confirmed that the endangered **Virginia big-eared bat** (*Corynorhinus townsendii virginianus*) was hanging out on Grandfather. Clark and Lee became the first to document the colony. The cave was a hibernaculum, a winter hibernation spot that researchers thought was safe for the bats because hiker traffic was light in winter. Research in 1986 found that even summer hiking groups rarely brought flashlights to the cave and only a few ventured into the first room. When construction of the Blue Ridge Parkway got close, cavers feared "alarmingly easy" access, and Currie led an effort that built a metal gate over the cave in 1986. The gate prevented people from disturbing the bats during hibernation, when they would exhaust fat stores and die when new food was not available. The gate was unlocked when the bats left in summer; but it was closed permanently, and the trail was closed in the early 1990s. The Virginia big-eared bat population grew and

Virginia big-eared bats spend winter hibernating in a number of caves on the mountain, and in the 1980s, that discovery sparked the closure of popular Black Rock Cliffs Cave. Cave gating expert Robert Currie of the U.S. Fish and Wildlife Service oversaw construction of the barrier intended to prevent human access. The gating crew sustained a lightning strike that didn't hurt anyone but knocked out an electrical generator. Photo by Randy Johnson.

stabilized, and in 2012, exciting research located the bats' summer roosts. Since these bats are a "cave-obligate species," their summer and winter roosts must be protected if the colony is to survive. Indiana State University biology professor Dr. Joy O'Keefe tracked the bats with tiny transmitters, temporary radio towers, and even an airplane, and the first maternity roost ever located in the state was found eight miles away on Beech Mountain. Efforts are being made to purchase and preserve the colony's summer refuge. That hopeful sign for an endangered species capped thirty years of bat research on Grandfather. Other bats have been found, among them the rare **northern long-eared bat** (*Myotis septentrionalis*); the **eastern small-footed bat** (*Myotis Leibii*), one of the East's smallest; and the **hoary bat** (*Lasiurus cinereus*), with an impressive 15-inch wingspan.

The Site of Soaring Birds

Interest in Grandfather's birdlife took off in 1984 with the Southern Appalachians' first reintroduction of the **peregrine falcon** (*Falco peregrinus*). By the 1950s, "egg-shell thinning" caused by DDT had so undermined breeding by peregrines that the species was extirpated from the East. DDT was banned in 1972, and by 1973, Dr. Tom Cade and the Peregrine Fund at Cornell University's Laboratory of Ornithology were bringing the bird back. In five years, 635 birds were released via the program's "hacking" technique. Born by captive breeding, the birds were caged at reintroduction sites in "hacking boxes," shelters where attendants surreptitiously fed them until the falcons were freed. In 1984, the Southern Appalachians were targeted, and Grandfather's ruggedness and growing research-friendly reputation made the location a likely candidate. The North Carolina Wildlife Resources Commission took the lead under the state's Nongame and Endangered Wildlife Fund.

Coordinator Gary Henry of the U.S. Fish and Wildlife Service explored the mountain with me and was impressed. He needed a perfect cliff, and I suggested a spectacular campsite I had found years before on a trailless, spruce-fir forested bulge below Watauga View that I called "Windy Bowl." Hemmed in by cliffs and sheltered among evergreens, the flat site even had a ledge for the hacking box. Hidden attendants could easily roll the birds' raw chicken dinners down a PVC pipe into the cage. By mid-May, the bird box and tent platform were ready for wildlife students Dan Audet, of Frostburg College, Maryland, and Bryant Tarr, of the University of Wisconsin. A media circus accompanied the birds' arrival and hike to the site with Marty Gilroy, Peregrine Fund program coordinator.

The students bore the burden of supplying themselves and their raptor charges. This was no easy task, as they had to carry their own food plus frozen whole chickens up 2,000 vertical feet on a 3-mile hike. The college guys toughened up, but volunteers helped, among them Robert Branch and later trail employee Ed Schultz. Audet and Tarr had to record every detail about the birds, spurred by agency warnings that the falcons' welfare "is strictly your responsibility." They named the male birds Beave and Artie and the females Shadow and Ev. The hack box was opened on May 21, 1984. The birds fledged, or first took flight, at different times, with Ev frightened into the air by a buzzing hang glider. The birds soon took control of Grandfather's airspace, hunting by "stooping" down on other birds like animal kingdom fighter jets. After first being alarmed, they "tail-chased" hang gliders and other species, including ravens, the mountain's monsters. Eventually we packed a ton of gear to the site as Hugh Morton photographed and filmed the project. Suddenly, the falcons and the backcountry were central to the mountain's media message. Morton reported bird sightings at "our peregrine site" to Peregrine Fund coordinator Jack Barclay, telling him he hoped "our birds are thriving." By early July, the falcons were gone. A second hacking program released six falcons on Grandfather in 1985, and as the birds were about to be released, attendants looked up to see Artie hovering over the place where he too had fledged. Peregrines were removed from the endangered species list in 1999, and in a 2005 book, *Peregrine Falcon: Stories of the Blue Meanie*, James H. Enderson argues that peregrine populations would have come back without reintroduction efforts. Others have called the birds' recovery the greatest conservation achievement of the twentieth century. Nevertheless, the drama that played out on Grandfather inspired many people to help save these swooping birds. To many High Country residents who spot peregrines over Grandfather's peaks, the falcons are still "our birds."

The falcon hacking site takes shape. Trail manager Randy Johnson works with North Carolina Wildlife Resources Commission biologist Gordon Warburton (who thirty years later became an early board member of the Grandfather Mountain Stewardship Foundation) and Gary Henry of the U.S. Fish and Wildlife Service. The birds' shelter box was secured to the cliff, and their food of thawed frozen chicken was dispatched down the plastic tube. North Carolina Collection, University of North Carolina Library at Chapel Hill. Photo by Hugh Morton.

The Rest of the Roost

After bats, David Lee targeted the mountain's overall bird life for study. In his oft-cited 1985 "Summer Bird Fauna of North Carolina's Grandfather Mountain," Lee and his peregrine attendant coauthors Audet and Tarr noted that Grandfather Mountain just wasn't known for birding. "People thought it was a tourist destination, not a natural area," Lee asserts. The entrance fee and long walk did not help. Lee was interested in how ecology and geography affect the distribution of bird species on a "mountain where I could work from below 2,000 feet all the way to 6,000 feet, and visit all the life zones and their transitional communities." Lee saw the mountain as we appreciate it today and helped set the stage for a "new view" of Grandfather. Lee would do for the modern inventorying of birds

what the Natural Heritage Program's Alan Weakley and Michael Schafale would do later that decade cataloging the mountain's flora.

Lee was fortunate. He camped during the summer of 1984, but his coauthors literally lived atop the mountain and hiked daily from mid-May through mid-July. Lee grew up in Maryland, so he easily noticed northern species not known to breed on the mountain. He documented the **hermit thrush** (*Catharus guttatus*), the **sharp-shinned hawk** (*Accipiter striatus*), the **black-billed cuckoo** (*Coccyzus erythropthalmus*), the **northern saw-whet owl** (*Aegolius acadicus*), and the **black-capped chickadee** (*Parus atricapillus*), calling the discovery of an "extant population" of nesting chickadees his "single most interesting find." Lee noted that destructive logging had eliminated the species from Mount Mitchell, and he speculated that Grandfather's ruggedness limited the severity of logging and preserved the population. He also looked at earlier vegetation research and concluded that "plant communities have not exhibited any major changes in the last 70 years," again evidence of lighter logging. Lee and colleagues "documented 84 species of nesting birds on Grandfather Mountain," and an "additional 20 to 30 could reasonably be expected," he wrote. He attributed that to "the variation of plant communities dictated by the elevational gradient" and concluded that "there is probably no other place in the Southern Appalachians where such extremes in elevation exist in such close proximity." The breeding bird population "comes closer to an entire mountain chain rather than a single peak." In summary, Lee concluded, "It is likely that nowhere else in North Carolina is such a rich diversity of breeding birds attained in such a restricted area" where "well over half the state's nesting bird fauna" were found in less than 10 square miles.

Lee was named the state's conservationist of the year in 2004 and regretted that he never studied the mountain further. But that was likely Grandfather's fault. His students were interested, but a single visit revealed "how much work was required." Lee also often wryly says research is more difficult on Grandfather because it's surrounded by dry counties and "it's too far to drive to get beer and too hard to carry it up the damn mountain." The surrounding counties are now wet, but hauling suds up the hill is as hard as ever, a fact known well by falcon attendants Audet and Tarr. They pointedly praised volunteer Robert Branch for the "beverages" he bestowed, the perfect accompaniment to Sunday night radio comedy on Appalachian State's student station. Lee, executive director of the nonprofit Tortoise Reserve conservation effort, helped Grandfather become an Important Birding Area, a global designation sponsored in the United States by the National Audubon Society. That program asserts that "the diversity of breeding birds at [Grandfather] is probably the highest of any site in North Carolina and probably the second highest in the United States. At least 118 breeding season species have been recorded and others are expected."

Massive Migration

Grandfather has more than its share of quintessential birds, including the state's largest colony of the **common raven** (*Corvus corax*), the largest population of any site south of New England and east of the Rockies. Lee said that makes Grandfather the "best place to watch ravens in the Southern Appalachians." The birds revered by Edgar Allan Poe are never more popular than on windy days when they soar, dive, roll, and tumble in blustery gusts. Ravens are songbirds, so beyond the unmistakable hoarse caw and gargling croak, their range of calls is impressive. They nest high on cliffs—one reason why Grandfather is a favorite. The mountain shines with high elevation bird species. According to Jesse Pope, "We have a very high quality of birds, with twenty-five species that you're not going to find many places in North Carolina." He points out **blackburnian warblers** (*Setophaga fusca*), **black-throated green warblers** (*Setophaga virens*), **rose-breasted grosbeaks** (*Pheucticus ludovicianus*), **pine siskins** (*Carduelis pinus*), **golden-crowned kinglets** (*Regulus satrapa*), **red crossbills** (*Loxia curvirostra*), **least flycatchers** (*Empidonax minimus*), and real anomalies such as **olive-sided flycatchers** (*Contopus cooperi*) and **mourning warblers** (*Geothlypis philadelphia*), "an extreme northern bird," asserts Pope.

One of Pope's favorite avifauna appreciation opportunities occurs in fall when raptors migrate south for the winter. The Appalachians and the Atlantic coast are the major flyways, and Grandfather is "incredibly important" as a stopover. No wonder. Imagine this: There they are, birds flying great distances, *sooo tired*, and suddenly, the Blue Ridge crimps in to a narrow strip of high summits. Dead ahead, there's an evergreen island in the sky, surrounded by a vertical-mile habitat hotel.

Who wouldn't peel off and check in? To assess that appeal, Grandfather has been participating in the annual Hawk Watch since about 2010. Daily public observations, often atop Linville Peak, are "wildly popular," says Pope. Species include **broad-winged hawks** (*Buteo platypterus*), **bald eagles** (*Haliaeetus leucocephalu*), **osprey** (*Pandion haliaetus*), **Cooper's hawks** (*Accipiter cooperii*), peregrines, kestrels, and more.

These migrating birds seek out thermals, rising columns of heat radiating off warm rocks, to lift themselves thousands of feet in the air. Then they coast off in search of another airy elevator, just like Grandfather's hang glider pilots of old. "MacRae Peak is one of the best places to watch thermals," Pope asserts, agreeing with Anthony Love, who loves that spot for rocky reasons. One day Pope was perched around MacRae's ladders with a Montreat College class when broad-winged hawks created a "perfect educational opportunity." He lectured on how groups of the birds, called kettles, caught thermals and "key off of each other. The second that came out of my mouth, there were a few more, then a handful more, then dozens more." Pope ended up with 250 hawks circling overhead, what he's called "a tornado of hawks." "Talk about a cool experience!" he exclaims. Target September 15 to 25 for the migration. If you want that kind of amazement on Grandfather, take a stewardship foundation or state park guided hike, or just point your binoculars above the autumn scenery.

Amphibians and the Aquatic Environment

The Southern Appalachians are home to more salamander species than any other place on the planet. Most salamanders are "lungless" and breathe through their skin. That reflects why misty forests and damp soil are essential and why destruction of evergreen forests by climate change or insect pests poses a threat. Maurice Brooks, author of *The Appalachians*, calls Grandfather "herpetological holy ground" because "no other Appalachian peak has yielded the first specimens of three salamander species." Emmett Dunn discovered the **Yonahlossee salamander** (*Plethodon*

yonahlossee). Worth Weller found **Weller's salamander** (*Plethodon welleri*). One of two closely related subspecies (*Plethodon welleri welleri*) may exist only on Grandfather. There's also the rare, very small **pigmy salamander**, or pygmy (*Desmognathus wrighti*). The tiny, four-inch-long **bog turtle** (*Glyptemys muhlenbergii*) prefers muddy hideouts and hibernates in winter. **Fingernail clams** were found on the mountain in 2005 by visiting educators from the North Carolina Museum of Natural Sciences. The rare, semiaquatic **southern water shrew** (*Sorex palustris punctulatus*), a small, mole-like mammal, lives near the Linn Cove Viaduct. The **long-tailed shrew** (*Sorex dispar*) ranges all the way to Canada's Gaspé Peninsula. The **star-nosed mole** (*Condylura cristata*), its snout ringed with fleshy feelers, can even smell underwater.

One of the mountain's most recent stories of discovery surrounds the eponymously named **Grandfather Mountain crayfish** (*Cambarus eesseeohensis*). According to Gary Peeples of the U.S. Fish and Wildlife Service, Roger Thoma, crayfish conservation biologist at Midwest Biodiversity Institute, "became aware of the possibility of a new species in 1978" and collected it on Grandfather in 2005, becoming the first to describe it for science. The crustacean lived only in the upper Linville River from the headwaters of Little and Big Grassy Creeks to Linville Falls. That got Jesse Pope thinking. The Linville and Watauga Rivers start a stone's throw from each other on the Eastern Continental Divide above Linville Gap. "It always fascinated me that a salamander could walk between two rivers that drain half a continent apart—so why couldn't a crayfish?" In 2008, he and staff conducted the first crayfish census in all the mountain's streams. Sure enough, the Grandfather Crayfish was in the Watauga River, too—but nowhere else on the mountain. That limited range nets the new species a Global Heritage Status Rank of G1 (critically imperiled).

Discovery happens in many ways under the Grandfather. When I moved to Linville to reclaim disappearing trails, I noticed a wooded knob rising above the Linville River at the corner of US 221 and NC 105. A long-gone roadside sign once read "Lenoir Park." Thinking I noticed a trail in the trees, I tossed cross-country skis into my Subaru one winter day and parked on Watauga Avenue. I recall thinking the park must honor the town of Lenoir, where Linville summer residents surely lived. Decades later, I realized this remnant of Linville's original design was all that's left to honor Walter Waightstill Lenoir, the man who sold Grandfather Mountain to the MacRaes. As I skied around the knob and paused above the frozen Linville River that day in 1978, the stream born on the mountain above was still hiding its secret crayfish. For Jesse Pope, finding a species that new shows "just how many secrets Grandfather has left to tell." With discoveries still being made and the mountain increasingly safe from development, I'm betting future generations will conclude that the natural world of Grandfather Mountain is even more significant than we thought.

Grandfather's frequent sea of clouds adds to the drama of a hike.
Here two hikers on MacRae Peak are silhouetted against the distant
Black Mountains. Photo by Randy Johnson

Introduction

Many people are confused from the get-go about visiting Grandfather Mountain. Not only do three separate entities manage the mountain, but one of them, the state park, is now responsible for property that used to be part of the Grandfather Mountain Attraction. To be specific, the backcountry and its highest peaks are a North Carolina state park, now public property where no entrance fee is charged. The Grandfather Mountain Attraction—the road to the Swinging Bridge, habitats, and Nature Museum—is still a privately owned tourist attraction where admission is charged. The Blue Ridge Parkway is a unit of the National Park Service where entry is free.

These three entities interface on the mountain's trails—hence the confusion, centered largely on where a hike starts. Even if you just hike from the attraction into the state park, you still pay to drive up that private road. Wherever a hiker starts, except at the attraction, he or she must fill out a state park hiking permit when a trail enters the park's backcountry—that includes hikers entering from the Blue Ridge Parkway and starting at a state park trailhead such as Profile. From either place, a hiker must stop at the state park sign and fill out the free permit registration form and review the latest rules (no alcoholic beverages, no rock or plant collecting, no hunting or trapping, and pets must be on a leash 6 feet or less, etc.). Campers should also register to camp and choose an unoccupied, first-come, first-serve campsite at the trail sign. Be aware that the park has begun the process of making some sites reservable online. In future more sites will be reservable, and a camping fee will probably be reinstated. Camping is only permitted from state park or Blue Ridge Parkway trailheads—never from inside the attraction. That road closes at night, and vehicles cannot be locked inside. Campers must also use designated state park campsites; camping is prohibited on Blue Ridge Parkway property except at Price Park's developed campground and one backcountry campsite.

All day hikers, whether they register at a state park trail sign or enter the trails from the attraction, must return by dark or the time posted on the sign or they may be considered lost and a search may be launched (especially in the attraction, where employees need to lock the gate). Attraction hikers generally must be off the trail an hour before closing time (always read the sign for seasonal hours). If you hike from the attraction and cannot return to your car, do not fail to call the attraction to avoid a search (828-733-2800 [Top Shop]; 828-733-4337 [gate]; or 828-733-1059 [Nature Museum]). Only campers registered from the valley trailheads are considered legitimate overnighters.

The most confusion involves hiking into the attraction. If you start at a state park or Parkway trailhead, you can enter the attraction by trail for free, to hike to the Swinging Bridge, for instance. But you must hike back or arrange in advance to have a friend drive to the top to pick you up (and they will be charged). You cannot walk down the attraction road, nor is there a trail or shuttle to the bottom. If you have no ride down from the Swinging Bridge, the friendly folks will be nice to you, but the best advice is have a plan in advance. It is *very difficult* to hike to the attraction and back in one day.

More confusing are similar names of overlooks and trails. The Boone Fork creek starts on Grandfather Mountain near the Blue Ridge Parkway's Boone Fork *Parking Area* (milepost 299.9) where the state park's Daniel Boone Scout Trail and Nuwati Trail start. However, Boone Fork creek flows miles away to form Price Lake. Oddly, the parking area beside that lake used to be named Boone Fork *Overlook* (milepost 297.2), presumably because the creek was still flowing under the water! (Smartly, this overlook's name was changed recently to Lake View Overlook). Also near the lake, the Boone Fork *Trail* is a 5-mile loop hike that follows Boone Fork *after* it reappears below the lake. Worse yet, the Tanawha Trail connects the Boone Fork Parking Area near the Daniel Boone Scout Trail to the Boone Fork Trail in Price Park.

Grandfather Mountain State Park's trail registration signs should be the first stop for hikers and campers heading up the mountain. This one is on the Blue Ridge Parkway's Tanawha Trail, just south of the Boone Fork bridge, and not far from the Asutsi, Nuwati, and Daniel Boone Scout Trails. Photo by Todd Bush/www.bushphoto.com.

Don't be one of those hikers who set out "to hike back to my car" and end up at the wrong part of Boone Fork. The name change at the overlook above will help, but it will take years for available information to catch up.

Be Prepared

On this mountain, the Daniel Boone *Scout* Trail rightly urges hikers to embrace the "Be Prepared" motto of the Boy Scouts. Grandfather's weather can be deadly, and people have died there from exposure, lightning strikes, and more. In full winter conditions, the trails can be waist-deep in snow or solid ice. The state park requires crampon-style boot traction devices (such as Yak-Trax or Kahtoola Microspikes). Snowshoes and trekking poles are good, too. In recent years, the attraction simply closes its state park trailheads when winter hikers would most like to use them. I have actually pulled

up to the gate with crampons, snowshoes, and arctic gear only to be told the trails are closed. The employee hands out photos to prove the summit looks like New Hampshire. Once I quipped, "Yep, that's what I'm here for!" Best winter bet: Start at state park trailheads.

Easy hikes around Grandfather require that you carry nothing, but summiteers should have a backpack, water bottle, snacks, spare clothing or rain jacket, first-aid kit (bandages, antiseptic, pain relief, sunscreen, moleskin for blisters), plus a permit and hiking map. Knowledge is most important. Read about trail safety, hypothermia, lightning, and winter hiking skills; this is a serious summit. Hypothermia can happen at any time of year, so have rain gear and, in colder months, gloves and a hat (most heat is lost from the head). On exposed peaks, frostbite is a major danger in winter, as is lightning in summer. Start early and be down

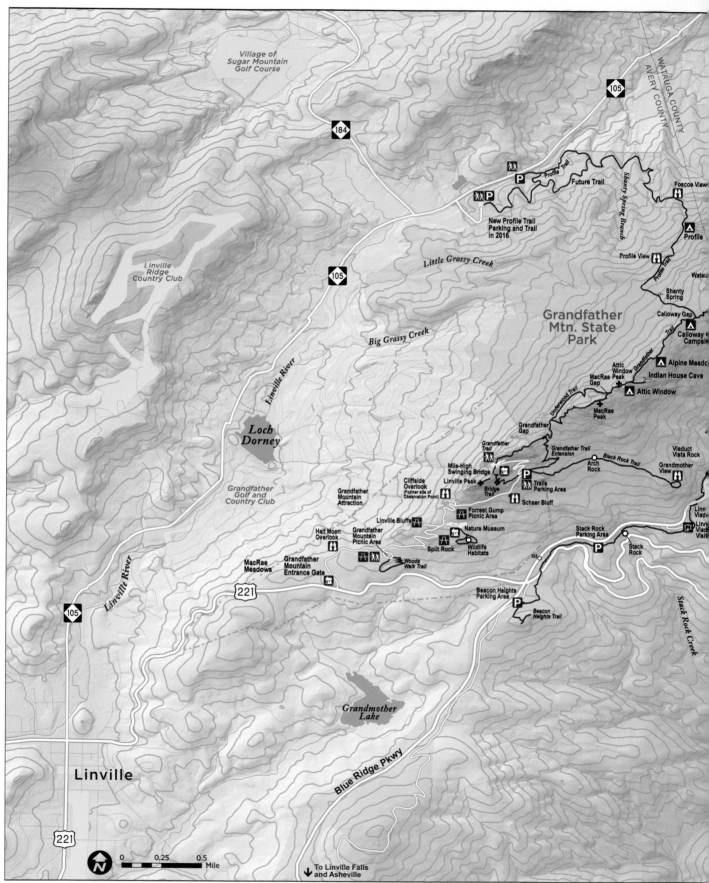

Grandfather Mountain Overview

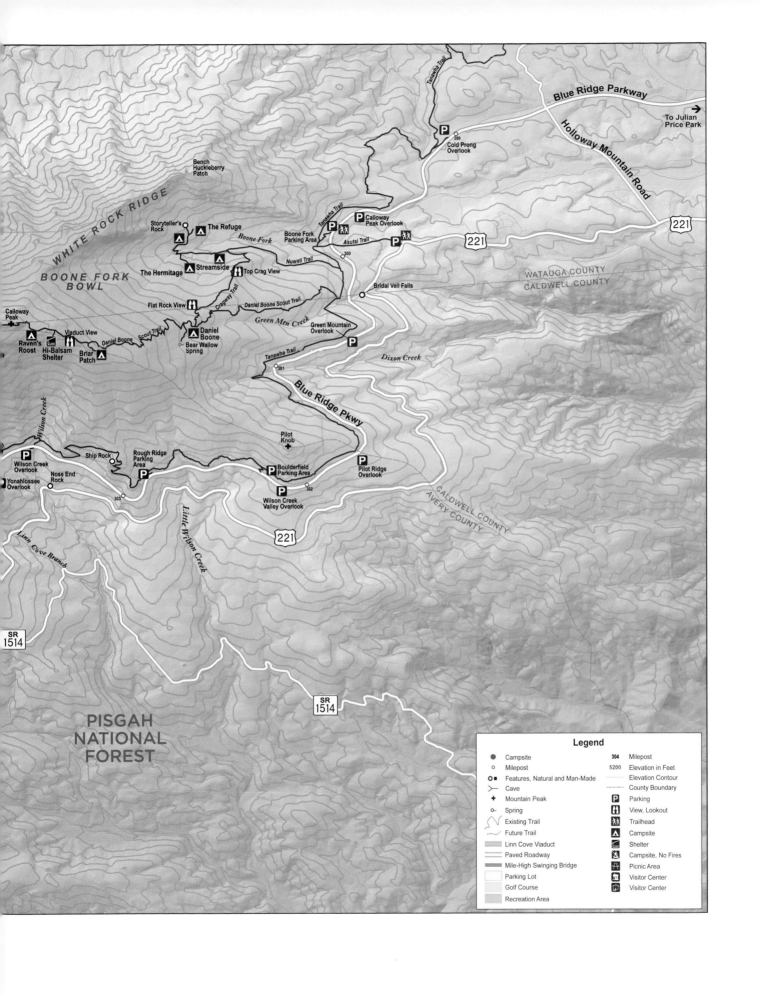

Blue Ridge Parkway

Holloway Mountain Road

To Julian Price Park

Cold Prong Overlook

Tanawha Trail

221

WATAUGA COUNTY
CALDWELL COUNTY

Calloway Peak Overlook

Boone Fork Parking Area

Asutsi Trail

Bench Huckleberry Patch

WHITE ROCK RIDGE

Storyteller's Rock

The Refuge

Boone Fork

The Hermitage

Streamside

Top Crag View

Nuwati Trail

BOONE FORK BOWL

Flat Rock View

Cragway Trail

Daniel Boone Scout Trail

Green Mtn Creek

Green Mountain Overlook

Calloway Peak

Viaduct View

Ravan's Roost

Hi-Balsam Shelter

Briar Patch

Daniel Boone

Scout Trail

Daniel Boone

Bear Wallow Spring

Bridal Veil Falls

Tanawha Trail

Dixon Creek

Blue Ridge Pkwy

Wilson Creek

Pilot Knob

Ship Rock

Rough Ridge Parking Area

Wilson Creek Overlook

Nose End Rock

Yonahlossee Overlook

Boulderfield Parking Area

Wilson Creek Valley Overlook

Pilot Ridge Overlook

CALDWELL COUNTY
AVERY COUNTY

221

Linn Cove Branch

Little Wilson Creek

SR 1514

SR 1514

PISGAH NATIONAL FOREST

Legend

●	Campsite	304	Milepost
○	Milepost	5200	Elevation in Feet
○■	Features, Natural and Man-Made		Elevation Contour
⤜	Cave		County Boundary
+	Mountain Peak	P	Parking
⟞	Spring		View, Lookout
	Existing Trail		Trailhead
	Future Trail		Campsite
	Linn Cove Viaduct		Shelter
	Paved Roadway		Campsite, No Fires
	Mile-High Swinging Bridge		Picnic Area
	Parking Lot		Visitor Center
	Golf Course		Visitor Center
	Recreation Area		

Icicle-adorned krummholz on Linville Peak stretches away to the distant Black Mountains. Photographer Skip Sickler became staff photographer for the Grandfather Mountain Stewardship Foundation in 2011, but his trail experience started on an Outward Bound expedition in 1980 when he helped rebuild Hi-Balsam Shelter. "It's still standing," he says with satisfaction. A few years later he started a fifteen-year career with "OB" as course director and base camp manager. "I have to credit Mr. Morton with fueling my photographic flames," he says. "The enthusiasm he demonstrated at the Nature Photography Weekend was an inspiration to many, myself included." Photo by Skip Sickler/http://skipsickler.zenfolio.com.

by afternoon thunderstorm time, or retreat if the weather deteriorates. Not everyone can afford high-tech outdoor gear, but Grandfather is a good place to wear garments that stay warm when wet (*not* jeans). Bring clothing for the worst weather the season can deliver. On easy Parkway trails, running shoes are fine, but hikes to Grandfather's peaks demand sturdier hiking boots. Do not even consider flip-flops.

Winter eradicates bothersome bugs and plants, but in summer, be on the lookout for bees and their nests. Grandfather's summits are mostly free of ticks, poison ivy, poison oak, and poison sumac. You'll be hard pressed to find a snake on the upper mountain, but near and below US 221, there may be timber rattlers and copperheads. Watch where you step. Don't reach or sit blindly behind logs

and rocks. Most animals in North Carolina are harmless, but Grandfather is bear country. Back away steadily and calmly from an encounter with a mother and cubs. Do not run or climb a tree. Do not take food into a tent, and hang bagged food away from camp. Read about bears. Carry clean water or treat it with a portable water filter. Even pristine-looking streams may contain waterborne *giardia lamblia*.

Leave No Trace

Grandfather is worth protecting. Go to the Leave no Trace website (www.lnt.org/) and follow their guidelines, especially for washing yourself and disposing of human waste. There are no back-country privies now, so make a "cat hole" and "go" at least 200 feet from surface water, trails, and

The Trails We Lost

A handful of trails we once hiked are an intriguing part of Grandfather's past.

Arch Rock Trail

The Arch Rock Trail linked the Grandfather Trail to today's Black Rock Trail. It descended from MacRae Gap, between MacRae and Attic Window Peaks, and passed through the formation called Arch Rock at its junction with the Black Rock Cliffs Cave Trail (which used to reach a now-closed fissure cave). At the trail's halfway point, Grand View Pinnacle offered memorable views. In 1991, Grandfather maintenance man Johnny Cooper claimed, "We built that one. Started up from the bottom." It seems likely that Clyde Smith at least designed it. He wrote "To Be Constructed" beside dashed lines he drew on a planning map. The plummeting path was closed in 1991 because it was "impossible to maintain," wrote Ed Schultz. I kept it open for the steep New England experience of terrain dictating trail design.

The Black Rock Cliffs Cave Trail

The current Black Rock Trail still follows the original track of the Black Rock Cliffs Cave Trail, but it ends at viewpoints instead of a cave in Black Rock Cliffs near Linn Cove Viaduct. The trail debuted in the fall of 1958 after an old logger "took Mr. Morton to the cave and we cut the trail to it," Cooper recalled. The path was likely built to bolster Hugh Morton's contention that the backcountry was a destination for attraction visitors that would be compromised by the Parkway's proposed "high-route." The 308-foot-deep, four-room fissure cave nevertheless had bona fide appeal (trailhead signs urged "Take a Flashlight"). An eye-widening surge of cold air greeted anyone stepping close to the entrance. One 60-foot-high chamber called the Chandelier Room required a belly-crawl. It was fun while it lasted. See Chapter 10 for more on how discovery of endangered bats led to the cave's closure.

Pilot Knob Trail

This trail climbed steeply from US 221 near Little Wilson Creek through the gap of Pilot Ridge to the Daniel Boone Scout Trail. It too was blazed to back up Hugh Morton's claim that construction of the Parkway's "high route" would compromise public use of the mountain. The path was little more than a corridor cleared through the woods, and all that's left of it today may be faint evidence of foot traffic beyond Bear Wallow Spring near the Boone Trail.

The Shanty Spring Trail and Calloway Trail

The western flank of Grandfather has seen more than two centuries of "hiking." That easily makes the Continental Divide between Linville Gap and the Grandfather summits one of the country's oldest recreational hiking routes. It also means the Shanty Spring Trail was likely just the latest of many tracks that came and went in that corridor over decades.

When Clyde Smith formalized the route in the mid-1940s, he called it the Calloway Trail to reflect its earlier name. The 1902 topo map in Chapter 3 supports that by showing a path veering off the Shanty Spring Trail route to descend a different ridge to the Grandfather Hotel, often called "Calloway's" and likely the source of the Calloway moniker. Smith kept the name Calloway, but he turned away from the old hotel site. At the sedge-covered swale I dubbed "the Glade" on 1970s trail maps (where the old topo map shows the trail veer right), his path dipped left to follow Little Grassy Creek, rejoining the later route of the Shanty Spring Trail closer to Linville Gap. By the 1970s, Smith's walk along the creek had grown closed, forcing hikers to follow the stairstep ridge below the Glade that we remember from Shanty Spring's 1980s heyday. By then, Smith's corridor along Little Grassy Creek was reduced to two side paths. The lowest led to a campsite and pretty waterfall; the highest, to another creekside camp below the Glade.

Eventually, the path began to be called Shanty Spring Trail, understandable with the spring being a landmark for centuries. Oddly, it's uncertain how the spring got that name. Undoubtedly a rustic "shanty" stood near the reliable water source at some point. The mountain had elusive residents, especially during the Civil War, and Johnny Cooper maintained it was "always known

Members of the Morton family and friends stage a campfire in Black Rock Cliffs Cave for a late 1950s Hugh Morton photo. Julia Morton is in the center by the fire. Daughter Judy is to her right, with Jim Morton behind Judy, and Hugh Morton Jr. to Jim's left. How times change. Today, an endangered species of bat prohibits the public from even entering the cave, much less building a campfire. North Carolina Collection, University of North Carolina Library at Chapel Hill. Photo by Hugh Morton.

as Shanty Spring—even while I was logging." That was in the early 1930s when there actually was a logging shanty at the spring. Cooper remembered, "We had a cabin just down the hill from the spring," and photographer George Masa saw the "shack and spring" in 1932. An early 1930s topo map appears to be the first map to call the stream below "Shanty Spring Branch." My guess: that's when the spring got the "Shanty" name. Had it been called that before the logging days, Shepherd Dugger and Margaret Morley might have alerted us in their writings decades earlier.

In a remarkable bonus insight, Cooper stated that "an old trail went right by the spring, up from Linville Gap, the old Calloway Trail." Despite Smith's desire to honor that earlier name, current usage dictated the path be called Shanty Spring Trail when I cleared it in 1978. But in my own nod to the past, I retained the historical name Calloway Trail for the uppermost section above Shanty Spring. In the 2000s, backcountry manager Luke Appling made the entire path to Calloway Gap the Profile Trail.

campsites. Stay on defined trails, don't shortcut switchbacks, and stick with a small group. Pack light and right and you won't be tempted to litter.

Camping causes significant impact. Above all, do not use vegetation of any kind for bedding or shelter. Daniel Boone you are not. State park camping is allowed only in thirteen sites and Hi-Balsam Shelter, all designated on the map and onsite. Some sites have tent platforms. Most sites are small and accommodate six at most. Calloway Gap on the Grandfather Trail and Daniel Boone, the midpoint on the Boone Scout Trail, have a number of tent platforms with a maximum capacity of twelve. Both of these big sites are designated "group" camp spots despite being very popular with small parties, who at this point have no other option but to bypass these longtime convenient campsites. It may take some time for the "group" versus "family" backpack site concept found in state parks to work itself out in a location like Grandfather. Fires are only permitted at low elevation sites, in existing fire rings (create no new ones). No fires are allowed on the ridgetop or at Hi-Balsam Shelter. Best bet: Read about clean camping and carry a gas stove. Grandfather has had all the challenges it needs. Please enjoy and protect the mountain safely and sensibly.

The Trails of Grandfather Mountain

THE GRANDFATHER TRAIL, UNDERWOOD TRAIL, AND GRANDFATHER TRAIL EXTENSION

Mileage: Via the Grandfather Trail Extension from Black Rock Parking Area, Calloway Peak is 2.7 miles one way, 5.4 miles roundtrip. From the summit parking area, Grandfather Trail is 2.4 miles one way to Calloway, 4.8 miles roundtrip.

Rating: Very strenuous

Blaze: Blue diamond for Grandfather Trail, yellow diamond for Underwood, red diamond for Extension

Trailhead: Park at the Black Rock Trail lots just past the "5000 feet" elevation sign. The Grandfather Trail Extension accesses Grandfather Trail from there. Don't start in the highest parking lot at the Top Shop, to preserve space for short-term visitors. To start there, just hike to the summit lot on the Bridge Trail (it begins across the summit road from Black Rock Trail parking). Walking the road is prohibited.

Overview: One of the South's most rugged, spectacular, and storied trails scales ladders and cables over cliffs across Grandfather's summit ridge to Calloway Peak, the highest (5,946 feet). If you may not be ready for this hike, experience the first part of it on Google Street View: bit.ly/GMstreetview.

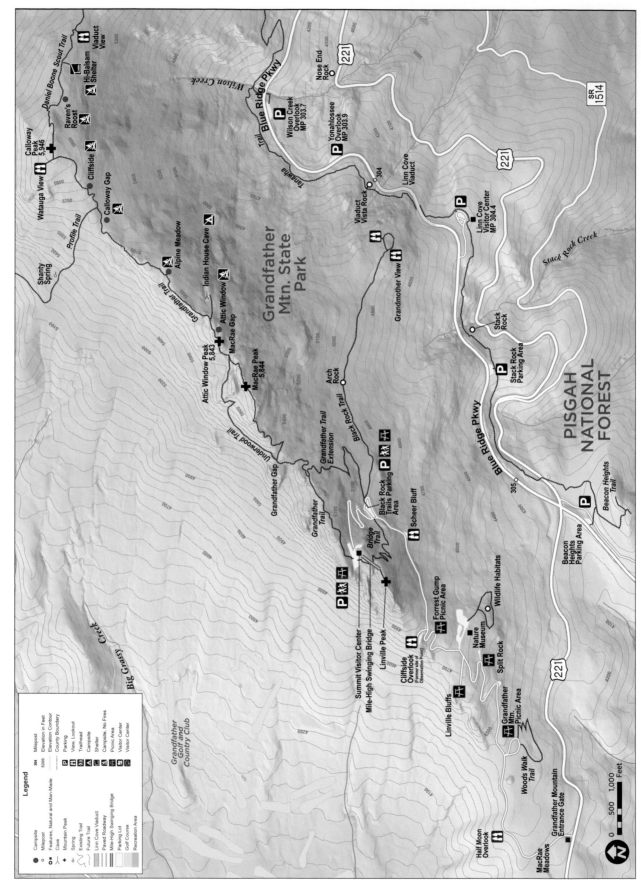

Grandfather Trail Corridor, Grandfather Attraction, and Blue Ridge Parkway

Legend

●	Campsite
○	Milepost
●=	Cave
⁜	Mountain Peak
○–	Spring
	Existing Trail
	Future Trail
	Linn Cove Viaduct
	Mile-High Swinging Bridge
	Paved Roadway
	County Boundary

304	Milepost
5200	Elevation in Feet
	Elevation Contour
	County Boundary
P	Parking
	View, Lookout
	Trailhead
	Campsite
	Shelter
	Campsite, No Fires
	Picnic Area
	Visitor Center
G	Golf Course

Features, Natural and Man-Made

Parking Lot

Recreation Area

Daniel Boone Scout Trail

Viaduct View

Hi-Balsam Shelter

Raven's Roost

Calloway Peak 5,946

Watauga View

Cliffside

Calloway Gap

Profile Trail

Shanty Spring

Alpine Meadow

Indian House Cave

Attic Window

MacRae Gap

Attic Window Peak 5,843

MacRae Peak 5,844

Grandfather Trail

Grandfather Trail Extension

Grandfather Gap

Underwood Trail

Black Rock Trail

Arch Rock

Wilson Creek

Blue Ridge Pkwy

Tanawha Trail

Nose End Rock

Wilson Creek Overlook MP 303.7

Yonahlossee Overlook MP 303.9

Linn Cove Viaduct

Viaduct Vista Rock

304

Grandmother View

Linn Cove Visitor Center MP 304.4

Stack Rock Creek

Stack Rock

Stack Rock Parking Area

PISGAH NATIONAL FOREST

Blue Ridge Pkwy

305

Beacon Heights Trail

Beacon Heights Parking Area

Grandfather Mtn. State Park

Black Rock Trails Parking Area

Scheer Bluff

Bridge Trail

Summit Visitor Center

Mile-High Swinging Bridge

Linville Peak

Cliffside Overlook (Former site of Observation Point)

Forrest Gump Picnic Area

Wildlife Habitats

Nature Museum

Split Rock

Grandfather Mtn. Picnic Area

Linville Bluffs

Woods Walk Trail

Half Moon Overlook

Grandfather Mountain Entrance Gate

MacRae Meadows

Grandfather Golf and Country Club

Big Grassy Creek

221

SR 1514

N

0   500   1,000
Feet

Trail Log

Go left from upper Black Rock parking on the Grandfather Trail Extension (Black Rock Trail goes right). At 0.6 mile, join Grandfather Trail at a bench. To reach that same spot from the summit parking area, scramble up a steep, rocky pitch, then turn right along a narrow rocky ridge. At a big boulder, pass under the right side or you'll discover why it's called "Head Bumpin' Rock."

The View: From the summit lot, just beyond the boulder, a cragtop view is a nice turnaround for a family stroll (otherwise, please park at lower trailheads to preserve parking). Straight ahead is MacRae Peak (5,844 feet). At about 10 o'clock on the cliffs are the ladders you'll climb. Left, or west, is the ten-story Sugar Top condominium so opposed by Hugh Morton.

Continuing from the summit lot, descend hand cables needed when the trail is a river of ice. At about 0.3 mile, reach the junction with the Grandfather Trail Extension from the Black Rock Parking Area. (Hikers starting at the top, subtract 0.3 mile from all mileages below—the Extension Trail is 0.3 mile longer). In grassy Grandfather Gap, at 0.7 mile, the yellow-diamond-blazed Underwood Trail goes left around MacRae Peak, avoiding the summit ladders. Go right on Grandfather Trail and the climb steepens, ascends a rocky face with a cable, traverses a new ladder, then turns right to another ladder in a fissure. A flatter section passes a breezy, wind-funneling gap by a cliff; then a series of ladders soar upward, cabled to cliffs. This is a real adventure, especially in a hair-whipping wind. If you're not a rock climber, you've lucked out. A boulder blocking the ledge at the top of the longest ladder once created a bona fide tricky traverse. When new ladders were installed in 2011, that rock was "removed." Pause on the ledge below the upper ladder to catch your breath—or a friend. The visitor center and Swinging Bridge are far below. Top the upper ladder, and stairstep ledges lead up alpinelike clifftops and across a sharp ridge. Beyond the next ladder, the squeamish can avoid a knife-edge ledge by stepping down left, then up beyond at wider footing. The house-sized boulder perched on the crest, an unnerving ladder cabled against it, is MacRae Peak (5,844 feet). Climb the ladder, hug the cable, and have lunch atop the rock amid stupendous views.

The View: Look east past the Blue Ridge Parkway as the land plummets to the Piedmont. Pilot Knob is just above the Parkway, with Rough Ridge below that. The next rocky summit out the ridgetop is Attic Window Peak, its face cloven by a couloir (the route of the trail). Banner Elk lies west, between Sugar Mountain (with the summit condo) and Beech Mountain (above Banner Elk). South toward the attraction, the massive ridge of the Black Mountains and Mount Mitchell ripple the horizon. Left, southeast, almost off to the Piedmont, you see the paired summits of Table Rock (left) and Hawksbill (right).

Descend a steep, rocky chute with cables to MacRae Gap. To loop back, go left on Underwood Trail, 0.5 mile through evergreens reminiscent of the far north. That trail descends a long ladder, then threads a mossy defile between huge boulders. This extremely rocky trail will be a challenge for the unsure of foot. Heading back on Underwood, the roundtrip is 2 miles from the upper parking lot—about 2.6 miles from Black Rock parking. Continuing out the ridge on the Grandfather Trail, leave wood-sorrel-covered MacRae Gap. Climb up three ladders through a maze of boulders reminiscent of New Hampshire's Ice Gulch or Maine's Mahoosuc Notch. Then it's straight up the massive split in Attic Window Peak. There's a secret "attic" in this peak. Halfway up, look left out of the cleft to notice a fissure in the rock. Traverse a bulge to the entrance and slide in. The ramplike floor leads between walls that grow dark, then brighten at the end of the tunnel. Suddenly, you're looking out the face at Banner Elk, far above a boulderfield. Below, at

Thousands of feet of air give clouds plenty of space to play below MacRae Peak. Hikers gazing out over the abyss are endlessly entertained. Photo by Randy Johnson.

November's clear, leafless, low-humidity days are made for knock-your-socks-off distant views from Attic Window Peak or anywhere on the mountain. This hiker is a 30-second walk from Attic Window's summit tent platform. Photo by Randy Johnson.

the bottom of a sloping rock, a flat landing spot has long tempted the adventurous. Retreat if the view is enough. Some descend to that ledge below and then, wriggling behind it, drop down into another even-walled corridor that leads back out into the chute about 15 feet below where you entered. You just missed it on the way up. There are other windows in this attic, but this one is the safest.

At the top of the cleft, Attic Window tent platform is to the right (no fires). A left tops the peak, one of the mountain's best views. Take the Grandfather Trail to the next gap and a ladder. A side trail leads right to Indian House Cave. Beyond the gap, a tree-line-like knife edge passes dramatic cliffs where two ledges offer geological insight (see Chapter 10). Descend into an alpinelike gap to idyllic Alpine Meadow campsite (no fires). Beyond the next craggy whaleback, a tiny gap is carpeted with wood sorrel. Calloway Gap is next, a popular campsite with tent platforms (no fires) at 1.9 miles, where orange-diamond-blazed Profile Trail descends left 0.3 mile to Shanty Spring (and on

to NC 105). Right on Grandfather Trail, the path climbs through a tiny meadow. A right reaches Cliffside campsite (no fires), with a spectacular ledge view to the east. Higher, through dense evergreens, arrive at the end of the trail at 2.4 miles. To the right, Calloway Peak (5,946 feet) is just 0.1 mile over one small ladder, on white-diamond-blazed Daniel Boone Scout Trail. Left, a short spur leads to Watauga View.

The View: West-facing Watauga View overlooks condo-crowned Sugar Mountain. On the horizon

Navigating the corridor of the Grandfather Trail, summer hikers thread an explosive rhododendron bloom near Alpine Meadow campsite. The trail continues across the whaleback of crags in the background to Attic Window Peak. Photo by Randy Johnson.

beyond, the Appalachian Trail runs left from grassy Hump Mountain to Roan Mountain. Below, the former ridge route of the Shanty Spring Trail drops to where NC 184 runs west from Linville Gap. That Eastern Continental Divide splits the Linville River, flowing left to the Atlantic, and the Watauga River, right, to the Mississippi. Just below the view, Profile Ridge bulges out where peregrine falcons were reintroduced. Hard right, White Rock Ridge runs northeast (a quartz mine possibly visible on its left side). The Boone Bowl lies right. Far left, Grandfather's ridge runs south, with the serrated Black Mountains beyond, Mount Mitchell on the left.

BLACK ROCK TRAIL

Mileage: 1.0 mile, 2.0 miles roundtrip
Rating: Moderate
Blaze: Gold circle
Overview: A level but rocky trail with a superb view of the plummet to the Piedmont and an interesting rock formation.
Trail Log

This gradual, lightly traveled trail across the mountain's eastern flank has rough footing in spots, but many families hike it. The first section is especially rich with the waxy, heart-shaped evergreen leaves of galax, long harvested for floral arrangements (just don't do it here). The leaves turn crimson in fall and winter, and the pungent smell of acidic soil may make city dwellers wonder what a bear might have done in these woods. The trail wanders through a tunnel of towering *Rhododendron maximum*, the tall, long-leaved, white-blooming variety (versus *Rhododendron catawbiense*, the smaller, red-flowering kind). In early July, these plants explode with softball-size blooms. Halfway along, a little stream gurgles through sheltering Arch Rock. The trail emerges from a New England–like mix of birches and spruce at an end loop where two small side trails each climb a ladder to great views amidst highbush blueberries (ripe in late August). The rounded peak with the TV tower is Grandmother Mountain, and Beacon Heights is below that. MacRae and Attic Window Peaks tower above (left and right), as does the Swinging Bridge. Even when the peaks are cloudy, views can reach to the Piedmont far below.

BRIDGE TRAIL

Mileage: 0.4 mile, 0.8 mile roundtrip
Rating: Moderate
Blaze: None
Trailhead: Leave the Black Rock parking lot and cross the road to enter the woods by a picnic table.

Grandfather's Classic Sampler Climbs

A number of Grandfather hikes are classics. Here's a short list of exciting encounters, a few for first-time hikers.

The Grandfather Sampler: Cragway Circuit

One hiker called this loop the Grandfather Sampler. "It has everything Grandfather is famous for, except ladders," he assured. "Evergreen forests, the grandeur of crags and cliffs, alpine scenery—and it's only half way up the mountain." The Cragway Circuit is a perfect starter hike. Climb Daniel Boone Scout Trail, have lunch at Flat Rock View, then descend alpine scenery on Cragway for a moderately strenuous 3.9 miles. Even easier is an out-and-back on the Nuwati Trail, three moderate miles, with rushing streams and a 360-degree view at Storyteller's Rock. Or combine the two.

The Swinging Bridge Sampler: The Real Attraction

Introduce friends to Grandfather at the attraction—but do it by trail. Park at Black Rock parking and hike up the Bridge Trail. See the Swinging Bridge from below, then above, and you've climbed Linville Peak by foot, not car. Head out the Grandfather Trail to a view of MacRae Peak, then take Grandfather Trail Extension back to your car. Total roundtrip, about 1.4 moderate miles. Perfect appetizer before a Grandburger at Mildred's Grill.

After a night at Daniel Boone campsite, this party of backpackers descends the alpine scenery of the Cragway Trail, one of state park superintendent Sue McBean's favorite paths on the mountain. Photo by Randy Johnson.

Overview: A short climb from the lower crags of Linville Peak leads to the rocky gap below the Swinging Bridge and the summit visitor center.

Trail Log

In the early 1990s, Harris Prevost suggested a trail from Black Rock Parking Area to the Swinging Bridge so visitors could hike rather than wait for a shuttle bus on busy days. The trail was built by Jim Morton and the Grandfather staff in the summer of 1995. "The scenery on the new trail is spectacular in places," Morton noted, "with a great new perspective on the Swinging Bridge from beneath it." Tight switchbacks separated by cable barriers and impressive stone steps meander into a spruce-fir forest among slabs of rock below Linville Peak. The trail passes below the Swinging Bridge and enters the upper parking lot from behind Convention Table Rock, the massive squarish summit that anchors the north side of the bridge. If you just want to see the bridge from below, it's a short, flat stroll to the photo op from the summit parking lot.

A Peek at the Peaks

Start at the attraction, and the most spectacular hike on the mountain climbs ladders across MacRae Peak and circles back via the Underwood Trail. It's one of the region's best, and just 2.6 miles from Black Rock parking. Combine this with the Swinging Bridge Sampler and you have the best of the backcountry and the attraction—all in 4 miles (it'll feel like 6).

Face-to-Face with Your Grandfather

The Profile Trail is an undertaking to Calloway Peak, so just hike to Profile View and see eye-to-eye with the old man. This 6.2-mile roundtrip is still strenuous, but besides getting up close and personal with your Grandfather, you can see Virginia's highest peaks emerge at Foscoe View.

For many hikers, starting out on the Grandfather Trail demands documenting the occasion. Photo by Randy Johnson.

WOODS WALK

Mileage: 0.4 mile

Rating: Easy

Blaze: None

Trailhead: Just past the first overlook on the attraction motor road, turn right into the picnic loop, where woodcarver Tom Wolfe has a studio. Circle past the restroom and park on the right at the sign.

Overview: This short, picnic-area loop is sometimes used for interpretive programs.

Trail Log

Wander the flat, flowery terrain of this hard-

The Tanawha Trail carries hikers over the Boone Fork bridge to the Asutsi, Nuwati, and Daniel Boone Scout trails. Photography instructor Tommy White went to extremes to get this shot, standing in the stream under an umbrella in the rain, taking long exposures to soften the splashing drops. "I constantly see the lack of planning in landscape photo shoots." he says. "We've all just grabbed a camera and traipsed into the woods, but I choose Grandfather as one of my favorite locations because it teaches the value of planning and giving that extra effort to get something that you can be proud of. The mountain's microclimates demand it." Photo by Tommy White Photography, www.tommywhitephotography.com.

wood forest among isolated evergreens. This is the solar side, so the sun beams into bright woods. The trail includes part of an early logging grade.

DANIEL BOONE SCOUT TRAIL

Mileage: 3.6 miles to Calloway Peak, 7.2 miles roundtrip

Rating: Strenuous

Blaze: White diamond

Trailhead: Reach the Boone Trail on the Blue Ridge Parkway's Tanawha Trail from Boone Fork Parking Area at milepost 299.9. In winter when snow closes the Parkway, year-round access is via the Asutsi Trail from US 221, 9.2 miles north of the Grandfather Mountain entrance. From Blowing Rock, take US 221 south about five miles to Holloway Mountain Road Parkway access and drive 1.5 miles farther on US 221 to the parking area on the right. The foundation of Florence Boyd's store is just 50 feet north of this trailhead.

Overview: Tracking up the "back side" of Grandfather, the Daniel Boone Scout Trail is the most gradual, easy climb to Calloway Peak, the mountain's highest, with a vertical rise of 2,044 feet. See Cragway Trail and Nuwati Trail for loop options.

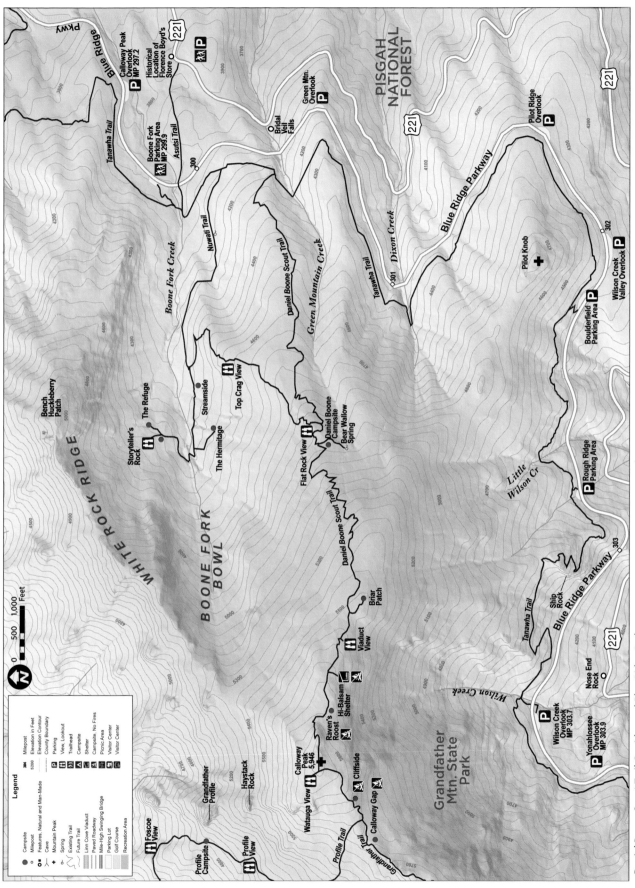

Daniel Boone Scout Trail Corridor and Blue Ridge Parkway

Trail Log

Leave Boone Fork Parking Area and avoid a left to the Parkway's Calloway Peak Overlook (an alternative if this lot is full). At the next junction, go left on the Tanawha Trail (right, Tanawha heads to Price Park). Cross the Boone Fork bridge, pass Asutsi Trail on the left (0.4 mile to US 221). Register at the state park sign and follow Tanawha over moderate climbs. A distinct level section is the old logging railroad grade of Boone Fork Lumber Company. Pass the Nuwati Trail on the right at about 0.4 mile, and at 0.6 mile turn right on Daniel Boone Scout Trail (Tanawha continues to Beacon Heights and the Great Smokies, as the Mountains-to-Sea Trail). As you pass through mixed deciduous and evergreen forest, note one almost paved portion of dry-gullied trail. This is one of the earliest parts of Clyde Smith's Boone Trail—likely chosen for evidence of use before the 1940s. Daniel Boone or D. R. Beeson may have trod this trail before you.

The trail passes a flat and then climbs to a rock outcropping and sign at 1.9 miles. Here Cragway Trail goes right to the Boone Bowl and the Nuwati Trail. Before continuing up, step onto Flat Rock View, a table-flat lunch spot and vantage point. The Boone Scout Trail continues left 0.1 mile over a rock-surfaced section of new trail built by the state park in 2013. At Daniel Boone campsite, a long-popular grassy flat at the trail's midpoint, tent platforms accommodate twelve (fires permitted). A side trail leads 100 yards through beautiful mixed deciduous and spruce forest to small, reliable, Bear Wallow Spring. Continuing, the Boone Trail switchbacks up through red spruce to Pilot Ridge and not-so-invitingly-named Briar Patch campsite on the left at about 2.7 miles (fires permitted). Beyond, the trail enters a dark, cool, spruce-fir forest carpeted with moss and wood sorrel. In 2015, the state park rerouted a portion of trail in this area that climbed a tricky crack up a rocky crag. Nearby, a signed trail leads left to Viaduct View. Soon another side trail goes left to Hi-

There are ladders all over Grandfather, most notably on MacRae Peak, but one of the biggest scales the crags of Calloway Peak. This local High Country hiker tackles that climb near the top of the Daniel Boone Scout Trail not far above the remains of a 1978 plane crash. Photo by Todd Bush/www.bushphoto.com.

Balsam Shelter, a cozy, low-lying lean-to that sleeps five (no tents or fires). Two hundred feet beyond, a tent platform called Raven's Roost (no fires) lies just across the trail from a path to a single-engine plane crash.

Then the trail stands on end, climbing steeply, using two long ladders, to Calloway Peak (5,946 feet), marked by a white and blue X at 3.6 miles. Continue 0.1 mile across the rocky, evergreen-covered crest and one small ladder to the Grandfather Trail. Just past the Grandfather Trail junction, Watauga View is the best vantage point to the west.

The View: From Calloway Peak, the mountain bulks against the developed western vista, focusing on the dramatic eastern drop to the Piedmont. Southwest, beyond the dark main ridge of the mountain, Mount Mitchell and the

An x marks the rock of Calloway Peak. Photo by Randy Johnson.

Black Mountains stagger the sky. Left of there, the V of peaks is Table Rock (left) and Hawksbill (right). The peak directly below left is Pilot Knob, with the Blue Ridge Parkway visible there and at Rough Ridge.

This eastern view—from Calloway, MacRae, or Attic Window peaks—is what made Michaux think he'd "climbed to the highest mountain of all North America." From Calloway, "one cannot command the circle of the horizon," Margaret Morley advised, so it's "necessary to get the view from two points, which is all the better." She means Calloway has the view south and east, and Watauga View is the outlook west. The roundtrip Boone Trail hike is just over 7.0 miles. To make a loop of about the same length, go left on Cragway, then right on Nuwati to Tanawha.

CRAGWAY TRAIL AND NUWATI TRAIL

Mileage: Individually, Cragway and Nuwati are 1.0 and 1.1 miles, respectively, but both require access on Tanawha Trail. That makes the out-and-back Nuwati hike 3.0 miles. A lower loop called the Cragway Circuit is 3.9 miles (most easily hiked up Tanawha and the Boone Scout Trail, then down Cragway, and back via Nuwati and Tanawha). Attaching that lower circuit to a Boone Scout Trail hike to Calloway Peak makes it 7.3 miles (versus 7.2 up and down the Boone Trail only).

Rating: Moderate for the Nuwati Trail and Cragway loop *downhill*, strenuous for the Boone Trail to Calloway Peak and for the *uphill* Cragway Circuit

Blaze: Orange circle for Cragway, blue circle for Nuwati

Trailhead: Start on the Tanawha Trail from the Blue Ridge Parkway's Boone Fork Parking Area, milepost 299.9. See Scout Trail for more.

Overview: These trails explore cirquelike Boone Fork Bowl. Nuwati Trail reaches spectacular Storyteller's Rock at the head of the valley, a moderate elevation gain of 580 feet. Campsites make that a nice beginner backpacking trip. Cragway links Nuwati to the Boone Trail, forming the Cragway Circuit, a classic lower loop with spectacular views and 920 feet of elevation gain. See "Grandfather's Classic Sampler Climbs" sidebar.

Trail Log: Nuwati Trail

In the early 1990s, then trail manager Steve Miller renamed this Nuwati Trail, the Cherokee word for "good medicine," referring to the healing power of wilderness (and complementing the Cherokee origin of the Tanawha name, "great hawk or eagle"). Leave Boone Fork Parking Area and take the second left on the Tanawha Trail. Cross Boone Fork bridge and register at the state park sign. At 0.4 mile, turn right on the blue-circle-blazed Nuwati Trail past another sign. The gradual rocky trail leads up the old logging railroad grade of Boone Fork Lumber Company. A spring gushes under the trail where quartz chunks litter the ground at 0.7 mile. The bowl-like shape of the valley emerges as the stream becomes audible on the right and the grade turns into a rhododendron tunnel fringed by lacey ferns. At 1.0 mile, the Cragway Trail goes left. Just beyond is Streamside campsite on the left (fires permitted). The trail crosses numerous streams, all bridged by trestles during logging days. A side trail left leads to The Hermitage campsite (no fires, but it has its own water source), and just beyond a large logging cable is wedged in the V of a tree. Cross Boone Fork, the last stream, and the path forks where old railroad ties and spikes are seen in the tread. Head right to The Refuge (fires permitted), a secluded tent platform and secondary tent spot, or go left to another platform campsite called

A yellow birch clutches a logging cable near the blue blazes of the Nuwati Trail. Hugh Morton and the scientists who theorized that glaciers had made grooves on nearby Storyteller's Rock walked right past the real culprit, metal rope used by loggers to drag virgin timber from Calloway Peak. In 2013, not far from this cable, the author found another artifact of the Boone Fork Lumber Company. Frank Aldridge later identified it as a broken brake shoe from a railroad flatcar. "They'd just toss 'em up into the woods when they made a repair," Aldridge explained. Photo by Randy Johnson.

Storyteller's Rock (fires permitted) beneath that namesake crag. To climb the prominent tooth of Storyteller's Rock (4,500 feet, at 1.5 miles) bear left, then right, to a short, steep scramble for a 360-degree panorama. The "glacial grooves" discussed in Chapter 10 are on the adjacent crag.

The View: Face southwest from Storyteller's Rock and look up the bowl to sculpted Calloway Peak. The "headwall" cliff of the supposed

The view from Storyteller's Rock is earned by a short, almost straight-up scramble that's well worth the effort. Photo by Randy Johnson.

cirque is just below it. To your right, the dome of White Rock Ridge rises above. The ridge runs farther right, to the heath bald peak of Bench Huckleberry Patch. Even farther right, east, the view stretches along the Blue Ridge Parkway to Blowing Rock and the distant Piedmont. Face Calloway again and, hard left, watch hikers on the rocky pinnacles of the Cragway Trail.

Trail Log: Cragway

The easiest way to hike the Cragway Trail is down. To do that, follow Tanawha past Nuwati and at 0.6 mile, turn right on the Boone Trail to reach Cragway at 1.9 miles (see Boone Scout Trail for more). Refill a water bottle at Bear Wallow Spring or check out Flat Rock View, then go right on Cragway. The trail winds down open crags and artfully breaches a small line of cliffs cluttered with rock tripe lichen

(*Umbilicaria*). The path abruptly opens into a heath bald at Top Crag, one of the best views on the mountain. Please pause here—be sure your party stays on the trail and only steps on rock to preserve low-growing vegetation. The switchbacks link rocky crags and great views, then level out before descending steps to Nuwati Trail at about 2.9 miles. Turn right, then left on Tanawha, to the Boone Fork Parking Area (3.9 miles). Or lengthen the hike by going left to include Storyteller's Rock, a 4.9-mile hike back to your car.

PROFILE TRAIL

Mileage: 3.9 miles, 7.8 miles roundtrip to Calloway Gap; 4.4 miles, 8.8 miles roundtrip to Calloway Peak; delete 0.8 mile if starting at original trailhead.

Rating: Strenuous

Blaze: Orange diamond

Trailhead: The new trailhead for the Profile Trail is located 0.2 mile north of Linville Gap, on an access road from NC 105 that diverges east just beyond the shopping center. The new parking area (expected by 2016) will hold 125 cars and include restrooms, a ranger office, and a maintenance facility.

Overview: This popular hike up the western flank of Grandfather Mountain gains just more than 2,000 vertical feet to Calloway Peak. The path was named for its face-to-face encounter with Grandfather's premier profile. As you climb, keep in mind that the steep trail route was dictated by the need to encroach as little as possible inside the property line of the Wilmor resort development once proposed for Grandfather's western flank. Today the land is safely preserved, but only rerouting the trail will make its challenging grade more gradual.

Trail Log

From the new state park parking area, the trail winds through New England–like forest and crosses a bridge above the headwaters of the Watauga River to join the streamside stroll of

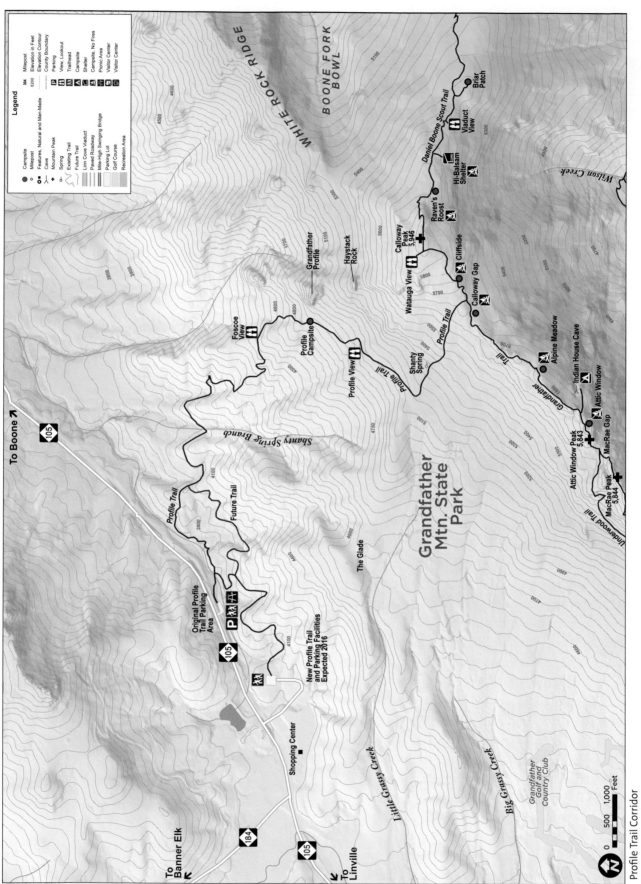

Profile Trail Corridor

Photographer Jim Morton spent years working on the Profile Trail, and he's seen the mountain's famous face in all kinds of weather. The old man appears all the more elderly in winter. Photo by James McKay Morton.

the original trail. Near a scenic drainage, the large, waxy, evergreen-leaved ground plant is Fraser's sedge. At about 1.8 miles, the trail dips across Shanty Branch, the source of Shanty Spring, 1.7 miles ahead. This lowest stretch of trail makes a nice kid's hike of 3.6 miles. It was designated as a Kids in Parks TRACK Trail in 2014, a system of popular family interpretive hikes that has quickly spread across the nation. To learn about nature, pick up one of the trail-head brochures (or download one at www.kids inparks.com/). The Rich Cove Forest brochure was designed especially for this trail by former Grandfather backcountry manager, now park ranger, Luke Appling. Kids can earn prizes and get fit with their family by hiking many such trails nearby in North Carolina. Past the stream, the trail threads a rocky fissure and rises into mixed evergreen and deciduous forest.

Climbing steadily out of a big drainage above lush vegetation, rocky switchbacks cross Green Ridge to Foscoe View at about 2.5 miles.

The View: Pause at the bench and interpretive sign at Foscoe View above the Watauga River Valley town of Foscoe. The second-highest and highest summits in Virginia, White Top (with its crescent-shaped meadows on left) and Mount Rogers (just visible on right) top the horizon. The Grandfather Community of old is just below. Repeated switchbacks reach Profile campsite's numerous tent spots and fire pit. The trail ascends pathways of natural stone; the longest is dubbed Peregrine Flight by primary builders Jim Morton and Kinney Baughman. Steep switchbacks end at a huge metaconglomerate boulder—note the obvious infused cobbles mentioned in Chapter 10. More steep steps pass a rock-paved shelter cave to Profile View at 3.1

miles. Savor the dramatic view of Grandfather's face. Traversing gradually, the trail makes an uphill turn where it joins the historic Shanty Spring Trail. At Shanty Spring, 3.5 miles, the water emerging below the cliff was "the coldest water outside of perpetual snow in the United States" to Shepherd Dugger. Beyond the cliff, Profile rises on the steep, rocky, historic route of the old Calloway Trail. Spruce and fir appear before the crest of Calloway Gap and the junction at 3.9 miles with the Grandfather Trail (see Grandfather Trail for connecting hikes).

The Trails of the Blue Ridge Parkway

Below Grandfather's peaks, the Blue Ridge Parkway has miles of trails that offer dramatic views of the mountain. One of those is the 13.5-mile Tanawha Trail from Beacon Heights (milepost 305.2) near the Grandfather attraction entrance to Price Park Campground (milepost 296.9) near Blowing Rock. Tanawha is part of North Carolina's Mountains-to-Sea Trail (MST), a 1,000-mile Appalachian Trail–style path from the Great Smokies to the Outer Banks. Trail access is from Parkway overlooks near Grandfather where most people hike out-and-back or spot a second car at another overlook. The best maps for these hikes are the Parkway's illustrated handouts for Tanawha Trail, Julian Price Park, and Moses Cone Park, available at the park website under "Plan Your Visit," at the "Brochures" link (http://www.nps.gov/blri/plan yourvisit/brochures.htm).

FLAT ROCK SELF-GUIDING LOOP TRAIL

Mileage: 0.7-mile loop
Rating: Moderate
Blaze: Yellow
Trailhead: Flat Rock Parking Area, milepost 308.3, about 3.2 miles south of the US 221 exit near Linville.
Overview: An intermediate foot or snowshoe loop hike or advanced Nordic ski tour with

A mom and her daughters catch some quality time atop Beacon Heights on the Blue Ridge Parkway below Grandfather. Nineteenth-century maps called it "Beacon Height." Photo by Randy Johnson.

interpretive signs and a great view of Grandfather Mountain.

Trail Log
This quick walk is great for nature study or a picnic in a northern hardwood forest at 4,000 feet. Not far above the parking area, the trail loop splits; head left (right is the absolute easiest direction). Interpretive signs describe trees and plants. Bear right at 0.2 mile with a yellow arrow marker and cross the big outcrop of Flat Rock.

The View: The 180-degree westward view looks down on Linville's golf course and out on the horizon where the Appalachian Trail crosses alpine-appearing grassy areas called "balds." As the ledge ends, and the trail dips back to its split near your car, look north to one of the Parkway's best Grandfather views.

BEACON HEIGHTS

Mileage: 0.7-mile roundtrip to the summit
Rating: Easy
Blaze: None from Parkway, white dots on the MST
Trailhead: Milepost 305.2, 0.1 mile south of the US 221 Parkway entrance near Linville, 1 mile

east from the Grandfather Mountain Attraction entrance.

Overview: One of the Parkway's short and popular "leg-stretcher trails" with spectacular views of Grandfather Mountain and its drop to the Piedmont.

Trail Log

From the trailhead, walk across a state road that parallels the Parkway and enter the woods where the sign says "Tanawha Trail Beacon Heights 0.2." At the first junction in the woods, turn right on the MST—also the Beacon Heights Trail to the top (left, Tanawha heads north). At the next junction, 0.2 mile, go left where the MST branches right. (Right, the MST descends into Pisgah National Forest). Shortly, the trail reaches a bench at about 0.3 mile.

The View: Right at the bench, a south-facing dome has great views of the Piedmont and the high peaks south along the Parkway, including Mount Mitchell and Linville Gorge. Left, the path ascends stone steps to another dome with spectacular views of the eastern flank and peaks of Grandfather Mountain above rippling foothills.

TANAWHA TRAIL TO LINN COVE VIADUCT

Mileage: 0.3-mile roundtrip for paved trail; 1.0-mile roundtrip to postcard view of the viaduct

Rating: Handicapped accessible to moderate

Blaze: Brown metal signs combine Tanawha Trail feather symbol and white dot of MST

Trailhead: Linn Cove Parking Area (milepost 304.4), about 0.7 mile north of the US 221 exit near Linville. Trail leaves lot at opposite end from Linn Cove Information Station.

Overview: A paved wheelchair path leads under the Parkway's stunning Linn Cove Viaduct, then continues as a rougher trail to a view of the viaduct popularized by photographer Hugh Morton.

Trail Log

The paved trail winds 0.15 mile to a viewpoint underneath the serpentine span. Beyond,

the path explores the jumbled terrain that required building this high-tech bridge. Using stone steps, the trail zigzags through towering rhododendron, hemlocks, and birches among huge boulders below Grandfather Mountain's Black Rock Cliffs. Cross the bridge over Linn Cove Branch, and at 0.5-mile, turn right at a small sign to scramble atop a roadside rock for a postcard-perfect view of the bridge.

TANAWHA TRAIL TO ROUGH RIDGE

Mileage: The closest view is only 0.6 mile round-trip. Out-and-back hikes of 1.2 and about 2 miles lead to the peak.

Rating: Easy to strenuous

Blaze: Brown metal signs combine Tanawha Trail feather symbol and white dot of MST.

Trailhead: Rough Ridge Overlook (Parkway milepost 302.8), Wilson Creek Overlook (Parkway milepost 303.6).

Overview: The Parkway's easiest path to a spectacular view. Dogs are not permitted past the stream bridges from either trailhead.

Trail Log

Startling vistas from boardwalks on alpinelike crags are just 0.3 mile from Rough Ridge Parking Area. Grandfather's three loftiest summits soar to nearly 6,000 feet, and far below, the rippling corduroy of the Pisgah National Forest descends to the Piedmont—total relief of nearly a vertical mile. The East's highest peak, Mount Mitchell, lies on the southern horizon, with Pilot Knob just to the north. From Rough Ridge Parking Area, ascend new steps and boardwalks built in 2015 and go left over an arching span (no pets past this point) into blueberry bushes and galax where eastern turkeybeard (*Xerophyllum asphodeloides*) flowers in June. Ascend to boardwalk views and interpretive signs past a distinctive stack rock. Please pause here. Be sure your party stays on the trail to preserve low-growing vegetation; endangered species surround you. Another 0.3 mile up rocky switchbacks leads to the summit,

Trekking Tanawha

Sections of the Tanawha Trail are busy day hikes, but it's easy to target the quietest stretches for solitude or turn Tanawha into a backpacking trip. Camping is prohibited along the Parkway except at designated sites, but if you use those spots, Tanawha can be a one- or two-night backpack. Deciding which way to backpack deserves some pondering. It's mostly downhill from Beacon Heights, but starting in Price Park lets you watch the mountain get closer, then cross it. Begin at either end, and the easiest itinerary is to camp in Grandfather Mountain State Park at the Nuwati Trail's streamside campsite, 6.5 miles from Price Park Campground, 8.6 miles from Beacon Heights. Trekking north, you can camp two nights: the first on Grandfather as above, an 8.6-mile first day, and then a second night at either Price Park Campground or Price Park's backcountry campsite on the MST near Boone Fork Trail. That's a 6.5-mile second day to the campground, 8 miles to the MST site. On day three it's a short walk out from either site: on the MST to Shull's Mill Road, or Old John's River Road to Sims Pond Overlook (milepost 295.5). Register at the Price Park Campground kiosk for either Parkway campsite.

Or don't camp. Fans of solitude or followers of Fido (leash required) can sample these lesser-used Tanawha sections. Try these:

Weller's Plunge: Beacon Heights to Linn Cove

This 1.6-mile section (3.2 roundtrip) is always quiet. You could start at Stack Rock Parking Area (304.8) between the two and hike out and back in either direction. Stack Rock, the famous Yonahlossee Road attraction since the 1890s, is a highlight near Linn Cove. A cliff on the stream above the pillar is where herpetologist Worth Weller fell to his death in 1931 (see Chapter 2).

Lost Linn Cove

The 1.3-mile stretch between Linn Cove Parking Area and Wilson Creek Overlook is rarely walked beyond the roadside viaduct view. By starting at Wilson Creek, milepost 303.6, you can reach that view of the viaduct

in just 0.7 mile while rarely seeing a soul (1.4-mile roundtrip). From Wilson Creek, go left on Tanawha.

Pilot Knob Ramble

The 3-mile stretch between Boulder Field Overlook (milepost 302.4) and the Boone Fork Parking Area is highly recommended for the mixed red spruce and deciduous forest around Pilot Knob (the summit is off limits for conservation reasons). Use two cars and walk it all downhill.

Cold Prong Escape

It's a quiet out-and-back or two-car hike between Cold Prong Overlook (milepost 299) and Boone Fork Parking Area. At the overlook, take the trail near the middle of

North of Grandfather, where the Tanawha Trail winds its way through miles of meadows, feather-emblazoned marker posts are often found. In one grassy expanse, a creative hiker added a real feather. Photo by Randy Johnson.

the lot and go left, then left again on Tanawha 0.2 mile below. There's a rich cove forest at about 1.2 miles, and near the Parkway you'll walk the old Boone Fork Lumber Company railroad grade. In 1940, National Park Service planners exploring this grade devised the controversial "high route," realizing it was "possible to climb higher and tunnel under Pilot Ridge," says the Parkway's Grandfather section history. At 1.9 miles, bear right at the junction, and the Boone Fork bridge has nice pools below (two lefts go to Boone Fork parking).

A rib of rock runs to clouds on Rough Ridge. At a magical moment like this, you can almost entertain Margaret Morley's inclination to step off onto the clouds. Photo by Tommy White Photography, www.tommywhitephotography.com.

where cable-defined pathways protect rare plants (1.2 miles roundtrip). Start at Wilson Creek Overlook for an out-and-back summit hike that eliminates the busiest boardwalk part of the trail. Pass under the Parkway road bridge and turn right where a trail bridge spans Wilson Creek. The meandering climb traverses a premier boulderfield forest just before the saddle where stone steps ascend the crag-capped Rough Ridge summit at 1.0 mile. Retrace your steps for a 2-miler. If you left another car at Rough Ridge parking, it's 0.6 mile downhill, for a 1.6-mile hike. Or walk the roadside back to Wilson Creek from Rough Ridge parking for a 2.4-mile hike.

Margaret Morley had a way with words when she rhapsodized about the High Country. This shot from the Holloway Meadow Loop recalls her observation that there's always a cool breeze in the high world at the back of the Grandfather. Photo by Randy Johnson.

Early Settlers History Hikes

TANAWHA TRAIL NORTH AND SOUTH FROM HOLLOWAY MOUNTAIN ROAD

Mileage: 2.4 miles for the Holloway Meadow Loop north (one of few MST loops), 1.6 miles for out-and-back hike to the south

Rating: Easy

Blaze: Brown metal signs combine Tanawha Trail feather symbol and white dot of MST; also wood posts.

Trailhead: Exit the Parkway at milepost 298.6, US 221 south of Blowing Rock. Turn right onto dirt Holloway Mountain Road and in 1.0 mile park in Tanawha/MST lot on left. Or take the Tanawha/Boone Fork Trail from Price Park Campground.

Overview: What was life like for early settlers in the lofty world "under the Grandfather"? Hikes from Holloway Mountain Road offer insight and heritage views.

Trail Log: Holloway Meadow Loop

The old homesites, graves, and former farms found on these hikes remind us to emulate a savoring style of foot travel Margaret Morley enjoyed before 1913 when High Country roads were more like trails. In *The Carolina Mountains*, she finds an abandoned cabin in this area where "its ice cold spring, the surrounding fruit trees, the signs of flowers once cultivated, gives you a strange impulse to stop here, like a bird that has found its nest." Take a picnic on these hikes; it's easy to step off the trail, circle a grove of trees, and find a glimpse of the Grandfather shared by only you, Morley, or that long-ago farmer. "Rest on the warm hillside fanned by the cool breeze," she urges, "for no matter how hot the summer sun, there is always a cool breeze in the high world at the back of the Grandfather." One little segment of that "high world," an informal loop hike knitted together in my FalconGuide *Hiking the Blue Ridge Parkway*, was formalized by the National Park Service in 2014 and named Holloway Meadow Loop.

From the kiosk in the parking lot, cross Holloway Mountain Road going north on a dirt road combination of Tanawha and the MST. The trail leaves, then rejoins, the grade to reach a fork near the edge of a meadow at 0.6 mile. Go right on the main grade, but just notice the left fork, your return route (unless you decide to hike that way). Enter the meadow into a historic farm and shortly pause at the grassy homesite sheltered by white pines. Foundation rocks hide nearby. Tall boxwood strands betray once-ornamental bushes unpruned for decades. An apple orchard struggles below. Nearby, three separate springs gush into a single water source, "such a spring as one is always looking for and always finding at the back of the Grandfather," Morley wrote.

Follow trail marker posts past the farm into an old orchard, then switchback down into trees and across two bridges. Among the ferns and white pines, a log farm structure recently disappeared into decay. At a signed junction at 1.2 miles, turn left with the MST onto Boone Fork Trail. (Right, the Tanawha and Boone Fork Trails head through Price Park Campground. Boone Fork goes to Price Park Picnic Area; Tanawha, to its terminus near the campground office in 0.5 mile. Both are optional starting points for this loop). Back in the meadow, Grandfather rises left. In the meadow at 1.5 miles, the Boone Fork Trail (and the MST) turns right, dipping to Boone Fork Creek, but turn left on an old farm road to enter arching rhododendron. Back in the meadow again, a hilltop view beckons left. Follow the old grade across the field and back into the trees at 1.8 miles, the junction you

passed earlier. Turn right, to your car, for a 2.4-mile roundtrip.

Trail Log: South of Holloway Mountain Road

South from Holloway Mountain Road parking, just at the top of the first meadow is a nice picnic site with Grandfather dominating the horizon. Cattle graze in the area, so pass through a stile below an old cemetery. Buried there are William C. and Adeline Coffey. Their son Andy was born prematurely after the couple escaped a Civil War raiding party led by the notorious guerrillas Keith and Malinda Blalock. Where the meadow ends, about 0.8 mile, turn around for an easy, airy picnic hike or ski tour of 1.6 miles. Continue, and the trail dips into woods and joins a farm road that passes a meadow with another homesite, possibly the Coffey's, at 1.1 miles. Hemlocks and white pines surround foundation stones and fruit trees. Continuing into woods beyond, at 2.0 miles, a link trail goes left to reach Cold Prong Overlook (milepost 229) at 2.2 miles. Starting there, the homestead is a rarely hiked 1.1 mile walk north, 2.2 roundtrip. If you do that, be sure to take the spur from the middle of the overlook going left, then turn right below on Tanawha.

PRICE LAKE TRAIL

Mileage: 2.5 miles
Rating: Easy to moderate
Blaze: None
Trailhead: Start at either of two lakeshore overlooks south of Blowing Rock—Lake View Overlook, reached by a spur road at milepost 297.2, or Price Lake Overlook at milepost 296.7.
Overview: This loop circles 47-acre Price Lake, the Parkway's largest. On clear days at any time of year, spectacular views include Grandfather Mountain and the bowl-shaped valley headwaters of the Boone Fork.
Trail Log

Price Lake is a wonderful walk, but if your one goal is just to see Grandfather, start in Price Lake Overlook and walk north across the dam to enter the trail. The mountain soars to the south, the Boone Fork Bowl gaping on the right. Photos can include foreground rocks, promontories, boaters in summer, and ice in winter. From Lake View Overlook, go south past the boat rental, and the first half-mile on the lakeshore is handicapped accessible (including stream and lake fishing spots) and a nice Nordic ski tour.

The path circles the lake through ferns, birches, and maples with a "Golden Pond" feel in the fall. Emerging at the Parkway, loop back left across the dam and reenter the woods where the path passes a restroom as it bisects campground Loop A, *the* premier place on the Parkway to set up a tent. Bring your kayak—or rent one May to October.

It's not unusual for Price Lake to be frozen in winter. If this hiker at the shoreline platform near the boat rental facility were on the far side of the lake, he'd see snowy Grandfather high above the ice. Photo by Randy Johnson.

The Trails of the Future

Grandfather's trail system is limited compared with that of many major summits. Except for small loops over MacRae Peak and Cragway, hikers climb up and down the same rugged trails. Look no further than the Tanawha Trail to appreciate that Grandfather could have a bigger network of gradual paths. Consider these potential loops that I have been dreaming about since starting the backcountry program in 1978.

Tanawha only connects to the peaks at the Nuwati and Boone Scout Trails, but if it also linked higher near the Swinging Bridge, hikers could loop the entire mountain, circuiting the Grandfather Trail above and Tanawha below. Also add a "second Tanawha Trail"

above the existing one, say, between the Black Rock Trail and the Daniel Boone Scout Trail at Cragway, and the entire eastern side of the mountain would be a gradual loop.

The Nuwati Trail was first called the Grandfather Trail Extension because I'd hoped it would continue past Storyteller's Rock and across White Rock Ridge to meet the Grandfather Trail at Calloway Peak. The dream was not only to create a spectacular loop with the Boone Trail around Boone Bowl, but to stretch the Grandfather Trail across the entire mountain, from the Swinging Bridge to the Parkway. The South's premier alpine experience! If another trail linked the Profile Trail to a trail on White Rock Ridge, say past Haystack Rock, an unprecedented

Imagine hiking a loop around the Boone Bowl, pairing the Daniel Boone Scout Trail and Cragway with a traverse of the now trailless White Rock Ridge. In the mind of the mountain's early trail manager at least, it's already one of the East's great hikes. This is the view from the Bench Huckleberry Patch, the northernmost peak of White Rock Ridge. Photo by Randy Johnson.

loop of Grandfather's highest peak would be possible via Profile Trail. And if a further connector went from the Profile Trail at Shanty Spring to the Grandfather Trail beyond MacRae Peak, that too would form a loop across the summits. Best of all, that lowest leg would have a gradual grade, making it easy for tired hikers to return from the Swinging Bridge while offering safe escape from the ice- and lightning-prone peaks.

No one would suggest that Grandfather's rare ecosystems be reduced to a playground for hikers at the expense of the environment. But if sited correctly and built to modern standards, an intelligently expanded trail network on Grandfather could increase our enjoyment of the mountain without negative impact. Only time will tell if that happens.

12 A Photographer's Guide to Grandfather

Finding yourself on Grandfather Mountain with camera in hand can be a transcendent experience. "My greatest joy was capturing the magic, those moments of ethereal beauty that happen everywhere on the mountain," says Helen Moss Davis, the attraction's staff photographer from 2007 to 2012. "Because the weather changes so quickly on Grandfather, the most valuable way to get great photos was to be up there in the middle of it: with my eyes, and my heart, wide open. I learned not to get stuck on the idea of shooting one thing or the other, but instead to watch the light and see where it took me." Photo by Helen Moss Davis/www.wildblueprints.com.

Photography and Grandfather Mountain have a special relationship. One-time owner Hugh Morton popularized the mountain in a career full of iconic images, many published in this book. We'll feature some of those photos to "see" how and where to take a great photo of the mountain. Smartphones may be everywhere, but Grandfather Mountain tempts people to bring real cameras—strong evidence that this summit is worth a special trip and extra effort to get the very best photos you can.

People, People, People

Morton knew the value of putting a person in a picture, especially on Grandfather, where the scale of the setting frustrates efforts to capture it. Put people in a lot of your photos, preferably walking, climbing, or gazing at the view—and not grinning at you (though you won't be able to avoid that on this mountain). Morton was the ultimate pro, with a second-nature sense of composition and a natural style that realistically represented people enjoying "his mountain." Nevertheless, early in Morton's career, his promotional shots looked pretty staged, especially obvious when wide-leg stances and hands on hips appear nostalgically orchestrated. But these images do one thing very well: They illustrate the importance of *delineating the elements of your photo*. That means carefully composing what is in, and out, of the picture. Place friends and family so they stand out from the shadows and are strongly separated from the busy detail of the scene—against the sky, close up on a foreground rock, illuminated against the background. Be sure they don't look like blobs—hence Morton's wide stances. Tell them, "Turn your head a little" so you see some profile. Avoid branches protruding from ears. It's easy to overlook those details when you are climbing a ladder on a cliff. And if you aspire to publication, clothes are important. Warn your subject in advance. Decades-old gear makes a photo look . . . decades old. "People and their experiences on the mountain are key to why Grandfather is so special to so many," advises Dr. William A. Bake, a master photographer of many books and widely associated with the Southern Appalachians, the High Country, and Grandfather Mountain.

The Technical Stuff

Lighting is critical, and Hugh Morton knew that choosing the best time for a photograph is important. Harris Prevost recalls many meetings with Morton that ended with a glance out a window. He "would notice that the light outside was perfect for the photograph he was trying to take and—meeting over," laughs Prevost. Plan ahead to get the right light. George Masa was a master, but one photo is a particularly failed photo op. Shooting south from Watauga View, Masa made a black

Hugh Morton called this shot "Grandfather Mountain masterpiece," in part perhaps because his future wife, Julia, was one of the two women posing perfectly with hands on hips. The photo appeared on the cover of *The State* magazine in September 1945. The couple married three months later. North Carolina Collection, University of North Carolina Library at Chapel Hill. Photo by Hugh Morton.

Bill Bake leading a 1980s photography workshop during a "Wildflower Weekend" sponsored by the North Carolina High Country Host organization. Photo by Randy Johnson.

Tommy White's panorama from Rough Ridge truly illustrates the spectacular photographic potential of Grandfather Mountain—and what a talented photographer can do with it. Photo by Tommy White Photography, www.tommywhitephotography.com.

bulge of the clifftops on the main ridge. Many a similar frustrating photo has been taken, usually in midday as hikers reach Calloway Peak and the sun is above and behind Attic Window and MacRae Peaks, what photographers call backlit. When the sun is coming from behind your subject and not directly illuminating it, the detail seen by the eye fades to shadow.

The backlighting bandit explains the shadow-faced family standing across the Swinging Bridge on Linville Peak at the same time of day. If you are shooting south into the sun, avoid shaded friends facing north by forcing your camera to flash so "fill-in flash" illuminates their faces. Or turn around and shoot the scene to the north with the sun directly on them. You could also sidelight your friends at an angle or "bracket" your exposure by using a feature that shoots three photos at different settings so you have more chances. You can also fool the meter. When your camera is blasted by incoming light, it closes down the aperture to let in less. You want to open up the lens, actually letting in more light, exposing for the darkness of the nearby ridge or people. Aim closely at the faces, step forward if you have to or fill the image mostly with the darker subject, then use the "exposure memory lock" button or partially depress the shutter button to focus and lock the exposure for the darkest subject. Then recompose and shoot. Face it, shadows can be too dark and competing sun too bright for success, but try anyway. Grandfather often creates explosive extremes, and once in a while they end up in your camera just as you remember them. In this book, it is apparent why

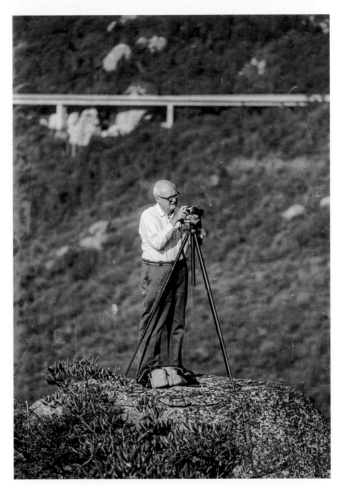

Hugh Morton was a frequent photographic visitor to Rough Ridge, starting in the mid-1980s before the Tanawha Trail boardwalks had hand railings to keep hikers from trampling fragile plant species. A version of this photo ran in *USA Today* announcing the 1987 completion and opening of the Blue Ridge Parkway. Photo by Randy Johnson.

From the striking vantage point of Montezuma Gap, Comet Hale-Bopp appears to leap over the sharp summits of Grandfather Mountain. Despite proliferating electric lights in the surrounding High Country and cities far below, Grandfather endures as a still-dark spot. Photo by Todd Bush/www.bushphoto.com.

(*Above and next page*) Hugh Morton was creative when it came to composition. More than once I saw him "craft" exactly the right setting, whether it was strictly natural or not. Keep in mind, such custom compositions are today against the rules wherever you are on the mountain. North Carolina Collection, University of North Carolina Library at Chapel Hill. Photo by Hugh Morton.

the great photographers, Hugh Morton among them, favor light in the morning, afternoon, or evening. A lower light source increases relief, and in pictures looking south from Watauga View, the farther the sun is to the left (morning) or right (evening), the more directly lit the sides of the mountain will be. So if the mountain is backlit for one photo, just choose another angle that is ready for its closeup.

A Special Place

For Bill Bake, Rough Ridge on the Blue Ridge Parkway is the mountain's premier photographic location. Morton spent a lot of time there, too. Bake likes Rough Ridge best, he reveals, "because it exemplifies the very best places for landscape photography. It's one of the best spots in Eastern North America to get a panoramic view. It offers such a grand sweep." That's pretty lavish praise. But there are best times to be there. "I'd suggest

doing your photography from dawn to before the sun is half way up to vertical," Bake counsels. At that time, the light is "extremely photographable. It's incredibly warmish, which recommends it to photography and painting." Another plus: "If you're in good shape you can get there in 15 minutes from the Parkway." Also, warns Bake, "the light goes behind the mountain in the afternoon," which is why the Linn Cove Viaduct almost vanishes in afternoon shade.

Another of Bake's favorite Grandfather photo spots is Flat Top mountain, a 2.8-mile (5.6-mile roundtrip) hike from Cone Manor House through meadows to a fire tower. "Above Cone Manor House, near the Cone graves, or at the fire-tower, if the clouds and sky are dramatic, the view can be spectacular," he assures. Clouds can be important in photos of Grandfather. A crystal blue day is nice, but Grandfather's way of building and shredding cloud castles and bathing them in spectacular

light recommends rowdy cloudy days. Park at Cone Manor, milepost 294, to take the Flat Top hike. At the carriage barn below the parking area, go left on the carriage road. Other great distant views of the mountain abound. Shoot the jagged peaks from Montezuma Gap between Linville and Newland, the Blowing Rock attraction, MacRae Meadows, and even Caldwell Community College campus on the US 321 bypass in Boone. Check Chapter 11 for hikes to Beacon Heights and the Flat Rock Trail on the Blue Ridge Parkway near Linville.

The Vision Thing

Even a great view has challenges. "It's easy to get some kind of photograph from Grandfather, but it can be hard to get something outstanding," Bake notes. Asserts the longtime national park photographer, "It's like Yellowstone—a natural paradise where so many absolutely trivial photos are taken." The ultimate key to a great photo is "vision," he says. "You can't tell somebody to have vision, but if you have it, Grandfather Mountain is a grand and suitable subject for the best images to happen." Bake has vision. As the last part of the Parkway was finalized, Parkway landscape architect Bob Hope and Superintendent Gary Everhardt asked Bake to give his blessing. They "showed him around the whole Grandfather Mountain Section," Hope remembered. Bake, whom Hope called "a great photographer," endorsed their Parkway vision. To achieve your own, Bake suggests, "you have to have experience, have studied great landscape painting and photography. It's really hard to just go out there and take an outstanding photo." The good thing is that some of the greats have photographed Grandfather, and their photos in this book speak volumes.

They're Only Pixels

The more time you spend on the mountain, the more likely you are to capture its beauty—especially the more photos you shoot. Take *a lot* of pictures. Hugh Morton's photo archive at the University of North Carolina includes nearly a quarter of a million color slides and negatives. Lucky for you and me, we no longer spend too much money on film and processing. It's all pixels now, so take five shots instead of one.

Photographer or not, it's the grand sweep of the cosmos that draws us to the summit. Countless pilgrims climbed Grandfather long before cameras existed. So snap away, but don't fail to put down the camera, take a deep breath, and just soak up the scenery in the company of friends and family.

Try the Nature Photography Weekend

Grandfather stages its annual Nature Photography Weekend after Memorial Day. The three-day, Friday-through-Monday event is a great way to improve as a photographer, explore the mountain's photo spots, and learn from photographers who know the mountain's scenery. The fee includes daily admission, and family members and guests receive a discount. Register early; the deadline is in early April.

Bibliography

INTERVIEWS

Aldridge, Frank. Interview by author, February 26, 2013.

Annand, Frederick. Interview by author, March 7, 2014.

Appling, Luke. Interview by author, November 20, 2013.

Beane, Wayne. E-mail exchange with and interview by author, Collettsville Historical Society, July 2011.

Blackburn, John. Interview by author, January 23, 2013.

Buck, Anita. E-mail exchange with author, August 2012.

Burnett, Jeffrey. Interview by author, November 30, 2013, and e-mail interviews, December 2013.

Burt, Devere. E-mail exchange with and telephone interview by author, October, November, 2012.

Byrd, Blanch and Howard. Interview by author, March 13, 2013.

Caudill, William. E-mail exchange with author, November and December 2013.

Chastain, Richard, and Dixie Chastain Lemons. Interview by author, September 6, 2012.

Church, Winston. Interview by author, April 12, 2013.

Clark, Mary K. Telephone interview by author, December 1988.

Conner, Elizabeth Hatcher. Interview by author, September 1990 and September 23, 2014.

Conway, Eustace. Interview by author, June 20, 2013.

Cooper, Johnny. Interview by Steven Miller and Edward Schultz, February 12, 1991.

Curtis, Carolyn Davis. Interviews by author, July 26 and September 27, 2013.

Dameron, Penn. Interview by author, March 11, 2014.

Dixon, William. Interview by author, November 7, 2013.

Everhardt, Gary. Interview by author, August 2, 2010.

Fox, Wade Hall. Interview by author, July 18, 2013.

Francis, Phillip. Interviews by author, August 2, 2010, and March 18, 2013.

Goodge, Grant. Interview by author, February 2014.

Gragg, Floyd Landis. Interview by author, September 2013.

Greene, G. Perry "Skip." Interview by author, November 21, 2013.

Hain, Frederick. Interview by author, March 27, 2013.

Hartley, Robert. Interviews by author, February and November 10, 2009.

Hope, Robert Allen. Interview by Mary Myers, North Carolina State University, November 4, 2000.

Houston, Gloria. E-mail exchange with and telephone interview by author, April 2014.

Hughes, James. Telephone interview by author, October 2013.

Johnson, Gary W. Telephone interview by author, July 20, 2012, and interview by author, September 11, 2012.

Johnson, Lois Bare. E-mail exchange with author August, September 2015.

Kelly, Josh. Interview by author, May 30, 2013.

Ledford, Lewis. Telephone interview by author, March 3, 2014.

Leonard, Michael. Telephone interview by author, April 10, 2013.

Love, Anthony. Interview by author, January 9, 2014.

MacDonald, Donald. E-mail interviews by author, November and December 2013.

MacRae, Hugh, II. Interview by author, March 25, 2013.

McBean, Susan. Interview by author, November 7, 2013.

Middleton, Lloyd M. Interview by author, September 11, 2012, and telephone interview, September 2012.

Miller, Steve. Interviews by author, May 2007 and March 4, 2014.

Morgan, Robert. E-mail exchange with author, August 4, 2012.

Morton, Hugh MacRae. Telephone interviews by author, April 19, 1991, and April 16, 1993.

Morton, Hugh MacRae "Crae," III. Interview by author, March 12, 2012.

Murray, Judy (Mrs. Stan Murray). Telephone interview by author, October 23, 2012.

Perry, Baker. Interview by author, February 7, 2014.

Pope, Jesse. E-mail exchanges with and interview by author, March 4, 2014.

Pottle, John F. Interview by author, June 1, 1980.

Pluchet, Régis. Interview by author, April 13, 2014.

Prevost Harris. Interview by author, October 16, 2013.

Randolph, Theodore "Ted" Fitz, III. Interview by author, June 2012.

Randolph, Theodore "Ted" Fitz, III, Jane Randolph, James Randolph, Serena Chesnut "Chessie" Randolph MacRae, and other Linville residents. Interview by author, August 3, 2012.

Raymond, Loren. E-mail exchange with and interview by author, January 15 and 16, 2013.

Ritch, Harvey. Interviews by author, July 2007 and fall/ winter 2013.

Ritchie, Fiona. Telephone interview by author, July 3, 2001.

Robbins, Spencer. Interview by author, October 7, 2013.

Scarborough, Pamela. Telephone interview by author, July 2013.

Schafale, Michael. E-mail interviews and document exchange with author, March and April 2014.

Shook, Agnes (Mrs. Ted Shook). Interview by author, April 3, 2012.

Smith, Sally J. E-mail exchanges with author, April 25, 30, July 16, August 6, September 19, 28, 2012, September 11, October 17, 2013, and January 3, 2014 (Clyde H. Smith daughter, Clyde F. Smith granddaughter).

Stout, Dewey. Interview by author, 1980.

Talbert, Margaret "Maggie." Telephone interview by author, July 26, 2012, and September 3, 2015.

———. "Shulls Mills: A Brief History of a North Carolina Community." *Blue Ridge Stemwinder*, Winter 1989.

Heller, Amos Arthur. "Notes on the Flora of North Carolina." *Bulletin of the Torrey Botanical Club* 18, no. 6 (June 1, 1891): 186–92.

Hendee, John C. Letter to Hugh Morton. June 26, 1981.

Hendee, John C., George H. Stankey, and Robert C. Lucas. *Wilderness Management*. Forest Service, U.S. Department of Agriculture, 1978.

Henderson, Bruce. "Blue Ridge Rivals Say They Aren't Making Mountain of Molehill." *Atlanta Journal Constitution*, May 20, 1990.

"Highlands Attraction Assn. Backs Morton." *Asheville Citizen Times*, March 28, 1962.

"Historic Trail Shelter Rebuilt." September 29, 1981. Grandfather Mountain press release.

Holler, Dr. Cato, Jr. N.C. Cave Survey letter to Randy Johnson. March 26, 1984.

Houston, Gloria. *The Year of the Perfect Christmas Tree*. Illustrations by Barbara Cooney. Penguin Young Readers Group, 1988.

Hudson, Arthur Palmer. *Folklore Keeps the Past Alive*. Athens: University of Georgia Press, 1962, 27.

Hughes, I. Harding, Jr. *Valle Crucis: A History of an Uncommon Place*. Bookcrafters, Inc., 1995.

Hughey, Miles. "'Angel of Mercy' in Mountains Devoted to Crippled Children." *Charlotte Observer*, April 5, 1953.

Igelman, Jack. *The View from the Top: The Battle over Mountaintop Development in WNC*. Carolina PublicPress.org. January 27, 28, 2014.

Inscoe, John C., and Gordon B. McKinney. *The Heart of Confederate Appalachia: Western North Carolina in the Civil War*. University of North Carolina Press, 2000.

J. G., Jr. "The Bagpipes in the Mountains of North Carolina." *Scottish-American*, February 13, 1907.

Jenkins, Charles F. "Asa Gray and His Quest for Shortia Galacifolia." *Arnoldia*, April 10, 1942, 13–28.

Johnson, F. Roy. *North Carolina Indian Legends and Myths*. Johnson Publishing Co., 1981.

Johnson, Randy. "Observational Research on the Social Side of Backcountry Use." *Appalachia Journal*, December 1978.

———. "Another Plane Hits Grandfather." *Sundown Times*, September 20, 1979.

———. "Backcountry Report." Unpublished report tendered to Hugh Morton, 1980.

———. "Ruggedly Packing the Grandfather." *Charlotte Observer*, June 27, 1980.

———. "Call It McCarolina: At the Highland Games, Everybody's Scottish." *Charlotte Observer*, "In the Mountains" column, July 11, 1980.

———. "The Nylon Wings of Man: Grandfather Event Soars in Hang Gliding Circles." *Charlotte Observer*, September 5, 1980.

———. "The Little Train That Could." *Tarheel*, May–June 1980, 60–62.

———. "The Grandfather Experiment." *American Forests*, October 1983, 22–27, 54–55.

———. "Case Study: Privately Owned Backcountry." Presentation at Fees for Outdoor Recreation on Lands Open to the Public, February 12, 13, 1984.

———. "Tanawha Trail to Soar Grandfather's Flank." *Mountain Times*, July 5, 1984, 1B, 7B.

———. "Life with the Falcons Was a Humbling Experience." *Mountain Times*, July 19, 1984, 15, 25.

———. "Beyond the Hypothetical: The Fee Trail Experience." Presentation at 1985 Outdoor Recreation Trends Symposium II, February 24–27, 1985.

———. "The Other Side of the Mountain." *The State*, September 1985, 10–12, 37.

———. Letter to Hugh Morton. October 6, 1985. Cave gating.

———. Rock climbing letter to Thomas Kelley. September 9, 1986.

———. *Southern Snow: The Winter Guide to Dixie*. Appalachian Mountain Club, 1987.

———. "Some Great New Sights to See: A View-by-View Guide to the Final and Most Exciting Link of the Blue Ridge Parkway." *The State*, August 1987, 20–21, 25, 28–29.

———. "Hugh Morton and the Viaduct." *Mountain Times*, September 10, 1987.

———. "Travel the Blue Ridge Parkway: Rolling along the Mountains' Newest Stretch of Highway." *USA TODAY*, September 11, 1987.

———. "Entrance Fees Could Stabilize Funding for State Parks in N.C." *Charlotte Observer*, September 7, 1990.

———. "Clearcutting: Controversy on the Mountainsides." *Blue Ridge Country*, November/December 1990, 24–25, 40–41.

———. "What's Next for the Clearcutting Controversy?" *Mountain Times*, August 15, 1991.

———. "Pay to Play: A Rationale for User Fees." *American Forests*, March/April 1991, 52–55, 72, 73.

———. "Grandfather Mountain. A Private U.S. Wilderness Experiment." *International Journal of Wilderness* 2, no. 3 (December 1996): 10–13.

———. *Hiking the Blue Ridge Parkway*. FalconGuides, 2003, 2010.

———. "Pivot Point of the Blue Ridge Parkway." *Subaru Drive*, Spring 2004, unpaginated.

———. "Hang Time: For Years Grandfather Mountain Served as the Launch Pad for High-Flying Gliders." *WNC*, August 2010, 22.

———. "The Grandfather Backcountry: A Bridge between the Past and Preservation." *Worth 1,000 Words: Essays on the Photos of Hugh Morton*. July 30, 2010.

Johnson, Randy, and James Thompson. "Clearcutting Series." *The Mountain Times*, June 2, 9, 16, 23, 30, and July 7, 14, 21, 28, 1988.

Johnson, Robert Underwood. "John Muir as I Knew Him." *Sierra Club Bulletin*, John Muir Memorial number, January 1916.

Jolley, Harley, E. *The Blue Ridge Parkway*. University of Tennessee Press, 1969.

Keith, Arthur. "Description of the Cranberry Quadrangle of North Carolina and Tennessee." *Geologic Atlas of the U.S.*, Cranberry Folio, no. 90. U.S. Geological Survey, 1903.

Keith, Edward. "Sawmill Operations." *Blue Ridge Stemwinder*, Winter 1989.

Kelley, Thomas. Rock climbing letters to Randy Johnson. August 11, September 18, and October 17, 1986.

Kelsey, Harlan P. "Shall Grandfather Mountain Be Saved?" *National Parks Magazine*, April–June 1944.

Kephart, Horace. *Our Southern Highlanders: A Narrative of Adventure in the Southern Appalachians and a Study of Life among the Mountaineers*. Outing Publishing Company, 1913.

"Killed on Logging Road." *Watauga Democrat*, March 15, 1923.

Lanman, Charles, "Novelties of Southern Scenery." *Appleton's Journal of Literature, Science and Art* 2 (1869): 1, 296, 327.

Lathrop, Virginia T. "The Little Jap." *The State*, September, 1953.

Lee, David. "Summer Bird Fauna of North Carolina's Grandfather Mountain." *The Chat*, Winter 1985, 1–14.

Lenoir, Walter Waightstill. Letter to Samuel T. Kelsey. April 15, 1887. Plans for mountain.

"Lenoir Isolated from Outside World." *Lenoir News*, July 18, 1916.

Leonard, Michael. Letter to Randy Johnson. August 4, 1986.

Leuschner, William A., Philip S. Cook, Joseph W. Roggenbuck, and Richard G. Oderwald. "A Comparative Analysis for Wilderness User Fee Policy." *Journal of Leisure Research* 19, no. 2 (1987): 101–14.

Lewis, Jehu. "The Grandfather of North Carolina." *Lakeside Monthly*, September 1873, 218–24.

Liles, Granville. "Grandfather Mountain and the Blue Ridge Parkway." Manuscript, February 1987, Blue Ridge Parkway (BLRI) Archives, Cone-Price Memorial Parks file (later published in *The State*, August 1987, 18–20, 24).

"Lightning Killed Young Man on Grandfather." *Watauga Democrat*. July 15, 1926.

Lillie, Robert J. "Blue Ridge Parkway, Geology Training Manual: Plate Tectonics and the Grandfather Mountain–Linville Falls Region." *Geoscientists-in-the-Parks* document, BLRI. National Park Service, Denver, Colorado, 1999.

Lindsey, T. H. *Lindsey's Guide Book to Western North Carolina: Illustrated*. Randolph-Kerr Printing Company, 1890.

"Linn Cove Viaduct: A Unique Segmental Project." *Dixie Contractor*, October 24 1980, 13, 17, 81.

The Linville Company. Special meeting of directors minutes, October 29, 1937. Authorized officers to sell right-of-way for parkway.

——. Special meeting of directors minutes, April 15, 1939. Authorized LC and road company to sell Yonahlossee Road to NC.

——. Annual meeting of stockholders minutes, April 7, 1943. Hugh MacRae gets peaks of Grandfather for "sundry cash loans."

——. Adjourned meeting of directors minutes, April 8, 1943. Eseeola closed summer of 1943.

——. Special meeting of stockholders minutes, October 2, 1944. Stockholders accept cottagers proposal to buy Linville holdings.

——. Special meeting of stockholders minutes, November 27, 1945. Morton praises working with Ranger Smith.

——. Directors meeting, May 9, 1952. Morton lends company money to improve toll road, secures same with deed of trust on mountain acreage, and urges dissolution of company.

Linville Improvement Company. Board of Directors meeting minutes, June 22, 1915. Endorsing Linville River Railroad right-of-way.

——. Stockholders meeting minutes, June 25, 1915. Approving railroad right-of-way and sale of company timber under "regulations of the US Bureau of Forestry."

——. Stockholders meeting minutes, February 8, 1922. Approved 99-year state lease on Yonahlossee Road.

——. Board of Directors meeting minutes, August 16, 1930. Approval of timber sale to Champion Fibre.

——. Special meeting of stockholders minutes, May 4, 1937. Adopted The Linville Co. name.

"Local Railroad Man Is Badly Hurt." *Watauga Democrat*, March 15, 1923.

Lord, Anthony J. "A Sawdust Reminiscence." *Blue Ridge Stemwinder*, Winter 1989.

Lord, William G. *The Blue Ridge Parkway Guide*. Stephens Press, 1963.

MacDonald, Donald. *America's Braemar, Grandfather Mountain and the Re-birth of Scottish Identity across the USA*. Southern Lion Books, 2007.

MacRae, Kim. "Hiking Grandfather's Trails." *Southern Living*, March 1987.

MacRae, Nelson. Linville Improvement Company, President's Annual Report to Stockholders, March 30, 1937. Came through Depression in "good condition," recommend change of name to The Linville Company, and positive prognosis for Observation Point and planned extension of the road, show value of Grandfather Mountain.

Masa, George. Letter to Roy ____. January 26, 1931. Carolina Mountain Club Archive. D. H. Ramsey Library, Special Collections, University of North Carolina at Asheville 28804. Reports logging damage after a Grandfather hike.

Maslowski, Karl. "Worth Hamilton Weller." *Cincinnati Museum of Natural History Quarterly* 21, no. 4 (Autumn 1988): 6–13.

Maslowski, Steve. "A Photographer's Guide to Blinds: Windows on Nature." *Bird Watching*, February 19, 2010.

Mathes, Hodge. "A Week among the Bears and Owls." Ca. 1950. D. R. Beeson Sr. Papers, 1830–1980. Archives of Appalachia, East Tennessee State University. Unpublished manuscript.

McCollum, Daniel W., and Annette Puttkammer. "Bibliography Related to Recreation Fees on Public Land." U.S. Forest Service, 1999.

McKeon, John B., John T. Hack, Wayne L. Newell, James O. Berkland, and Loren A. Raymond. "North Carolina Glacier: Evidence Disputed." *Science*, April 5, 1974, 88–91.

Mickey, Joseph Jr. "Boone Fork Trout Stream Management Report." June 27, 1983.

Mitchell, Elisha. *Diary of a Geological Tour by Professor Elisha Mitchell in 1827 and 1828*. James Sprunt Historical Monograph, with introduction and notes by Kemp P. Battle. University of North Carolina, 1905.

Moore, Ruth. "Lofty Mountain Thrills Traveler." *Greensboro Daily News*, August 27, 1937.

Morgan, Robert. *Boone: A Biography*. Algonquin Books of Chapel Hill, 2007.

Morley, Margaret. *The Carolina Mountains*. Houghton Mifflin, 1913.

Morris, Peter. "Grandfather Mountain Has New Trail under Its Mile High Swinging Bridge." *Mountain Times*, November 16, 1995.

Morrison, Clarke. "Morton Chooses Nature over Dollars." *Asheville-Citizen*, February 19, 1991.

Morton, Catherine. "Mildred, My Father & Me." *High Country Magazine*, July/August 2006, 22–25.

——. "Morton Family Turns Grandfather Mountain over to North Carolina." *Carolina Mountain Life*, Winter 2008–9, 26–27.

"Morton Claims Park Service Trying to 'Steal' Mountain." *Raleigh News and Observer*, March 8, 1962.

Morton, Hugh MacRae. Grandfather Mountain press release. *Asheville Citizen-Times*, February 6, 1956.

——. Letter to George D. MacRae. January 4, 1966.

——. Letter to Robert Hartley. 1968.

——. "Hang Gliding at Grandfather Mountain." 1977. Unpublished article.

——. Letter to Gary Everhardt. May 15, 1980. Grandfather Mountain access easement, road rights of way under Parkway, and "haul road" at Wilson Creek.

——. Letter to Dr. Cato Holler Jr., N.C. Cave Survey. May 1, 1984. Existence of bats.

——. Letter to Jack Barclay, The Peregrine Fund. March 1, 1985. Embraces "our birds."

——. Letter to Randy Johnson. April 9, 1993. Wilmor tract and acreage figures.

——. *Mildred the Bear and Her Cubs at Grandfather Mountain*. 1st ed. Undated.

——. *Mildred the Bear*. 4th ed. 1979.

——. *Sixty Years with a Camera*. North Caroliniana Society, Inc., and North Carolina Collection, 1996.

——. Letter to Randy Johnson. April 1, 1996. Charlotte chamber honor and role of environment in business.

——. Letter to Randy Johnson. May 25, 2004. Author's article about Grandfather Mountain in *Subaru Drive*, author's presentation of Society of American Travel Writers' Phoenix Award to Morton, "Grandfather Mountain alumni."

Morton, James McKay. "John Muir's Visit to Grandfather Mountain." *Appalachian Voices*, April 8, 2007.

Muir, John. Letter to Charles Sprague Sargent. June 21, 1898. University of the Pacific Library, Holt-Atherton Collections.

——. Letter to wife Louisa Wanda Muir. September 25, 1898. University of the Pacific Library, Holt-Atherton Collections.

——. Letter to daughter Helen Muir. September 26, 1898. University of the Pacific Library, Holt-Atherton Collections.

——. Letter to wife Louisa Wanda Muir. September 30, 1898. University of the Pacific Library, Holt-Atherton Collections.

Murray, Stanley A. Letter to Clyde F. Smith, October 21, 1966. From AT Conference chairman, Smith's sign making offer an "answer to a prayer."

"New Hiking Trails Open on Grandfather Mountain." August 1, 1983. Grandfather Mountain press release.

"New Visitor Center Built atop Grandfather Mountain." *Asheville Citizen-Times*, October 15, 1961.

Nihlean, Janet. "Carolina Mountain Club Trip Report: Grandfather Mountain from Linville Gap." May 14–15, 1932. Carolina Mountain Club Archive. D. H. Ramsey Library, Special Collections, University of North Carolina at Asheville 28804.

Norman, Eliane N., Walter Kingsley Taylor, and Charlie Williams. "The North American Travels of André Michaux: Plants, People, and Places." In development for the University of Alabama Press; publication expected by 2018.

"North Carolina Trail Association/ Grandfather Mountain to Sponsor Second Trail Construction Workshop." April 27, 1984. Grandfather Mountain press release.

Oakley, Shawn W., Michael P. Schafale, and Sam H. Pearsall. *Grandfather Mountain Site Conservation Plan*. Nature Conservancy, 1996.

O'Donnell, Kevin, and H. Hollingsworth, eds. *Seekers of Scenery: Travel Writing from Southern Appalachia, 1840–1900*. University of Tennessee Press, 2004.

Parker, Francis. "Boone Fork Lumber Company: A Corporate History." *Blue Ridge Stemwinder*, Winter 1989.

Parker, Warren T. U.S. Fish and Wildlife Service cave gate letter to Hugh Morton. October 3, 1985.

Parris, John. *Mountain Bred*. Citizen-Times Publishing Company, Asheville, 1967.

Peek, Charlie. "Adversaries Found That Morton Was a Man to Match His Mountain." *Winston-Salem Journal*, September 6, 1987, 1c, 7c.

Pegram, Charles B. "Illness Claims Life of James C. Shuford." *Hickory Daily Record*, April 1974.

Pezzoni, J. Daniel, ed. *The Architectural History of Watauga County North Carolina*. Watauga County Historical Society, 2009.

Pluchet, Régis. "Michaux Mysteries Clarified." *Castanea: Occasional Papers in Eastern Botany*, no. 2 (December 2004): 228–32.

——. *L'extraordinaire voyage d'un botaniste en Perse*. Éditions Privat, 2014.

"Preservation Plan for Big Grandfather Mountain Area Urged." *Asheville Times*, July 13, 1935.

Prevost, Harris, Catherine Morton, et al. "Grandfather's Voice: A Newsletter for People Who Appreciate Grandfather Mountain." March 1996–Spring 2006.

Quinn, Joseph. "William S. Whiting's Logging Railroads: An Historical Geography, 1900–1925." Master's thesis, Appalachian State University, 2003.

Rapport, Leonard. Letter to J. O. Kilmartin, Board of Geographic Names. November 8, 1960. Carolina Mountain Club Archive. D. H. Ramsey Library, Special Collections, University of North Carolina at

Asheville 28804. Carolina Mountain Club member supports naming of Masa Knob.

Raveson, Betty. "Invershiel: A New Old World." *Palm Beach Life*, September/October 1967.

Raymond, Loren A., and Anthony B. Love. "Pseudobedding, Primary Structures and Thrust Faults in the Grandfather Mountain Formation, NW North Carolina, USA." *Southeastern Geology* 44, no. 2 (June 2006): 53–71.

Ritchie, Fiona, and Doug Orr. *Wayfaring Strangers*. University of North Carolina Press, 2014.

"Road Engineers Disagree with Hugh Morton." *Raleigh News and Observer*, May 17, 1962.

Roberts, Claudia P. "Linville National Register of Historic Places Inventory Nomination Form." November 2, 1978.

Saunders, Paul Richard. "The Vegetational Impact of Human Disturbance on the Spruce-Fir Forests of the Southern Appalachian Mountains." Ph.D. diss., Duke University, 1979.

Schlosser, Jim. "Hugh's North Carolina: Hundreds Attend Memorial for State's Late 'Hero.'" *News & Record*, June 10, 2006.

"Shelter: 40-Year Old Structure Is Rebuilt." *Watauga Democrat*, July 6, 1981.

Shook, Theodore. "Grandfather Mtn. Acquired Its First Haircut in 1930." *Watauga Democrat*, June 29, 1976.

——. *The Grandfather Community*. Puddingstone Press, 1985.

"Shortia galacifolia: A Plant Rediscovered." Harvard University Asa Gray Bicentennial Celebration, 1810–2010. Harvard University Library. http://botlib.huh.harvard .edu/libraries/Gray_Bicent/gray _main.htm. Last updated July 2010

Sidebottom, J. "The Christmas Tree Industry in Western North Carolina." In *National Proceedings: Forest and Conservation Nursery Associations—2008*, coordinated by R. K. Dumroese and L. E. Riley, 71–73. Proc. RMRS-P-58. Fort Collins, Colo.: U.S. Department of Agriculture, Forest Service, Rocky Mountain Research Station, 2009.

Smith, Clyde F. "A Summer on the Dome." 1926 Diary of Carter Dome fire tower duty. Collection of Christopher Whiton.

——. Comments recorded in Mount Cardigan summit register, July 22, 1945, and September 3, 1947. Appalachian Mountain Club Library and Archives, Boston, Mass.

Smith, Clyde H. "Meeting the Mountains." *New Hampshire Profiles*, March/April 1981, 62–66.

Smith, Hilda. Diaries in single and multiyear volumes for 1937, 1938, 1939, 1950–54, 1955–59, 1960–64, 1965–69, 1970–74, 1975–79.

Stasio, Marilyn. "Heritage Drama." *Hemispheres Magazine*, May 2000, 102–11.

Stephenson, Martha. Letter to the editor. *Charlotte Observer*, August 9, 1992.

——. Letter to Hugh MacRae Morton. April 9, 1993.

Stewart, Chris, and Mike Torrey, eds. *A Century of Hospitality in High Places: The Appalachian Mountain Club Hut System, 1888–1988*. Appalachian Mountain Club, 1988.

Stewart, Kevin G., and Mary-Russell Roberson. *Exploring the Geology of the Carolinas: A Field Guide to Favorite Places from Chimney Rock to Charleston*. University of North Carolina Press, 2007.

Swanson, Drew A. "Marketing a Mountain: Changing Views of Environment and Landscape on Grandfather Mountain, North Carolina." *Appalachian Journal*, Fall 2008, Winter 2009, 30–53.

Tager, Miles. *Grandfather Mountain: A Profile*. Parkway Publishers, 1999.

Tarvit, Jim. *Scottish Steam Drifters*. St. Ayles Press, 2004.

Thompson, Roy. "Two Claim Proof of Glacier in N.C." *Winston-Salem Journal*, March 31, 1973.

Thuersam, Bernhard. "General William MacRae: Lee's Fighting Brigadier." Cape Fear Historical Institute Papers. www.cfhi.net.

Timblin, Carol Lowe, and Leslie Banner Cottingham. *The Bard of Ottaray: The Life, Letters, and Documents of Shepherd Monroe Dugger*. Puddingstone Press, 1979.

Tipton, Ron, and Randy Johnson. "Backpacker Forum: Price Hikes / You Get What You Pay For." *Backpacker Magazine*, July 1984, 36–42.

Trotter, William R. *Bushwhackers The Civil War in North Carolina: The Mountains*. J. F. Blair, 1988.

U.S. National Transportation Safety Board. Aircraft Accident Reports, IAD78FA062 (May 12, 1978), IAD79FA082 (September 16, 1979), and IAD80FA037 (April 7, 1980).

U.S. Secretary of Agriculture. *A Report of the Secretary of Agriculture in Relation to the Forests, Rivers, and Mountains of the Southern Appalachian Region*. 1902.

"Viaduct Built from Top Down: Sharply Curved and Superelevated Structure Leaves Slope Unscathed." *Engineering News-Record*, October 28, 1982, 22–25.

"Vive la Grandfather: André Michaux Descendant Retraces Family Footsteps." *Watauga Democrat*, April 16, 2014.

Waite, John R., ed., and Chris Ford, art director. *Blue Ridge Stemwinder*. 62 vols. 1988–2007.

——. *The Blue Ridge Stemwinder*. Overmountain Press, 2003.

Walker, Charles F. "Description of a New Salamander from North Carolina." Proceedings of the Junior Society of Natural Sciences, July 31, 1931.

Warner, Charles Dudley. "On Horseback." *Atlantic Monthly*, July, August 1885, 88–101, 194–207.

Wauer, Roland H., "Ro." Letter to Randy Johnson. May 1, 1986. Acknowledges receiving proposal to designate Grandfather Mountain as a United Nations Biosphere Reserve.

Weakley, Alan S. "Grandfather Mountain Corridor (Blue Ridge Parkway) Natural Area." September 1986. North Carolina Natural Heritage Program report.

——. "Hugh Morton and North Carolina's Native Plants." *Worth 1,000 Words: Essays on the Photos of Hugh Morton*. June 15, 2010.

Webb, Thomas, et al. "Sawmilling in Linville, NC." *Avery Post*, June 23, 2004.

Wecker, David. "Exhibit Has Tragic History." *Cincinnati Post*, April 25, 2000.

Weller, Worth Hamilton. High School Diary, Cincinnati Museum Center,

Cincinnati, Ohio. Ca. 1930–31. Transcription by Helen Walland.

Whisnant, Anne Mitchell. *Super-Scenic Motorway: A Blue Ridge Parkway History*. University of North Carolina Press, 2006.

Whiting, William S. Letter to J. C. Shull. August 15, 1917.

Whyte, Thomas R. "Prehistoric Sedentary Agriculturalists in the Appalachian Summit of Northwestern North Carolina." *North Carolina Archaeology*, October 2003, 1–19.

——. "Collision at the Crossroads: Confusion in the Late Woodland Period (AD 800–1400) of Northwestern North Carolina." In *The Archaeology of North Carolina: Three Archaeological Symposia*, North Carolina Archaeological Council Publication number 30, 2011.

——. "Archaeological Investigation of Indian House Cave, Grandfather Mountain State Park, North Carolina." Report submitted to the North Carolina Office of State Archaeology and the North Carolina Division of Parks and Recreation, Raleigh, 2015.

Wildlands Philanthropy: The Great American Tradition. Earth Aware Editions, 2008.

Wilkins, Kay. "Cy Crumley— A Railroading Man." *Johnson City Press-Chronicle*, July 4, 1976.

Williams, Charlie. "André Michaux, a Biographical Sketch." *Castanea: Occasional Papers in Eastern Botany*, no 2 (December 2004): 16–21.

Wilson, E. E., ed. *The Linville Ledger, Diamond Jubilee Edition*. Linville Resorts, Inc., 1967.

"Would Locate National Park." *Watauga Democrat*, November 13, 1924.

Wright, Susan. "The Wild and the Wind: John Muir's Presence in the California Hall of Fame Might Bemuse Many People on This Side of the Atlantic." HeraldScotland.com. April 21, 2013.

Zeigler, Wilbur G., and Ben S. Grosscup. *The Heart of the Alleghenies*. A. Williams & Co. and W. W. Williams, 1883.

TELEVISION/VIDEO PROGRAMS

Burns, Ken. *The National Parks: America's Best Idea*. 2009.

Bonesteel, Paul. *The Mystery of George Masa*. Bonesteel Films, 2003. http://www.bonesteelfilms.com/.

Grove, Kyle. *Just a Stop along the Way*. 2010.

Smith, Clyde H. *Mount Cardigan*. 2000.

Acknowledgments

I have been visiting, researching, writing about, and living below Grandfather Mountain's peaks since the 1970s. A handful of years ago I focused all of that experience on writing this book, what the University of North Carolina Press hopes will be "the definitive book on the mountain." Four solid years of recent research and writing became the biggest challenge of my life as a writer. I am grateful to say that it was easier and more inspiring because of all the help I received from people who love my favorite mountain.

The fact that Grandfather is esteemed by so many is the biggest reason why I set out to write a "comprehensive" book about it. My goal has been to track the breadth of topics that account for why people are so passionate about this place. In pursuing that mission, I have met countless folks who immediately pause with a faraway look in their eyes, only to confess "that mountain" is a prized part of their lives.

I am one of those people. Meeting so many more of you has been a moving, enriching experience. Whether we've met in libraries, museums, or archives of historic images and records, I thank you. Valuable assistance came from Greta Browning and Dean Williams at Appalachian State University's W. L. Eury Appalachian Collection; Laura Smith at East Tennessee State University's Archives of Appalachia; Gene Hyde and Colin Reeve at UNC-Asheville's Ramsey Library Special Collections; Eric Blevins of the North Carolina Museum of History; Stephen Fletcher, Keith Longiotti, and Michael Milner at UNC-Chapel Hill Library and the Hugh Morton Collection; Zoe Rhine at Asheville's Pack Memorial Public Library; Jacqueline Holt, curator at the Blue Ridge Parkway; and Rob Burbank and Rebecca M. Fullerton at the Appalachian Mountain Club, among others. As my research progressed, it was humbling indeed to find myself requesting to use historic images and documents from the nation's premier archival repositories, among them Ben Franklin's American Philosophical Society, the nation's oldest scientific organization.

Many of those who helped me made indispensable efforts on my behalf in their own quest to honor Grandfather Mountain. That can be said for many very elderly residents of the Grandfather Community and the High Country area, including the relatives of historically important individuals who have figured in the tales I tell. To appreciate the long list of people to whom I am indebted for graciously granting me interviews, turn to the bibliography. Some are no longer among us. That list includes people whose life's work has helped usher the mountain into public ownership—and their names and contributions are a prominent part of the story I strive to tell. Some of those interviews were recorded thirty-five or more years ago, when my study of the mountain was starting. As a result, I have culled comments from many of my own articles that appeared decades ago in a long list of local and national publications, among them the *Charlotte Observer*, *USA Today*, *Hemispheres Magazine*, the *Mountain Times*, *High Country Magazine*, *Carolina Mountain Life*, and so many more.

Most importantly, the people who have helped make this book what it is include many who shared their family's historic images and almost secret stories. This book's assortment of anecdotes and rich trove of images was provided by people whose work on my behalf helped them realize they too have their own collection of precious materials worthy of historical stewardship. I am honored to have helped some of those artifacts find their way into museums and archives.

Thanks to Appalachian State University for the expertise of its authorities. Anthropologist Thomas Whyte aided my research on Native Americans. He vetted my conclusion that Indian House Cave likely was not a Native American ritual site and added welcome certainty when he and his students followed up with a dig at the cave. Geography professor Baker Perry helped shed light on Grandfather's climate. It was gratifying to notice an old copy of my book *Southern Snow: The Winter Guide to Dixie* in his office. And without the help of Anthony Love and Loren Raymond I would never have understood the geology of Grandfather Mountain much less been able to explain it.

On the art side, I owe a significant debt to professional photographers who graciously offered their own photographs. These contributions are freely given evidence of the love these people feel for Grandfather. Talented photographers such as Tommy White, Skip Sickler, Todd Bush, Helen Moss Davis, and Robert Moore (of the *Watauga Democrat*) offered their spectacular images at no cost. Sickler and Davis, current and onetime staff official photographers at the Grandfather attraction, stepped beyond their contractual relationship to illustrate the mountain you see here.

And there are artists, too. For decades, Richard Tumbleston's paintings have captured my appreciative eye, the High Country, and his favorite mountain. Among collectors, his iconic images are synonymous with our area. I am truly honored that his work *Grandfather*, in Chapter 5, was painted specifically for this book. Artist Jason Drake's painting *Grandfather Mountain Reverie*, also in Chapter 5, is evidence aplenty that he too is inspired by our Grandfather. Graphic artist Chris Ford permitted me to use his wonderfully detailed, microscopically researched map of Tweetsie Railroad in Chapter 5 as well. An original version appeared in his friend John Waite's classic book *Blue Ridge Stemwinder* (for which Ford was art director). But it's not exactly the same map. Chris graciously added logging board roads, the Boone Fork Lumber Company railroad grades, and other details revealed by my own research. For that and for images from John Waite's collection, I thank John's wife, Sharon Waite, and Overmountain Press, publishers of John's and Chris's highly recommended book on Tweetsie.

I'm also grateful to those who have helped shape my hike to an outdoor life. Without Hugh Morton's encouragement, I never could have created my own job at Grandfather Mountain and worked to preserve public access and encourage conservation. Also at Grandfather, I am grateful for the help and friendship of Harris Prevost, Jesse Pope, Winston Church, Steve Miller, and other members of the Morton family, including Catherine and Jim Morton. Without the volunteer effort of many close friends, among them Robert Branch, Steve Owen, Jerome Barrett, Jack Corman, Richard G. McDade, and many, many more, I would not have been able to establish the mountain's early trail management program, a story I tell briefly in this book. That includes my son Christopher and his mother, Elizabeth Johnson.

Credit for any book goes way beyond the writer, and the best thing about writing about a mountain or trails in general is working with rangers, managers, and park employees, most recently the staff of the new Grandfather Mountain State Park. I am privileged to have been asked to serve on Grandfather's State Park Advisory Committee. Dedicated, enthusiastic, and in many cases woefully underpaid, state and federal park employees work tirelessly to protect the nation's special places, many now preserved in a state park system that celebrates its first century in 2016. When you meet them on the trail, please take time to thank them.

Sincere gratitude goes to the skillful, encouraging staff at UNC Press for helping make this book on Grandfather Mountain possible. Their perseverance and advice were pivotal as the manuscript evolved, expanded, and contracted. I'd especially like to thank Editorial Director Mark Simpson-Vos for his patience and professionalism while the manuscript developed its own voice. Thanks also to Associate Editor Lucas Church, Assistant Managing Editor Stephanie Wenzel, and Design Director Kim Bryant. Also thanks to David Perry, retired former UNC Press editor in chief, with whom this project got started. Though not employees at the Press, its "independent readers" deserve special gratitude for the invaluable role they played in shaping the book you hold in your hands: Dan Pierce, professor of history at UNC-Asheville, and Vicky Jarrett, former editor in chief of *Our State*.

I thank those mentioned above and many others for encouraging me to make backcountry the backdrop for my life. This book celebrates the love we share for wild places so often far from the path we tread in living our lives. Despite my eventually editing an international travel magazine and traveling the globe, a worldly U.K. acquaintance once looked at me with surprise and pronounced his quizzical realization, "You, you're a *hiker person*." Spot on. I am proud that my passion for wilderness and backpacks was only enhanced by packing carry-on bags for international flights. My involvement with trails has been long and life-transforming—which brings me to you. Here's hoping you find inspiration in these pages, but I am certain you will be inspired by the places this book leads you to on Grandfather Mountain.

Last, I thank the person and the pet who got me over the finish line when my most recent research and then the writing and rewriting of this book stretched to almost four years of six-plus-day weeks. First is my wife, Cathy, an essential source of strength and support. Many times her belief in this book was all I had to go on. Second is a black cat not so creatively named Kitty-Boy. One winter day, my dog Pepper, wagging her tail in welcome, pointed out a skinny, shivering refugee who'd melted himself to the ground through High Country snow. After Kitty-Boy came in from the cold, he was always able to make me smile and urge me on, even after I'd two-finger mistyped "Linville" as "Lincille" for what felt like the five millionth time.

Index